Child Sponsorship

Child Sponsorship

Exploring Pathways to a Brighter Future

Edited by

Brad Watson
Senior Lecturer, Avondale College of Higher Education, Australia

Matthew Clarke
Head of School, Faculty of Arts, Deakin University, Australia

palgrave
macmillan

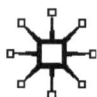

First published 2014 by
PALGRAVE MACMILLAN

Palgrave Macmillan in the UK is an imprint of Macmillan Publishers Limited, registered in England, company number 785998, of Houndmills, Basingstoke, Hampshire RG21 6XS.

Palgrave Macmillan in the US is a division of St Martin's Press LLC, 175 Fifth Avenue, New York, NY 10010.

Palgrave Macmillan is the global academic imprint of the above companies and has companies and representatives throughout the world.

Palgrave® and Macmillan® are registered trademarks in the United States, the United Kingdom, Europe and other countries

ISBN: 978-1-137-30959-4

This book is printed on paper suitable for recycling and made from fully managed and sustained forest sources. Logging, pulping and manufacturing processes are expected to conform to the environmental regulations of the country of origin.

A catalogue record for this book is available from the British Library.

A catalog record for this book is available from the Library of Congress.

Contents

List of Figures

List of Abbreviations

ADP	Area Development Program
BWAA	Baptist World Aid Australia
CCCD	Child Centred Community Development
CCCDA	Child Centred Community Development Approach
CCF	Established in 1938 as China Children's Fund, renamed Christian Children's Fund in 1951. The organization is now known as ChildFund
CDCS	Community Development Child Sponsorship
CI	Children International
CRC	Convention on the Rights of the Child
CS	Child Sponsorship
DAC	Development Assistance Committee of the Organisation for Economic Cooperation and Development
GCE	Global Citizenship Education
GDP	gross domestic product
GIK	Gifts-in-Kind
GROs	Grassroots Organizations
HDI	Human Development Index
IFCS	Individual/Family Child Sponsorship
IICS	Individual or Institutional Child Sponsorship
INGO	International Non-Governmental Organization
LAR	Latin American Region
LWA	Lutheran World Action
MDGs	Millennium Development Goals
MELF	Monitoring, Evaluation and Learning Framework
MSC	Most Significant Change
NFE	Non-Formal Education
NGDO	Non-Governmental Development Organization
NGO	non-governmental organization
NJC	National Joint Committee
PLAN	Plan International
POEM	programme outcome effectiveness measurement
PVO	private voluntary organization
QUAKERS	Society of Friends
RBA	rights-based approach
RBCS	Rights-Based Child Sponsorship

SAO	Support an Orphan (when established in 1970; now known as Share an Opportunity)
S.C.F.	Save the Children Fund
UNCRC	UN Convention on the Rights of the Child
UNHCR	United Nations High Commissioner for Refugees
UNICEF	United Nations Children's Fund
USAID	USA's Agency for International Development
WFP	World Food Programme
WHO	World Health Organization
WVI	World Vision International

Foreword

As someone located in a nation where enormous wealth is generated by a few, while significant millions are trapped in a web of entanglement, it is my great privilege to introduce a text that demystifies the origins of child sponsorship (CS), documents the diversity in sponsorship funded programmes and opens the way for a deeper and more considered discussion of its power and potential to impact all members of society. The task of leading 2,000 staff who serve over 2.5 million children in 5,000 communities has provided innumerable opportunities to learn from the many challenges involved in implementing CS funded programmes. However my colleagues and I find CS provides an important ongoing opportunity to address issues of inequality.

There are several types of sponsorship funded programmes documented in this text, but for us sponsorship provides crucial engagement with long-term development processes in partnership with civil society, NGOs and the Government. These development processes primarily occur in urban, rural and isolated tribal areas, and focus on tackling child mortality rates, poor health, lack of education, inadequate or unsafe water, food insecurity, low income, marginalization and exclusion.

Taking full advantage of hindsight and the lessons learnt over many years from those who live and work among the poor, I would like to offer a perspective on child sponsorship informed by close engagement with those frontline staff who live and work among the poor. I offer five observations for your consideration.

Firstly, CS that emphasizes systemic poverty reduction reminds us that sustainable, equitable development and transformation must target those who are on the margins of society. Opting to take the side of the child is a political choice, and moral imperative, especially in an industry whose metrics tend to be adult-centric. The sponsorship of children is more than a tool for mobilizing resources. It is partially because of CS in the humanitarian industry that we pay attention to the often forgotten people on the margins, namely children. In India, where I am based, CS draws the attention of the powerful into considering the poor. It brings a human face to our development conversations.

Secondly, CS is a great tool for the redistribution of wealth and a meaningful reversal of the economic status quo. We may consider CS in many different ways. For me as a sponsor, it might simply be an emotional act of doing good. For another it might be investing for returns in a deserving child many miles away from home. However there is no running away from the fact that because of CS there is a definite, sizeable and ongoing transfer of resources from the haves to the have-nots. How else would millions consider and sustain their interest in the poor? Because of CS there is space created in the living rooms of our middle-class homes in India, to talk about poverty and meaningful interventions. There is really no other tool that has the potential to engage millions (a pre-requisite to trigger movements) to consider the poor on a personal level. All the funding from all the major donors and corporates could not have achieved the engagement of the ordinary middle class for a single cause. Sociological studies have shown that movements are often triggered when the middle class are mobilized for a cause and CS has the potential to do just that. Although CS has historically been thought of as benefactors in the global North assisting children in the global South, today we have sponsorship engagement growing in the global South as well, making sponsorship a significant instrument capable of mobilizing a global voice on behalf of the marginalized.

Thirdly, CS continues to draw the attention of the humanitarian industry to the importance of personal and collective empowerment in the broader development agenda. As the logical next step in the early CS programmes described in this book there was a major shift to invest in the child's well-being, values and personality. The renewing of the mind and holistic well-being can matter in CS as much as material measures of poverty. However, from the 1980s child sponsorship raised questions about the need for educating sponsors and donors, and challenging their worldview as well. I have often come back more transformed from my interaction with sponsored children than I would from other visits and am reminded that genuine transformation is always mutual – a lesson so alien to our engagement with major donors and grants!

Fourthly, CS that emphasizes child activism challenges the powerful. In an industry that is so adult-driven and measured by adult-centric metrics, it is CS that calls attention to the validity of child well-being metrics – an awkward choice it would seem for many development gurus. To our advocates in the corridors of power, and especially in some cultures, children are a disruption to serious adult conversation or at best their participation is a form of mere tokenism. The emphasis on empowerment of children is a political choice an organization makes – more than a marketing tool or a brand choice. It raises fundamental questions about our development models. Can sustainable models of development that seek to measure the future relevance of current investment, ignore the child? Can we measure sustainability without considering the impact on the child? It is time we redefined development, sustainability, empowerment, advocacy, transformation and other familiar humanitarian parameters from the point of view of the child, especially young adolescents and youth. Thanks to some innovative CS programmes we have the possibility of an alternative view, especially when children and youth are meaningfully engaged in project design, monitoring, evaluation and as agents of change in their communities.

Finally, innovative child sponsorship programmes and consequent investments in children provide us an opportunity to empower a cadre of agents of change. Recently I was at a congress of children. The children made their speeches, presented their demands and offered their solutions. To my delight, none of the children needed to be reminded of the need to be inclusive, the value of values, and the possibility of being joyful and resilient in the face of intense poverty and oppression. If it was an adult conversation in a community or among advocacy experts, these would be alien factors to be forced into the conversation. For development gurus these would require 'politically correct' speeches. For the congress of children these were natural. It is because of CS that we have children who can proudly sit along with politicians and policy makers in New Delhi, Bali and New York, offering another alternative point of view. The poor in our communities need not fear; there is fast emerging a politically conscious cadre of children, who will naturally challenge status quo.

As I commend this book, so rich in its research, bringing history and contemporary insights together, let me say that it is time to exploit the full potential of child sponsorship to fund innovation. In my view it is an undersold opportunity whose full potential is yet to be realized. If we limit child sponsorship to merely being a component in a 'revenue model' of a humanitarian enterprise, we have lost an opportunity to transform our nations and trigger a movement. With CS we have a paradigm as well as a tool for development and transformation, that has the potential to challenge the status quo, redistribute wealth, challenge flawed assumptions in the humanitarian industry, transform thinking, mutually impact all stakeholders, equip a cadre of young minds who will dare to break the cycle of poverty and oppression, and trigger a worldwide movement interested in justice for the poor.

I stand as one who is thankful for the 'discovery of child sponsorship' in the humanitarian industry and I dare say that when it is done well it challenges some popular, flawed assumptions in our critique of synergies between CS and development theories. As you read this book I encourage you to consider and explore the possibility of new frontiers in poverty reduction, community development and social activism that harness child sponsorship as a powerful agent for change and recognizes its potential. In this context I commend this book as being foundational for a considered discussion by scholars and practitioners of what CS has been in the past, continues to be today, and can be tomorrow.

Jayakumar Christian
Director, World Vision India

Acknowledgements

Like all books, this one would not have been possible without the remarkable support of many individuals. Apart from the contributors who so generously provided their insights, the editors would like to especially acknowledge Kathleen Holt and Christy Howard for their enthusiasm, encouragement and unfailing support. The archivists responsible for the Cadbury Collection at the University of Birmingham were fantastic. Christina, Ambra, Shirley and the team at Palgrave were a pleasure to work with, as was Harwood Lockton whose eye for detail proved invaluable. Finally, the editors would like to thank their long-suffering families. Special thanks go to Fiona, Caleb, Zoey and Zac for your patience with a preoccupied husband and father.

Notes on Contributors

Matthew Clarke is a professor in the Faculty of Arts and Education at Deakin University, Australia. His research interests are in religion and development, aid effectiveness and development in the Pacific. Professor Clarke also undertakes regular evaluations of community development programmes in the Asia-Pacific region.

Jim Cook is President and CEO of Children International, a child sponsorship organization that provides direct support and community assistance to approximately 335,000 children, youth and their families in 11 countries worldwide. An accountant by trade, Jim was asked to join CI's board of directors in 1985 and became the organization's executive vice president in 1987. He has served as President since 1996.

Han Dijsselbloem studied engineering in the Netherlands and taught in Bolivia as a volunteer with Dutch SNV. He joined Plan International in 1979 where he has worked in a variety of managerial and trainer roles and locations. He is currently based in Panama as the Regional Administrator for Plan's Latin American operations.

Amy Jo Dowd is Senior Director for Education Research at Save the Children and is a graduate of Stanford (MA) and Harvard's (MEd, EdD) Graduate Schools of Education. She is passionate about using rigorous research to improve practice and led the development of Literacy Boost, an evidence-driven system for improving children's learning.

Justin Fugle is a Senior Program Advisor at Plan International USA. He has nearly 20 years of experience designing and implementing participatory community development programmes across more than 35 countries in Africa, Asia and Latin America. He led the design and implementation of Plan Bolivia's second Country Strategic Plan, which invested more than $50 million in partnership with more than 1,000 communities across the nation. An expert resource and trainer on Plan's child-centred, community development approach, Justin lives with his wife and children in Arlington, VA.

Uwe Gneiting is a Research Associate with the Transnational NGO Initiative at Syracuse University where he worked with Plan International on two collaborative research projects in 2009 and 2011.

He is currently completing his PhD in Political Science at the Berlin Graduate School for Transnational Studies of the Freie Universität in Berlin, Germany.

Damon Guinn joined Children International in 2001. He has worked as a staff writer and an editorial manager.

Céline Gustavson is Sponsorship Program Advisor at Save the Children. She is a graduate of Mount Holyoke College and Georgetown University. She has supported the development and implementation of Save the Children's approach to Child Sponsorship programming for over a decade.

Christabel Kalaiselvi has over 23 years' experience working with World Vision India and has headed the field operations since March 2012. She served as Associate Director for the monitoring and evaluation of 18 ADPs for two years before becoming Director of Capacity Investment and Staff Care.

David P. King is the Karen Lake Buttrey Director of the Lake Institute on Faith and Giving as well as Assistant Professor of Philanthropic Studies within the Indiana University Lilly Family School of Philanthropy and adjunct faculty of Religious Studies at Indiana University-Purdue University Indianapolis (IUPUI). He earned his PhD from Emory University with a specific interest in American religious history and its intersections with the growing field of world Christianity. His current research focuses on the rise of evangelical relief and development NGOs, religious humanitarianism and religion's engagement with international affairs. David has recently been named one of ten Young Scholars in American Religion for 2013–2015 by the Center for the Study of Religion and American Culture.

Harwood Lockton is a former senior lecturer in international development at Avondale College of Higher Education, Australia and development NGO worker. In retirement he is an adjunct lecturer in development at Avondale and Pacific Adventist University in PNG as well as being a committee member on both the Australian NGOs code of conduct committee and a national advocacy consortium.

Earl Moran is Associate Vice President of Management Support at Save the Children and is a graduate of the University at Buffalo (BS) and Vanderbilt University (MBA). He has over 20 years' experience of NGOs, including time in headquarters and the field with a focus on strategic and cross-functional projects that create measurable results for children. He has lived and worked in Botswana, Pakistan and Afghanistan.

Manohar Pawar is Professor of Social Work, School of Humanities and Social Sciences, Charles Sturt University, Australia and the president of the International Consortium for Social Development, Asia-Pacific Branch. His first job was with an Indian community development and child sponsorship agency. Recent books include *International Social Work: Issues strategies and programs* (2nd ed., 2013), *Social and Community Development Practice* (2014), *Water and Social Policy* (2014, Palgrave Macmillan) and *Social Work Practice Methods* (2014).

Mark Peters is Global Initiatives Director, Compassion International, Voyager Parkway, Colorado Springs, Colorado, USA.

Brett Pierce is Senior Sponsorship Programming Specialist – Strategy and Special Projects at World Vision International. For the past 13 years, he has focused on developing effective programming approaches and tools for child sponsorship. His background includes programming, education, and marketing. He also served as consultant to Baptist World Aid during their transition to developmental approaches to child sponsorship.

Frances Rabbitts is a PhD graduate of the Geography Department at the University of Exeter, UK. Her research interests encompass various themes related to charity, giving and international development, and her doctoral work focuses specifically on how child sponsorship schemes are managed and experienced within 'donor' countries.

Anthony Sell was appointed Director of Programs at Baptist World Aid Australia (BWAA) in 2010 and was heavily involved in the transition of the child sponsorship programme. Previously, he worked for African Enterprise for more than two years, an African mission and development agency focused on ten countries in sub-Saharan Africa and worked with children for more than ten years in various community service sectors.

Alistair T.R. Sim is Global Program Effectiveness Research Director for Compassion International, Voyager Parkway, Colorado Springs, Colorado, USA and Conjoint Professor, Faculty of Health & Medicine, The University of Newcastle, Australia.

Rachel Tallon is based in Wellington, New Zealand. A trained secondary school teacher, Rachel is passionate about the social sciences learning area and how young people learn about distant countries in this rapidly globalizing world. In addition to teaching, Rachel is also an experienced education resource writer and has worked in various capacities with not-for-profit organizations in New Zealand. She currently divides her time between education consultancy work and teaching undergraduate Geography and Development Studies at Victoria University. She holds a doctorate in Development Studies.

Anthony Ware lecturers in International and Community Development at Deakin University in Australia where he is actively involved with the Australia Myanmar Institute, Centre for Citizenship, Democracy and Human Rights, and Alfred Deakin Research Institute.

Brad Watson is Senior Lecturer in the International Poverty and Development Studies Program at Avondale College of Higher Education, Australia. Brad has an ongoing interest in child sponsorship, including its origins, evolution and usefulness as a vehicle for poverty reduction. Brad enjoys evaluating child sponsorship programmes and working with NGOs to maximize positive impacts of project activity.

Felicity Wever worked at BWAA for almost seven years and also played a key role in the transition of the child sponsorship programme. She has worked in the development sector since 2001, working with Caritas and UNICEF more recently.

1
Introduction to Key Issues in Child Sponsorship

Brad Watson and Matthew Clarke

Introduction – The child sponsorship phenomenon

Child Sponsorship (CS) is a humanitarian phenomenon and its broad popularity combined with a prodigious ability to mobilize funds for international non-governmental organizations (INGOs) is unique in the humanitarian aid sector. Writing in the mid-1990s, Smillie (in Sogge et al, 1996, p.99) described CS as 'the bedrock of several of the older organizations' and 'one of the most enduring success stories in private aid agency fundraising'. In the same year that the Millennium Development Goals (MDGs) were launched, Brehm and Gale (2000, p.2) noted that 'agencies which run such programmes report a year-on-year increase in both the number of children sponsored and the amounts of money raised'. The prominence of CS as a fundraising device has continued with the first decade of the twenty-first century witnessing sustained growth in what can be loosely termed the CS sector. In North America, Europe, the United Kingdom and Australia, INGOs that have invested in CS as a key marketing tool are amongst the largest private aid agencies in terms of annual funds raised. The volume of children assisted is especially noteworthy. According to Wydick et al (2009, p.1) in 2009 the number of children in the world who were sponsored was between eight and 12 million, and the subsequent flow of funds exceeded US$3.1 billion. By such accounts it is possible that over two decades CS has generated international transfers in excess of US$50 billion.

Although there are numerous INGOs utilizing CS, a small number of them tend to be more prominent in Northern countries. For example, in 2007 the three largest Canadian CS INGOs generated 'more than ten times as much money from the public as the three top non-sponsorship organizations' (Plewes and Stuart in Bell and Coicaud, 2007, p.30). The situation in Australia, where World Vision is the largest INGO, is even more intriguing. World Vision Australia's annual 2008–2009 income was more than five times greater than the next largest INGO (ACFID, 2012). In the year 2010–2011, total international income for Save the Children, World Vision, Compassion, Plan, Children International and ChildFund exceeded US$6 billion, at least US$2.5 billion of which derived from CS. Far from being a spent force, CS is a tool that has paved the way in some INGOs for rapid growth and leverage to access government grants (Maren, 1997, p.145), a sustainable income stream, a more diversified funding base and the consolidation of a small number of INGOs into 'super-sponsors.' The success of CS in mobilizing public donations has elevated several CS INGOs (especially the early adopters) into an elite category of fundraisers. As a 'product' in the market place, CS can therefore be considered a great success and the fact that CS fundraising methods have remained relatively popular over time is remarkable.

Although CS activities across INGOs are not uniform, they do have a number of common characteristics including a historic emphasis on regular giving, the motivation of donating to benefit individuals, and the provision of regular updates for the benefit of sponsors. In linking individual children to geographically distant donors, CS is credited with personalizing giving and making, as Fowler (1992) suggested, distant obligation seem immediate and personal. Children are key to the enduring appeal of CS to donors and while there is a continuum of modes for utilizing the funds raised through CS (from direct cash handouts to beneficiaries, to larger community development activities and community mobilization) the child as core has remained largely intact over time. Consequently the reputations and identities of CS INGOs are inextricably and profoundly linked to children although the extent to which children serve INGOs as symbols of world harmony, seers of truth and embodiments of the future (Bornstein, 2003, p.7) is debatable.

The emphasis of CS INGOS on children and their needs has legitimized and depoliticized their activities historically. It is argued by Manzo (2008, p.632) that the iconography of childhood expresses institutional ideals and key humanitarian values of solidarity, impartiality, neutrality and humanity. However, there can be no doubt that as a motivator for private donors and a legitimizing imperative for INGOs, the sponsorship of children works. Commenting on aid appeals in general, Coulter (1989, p.1) observed that 'the wide-eyed child, smiling or starving, is the most powerful fundraiser for aid agencies.' Notably, much of the contentious historic debate over CS fundraising has focussed on its truthfulness and the extent to which CS INGOs have portrayed developing country beneficiaries with respect and dignity (Mittelman and Neilson, 2009, p.64). This has led some to question whether the formation of a relationship based on exchange of money 'may perhaps be a source of dissonance in sponsors' (Yuen, 2008, p.50).

The CS literature

Scholarly scrutiny of CS interventions has been very limited and there is an acute shortage of quality research regarding the impact of historic interventions. In one attempt at a literature review, Brehm and Gale (2000, p.1) observed that there was '...a scarcity of empirical research-based evidence about the impact of child sponsorship on recipient families and communities'. Unfortunately, the situation remains little changed at the time of writing this chapter. Available information about CS typically falls into the three broad categories of easily accessible journalistic exposé, carefully selected in-house publications (including consultancy reports) and a fragmented scholarly literature. Despite some exceedingly rare efforts to quantify the impact of sponsorship interventions (Wydick et al, 2013), and a small number of contributions from anthropologists (Bornstein, 2001, 2003), CS interventions are characterized by an abundance of anecdotal, often negative accounts dating to the 1980s. Such accounts have continued to inform the widespread criticisms of CS that emerged when the *New Internationalist* magazine addressed the topic in several issues during the 1980s (Stalker, 1982).

Generally speaking, CS is heavily contested, poorly understood and under- researched, a point made in Chapter 4 which deals with historic criticism of CS. That so few scholars and industry insiders have sought to interrogate the emergence, evolution and contribution of CS INGOs makes it difficult to evaluate their legitimacy, especially in the absence of a large body of evidence on the impact and effectiveness of non-CS INGOS noted by Edwards and Hulme (2002, p.6).

A technical approach to evaluating the legitimacy of INGOs involves comparative judgments based on perceptions of accountability, representativeness and performance (Lister, 2003, p.3). Fowler (1997, p.188) asserts for example that demonstrating satisfactory levels of achievement is the first step on the legitimacy ladder. Like other INGOs, CS

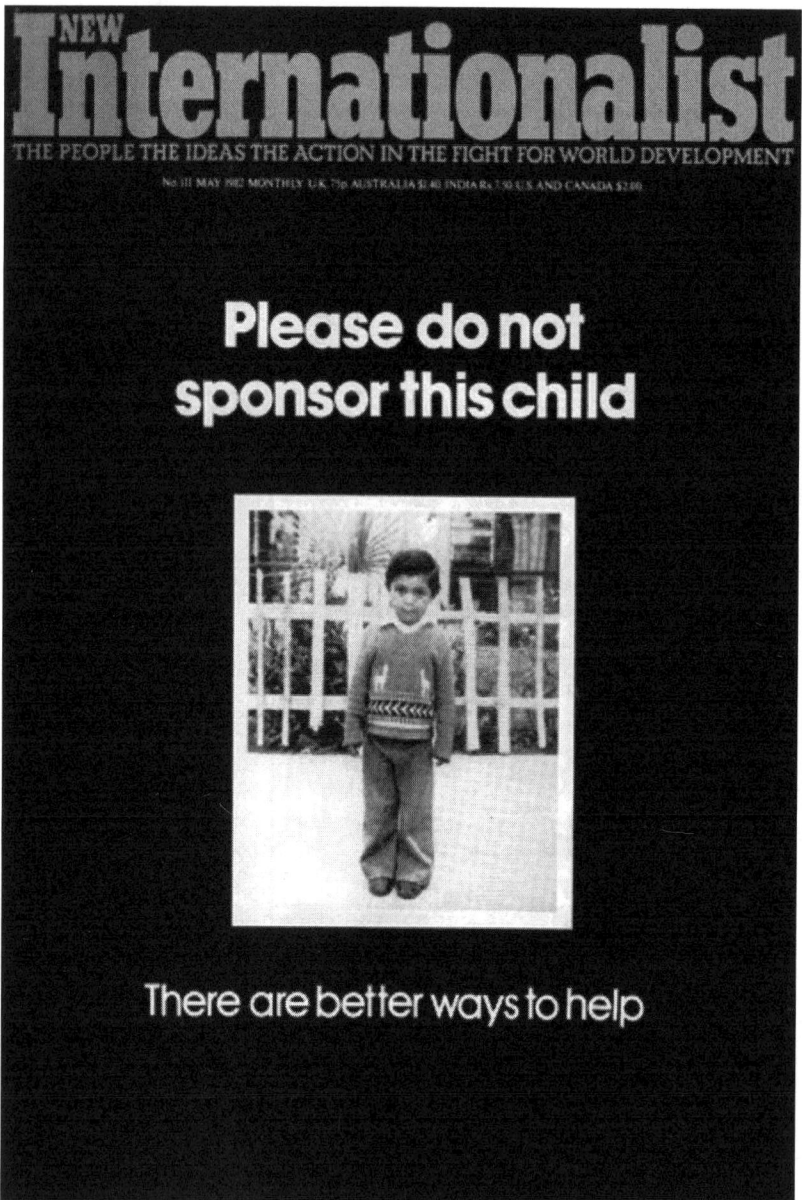

Figure 1.1   New Internationalist front cover
From the early 1980s the individual support of children through CS was increasingly questioned (Stalker, 1982, p.1)

organizations are eager to do good and consequently they are prone to critical self-reflection. Meadows (2003, p.109) asks, 'Does Child Sponsorship ever go wrong? Of course. Is that a good enough reason to abandon the concept?' It is perhaps the pre-eminent question that has occupied staff in CS INGOs for the past 20 years as they have considered both marketing imperatives and the impact of CS-related humanitarian interventions in terms of what really makes an impact. This question of efficacy and legitimacy is paramount. Harris-Curtis (2003, p.1) observes that in addition to INGO self-reflection 'The reality for NGOs today is that they are increasingly challenged by the media, public, governments and academia.' While this may be the case, large CS INGOs have been especially sensitive to criticism that programmes are out of step with 'best practice'.

At a time when the 'halo of saintliness' around INGOs is under threat (Racelis in Bebbington et al, 2007, p.203) can it be demonstrated that CS INGOs are thinking, learning organizations committed to improvement even though they may not have transitioned from a mind set of aid for individual welfare, to development as delivery beyond to development as leverage? (Edwards et al, 1999, p.15). Is CS an impediment to change or a vehicle for innovation? In Chapter 5 Moran and others argue that for Save the Children International CS has, over the past decade, become a flexible source of funding for creative, lasting change. Chapter 3, which features the evolution of the ChildFund and Plan International's programmatic approach, proposes a typology of CS funded activity. It suggests that change and critical self-reflection is a feature of large CS funded INGOs though to what extent expectations of sponsors contribute to mandates for change is unclear.

Keeping in mind Fowler's 'onion-ring' strategy for INGOs, we might ask if CS INGOs have a credible 'core' of projects and successive 'skins' or 'layers' of important activity including research, evaluation, advocacy, campaigning and public education, with a commitment to human rights and structural reform? Or are they merely 'ladles in the global soup kitchen', prone to choosing a path of least resistance? (Fowler in Edwards and Fowler 2002, p.22). In Chapter 9 of this book Sim and Peters discuss the Compassion model of intervention, an approach that places holistic child development at the centre or core of intervention logic. In keeping with UNICEF's argument that children living in poverty 'experience deprivation of the material, spiritual and emotional resources needed to survive, develop and thrive' (UNICEF in Minujin et al, 2006, p.485) Sim and Peters prod us to consider who decides which CS core activities are credible and whether religion and child development are synergistic.

Although there appears to be a dearth of published research demonstrating CS INGO engagement in robust evaluation, most large CS INGOs do capture data to identify programme impact, flaws and tensions. Although such information has often been lost in the 'grey literature' of confidential INGO project records there is a recent, albeit limited trend to publicize findings and learnings, examples of which are found in Chapter 6 where the authors discuss the transition of Plan International's development programming from a traditional service delivery model towards a rights-based approach and how this strategic shift has interacted and is interacting with Plan's sponsorship model. Given its emphasis on rights-based interventions, Plan may be seen as an organization committed to a theory of change model in which 'capacity changes of young people and duty bearers are expected to trigger citizenship changes whereby young people become aware of their power and use this to effectively participate in decision-making processes' (Williams and Kantelberg, 2011, p.2).

The tensions evident in CS advertising have received considerable attention from academics however given that CS is one of the primary portals through which private donors in the North may view (and to an extent experience) the South, how can CS INGOs not only educate their supporters, but deepen understanding of structural causes of poverty so that sponsors become partners, advocates and activists? In her chapter Tallon addresses the issue of global citizenship education for school students and asks how CS INGOs can engage in development education in ways that dignify the poor, avoid harmful stereotypes and deal with the causes of poverty rather than the symptoms. Critical to such an approach is avoidance of aid discourses that rely on the benevolence and politics of poverty associated with charity and what has been disparagingly referred to as the White Man's Burden (Jefferess, 2008, p.34). Accordingly, CS INGOs are said to embrace a test of their credibility when moving beyond the self-serving task of marketing children as passive products, to the more complex task of advocating with children and their communities, for the realization of child rights as a purposeful way of reducing poverty.

Child: Product or purpose?

The post-World War Two era saw the United States and Western Europe prosper, an acceleration of globalization, and a growing interest in the conditions of the poor in 'undeveloped nations' accompanied by the running down of the era of traditional missionary endeavour and direct colonialism. In this nexus of events, it had never been so easy to offer direct support to individuals in far-flung places. The widespread dissemination of a note, found pinned to a small child by either journalist John Langdon-Davies or relief volunteer Eric Muggeridge during the Spanish civil war in 1937, is characteristic of many post-World War Two appeals for sponsorship that would prove popular: 'This is Jose. I am his father. When Santander falls I shall be shot. Whoever finds my son, I beg him to take care of him for my sake' (in Mittelman and Neilson, 2011, p.371). This emotive, brief request contains several potent themes of past CS marketing including urgency, appeal to paternal or maternal instinct, lost innocence and a sense of very personal need. This poignant message first informed, then sought compassion and finally urged action, enlisting members of the general public in the ongoing provision of food, shelter, education and child-oriented services for the benefit of individual children. However, this was certainly not the first foray into CS.

It is interesting that to date there has been a lack of consensus on which organization pioneered CS. The origin and characteristics of early CS programmes are discussed by Brad Watson in Chapter 2, which traces early CS practice to at least 1919, in a joint sponsorship programme run between the newly established Save the Children Fund in the UK and the Society of Friends in the Austria. There it was initially used for the provision of food rations to middle-class children who were not eligible for aid provided by the American Relief Administration feeding programme. The common perception that CS did not emerge until the late 1930s and early 1940s is incorrect. Referring to Save the Children Fund sponsorship of British children, Freeman (1965, pp.49 & 89) observed that during the Great Depression there were British children 'with limbs like broomsticks' and 'grotesque swollen abdomens'. Save the Children UK responded indicating that 'individual children put forward by teachers or medical officers as in great need of help were "adopted" by benefactors who not only paid the sponsorship subscription, but took an interest in the child or family or school with letters, presents and even visits'. It would seem that in the 1930s CS was offered to a small number of citizens in the UK and USA for the support of children in their own countries.

Freeman notes that by 1963 there were just 715 individual children and 169 families being helped by UK friends in 'other' countries. Nevertheless, despite its humble beginnings, popular support for international CS increased dramatically and was adopted with great success by other organizations such as World Vision, featured in Chapter 7. This may be attributable to a combination of effective marketing and the fact that although many donors have been overwhelmed at the seeming futility of addressing global poverty, 'the genius of sponsorship is that it links a caring donor with a needy child in the Third World' (Waters, 2001, p.5). In some cases it has nurtured direct contact with families of sponsored children. Freeman (1965, p.142) remarks on the personal link forged between some sponsors and adult beneficiaries, quoting a letter from a widow in a German refugee camp to her sponsor: 'It is thanks to you that I did not lose my courage... What a comfort to know that someone, however far away, knows your name and that of your children. Around here is no one, only misery, but your help is a solid rock beneath my feet.'

Bornstein (2001, p.601) reminds us that the western perception of children as valuable for their innocence and emotional value may not be consistent with the way children are viewed in their community of origin. Commentators have also observed the potential for negative impacts of some CS funded interventions on recipients, referred to in media exposés as formation of unrealistic expectations, development of dependency and arousal of divisive jealousies. In her study of a faith-based CS INGO Bornstein (2001, p.609) writes, 'The irony of child sponsorship is that as much as child sponsorship links people across nations in transnational relationships of a global 'Christian family', it divides people locally and has immense potential to inspire jealousy.' The success of CS fundraising has not been without more pointed criticism. CS INGOs are said, especially in the 1980s, to have made repetitive, extensive, though not exclusive use of babies, starving children and graphic, emotive imagery of supplicant, helpless 'others' to elicit donations in what Smillie (1995, p.136) refers to as the 'pornography of poverty'.

Smillie (2000, p.121) notes that the CS format of marketing has emerged as 'the pre-eminent lens through which a very large and growing number of Northern citizens view the South.' Because of their significant reach, and the level of trust extended by private donors, CS INGOs continue to exercise considerable influence, shaping the public's perception of what causes poverty, what works, how children are best helped and what is sustainable. It is not surprising then that CS INGOs have faced a high level of scrutiny regarding their marketing and public communications strategies which has led to heated debate at times. The extent to which these observations can be applied across

CS INGOs is however questionable. For example, Mittelman and Neilson's (2011, p.387) study of 1970s Plan Canada print advertising concluded that the organization '...did not cross the delicate line between showing the hardship and realities of life in the developing world...and what became known as "development porn."' Arguing that CS organizations have historically been the biggest users of negative images, Plewes and Stuart (in Bell and Coicaud, 2007, p.30) acknowledge that there has been a shift in CS fundraising, 'from miserable, starving children' to 'picking winners', a view partially echoed by Cameron and Haanstra (2008, p.1478) who observe a growing preference for images of self-reliant and active people. The strict codes of conduct designed and embraced by leading CS INGOs have played a role in this trend.

Historic criticism of CS endorsed the view that pre-1990s CS advertising was often paternalistic, misleading or dependent on 'a particular construction of the relationship between the First World and the Third World' (Maddox, 1993, p.91). Although not specifically commenting on its own advertising, the Save the Children UK website (2012) acknowledges that coverage of famines in the 1980s '...perpetuated negative and destructive stereotypes of people in developing countries, who were seen as dependent and helpless.' In his analysis of sponsorship telethons Jefferess (2002, pp.6–7) warns of the potential construction of a neo-colonial discourse in which viewers may identify more with the spokesperson describing the suffering than with the victims themselves. Although most sponsors have little interest in questioning their mental constructs of poverty and the Other, this issue is deeply important from a development education perspective.

Writing at a time when many of the large CS INGOs were modifying the way they communicated with the public, and the ways in which they intervened through projects, Smillie (1995, p.136) gave voice to the commonly expressed concern that although CS had proven to be exceptionally successful as a form of fundraising 'Direct correspondence with a child is very expensive.' In his scathing journalistic exposé of the domestic sponsorship programme of Save the Children USA, journalist Michael Maren (1997, pp.144–147) argued that, 'The total of the sponsors' dollars that actually went in grants to field programs was...less than 50%.' Echoing this concern with cost efficiency, the 1993 Human Development Report (UNDP, p.89) unilaterally declared that, 'Agencies that receive money from child sponsorship organizations...have to spend much of their time collecting copious quantities of personal information about the sponsored children and employ large teams of "social workers" for this.' The extent to which such generalizations were or remain valid is debatable, especially for smaller, more cost-efficient organizations. Some CS INGOs clearly did not employ large teams of social or administrative workers and diversity in historic CS is evident. Currently it would be difficult to maintain the claim that the projects of large CS INGOs are small and parochial. Indeed, in Chapter 7 Pierce explores the shift to long-term capacity building and integrated community development in World Vision's very large Area Development Programs (ADPs) and beyond to a development programming approach.

CS INGOs as partners in poverty reduction

CS is firmly rooted in forms of western philanthropy preoccupied with the innocence of children. In choosing a symbol for her work, Eglantyne Jebb used the same swaddling-clothed child for the Save the Children Fund that had been created in 1419 for the Foundling Hospital in Florence where care was provided for the city's destitute children (Freeman, 1965, p.139). Jebb herself famously observed that, 'The only international language in the world is a child's cry' (Jebb and Save the Children Australia, 2008, p.17). This emphasis on children and child poverty by contemporary INGOs that utilize CS is rarely contested. It is estimated, for example, that more than 30 per cent of all children in developing countries live in absolute poverty, characterized by an income of less than US$1 a day (UNICEF, 2011). CS INGOs argue that life for these 600 million children, and a further 500 million who live on less than US$2 per day, is precarious. It is characterized by multi-dimensional facets of disadvantage, often including ill health, illiteracy, violence, inadequate shelter, limited access to clean water or sanitation, economic uncertainty, exclusion from vital services and higher rates of premature death. To date the 1989 Convention on the Rights of the Child is the most widely endorsed human rights treaty in history, ensuring that 'Children's survival, development and protection are now no longer matters of charitable concern but of moral and legal obligation' (UNICEF, 2006, p.1). CS INGOs have often, with broad public approval, placed child welfare at the centre of a moral framework of action and increasingly place them at the centre of a rights-based theory of change.

CS INGOs have shaped, and are being shaped by the international child rights agenda. Save the Children has been at the forefront of child rights campaigning and advocacy since 1919. In Chapter 2 of this book Save the Children is recognized as a world leader in child rights, the earliest pioneer of CS and recent innovator in use of CS funding. As a network with partners which have both rejected and embraced sponsorship, Save the Children exemplifies the experience of many CS INGOs as they have sought to transition individual support of children to inclusive models of community development (Gnaerig and MacCormack, 1999, pp.145–146). For INGOs that function in a loose federation, with high levels of autonomy for various country offices, it has been especially difficult to coordinate policy development and new programmatic interventions incorporating CS.

Change is by nature divisive, a fact not lost on Hickey and Sell, of Baptist World Aid Australia. In Chapter 10 they explore the complexity and ethics of a small, Australian organization moving rapidly from individual child support to interventions based on ideals of community development and empowerment. It should be noted that while many of the larger CS INGOs have transitioned to community development utilizing sponsorship as a fundraiser, the extent to which smaller CS organizations should, or can follow, poses interesting dilemmas. Micro-sponsors, defined here as CS organizations with less than 1,000 supported children, may not have the resources to transition or up-scale. How should their legitimacy be measured?

The bigger CS INGOs in Northern countries are cognizant that the international community has embraced its legal and moral obligation to poor children by prioritizing them in four out of the seven nation-based MDGs. Children or young people are expressly targeted in goals relating to the reduction of poverty, provision of universal education, achievement of gender equality and improvement of child health. UNICEF's (2006) claim that poverty reduction begins with children is widely endorsed by CS INGOs for pragmatic reasons, if not for the moral imperative of helping first those who suffer most, yet wield least power. Though they are motivated by the plight of children, and operate in a paradigm of international aid preoccupied with concepts such as sustainability, capacity building and rights-based development, the reality is that contemporary CS INGOs maintain different ways of responding and have evolved over time. Quoting personal correspondence with World Vision staff, Jefferess (2002, p.5) notes, 'eventually, as development experts discovered putting money in to one person's hands was not the ideal formula for improving a person's situation, the idea of a full community development project was hatched'.

Taking exception at such simplistic analysis, and the lack of a typology of CS interventions, Watson (Chapter 3) proposes four basic types of sponsorship funded intervention: individual support of children in institutions such as orphanages or schools where the large majority of funding benefits a child; individual support of children in a community setting where children and immediate family benefit from a majority of funding via cash transfers, provision of goods or direct service delivery; support of children in community development projects where individual children might ultimately benefit from pooled funding; and support of children in rights-based development activities where all members benefit from community development and community empowerment initiatives. To some extent Watson's typology reflects David Korten's generations of INGO (see De Senillosa, 1998, pp.2–3), beginning with welfare and progressing to development of sustainable systems. A critical question is, are all four types of CS INGO identified in this book effective partners in this multi-pronged quest to improve children's lives? To what extent do CS INGOs catalyse poverty reduction with what UNICEF refers to as quick impact initiatives, rights-based approaches and deeper structural reform, policy change and international networking? Further, does such a typology stand up to scrutiny or is it overly simplistic?

The intersection of faith and religion with CS is a rich area of inquiry. It is notable that the majority of early CS INGOs began their work in an era when many Northern countries were still classified as Christian. In one review of 1,600 secular and religious private voluntary organizations (PVOs) that registered with the US Federal Government between 1939 and 2004, it is possible to see the decline of Jewish and Catholic PVOs after World War Two, the rise of Evangelical PVOs and then rapid growth of secular PVOs in the mid-1980s to mid-1990s (McCleary and Barrow, 2008, p.512). In keeping with this trend there are two notable areas of interest explored by David King in Chapter 12. First, the common but not exclusive popularity of CS within Christianity. Second, and more importantly, the transition of some leading CS INGOs from direct evangelism to humanitarianism informed by religious principles. King's case study of World Vision's transition illustrates this well.

Yuen (2008, p.46) observes that sponsorship enables Christians to, 'find a way to actively enact their faith; the compassion one feels...is actually the voice of God speaking to Christians to act.' The role of sponsorship in the lives of sponsors, and the meaning derived from the act is explored in more length by Rabbitts in Chapter 13. Clearly, the spiritual dimension and meaning making attached to giving for some sponsors is sometimes matched by a spiritual interpretation of receiving on the part of sponsorship beneficiaries. Bornstein (2001, p.599) relays the words of Albert, a boy who had been sponsored in Zimbabwe and was interviewed as an adult: 'then came the sponsor and everything looked up...the Lord came to my rescue in the form of a sponsor and He was there as a provider.' Though Christian CS INGOs do not claim a monopoly on CS , the widespread promotion of sponsorship within faith-based organizations has resulted in mixed expectations of child-saving and they have often struggled with an ongoing tension between direct evangelism and faith-based foreign aid. David King's (2011) exploration of the transition of World Vision from evangelical to a faith-founded and faith-inspired Christian organization is a case in point. Whaites (1999, pp.410–412) describes World Vision in its early days as 'missionaries fighting Marxism' whereas by the 1990s it had become a diverse partnership exhibiting a shift away from a 'homogenous set of evangelical core beliefs'.

Despite a historic dearth of information about CS from the 1950s to the 1990s, there is a resurgence of interest in the topic, informed perhaps by the continued growth of CS INGOs, emergence of codes of conduct regulating CS INGO activities (see Chapter 15 for a discussion of the future of CS), willingness of large CS INGOs to publish evaluations and emerging scrutiny of academics. A startling omission is the lived experience of sponsored individuals, and the sponsors themselves, whose voices have largely been absent in debate and marginalized in discussion over the complex meaning making that occurs in the construction of transnational relationships. For this reason Chapter 11 gives voice to six sponsored individuals while Chapter 13 by Frances Rabbits calls for a more nuanced appraisal of the impact of sponsorship on donors. Chapter 14, by Tallon and Watson, calls for more effective development education in schools by CS INGOs marked by a more holistic understanding of poverty and the poor, rather than paternalistic charity.

Conclusion

In State of the World's Children (2006, p.1), UNICEF called for immediate action on child poverty at three levels. First, a massive push to boost access to essential services, dubbed 'quick impact initiatives' that 'provide a vital kick-start to human development and poverty reduction'. Second, longer-term initiatives rooted in rights-based approaches to development and national capacity building. Third, deeper approaches that integrate policy reform with governments, civil society, donors, international agencies and media. This focus on children is implicit for many CS INGOs whose international programmes seek to improve the lives at the community level through direct welfare, child development, service delivery or capacity-building activities and advocacy. However, as a whole the CS literature is fragmented, disjointed, prone to generalization and reliant on anecdotal evidence. While CS critics would rightfully decry any stereotyping of the poor, CS INGOs routinely find themselves subject to ongoing stereotyping and critique that neglects their evolution over time. This is partially the fault of the CS INGOs themselves. Although a number of the larger organizations have produced quality books about their own work, these are often dated and academic case studies of change in CS INGOs are rare. Hopefully, this book will play a role in furthering discussion and awareness.

CS advertising seems to have provided a minor field of inquiry for communication and semiotics specialists (Manzo, 2008), but the literature is largely populated with dated analysis of advertising from an era of CS that may well have passed for larger CS INGOs bound by self-enforced codes of conduct. A small number of anthropologists have turned their attention to CS (Bornstein, 2001) however there is little recognition in the literature of the historical diversity in CS interventions, the stance of progressive CS INGOs and current CS advertising, advocacy and programmatic interventions. Like many issues in CS, the portrayal of Southern children in Northern nations is overdue for review. Further, abundant, largely anecdotal criticism of individual CS in the 1980s and 1990s (see Chapter 4) is contrasted with a tremendous shortage of research-based evidence regarding the impact of CS on recipient families and communities (Brehm and Gale, 2000, p.2). The few studies that do exist (such as Wydick et al, 2013) are as interesting for their findings as for their rarity.

Despite the popular misconception that there has been relatively minor change to the CS model of marketing and to programmatic interventions, the larger sponsorship organizations are best seen as ethical organizations, committed to child poverty reduction as they continue to grapple with complex issues. As a fundraising tool, CS has successfully raised billions of dollars that have been used with differing degrees of success by INGOs to work towards improving the living conditions of children and more recently, their communities. That many CS INGOs have shifted from a paradigm of individual welfare to community development is reflective of a broader shift in the evolution of humanitarian aid and indicates that CS INGOs are receptive to, and in some cases are leading change. That there are still 600 million children in desperate material poverty suggests that poverty is more ingrained and difficult to overcome than allowed for in the optimism of the MDG timeline. CS INGOs will continue to be important partners in the twenty-first century quest for a world in which all children may develop to their full potential. Arguably, the impact of their contribution will ultimately be determined by the extent to which they have, or continue to 'move beyond charity-based partnerships – seeking out children and their families as partners and rights-holders to be empowered and enabled in making their capacities and vulnerabilities known and acted upon' (UNICEF, 2006 p.88). To what extent child sponsorship fundraising complements this move is perhaps the central question facing all CS INGOs as they seek to maximize impact and pursue sustainable change.

Bibliography

ACFID (2012) *Facts and Figures in 2008 and 2009*, http://www.acfid.asn.au/ resources/facts-and-figures, date accessed 12 October 2010.

Archer, D. (2010) 'The evolution of NGO-government relations in education: ActionAid 1972–2009', *Development in Practice*, 20, 4–5, 611–618.

Bebbington, A., Hickey, S. and Mitlin, D.C. (2007) *Can NGOs Make a Difference? The Challenge of Development Alternatives* (New York: Zed Books).

Bell, D.A. and Coicaud, J.M. (eds) (2007) *Ethics in Action. The Ethical Challenges of International Human Rights Nongovernmental Organisations* (Cambridge: Cambridge University Press).

Bornstein, E. (2001) 'Child Sponsorship, evangelism, and belonging in the work of World Vision Zimbabwe', *American Ethnologist*, 28, 3, 595–622.

Bornstein, E. (2003) *The Spirit of Development: Protestant NGOs, Morality, and Economics in Zimbabwe* (New York: Routledge).

Brehm, V. and Gale, J. (2000) 'Child sponsorship: A funding tool for sustainable development?' *Informed: NGO Funding and Policy Bulletin NGO Sector Analysis Programme Bulletin*, 3, November, 2–6.

Cameron, J. and Haanstra, A. (2008) 'Development made sexy: How it happened and what it means', *Third World Quarterly*, 29, 8, 1475–1489.

Coulter, P. (1989) 'Pretty as a picture', *New Internationalist* http://www.newint. org/features/1989/04/05/pretty/, date accessed 17 April 2012.

De Senillosa, I. (1998) 'A new age of social movements: A fifth generation of non-governmental development organisations in the making?' *Development in Practice*, 8, 1, 40–53.

Edwards, M. and Fowler, A. (2002) *The Earthscan Reader on NGO Management* (London: Earthscan).

Edwards, M. and Hulme, D. (2002) *Non-Governmental Organisations: Performance and Accountability Beyond the Magic Bullet* (London: Earthscan).

Edwards, M., Hulme, D. and Wallace, T. (1999) 'NGOs in a global future: Marrying local delivery to worldwide leverage', *Public Administration and Development*, 19, 17–136.

Fowler, A. (1992) 'Distant obligations: Speculations on NGO funding and the global market', *Review of African Political Economy*, 26, 55, 9–29.

Fowler, A. (1997) *Striking a Balance: A Guide to Enhancing the Effectiveness of Non-Governmental Organisations in International Development* (London: Earthscan).

Freeman, K. (1965) *If Any Man Build: The History of Save the Children Fund* (London: Hodder and Stoughton).

Gnaerig, B. and MacCormack, C.F. (1999) 'The challenges of globalization: Save the Children', *Nonprofit and Voluntary Sector Quarterly*, 28, 4, 140–146.

Harris-Curtis, E. (2003) Northern NGDOs, Inclusion and Extreme Poverty, paper presented to IDPM Chronic Poverty Conference 'What Role Do NGOs Play in Alleviating Chronic Poverty?' Manchester University, April 2003.

Jebb, E. and Save the Children Australia (2008) *Lessons in Leadership from a Spinster in a Brown Cardigan/Eglantyne Jebb* (East Melbourne, Victoria: Save the Children).

Jefferess, D. (2002) 'For sale – Peace of mind: (Neo-) colonial discourse and the commodification of third world poverty in World Vision's "telethons"', *Critical Arts*, 16, 1, 1–21.

Jefferess, D. (2008) 'Global citizenship and the cultural politics of benevolence', *Critical Literacy: Theories and Practices*, 2, 1, 27–36.

King, D.P. (2011) 'World Vision: Religious identity in the discourse and practice of global relief and development', *The Review of Faith & International Affairs*, 9, 3, 21–28.

Lister, S. (2003) 'NGO legitimacy: Technical issue of social construct?' *Critique of Anthropology*, 23, 2, 175–192.

Maddox, M. (1993) 'Ethics and rhetoric of the starving child', *Social Semiotics*, 3, 1, 71–94.

Manzo, K. (2008) 'Imaging humanitarianism: NGO identity and the iconography of childhood', *Antipode*, 40, 4, 632–657.

Maren, M. (1997) *The Road to Hell: The Ravaging Effects of Foreign Aid and International Charity* (New York: The Free Press).

McCleary, R.M. and Barrow, R.J. (2008) 'Private voluntary organizations engaged in international assistance, 1939–2004', *Nonprofit & Voluntary Sector Quarterly*, 37, 512–536.

Meadows, P. (2003) *Rich Thinking about the World's Poor: Seeing the World through God's Eyes* (Carisle, Cumbria: Spring Harvest Publishing Division and Authentic Lifestyles).

Minujin, A., Delamonica, E., Davidziuk, A. and Gonalez, D. (2006) 'The definition of child poverty: A discussion of concepts and measurements', *Environment and Urbanization*, 18, 481–500.

Mittelman, R. and Neilson, L.C. (2009), 'I saw a picture of a child living on 14¢ a day and I nearly choked on my $12 Scotch', Plan Canada's marketing of child sponsorship programs: A content analysis of print advertisements from the 1970s and 1980s in T.H. Witkowski (ed.) *Rethinking Marketing in a Global Economy: Proceedings of the 34th Annual Macromarketing Conference*, Kristiansand, Norway.

Mittelman, R. and Neilson, L.C. (2011) 'Development porn? Child sponsorship advertisements in the 1970s', *Journal of Historical Research in Marketing*, 3, 3, 370–401.

Plewes, B. and Stuart, R. (2007) 'The pornography of poverty: A cautionary fundraising tale', in D. Bell, and J. Coicaud (eds) *Ethics in Action. The Ethical Challenges of International Human Rights Nongovernmental Organisations* (UK: Cambridge University Press).

Racelis, M. (2007) 'Anxieties and affirmations: NGO-donor partnerships for social transformation', in A. Bebbington, S. Hickey and D. Mitlin (eds) *Can NGOs Make a Difference? The Challenge of Development Alternatives* (London: Zed Books).

Save the Children (2012) *History: Save the Children*, http://www.savethechildren.org.uk/about-us/history, date accessed 17 April 2012.

Smillie, I. (1995) *The Alms Bazaar: Altruism under Fire – Non-Profit Organisations and International Development* (London: IT Publications).

Smillie, I. (2000) 'NGOs: Crisis and opportunity in the New World Order', in J. Freedman (ed.) *Transforming Development: Foreign Aid for a Changing World* (Toronto: University of Toronto Press).

Sogge, D., Biekart, K. and Saxby, J. (eds) (1996) *Compassion and Calculation: The Business of Private Foreign Aid* (London: Pluto Press).

Stalker, P. (1982) 'Please do not sponsor this child', *New Internationalist*, http://www.newint.org/issues/1982/05/01/, date accessed 17 April 2012.

UNDP (1993) *Human Development Report* (Oxford: Oxford University Press).

UNICEF (2006) *State of the World's Children 2006*, http://www.unicef.org/mdg/poverty.html, date accessed 16 April 2012.

UNICEF (2011) *Millennium Development Goals*, http://www.unicef.org/mdg/poverty.html, date accessed 8 May 2012.

Waters, K. (2001) 'The art and ethics of fundraising', *Christianity Today Magazine*, http://www.christianitytoday.com/ct/article_print.html?id=7970, date accessed 19 January 2010.

Whaites, A. (1999) 'Pursuing partnership: World Vision and the ideology of development – A case study', *Development in Practice*, 9, 4, 410–423.

Williams, L.G. and Kantelberg, R. (2011) *Evaluation of Plan UK-DFID Partnership Programme Agreement: The Governance Program*, The IDL Group, http://www.plan-uk.org/resources/documents/Plan_UK-Governance_evaluation.pdf, date accessed 8 May 2012.

Wydick, B., Glewwe, P. and Rutledge, L. (2013) 'Does international child sponsorship work? A six-country study of impacts on adult life outcomes', *Journal of Political Economy*, 121, 2, 393–436.

Wydick, B., Rutledge, L. and Chu, J. (2009) *Does Child Sponsorship Work? Evidence from Uganda Using a Regression Discontinuity Design*, http://emlab.berkeley.edu/~webfac/bardhan/wydick.pdf, date accessed 11 September 2013.

Yuen, P. (2008) '"Things that break the heart of God": Child sponsorship programs and World Vision International', *Totem: The University of Western Ontario Journal of Anthropology*, 16, 1, 39–51.

2
Origins of Child Sponsorship: Save the Children Fund in the 1920s

Brad Watson

Introduction

The origins of child sponsorship (CS) are poorly understood. Ove (2013, p.56) comments that 'If there is one "true" origin of child sponsorship, it appears to be lost in the mists of time or to the vagaries of marketing personnel.' It is true that the passing of time does seem to have obscured recollection of its early use to the point that at least three CS organizations have been incorrectly credited with founding CS in the 1930s or 1940s when in fact it was pioneered much earlier. Importantly, while CS has been enduringly popular and widely used, there has been little analysis of its historic precursors. Those interested in early CS are invariably left with important questions. When and where did it begin? How did it function? What challenges and achievements are evident in early CS programmes? This chapter seeks to answer these questions with extensive reference to Save the Children Fund archival sources, allowing where possible for the sources to speak for themselves.

Lynch (1986, p.13) describes the search for the origin of institutions, customs and inventions as an important task of scholars. Accordingly, this chapter seeks to set the record straight and argues that contrary to claims surrounding the invention of CS in the 1930s by China Children's Fund (CCF is now referred to as ChildFund), Foster Parents Scheme for Children in Spain, or Save the Children USA, the origins of individual CS are readily traced to 1919, in the post-World War One work of The British Save the Children Fund (S.C.F.), the Society of Friends and various relief missions in Europe. At that time CS was couched in terms of 'child adoption' or 'godparenting' and primarily involved short-term provision of food rations to children and ongoing support of orphans. Referring to sponsors in the UK as godparents, it seems evident that the early 'adoption' scheme of the S.C.F. was firmly rooted in the Christian tradition of sponsorship and provision of a godparent at the point of baptism, a non-biblical custom dating to the second century CE. To some extent this may account for the popularity of international non-governmental organization (INGO) facilitated child sponsorship in countries with historic connections to Christianity.

Competing claims

Tise's (1993, p.5) history of Christian Children's Fund (formerly China Children's Fund and now ChildFund) credits the invention of CS to its American founder, John Calvitt Clarke. Referring to very rapid growth in fundraising in the 1940s and the care of children in Chinese orphanages, Tise writes:

> The secret to the miracle was CCF's very popular 'adoption' program developed sometime prior to 1941. According to this plan, individual donors could contribute a set amount of money per month and per year and 'adopt' an orphaned child in China.

Noting that regular installments totaled US$24 per year, Tise concluded that '...CCF was the earliest of the various international child assistance organizations to employ this form of "adoption" as a mechanism for raising funds'. Key to this narrative is the idea that CS was conceived by an American, adapted for orphan care in China, popularized in the United States and replicated by other INGOs for worldwide use.

Contrary to Tise's understanding of the origins of CS, an earlier history of Foster Parents Plan International attributes conception of the idea to British journalist John Langdon-Davies in 1937:

> While covering the war in Spain for the London News Chronicle, Langdon-Davies conceived the idea of a personal relationship between a refugee or orphaned child and an English sponsor. In England he enlisted the support of the Duchess of Atholl, a prominent conservative member of parliament... (Molumphy, 1984, p.2).

In this narrative the invention of CS is attributed to a brave, well-connected British journalist, for direct support of costs associated with children's colonies in war-affected Spain. The Duchess of Atholl is presented as an influential supporter of Langdon-Davies' fresh idea.

A third claim is commonly made, presuming that CS was first used in the USA by Save the Children. Referring to Save the Children USA historical accounts available in the 1990s, Journalist Michael Maren wrote, 'The organization pioneered this fund-raising technique with Appalachian children in the 1930s. It has since been adopted by dozens of other charities around the world...' (Maren, 1997, p.139). In similar vein Ove (2013, p.57) cites a Save the Children USA historical account in which:

> Save the Children US, which was established to help poor children in Appalachia, claims to be the first instance of a sponsorship program in 1938 – a program in which individuals could sponsor schoolhouses and provide the children who attended them with 'meals, books and school supplies'.

Although ChildFund, Plan and Save the Children USA used CS in their early years, by then it was an already well-used fundraising device. By 1939 the sponsorship of children had been utilized for some 20 years by the S.C.F. in the UK and Quakers (otherwise known as the Society of Friends) whose relief mission was one of many based in post-World War One Europe.

S.C.F. and the Society of Friends in post-World War One Europe

Individual CS was used as early as 1920, as a direct response to widespread poverty and famine in war-torn Europe. From October 1, 1920 the recently established British Save the Children Fund (S.C.F.) published *THE RECORD of the SAVE THE CHILDREN FUND*, a monthly publication designed to advocate for improved child welfare and to raise funds for famine relief in what it referred to as 'the stricken lands.' It was described by the Glasgow Bulletin as 'the most melancholy magazine in existence' (S.C.F., 1920c, p.38). By 1922, when it was renamed *The World's Children: A Quarterly Journal of Child Care and Protection Considered from an International Standpoint*, circulation was 5,000 and sold for three pence per copy (Mahood and Satzewich, 2009, p.59).

The widely-circulated periodical played a key role in mobilizing support for British funded relief efforts, in stark contrast to the grim war propaganda prevalent in previous years and strident, ongoing calls for reparations. Referring to the plight of post-war Germany it described in its first edition (S.C.F., 1920a, p.5), 30,000 tuberculous children in Berlin, a million children dead from hunger and consumption since the cessation of hostilities and 'school children with hollow chests and lifeless eyes, the corpse-like babies dying in the wards'. With Christmas 1920 approaching in Britain, S.C.F. staff adapted war language in their appeal for humanitarian aid, observing that:

> The most dreadful siege in history is taking place in Europe to-day – a short journey from where you are reading now. Famine, Cold and Disease are the besiegers. The daily casualties, numbering always hundreds and often thousands, are innocent little children – not strong fighting men. And this siege had been going on for two years – two years during which Millions of Children have Died! (S.C.F., 1921a, p.64).

Poignant commentary and urgent appeals were designed to arouse a complacent, war-weary public, declaring to readers in Europe, 'All hope gone, Death is staring them in the face unless you, or others like you, come to their assistance' (S.C.F., 1921a, p.64).

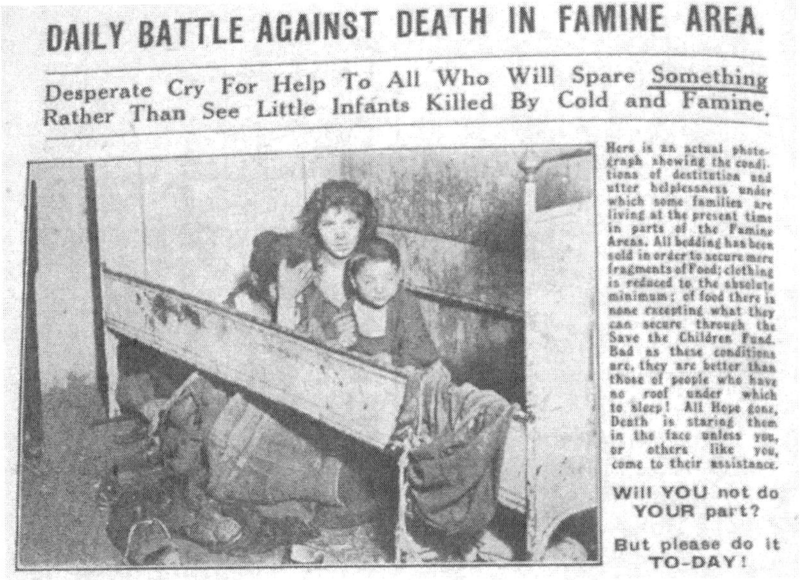

DAILY BATTLE AGAINST DEATH IN FAMINE AREA.

Desperate Cry For Help To All Who Will Spare Something Rather Than See Little Infants Killed By Cold and Famine.

Here is an actual photograph showing the conditions of destitution and utter helplessness under which some families are living at the present time in parts of the Famine Areas. All bedding has been sold in order to secure mere fragments of Food; clothing is reduced to the absolute minimum; of food there is none excepting what they can secure through the Save the Children Fund. Bad as these conditions are, they are better than those of people who have no roof under which to sleep! All Hope gone, Death is staring them in the face unless you, or others like you, come to their assistance.

Will YOU not do YOUR part?

But please do it TO-DAY!

Figure 2.1 1920 S.C.F. appeal
Picture of mother and child in dirty room without bedding, mattress or adequate clothing (S.C.F., 1921a, p.64)

Levels of sympathy in Britain for children in post-World War One Europe varied. Referring to 1921 S.C.F. announcements that it would send aid to starving Russian Children, Mahood and Satzewich (2009, p.55) describe Fund supporters and detractors influenced by anti-Russian, anti-German and anti-alien sentiment with consequent reservations about fuelling Bolshevism and feeding enemy children. However, where it existed concern was linked to pity for starving children, ill women, abhorrence for post-armistice sanctions and sureness of British generosity at a time when the gruesome after-effects of the war had become well publicized. Referring often to the plight of 'thousands of little ones standing in daily peril of death from starvation' (S.C.F., 1920a, p.1) S.C.F. publications also mentioned 'the evil structure of international relations' (S.C.F., 1921e, p.201) with one influential contributor arguing that 'The money we send to feed the children is thus not so much alms as blood-money. It is the compensation which the Koran and other codes have allowed to be paid for murder' (Zangwill in S.C.F., 1921e, p.216).

Noting that 'there is no more generous people in the world than the British people,' (Snowden, 1921, p.68). Mrs. Philip Snowden, described by some as the most eloquent Englishwoman alive, observed that childhood's 'beautiful innocence and helplessness appeals to the best in all. It is bigger than nationality, purer than ambition, greater than material wealth. It must be saved if civilization is to be saved, and the kingdom of heaven achieved.' Snowden's comments were not representative of some strands of public opinion which had branded those who helped German children as Hun lovers. Nevertheless, she also speculated that when the history of the times came to be written by the historians of the future, 'to no body of people will a warmer tribute be paid than to those who organised themselves for the work of saving the children of Europe' (Snowden, 1921, p.69). The adoption of the Della Robbia Bambino by the S.C.F. symbolized its role in appealing, on behalf of countless imploring children, to charity and the beneficence of civilized Europe.

Sympathy for post-war Austria was especially strong in 1920 and 1921 in S.C.F. writings and is partially attributable to British government pound-for-pound grants to relief societies active in Poland and Austria (S.C.F., 1920a, p.10). Although S.C.F. writers commented that 'The state of Austria outside Vienna is not so distressing,' (S.C.F., 1921b, p.102) they also took pains to describe to readers '...the pauperization and demoralization of the people,' concluding that 'Vienna must be regarded as a dying city' (S.C.F., 1920a, p.4). It was in this

Figure 2.2 The S.C.F. Dela Robbia Bambino
Dela Robbia Bambino (S.C.F., 1921d, p.185)

context that the fledgling S.C.F. made its first international grant on May 28 1919, to work in Austria, almost a month before it was registered under the War Charities Act (S.C.F., 1922b, p.11). Grants to Armenia and Germany were also made in June 1920. More approving of the grant to Armenia, the secretary of the American Near East Relief Administration reported that Armenian refugees had, by contrast, lost everything and 'have no houses, no clothes, no tools' (S.C.F., 1920a, p.3). Notably, by 1919 the Americans had already fed 160,000 children in Austria as part of its massive relief effort (S.C.F., 1920a, p.2). Similar feeding programmes were envisaged by S.C.F., sure that 'The Coming Winter will be A TIME OF Crisis' (S.C.F., 1920a, p.16).

Although it prioritized food and medical aid, S.C.F. emphasized other needs on the basis that '...the rigors of the food famine are considerably increased by the lack of linen, clothing and soap' (S.C.F., 1920a, p.1). Early communication from S.C.F. mentions a range of problems including what it referred to as a 'clothes famine' (S.C.F., 1920a, p.2), manifested in 'unhappy little ones wrapped in newspapers' (S.C.F., 1920a, p.3) and a scarcity of linen so great that in some schools 'between forty and fifty percent of the children have only one shirt each' (S.C.F., 1920a, p.1). The situation reported by one eye-witness in 'Czecho-Slovakia' is especially interesting. Arguing that the term 'house' was too dignified, the worried observer noted that:

> Hovel or hole is a better word for these inhabitants. The squalor is almost beyond belief. Six or seven people – if one can call them people – in one stuffy hole and a half-dozen hens or rabbits besides. One picked the fleas off oneself coming out. Idiots and cretins abound, and there is a goiter or two (colossal in size) in every family (S.C.F., 1920a, p.4).

Though a twenty-first century reader is likely to find such descriptions judgmental and insensitive, the issues raised were nonetheless serious. Concern is evident for overcrowding, unhygienic homes with plague carrying fleas, dietary deficiency, untreated medical conditions and disability linked to malnutrition. The specter of typhus, plague and TB loomed large for those who worried about child welfare in the immediate post-war years.

Other voices were less critical though no less passionate about the situation in the 'stricken lands' in 1920. In Hungary, a Mr. Cournos noted the urgent need for '...milk for the children and linen and rubber goods for the hospitals' with schooling for children forced to leave at age 12 but barred from entry to a trade until 14 (S.C.F., 1920a, p.5). U.S Army Medical Core representative Col. Gilchrist summed up the need of Poland in terms of an imminent typhus epidemic with potential to '...threaten the whole of Europe' (S.C.F., 1920a, p.6). In Russia, Miss Francis, senior sister of Lady Muriel Paget's Hospital at Sevastopol declared that throughout the Crimea '...people are living on bread and soup...everywhere there is very grave poverty, people of all classes are selling everything they have...' (S.C.F., 1920a, p.6). The depth of concern is mirrored in the urgency of early S.C.F. communications. Monthly advertising noted that 'The Coming Winter will be A TIME OF CRISIS to many millions of suffering children in the war-stricken lands of Europe and Asia Minor. Even now thousands hover between life and death' (S.C.F., 1920a, p.16). Apart from provision of milk and food rations, arrangements were made '...for children to be "adopted" in Austria and the towns of Germany, and also in Estonia, Poland and Armenia' (S.C.F., 1920b, p.21). It is in this adoption programme that we see use of CS by S.C.F. and the Society of Friends as a fundraising tool.

Figure 2.3 S.C.F. picture titled 'Orphaned and Destitute Two little Armenians who might be saved'
(S.C.F., 1921a, p.52)

Early child sponsorship at S.C.F.

Subsequent to announcements of the establishment of a child welfare department at S.C.F., early editions of The Record make increasingly frequent references to CS, commonly referred to as the 'Adoption scheme'. By November 1920, approximately 18 months after making its first international grant, The Record could already report that:

The 'Adoption' Scheme, whereby the individual subscriber of 2S.[shillings] a week, or an equivalent monthly or yearly sum to the S.C.F., provides a daily meal for a specific child in the famine area, has proved immensely popular, and is fast becoming a concrete reality. The names and addresses of 1,000 Slovak children, of 1,500 Budapest children, and of a number of Serbian children, have been received and sent to the 'godparents' with all available detail (S.C.F., 1920b, p.21).

A follow-up article in December 1920, noted strong support in Britain from individuals, Women's institutes, Girl's Friendly Societies, Brotherhood meetings, congregations and staff of shops and offices. Within a short period of time S.C.F. sponsorships had grown and included 451 children in Serbia, 2,000 in Slovakia, 2,000 in Budapest (Hungary) 350 in Leipzig (Germany) and 800 in Dvinsk (Baltic Provinces) (S.C.F., 1920c, p.45). By January 1921 S.C.F. could announce with some satisfaction that 'The adoption scheme is going forward rapidly...' and 'The promises of adoption number 15,045' (S.C.F., 1921a, p.60).

Writing in 1922, Eglantyne Jebb attributed development of the adoption system, (now known as child sponsorship) to S.C.F. in Britain, with the first adoptions taking place in S.C.F. funded projects in Austria and Europe in 1919 and 1920. Offering her readers the insight that '...twelve hundred specially necessitous children were fed by the society of Friends under the Adoption Scheme, and five hundred more by various institutions selected by the International Commissioner' (Jebb, 1922, p.20) she also took pains to point out that 'The adoption system, which was first initiated by the Save the Children Fund, was widely copied by other organizations, the merit of the scheme consisting in the fact that individual donors could, if they wished, interest themselves in individual children' (Jebb, 1922, p.19). Significantly, Jebb's account indicates that S.C.F.'s Adoption Scheme was already successful enough to have, within two years, been replicated and adapted by various other organizations providing relief in Europe.

It seems likely that the copying of the 'Adoption Scheme' referred to by Jebb may be attributed to two factors if we are given room to speculate. Firstly, competing fundraisers noted S.C.F.'s success and adopted the fundraising technique. Secondly, as S.C.F. worked with other organizations and institutions that had complementary non-S.C.F. income streams, these partners began their own 'adoption' programmes. A good example is the Society of Friends (Quakers). A letter from Friend's volunteer Mary Houghman to Miss E. Sidgwick refers to '...one of our early adoptions in Vienna, about August 1919 to 1920...' (Houghton, 1922a). Though Houghton attributes early funding of 'adoptions' to the S.C.F., and refers to a 'joint adoption plan', by 1922 the Friends in

Vienna had developed their own 'adoption' programme and started '...a special American branch of our Adoption Scheme by which children carefully chosen from amongst the needy families without regard to nationality, religion, or class, receive monthly food parcels worth about $2' (Houghton, 1922b, p.2).

While the Friends were recruiting sponsors in the USA, S.C.F. publications promoted 'adoptions' worldwide. In a short piece of writing titled 'The Empire and the Save the Children Fund' support is recorded from Australia, New Zealand and Canada (S.C.F., 1922a, p.143). In 1923 S.C.F.'s 'Overseas Department' was praised for:

> making great headway with the 'adoptions' scheme, and there are now subscribers scattered all over the world who are bearing a part in this most effective method of help. In South Africa, particularly, the scheme seems to have attracted schools and institutions (S.C.F., 1923, p.149).

Awareness of adoption or child sponsorship, was also evident in the USA in the early 1920s through the Quakers and those who received S.C.F. publications. Although we cannot be sure that the S.C.F. programme was being referred to directly, in December 1921 The Record reported that the president of the United States of America had '...issued an appeal to the American people to contribute to the relief of the children of Central Europe who are facing starvation. He announces that he will adopt 20 of these children as his own temporary wards' (S.C.F., 1921a, p.61). It may well have been that President Wilson, the 29th president of the United States of America, was an early child sponsor though further inquiry is needed to confirm the nature of his 'adoptions' and links to S.C.F. or the Society of Friends.

Unfortunately, it is not clear whether the original idea for promoting 'adoptions' of individual, war-affected children through a system of monthly donations originated with S.C.F. British staff, one of the S.C.F.'s many partners or with other charitable organizations. Members of the early S.C.F. executive committee included Catherine Booth, a Brigadier in the Salvation Army, and Ruth Fry, a representative of the Quakers. When the International Save the Children Union was formed and based in Geneva, it was with the strong support of Etienne Clouzot, Head of Secretariat, the International Committee of the Red Cross. While Jebb herself claimed that S.C.F. invented the 'Adoption Scheme' it may well be that her knowledge of its genesis was incomplete. Nevertheless, in the absence of other claims prior to 1920, the

British Save the Children Fund should be cautiously accorded credit for pioneering CS in the post-World War One period.

How did it function?

Children who were sponsored in the early years by S.C.F. were referred by various relief agencies active in each country. The December 1920 edition of The Record reassured readers in Britain and its Dominions that:

> The administration abroad is in the hands of the various relief agencies, viz., the Serb-Croat-Slovene Association for Child Welfare, Lady Muriel Paget's mission to Czecho-Slovakia, Action Lodge Famine Relief Fund in Budapest, the Committee for Feeding Undernourished Children in Leipzig, and Lady Muriel Paget's Mission to Eastern Europe (S.C.F., 1920c, p.45).

S.C.F. encouraged European-based relief missions to select needy children and forward lists to the UK where appeals for funding in general and adopters in particular had already been made (see advertising below in Figure 2.4). Eager to explain how needy children were identified, Record staff wrote:

> Each child has been selected through the schools by the relief workers, in itself no light task, and the fullest possible particulars have been forwarded for the god-parents. Everywhere the schoolteachers have given ungrudging assistance (S.C.F., 1920c, p.45).

It is noteworthy that in Serbia most of the children selected for sponsorship were in orphanages and orphan homes, or were orphans living with family members. Although sponsorship of orphans provided daily meals at home or in institutions, it was reported that 'In Slovakia the feeding is done chiefly in the school-kitchens of the villages... We have photographs showing the children watching the cook or happily grouped in little picnic parties...' (S.C.F., 1920c, p.45).

In 1920 and 1921 the first sponsorship advertising became evident in S.C.F. publications as an alternative to lump sum donations for unspecified needs. An example of this can be seen below where donors were given the option of choosing the nationality of their godchild and making a commitment to weekly or monthly support prior to receiving child details by mail. At this point in time it appears that

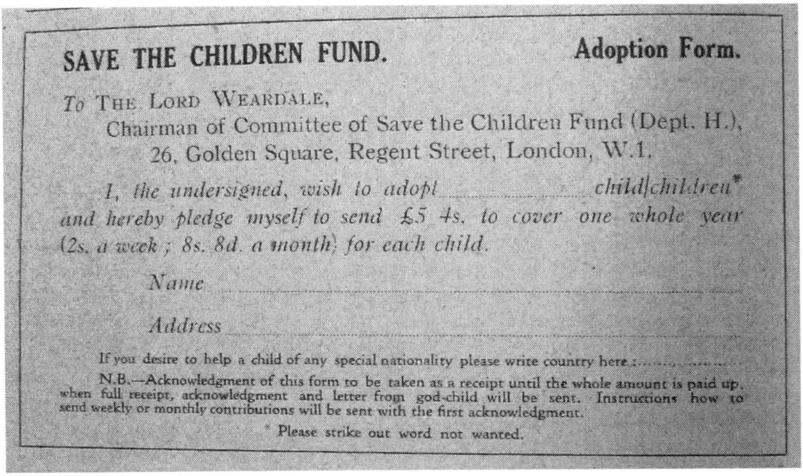

SAVE THE CHILDREN FUND. Adoption Form.

To THE LORD WEARDALE,
Chairman of Committee of Save the Children Fund (Dept. H.),
26, Golden Square, Regent Street, London, W.1.

I, the undersigned, wish to adopt .... child/children and hereby pledge myself to send £5 4s. to cover one whole year (2s. a week ; 8s. 8d. a month) for each child.*

Name ....

Address ....

If you desire to help a child of any special nationality please write country here :..................

N.B.—Acknowledgment of this form to be taken as a receipt until the whole amount is paid up, when full receipt, acknowledgment and letter from god-child will be sent. Instructions how to send weekly or monthly contributions will be sent with the first acknowledgment.

* Please strike out word not wanted.

Figure 2.4 1920 S.C.F. Adoption Form
Early adoption form referring to beneficiaries as a 'god-child' (S.C.F., 1920c, p.46)

godparents provided a cash payment first, and were later sent details of a specific child. In some sources this was referred to as 'pairing' (Gilmore, 1922, p.1).

A letter from S.C.F. staff to children in Britain and its dominions illustrates the basic mechanism of sponsorship:

> My Dear Boys and Girls, ...No doubt you know all about our 'adoption' scheme. What you do is to pay 2S. a week, which provides a little boy or girl with a good meal each day for a week. Those people who promise to pay their 2S. regularly for a whole year become 'god-parents' and they write to the little children they are saving. At Christmas some of the 'god-parents' sent presents to their 'adopted' sons and daughters and they replied very nicely... (S.C.F., 1921c, p.176).

S.C.F. in Austria

The conclusion of World War One with an armistice in 1918 and subsequent Treaty of Versailles in June 1919, resulted in an end to the devastating Allied naval blockade in the North Atlantic. Sympathy for Austria ran deep in S.C.F. publications. The May 1921 edition of The Record featured an article by Sir Phillip Gibbs entitled 'By Austria's

Deathbed. An Impression of Vienna' (S.C.F., 1921e, p.199). In it he wrote 'It is a ghoulish thing to sit at the deathbed of those Austrian people, as I have done, studying the symptoms of this mortality, watching the death agony...' In his descriptive assessment Gibbs described a babies' clinic as 'filled with haggard, anemic women who had brought their terrible little babes, all scrofulous and boneless, for medical examination...' and remarked on the '...bewildering contrasts between reckless luxury and starving poverty, between gaiety and despair...' (S.C.F. 1921e, p.200). Appalled by the impact of the blockade and trade restrictions, Gibbs also expressed sympathy for a doctor who was living on cabbage soup while persevering with a suit dating from before the war.

As a consequence of the sympathies of key S.C.F. supporters like Gibbs, Austria's accessibility, close proximity to Switzerland, prevalence of capable relief missions and priority for allied food and medical aid, S.C.F. support for Austria in the period 1919–1923 was significant, with provision of £150,000 to the Society of Friends and £5,000 to the Vienna Emergency Relief Fund (S.C.F., 1920c, p.38). It is noteworthy that:

> Vienna was the first place to receive the succour of the Save the Children Fund, the initial consignment of food – the very first consignment to be bought with British funds – being purchased in Switzerland in the early spring of 1919 (Jebb, 1922, p.18).

In her factual account of S.C.F.'s work in Austria, Eglantyne Jebb reported that the Friends were actively involved in provision of rations or meals, and '...had 70,000 of these children on its books in the winter 1920–21' (Jebb, 1922, p.18) most of whom were under the age of six. In addition to food distribution and child feeding, the Friends had partnered with an Austrian child welfare agency which operated 69 centres in Vienna, providing free medical consultations, crèches and food depots where mothers could purchase cheap rations.

Austria is also significant because it was one of the first sites, if not the definitive first site, for S.C.F. 'adoptions'. A letter from Miss Haughton, in the Friends Relief Mission Vienna, mentions an early sponsor in August 1919 (Houghton, 1922b), just three months after S.C.F.'s first cash grant to Austria. In a letter home from one of the Friend's Relief Workers, the writer explains that 'The idea of the "Adoption" Scheme originated with the "Save the Children" Fund who have given us a grant which enables us to adopt over 1,300 children, to which we have added various small grants and gifts from individual "adopters", which have brought our numbers up...' (Friends volunteer, n.d., p.4).

Concluding that it would be impossible to continue feeding large numbers of Austrian children for a third consecutive year, when dire need existed elsewhere (for example Russia) Jebb observed that S.C.F. '...determined therefore to concentrate its assistance in two main directions: (1) Feeding a number of specially-selected cases of children through its 'adoption' system... (2) Subsidizing local institutions...' (Jebb, 1922, p.19). The support of local institutions was justified by observations that Austria already had noble institutions and welfare departments, but little funding. Although the word sustainability was not used, the issue was clearly one of temporary support until local organizations could once again sustain their activities on behalf of orphans, disabled children and the poor.

Jebb hinted at a unique feature of the Austrian Adoption Scheme when she wrote:

> Vienna was a particularly suitable locality for the working of this scheme, partly because it was easier here than in less settled areas to keep track of children, and partly because there were so many who were specially suitable for 'adoption' in that they did not fall into any one of the recognized categories for relief (Jebb, 1922, p.19).

The question is, what was Jebb referring to when she mentioned adoption of children who did not fall into recognized categories and who were, in likelihood, not eligible for food distributed in the American or other food programmes? Clues to the nature of Jebb's special category are found in correspondence from Quaker staff in Austria. A 1922 Letter to S.C.F. supporters stated that 'An interesting feature of our work is that whilst a large number of our children belong to the working-class, the majority of them are drawn from the families of brain-workers, pensioned War invalids and State officials' (Houghton, 1922c, p.2).

One class-conscious Friend was quite explicit in her criteria for child selection, stating in a letter home:

> I am so glad to be able to open my doors to all and sundry, making only such general distinctions as, that the children must come from decent families, keeping up standards of cleanliness, so that we need feel no scruples in letting them stand in the 'que' together, when they come along for their monthly Food Parcel (Friends Volunteer, n.d., p.4).

Excluding poorly dressed, lower-class children from the sponsorship programme so as not to offend middle or upper class children who required charity seems contrary to Quaker principles of non-discrimination. Rather than view this as evidence of systemic prejudice and lack of compassion, it is perhaps better understood as evidence that the 'Adoption Scheme' was promoted to affluent supporters sympathetic to the plight of educated Viennese who had fallen on hard times and whose children may not have been eligible for assistance under other feeding schemes. In correspondence to S.C.F. supporters it was noted that:

> All the women have been personally visited and last winter it was possible to discontinue the rations to some children whose circumstances had improved and give them to others who were more needy. Almost half are children of widows, pensioners or invalids... (Houghton, 1922d, p.1).

To illustrate the human dimension of the process for its readers, Record staff added a copy of a hand-written letter by a sponsored boy named Paul:

> Dear Foster Parent No 4306, Many thanks for the kind gift of 524 Crowns You've been so kind to send me for Christmas Mama brought me a pair of boots from it. Father knows and loves Great Britain and Ireland he studied there for a year – I have got a little brother, two years old, his name is Laszeo Mother is often ill Father is art-teacher I am a pupil of a state grammar school of the 1 Class. I would like to know your children by name. I am dear Foster parents Yours very gratefully, Paul Baronski Budapest... (S.C.F., 1921c, p.176).

In this instance, it was clear to British readers that the sponsored boy was from an educated family adversely affected by post-war conditions. The report excerpt below indicates a strong bias in the Austrian Scheme. Though the terminology is dated, Mittelstand may be taken to refer to the families in the middle-upper classes, and of 1221 families supported, 981 were classified as such.

There were certainly procedures to eliminate inappropriate sponsorship. For example, a request by the Swedish Y.W.C.A. to find a sponsor for one Florian Richter was considered due to the fact that his father had been a doctor of medicine missing since 1915, presumed dead.

```
            Statement made from Case Records in our Office.
                                                    % of totals:
    Total of families . . . . . . . . . .  1221

    MITTELSTAND:-
        No.of Mittelstand Families . . . . .    981
        Professors & Teachers (included in. .   128
                        figure )
    Widows . . . . . . . . . . . . . . . .      137          13%
    Invalids and Pensionists . . . . . . .       71           7%
    Tuberculosis in family . . . . . . . .      184          20%

    WORKING CLASS:-
        No.of Working Class Families . . . . .  220
    Widows . . . . . . . . . . . . . . . .       48          25%
    Invalids and Pensionists . . . . . . .       15           6%
    Tuberculosis in family . . . . . . . .       72          33%

        Total of Widows (Middleclass and Working Class)185. . 16%
          "    "  Invalids and Pensionists . . . . .  86. .  7%
          "    "  Tubercular Cases . . . . . . . . .  256. . 22%
```

Figure 2.5   Report of Save the Children Fund adoption scheme
(Anon, 1922a, p.1)

However, an assessment based on a family visitation reported that the home was comfortably furnished, income was sufficient and the boy was in boarding school. 'In our opinion this is not a needy case and would not be helped from our funds' (Mission Der Freunde Mittelstand, n.d., p.1).

Documentation from S.C.F. archives indicate that sponsored children in Vienna received home visits from Friends who functioned as case workers whose task was to assess levels of family need. In 1922 the Friends reported to S.C.F. that 'Visits of Investigation paid to the homes of the children...' numbered 1,433, and that 350 most urgent cases should be supported during the following winter (Anon, 1922a, p.2).

A second important feature of the joint S.C.F. and Friends Austrian Adoption Scheme was its short-term nature. Unless in an institution, children received food parcels for periods typically around six months, with preference for support over the winter months. Institutionalized children received subsidized daily meals or fresh milk. While 12 month adoptions were encouraged, it seems that six month adoptions were more common. A 1922 letter from S.C.F. asked for information on the conditions of two adopted children, noting that 'They were six month adoptions, but the adopter awaits your view to decide whether to go on, or change to some more necessitous child elsewhere' (Anon, 1922b, p.1). However, in denying a request to use sponsor funding to support one child for the first six months, and another for the second six months, an earlier letter from S.C.F. staff stated firmly 'With regard to substituting other children for the second six months, I am sorry we cannot agree to this. Our scheme provides for the feeding of the same child for one year and the foster-parents understood this from the beginning' (Anon, 1921 p.1).

It seems evident from the account above that the expectations of S.C.F. staff in the UK determined the length of support provided to individual children rather than the expert opinion of staff in Austria who preferred greater flexibility. It is notable that there appears to be no preference in early years for younger children or for the poorest of children. Another interesting feature of the 'Adoption Scheme' in Austria was the nature of tangible support provided to children through food aid and gifts. Food parcels funded by S.C.F. and distributed by the Friends seem to have been generous, as seen in this description:

> It is an interesting sight to see our little family of children of all ages coming along with knapsack on back, or capacious bag in hand to fetch their precious gifts of milk, fat, sugar, cocoa, white flour, and rice, and last, but not least appreciated, a cake of good quality washing soap, treasures which it is utterly beyond their parent's power to buy in the open market, owing to the terrible depreciation in the value of the Krone (Anon, 1922c).

Not all children were assisted in this manner. Children in institutions benefited from food supplied directly to the institution, typically milk. The Friends had already experimented with importation of dairy cattle to supply milk to malnourished children in institutions, and in 1922 the Friends raised the issue with S.C.F. of appropriate support for older children, advocating for:

> ...a hot mid-day meal to such of the older children as are best fitted for this type of help, namely those who owing to advanced study had to be away from home all day and only take a little plain lunch (often just black bread) with them. The parents are delighted at the suggestion and these big boys and girls do not need fresh milk so much as plenty to eat at mid-day' (Anon, 1922f, p.1).

It seems then that the S.C.F.-funded Joint Adoption Scheme provided three variations of support: daily milk rations for malnourished children; monthly rations for predominantly middle-class children in need of temporary assistance; and in some cases daily midday meals, generally over a period of six months to 12 months. In some cases rations were supplemented with cod liver oil, boots and clothing.

A final feature of S.C.F. funded adoptions in Austria was the personal touch incorporated in experimentation with letter writing and gift giving. In the Austrian joint adoption scheme it appears that it was the Friends who actively pursued communication between godchildren and their adoptive parents. A February 1921 letter from the Friends in London to S.C.F. acknowledges receipt of a cheque from S.C.F. of £4,420 to cover the costs of 850 adoptions and concluded with this pointed advice to S.C.F.

> We are posting to you to-day a further number of the cards written by the children who have been adopted. We feel that this may be very valuable in making more real the connection between the children, and those who have contributed towards their help. We have asked Miss Houghton, our representative in Vienna...to keep you supplied with reports as to its working, and to make the contact between the children and their 'god-parents', as they like to call them, as living as possible (Henderson, 1921, p.1).

Such correspondence seems to indicate that while S.C.F. originated the idea of sponsoring individuals, it was the Friends who played a very active role in nurturing ongoing contact between children and their adoptive parents, paving the way for monthly and yearly reports on child progress that became common in later years.

One such letter is as follows:

> Dear Godparents, Thank you very much for your good gifts. They tasted very good, but I am sorry I have already started on the last parcel. I have two big brothers, and sometimes I gave them some of the cocoa to taste. My parents have an allotment in the Prater, and we shall soon have the first things grown in it. My school report is good. In Languages, Singing, Writing, General Deportment Drill, I got 'good'. In Arithmetic, Reading, Scripture, Home-work, Nature Study and Industry, I got 'Very Good'. I am in the fourth class, and I love reading. At home, they call me the Book-worm. Two years ago I was in Sweden, in Goteborg, where I had a good time. I am sending you two drawings. One is the little house father is building, and I am going to help him and then I am to have my own bed. Where do you live, dear Godparents? I am so glad Spring is coming,

and that the cold weather is over. With much love, Your thankful godchild (Austrian Godchild, 1922, p.1).

The formula of this letter is simple and much replicated. A salutary greeting is followed by, in various order, an expression of thanks, description of school achievement, polite question or two to the sponsor, commentary on weather or play activities and closing statement of gratitude. Remarkably, the contents are not dissimilar to millions of letters written to sponsors since.

By 1923 crises elsewhere had made it difficult for S.C.F. to justify a continuation of support for children in Austria. Letters exchanged between the Friends in Vienna and S.C.F. in Britain reveal pleas for ongoing assistance and launch of new appeals. By this time however S.C.F.'s attention had turned elsewhere and the Friends Relief Mission struggled to actively recruiting adopters. A January 30 1923 Letter to S.C.F. reveals that in a new fundraising drive a '...total of 500 children has been reached, a good many of these are covered by private adopters from America or Vienna, and some are paid for by the Mission' (Gilmore, 1923, p.1). As early as 1922 the Friends in Vienna had reported that adopters existed in '...England, America, Canada, or Australia...' (Anon, 1922c, p.1).

S.C.F. did not only sponsor children in mainland Europe. Referring to the 'adoption' of children in the British Isles in the photo-card adoption scheme, *The Record* (S.C.F., 1925, p.36) noted that names of British children were gathered from the Invalid Children's Aid Association and help usually consisted of sending the child away to the countryside or sea for a holiday, then rations of cod liver oil or milk, for the rest of the year. For example, 'A clergyman, in poor circumstances, was given five (pounds) to provide milk for a little ailing son... one donor gave ten (pounds) that that the mother of five children – herself tubercular – might go away with the youngest two children, aged four and two respectively, for a holiday'. The use of photographs in the British scheme resulted in some 'parents' taking '...great interest in selecting their children – not only by nationality but by personal circumstances and characteristics' (S.C.F., 1925, p.36).

Experimentation with sponsorship had not been without its difficulties. Key problems included ongoing confusion and miscommunication over lists of adopted children, discrepancies in payments made by godparents, difficulty in administering gift giving, concern that short-term sponsorships left children vulnerable in coming winters, a strong feeling that some families should pay a portion of the costs of their food parcels to avoid the demoralization of dependency, and '...a good deal of disappointment on the part of some of the children at not having had any communication from their Adopter...' (Houghton, 1922c, p.5). The allocation of children by staff was sometimes problematic. In one case staff in the S.C.F. Allocation's department wrote 'The foster-parent has had a nice little letter from him but she is not pleased, because she declares we have given her a Jew, when she particularly desired otherwise' (Anon, 1922d, p.1). A subsequent family visit revealed that 'They are no Jews, but of Polish peasant type, and Roman Catholics... (Anon, 1922e, p.1). The short-term nature of some sponsor support also provided challenges, with the S.C.F. Allocations Department observing in 1922 that 'we have not many...that we can safely allocate: since some fosterparents in these hard times, pay installments for a couple of quarters, and then cease' (Anon, 1922g, p.1).

Nevertheless, the Adoption Scheme was praised for its ability to mobilize funds, in a personal way in which 'Love has blessed the gift. The children look upon the English friends as true god-parents, and these links of friendship will endure, witnessing to the reality of international goodwill' (Houghton, 1922d, p.1). Further, Quaker staff noted that a fine piece of work had been accomplished by S.C.F. in supporting individual children in their homes 'which often proves to be a more satisfactory way of helping them – especially the younger ones – than by taking them out of their own surroundings' (Houghton, 1922c, p.4).

The S.C.F. CS programme endured the Great Depression and operated more or less continually until the outbreak of World War Two. In January 1937, with the specter of another world war looming, the S.C.F. publication (now referred to as The World's Children) stated that 'The total number of adoptions at April 30th, 1936, was 669. Of these 458 were foreign cases. 211 were British children from the distressed areas of South Wales and the North of England, and from poor districts in London' (S.C.F. 1937a, p.58). Internationally sponsored children came from Austria, Armenia, Bulgaria, Czechoslovakia, Estonia, France, Germany, Hungary, Latvia, Poland, Turkey and Yugoslavia, suggesting that the programme had shrunk considerably from the 1920s yet maintained its geographic diversity. In Britain, S.C.F. staff relished the opportunity to encourage adoptive parents to provide an annual holiday for disadvantaged children, asserting that 'a holiday by the sea, or in the mountains or the open countryside, is little less than a glimpse of heaven' (S.C.F., 1937b, p.131).

Conclusion

The tumultuous period between the conclusions of World War One and onset of World War Two, a lack of readily accessible historical information, and the emergence of many new INGOs globally, may be partially responsible for well-intentioned though inaccurate claims about the origins of CS. However, while John Langdon-Davies and the Duchess of Atholl have been credited with founding CS to support displaced Spanish children in 1937 and 1938, it is more likely that the Duchess was already well familiar with foster parent schemes involving what we now refer to as sponsorship. In 1921 her husband, His Grace the Duke of Atholl, was preparing to take over as president of the British S.C.F. In a speech at Edinburgh at that time the Duchess of Atholl had expressed her pride in S.C.F.'s work, describing it as 'A task of Unprecedented Magnitude' (S.C.F., 1922c, p.105).

Debunking the claim that American J. Calvitt Clarke independently conceived the idea of child sponsorship as a tool for fundraising is also not difficult. CS had been publicized in the USA since at least 1921 via S.C.F. and the Society of Friends. According to CCF history Clarke was involved with the American Near East Relief programme until 1931 and had visited Armenia personally in 1924 at a time when S.C.F. was already sponsoring children there. As Co-Founder of Save the Children Federation (USA) in 1932 and southern Director from 1934–1937 it seems likely he would have been familiar with Save the Children literature, including sponsorship appeals, especially given that sponsorship was provided to children during the Great Depression in American Appalachia (Maren, 1997). Rather than being credited for inventing CS, it seems likely that J. Calvitt Clarke replicated an existing fundraising mechanism when he established CCF for the support of Chinese orphans.

CS was clearly used by S.C.F. and the Society of Friends in several European countries in the aftermath of World War One. In the absence of further information, S.C.F. and the Society of Friends should cautiously be credited as early pioneers of CS as a fundraising tool utilized to 'pair' international donors with disadvantaged children for the purpose of short-term provision of rations in post-conflict settings. Key ingredients of the early adoption scheme continue in CS programmes 90 years later, including monthly payments for the support of individual, identifiable children utilizing personal correspondence to encourage a sense of personal connection.

Acknowledgements

This chapter would not have been possible without the invaluable assistance provided by staff at the Cadbury Archives, University of Birmingham and Amy Bang from Save the Children.

Bibliography

Anon (1921) *Letter to Miss Hilda Clarke*, 2 June 1921 p.1 SCF Box A398 EJ32.
Anon, (1922a) *REPORT OF SAVE THE CHILDREN FUND ADOPTION SCHEME* p.1 SCF Box A398, EJ32.
Anon (1922b) *Letter to Miss Levin*, 4 August 1922 p.1 SCF Box A399, EJ38.
Anon (1922c) *Friends Relief Mission Adoption Scheme*, Vienna, 8 February 1922 pp.1–2 SCF Box A398 EJ32.
Anon (1922d) *Letter to Miss Houghton*, 16 May 1922 p.1 SCF Box A398 EJ32.
Anon (1922e) *Letter to Miss Sidgewick*, 8 June 1922 p.1 SCF Box A398 EJ32.
Anon (1922f) *Letter to Miss Sidgewick*, 1 December 1922 p.1 SCF Box A398 EJ33.
Anon (1922g) *Letter to Miss Levin*, 2 May 1922 p.1 SCF Box A399, EJ31.
Austrian Godchild (1922) *Letter to Godparents*, 6 April 1922 p.1 SCF Box A398, EJ32.
Friends Volunteer (n.d.) *Extracts from a Home Letter of one of the Friends' Relief Mission Workers* pp.1–6 SCF Box A398 EJ32.
Gilmore, E.J. (1922) *Letter to Miss Sidgwick*, 29 October 1922 pp.1–2 SCF Box A399 EJ33.
Gilmore, E.J. (1923) *Letter to Miss Sidgewick*, 30 January 1923 p.1. SCF Box A398 EJ31.
Henderson, J.B. (1921) *Letter from Friends' Emergency & War Victims Relief Committee*, 18 February 1921 p.1 SCF Box A398 EJ31.
Houghton, M. (1922a) *Letter to Miss Sidgewick*, 23 August 1922 p.1 SCF Box p.1 A398, EJ32.
Houghton, M. (1922b) *Friends Relief Mission Adoption Scheme*, 8 February 1922 pp.1–2 SCF Box A398, EJ32.
Houghton, M. (1922c) *A Letter addressed to the Adopters who have helped the CHILDREN of VIENNA*, May 1922 pp.1–6 SCF Box A398 EJ32.
Houghton, M. (1922d) *Appeal to Adoptors*, Vienna, July 1922 p.1 SCF Box A398 EJ32.
Jebb, E. (1922) British Relief in Austria, *THE RECORD of the SAVE THE CHILDREN FUND* Vol. 3, No. 1, October 1922, pp.18–20, SCF Box A670.
Lynch, J.H. (1986) *Godparents and Kinship in Early Medieval Europe* (Princeton, NJ: Princeton University Press).
Mahood, L. and Satzewich, V. (2009) 'The Save the Children Fund and the Russian famine of 1921–23: Claims and counter-claims about feeding "Bolshevik" children', *Journal of Historical Sociology*, 22, 55–83.
Maren, M. (1997) *The Road to Hell: The Ravaging Effects of Foreign Aid and International Charity* (NY: The Free Press).
Mission Der Freunde Mittelstand (n.d.) *REPORT on: Richter XII* SCF Box A399 EJ3.

Molumphy, H.D. (1984) *For Common Decency: The History of Foster Parents Plan 1937–1983* (Warwick, RI: Foster Parents Plan International).

Ove, P. (2013) *'Change a Life. Change Your Own': Child Sponsorship, the Discourse of Development, and the Production of Ethical Subjects.* Doctoral thesis, Faculty of Graduate Studies, University of British Columbia.

S.C.F. (1920a) *THE RECORD of the SAVE THE CHILDREN FUND*, 1, 1, October 1920 pp.1–16 SCF Box A670.

S.C.F. (1920b) *THE RECORD of the SAVE THE CHILDREN FUND*, 1, 2, November 1920, pp.17–32 SCF Box A670.

S.C.F. (1920c) *THE RECORD of the SAVE THE CHILDREN FUND*, 1, 3, December 1920, pp.33–48 SCF Box A670.

S.C.F. (1921a) *THE RECORD of the SAVE THE CHILDREN FUND*, 1, 4, January 1921, pp.49–64 SCF Box A670.

S.C.F. (1921b) *THE RECORD of the SAVE THE CHILDREN FUND*, 1, 7, February 1921, pp.97–112 SCF Box A670.

S.C.F. (1921c) *THE RECORD of the SAVE THE CHILDREN FUND*, 1, 11, April 1921, pp.161–176 SCF Box A670.

S.C.F. (1921d) *THE RECORD of the SAVE THE CHILDREN FUND*, 1, 12, May 1921, pp.177–196 SCF Box A670.

S.C.F. (1921e) *THE RECORD of the SAVE THE CHILDREN FUND*, 1, 13, May 1921, pp.197–214 SCF Box A670.

S.C.F. (1922a) *THE RECORD of the SAVE THE CHILDREN FUND*. S.C.F., 2, 9, January 1922 pp.135–150 SCF Box A670.

S.C.F. (1922b) *The World's Children: A Quarterly Journal of Child Care and Protection Considered from an International* Viewpoint, 3, 1, October 1922 pp.1–66 SCF Box A670.

S.C.F. (1922c) 'The Duchess of Atholl and the Save the Children Fund', *The World's Children: A Quarterly Journal of Child Care and Protection Considered from an International Viewpoint*, 3, 2, December 1922 pp.67–108 SCF Box A670.

S.C.F. (1923) *The World's Children: A Quarterly Journal of Child Care and Protection Considered from an International* Viewpoint, 3, 3, April 1923 pp.109–156 SCF Box A670.

S.C.F. (1925) *The World's Children: Journal of Child Care and Protection Considered from an International Viewpoint*, 5, 2, November 1925 pp. 21–38 SCF Box A670.

S.C.F. (1937a) *The World's Children: The Official Organ of the Save the Children Fund and of the Declaration of* Geneva, 17, 4, January 1937 pp.56–58.

S.C.F. (1937b) *The World's Children: The Official Organ of the Save the Children Fund and of the Declaration of* Geneva, 17, 9, June 1937 p.131.

Snowden, P. (1921) 'THE CRY OF THE CHILDREN', *THE RECORD of the SAVE THE CHILDREN FUND*, 1, 5, January 1921 pp.67–68 SCF Box A670.

Tise, L.E. (1993) *A Book about Children: The World of Christian Children's Fund 1938–1991* (Falls Church, VA: Hartland Publishing).

Zangwill, I. (1921) 'BARGAINS IN BENIFICENCE', *THE RECORD of the SAVE THE CHILDREN FUND* Vol. 1, No.14, June 1921 pp.215–216 SCF Box A670.

3
A Typology of Child Sponsorship Activity

Brad Watson

Introduction – Questions of legitimacy

Critique of international non-governmental organizations (INGOs) is often framed by comparisons of efficacy, accountability and transparency, culminating in broad conclusions about their legitimacy as change agents. For Fowler (2000, p.220) 'The most important factor for NGDO [non-governmental development organization] credibility and legitimacy is demonstrating effective performance'. Mindful of this emphasis on performance and impact, the Bond Network (2006, p.6) emphasizes that the quality of an INGO's work '...is primarily determined by the quality of its relationships with its intended beneficiaries'. Although Riddell (2008, p.307) has wisely cautioned against 'drawing overall, general conclusions about the impact of different NGO development initiatives' it is important to clarify the nature of specific approaches to helping children through Child Sponsorship (CS) rather than to assume that CS is much the same everywhere and similar today when compared to CS practice in the past. Mindful about ongoing critique of CS, this chapter seeks to position CS INGO interventions in a landscape of contested ideas and argues that informed critique of CS is best achieved through a typology of CS funded interventions.

Generalizing about child sponsorship from 1940 to 1980

In the era 1940 to 1980 CS INGOs often, though not exclusively, emphasized the support of individual children in institutions (especially orphanages and schools) or they prioritized cash transfer and service delivery to disadvantaged children and families in the context of their communities or homes. Of 26 CS INGOs identified by Livezey (1981, p.2) in the early 1980s it was apparent that 'Some help children in institutional settings such as orphanages and schools. Others help children in their homes settings'. However, throughout the 1960s and 1970s, CS for beneficiaries in home settings typically involved direct handouts, service provision and cash transfers to children and their families for food, medicine and school needs. Notably, both broad models of sponsorship funded intervention were predicated on the idea that disadvantaged children required targeted help (child welfare interventions) from powerful, external agents (INGOs). Both prioritized ongoing support for child welfare and education. While some CS INGOs were experimenting more and more with '...self-help uplift projects – such as well digging, sewer building, and introducing new farming techniques...', the majority prioritized institutional care and direct assistance to children and families.

ChildFund (previously CCF was used as an acronym for Christian Children's Fund or China Children's Fund) is a case in point. In his *Book About Children* Tise (1993, p.7) describes an American organization dedicated in its formative years to 'hordes of homeless children' in China who needed a safe haven (p.38), preferably orphanages. Accordingly, Tise (1993, p.7) points out that by November 1944 Child Fund was providing funding to 45 Chinese orphanages. This is best seen as an institution-based child welfare programme formed in response to wartime conditions in which state welfare agency was dysfunctional, non-existent or overwhelmed. The primary objectives of ChildFund at this time were the rescue of vulnerable children, protection in a safe haven, provision of educational opportunities and delivery of religious instruction. As a matter of expedience, in its early years the pioneering staff at ChildFund readily though not exclusively partnered with Christian missions that had pre-existing orphan care programmes and schools.

Tise attributed the rapid growth of ChildFund to the '...very popular "adoption" plan developed sometime prior to 1941' (Tise, 1993, p.7). Promoted widely by founder John Calvitt Clarke, the 'adoption plan' encouraged individual donors in the USA to contribute monthly for the support of a Chinese orphan. 1941 board minutes reveal that Clarke thought the 'plan was working very well and that the current rate of $24 per child per year should be continued even though it "is now costing more than $24 per year to take care of these orphans"' (Tise, 1993, p.7). ChildFund's role was relatively simple. It raised funds in the USA and transferred them to foreign missionaries and mission institutions. In some cases ChildFund planned and constructed its own institutions. For example, the purpose-built, innovative Hong Kong Children's Garden (constructed in the mid-1950s) eventually housed 1,000 children in 98 cottages, each with houseparents, providing both formal and vocational education in what was widely lauded as an example of best practice in orphan care. However, most ChildFund supported orphanages appear to have been run like Hong Kong's Faith Love Orphanage with dormitories, regimented programmes, strict discipline and traditional, institutional approaches to orphan care (Tise, 1993, pp.44–45).

As a fundraising device, CS for orphan care provision provided a potent mechanism for mobilization of support in geographically diverse areas. By 1946 'funds were being sent to orphanages in the Philippines and Burma. Only a year later operations were being expanded into Japan, Korea and other realms of the Asian Continent'. At the peak of its orphan care assistance programme in Korea in the late 1950s (by which time ChildFund was known as Christian Children's Fund rather than China Children's Fund), it was assisting more than 38,000 children in 72 orphanages (Tise, 1993, p.64). The level of need reported was often touching. Reflecting on his early work in China, Reverend Verent Mills reminisced that the youngest of the 700 Chinese children in his care was discovered by a cluster of bamboo.

> And right beside the road there was a little boy. He looked more like a monkey than a human being thin, drawn, the skin on his face parched and wrinkled. The child was starving to death. He couldn't stand up, he couldn't cry, he just made moaning sounds. He was probably two and a half or three, and there he was, sitting in his own mess, too weak to move... (Mills in Tise, 1993, p.10).

In his poignant account of rescue and rehabilitation of the child (named Lo Duk, or Begotten of the Road), Mills provided a touching account of the potential for individual CS in a well-run orphanage to radically change a child's life through an act of love. Although such narratives would later be deemed simplistic and misleading in a context of poverty reduction, in the context of war-time orphan care they were generally deemed legitimate.

The rescue and protection of children like Lo Duk resulted in widespread acclaim for ChildFund's founder insofar as 'Everywhere he went, Clarke was treated with honor and glory. He made endless addresses, was feted at luncheons and dinners, and entertained by children at each of CCF's orphanages...' (Tise, 1993, p.8). To a large extent Clarke's vision of an international child adoption agency for war-affected children was legitimated in the 1950s by orphan care practice in his own country, affirmed by evangelical missionary zeal and promoted as an antidote to communism via an act of civic responsibility. Under Clarke's leadership CCF advertising depicted an emaciated child on a benefactor's lap, declaring that 'The road to communism is paved with hunger, ignorance and lack of hope' (in Klein, 2003, pp.155–159). In the context of emergent cold-war hostility and American confidence in its mandate to spread democracy, CS for orphans was embraced by some sponsors as an act of civic duty, Christian responsibility and demonstration of patriotic zeal.

ChildFund severed all ties with Clarke in 1963. His demise was accompanied by an irony apart from the harsh reality that he had been orphaned by the organization he had founded. That is, ChildFund's support for orphanages had peaked as the rapid demise of traditional American orphanages accelerated. Shughart and Chappell (in McKenzie, 1999, pp.153–154) have observed that in 1933 144,000 children were cared for in American orphanages in the USA. However, by 1977, only 43,000 children remained in institutions with family care viewed as a more legitimate and cost-effective response. The tide had clearly turned against the institutionalization of children in the USA by the 1960s, as it had against Clarke and his plans for an expanded orphan care programme.

Despite its historical work being centred on orphan care, by the 1960s ChildFund had begun to transition its programmatic approach while retaining individual sponsorship as a fundraising mechanism. The shift required a move to what it called Family Helper projects. Informed by American advances in the realm of social work utilizing case workers, the 1960s experimental Family Helper programme employed centres of social services, complete with supervisor, case workers, library books, classrooms and recreation spaces. High school graduates interested in social work were initially enlisted to visit homes, develop case reports on families and invite participation in ChildFund's programme (Tise, 1993, p.74). Cash grants were paid directly to families of eligible children '...to help you buy your groceries, and help you with your home. But every child of school age, five years and older, must go to school' (Tise, 1993, p.75). Additionally, mothers were encouraged to attend classes in nutrition, literacy, budgeting and sewing, or avail themselves of volunteer doctors who '...came to the center to give the children inoculations' (Tise, 1993, p.75). For ChildFund staff, the move towards case work represented an effort to adopt best-practice child welfare programming in an international context.

ChildFund's experimentation with individual child welfare in the Family Helper programmes of the 1960s and 1970s is evidence of a programmatic shift that was, arguably, out of step with emergent and soon to be dominant emphases on community development and poverty reduction. In a candid assessment of the experimental Family Helper programmes, staff member James Hostetler (Hostetler in Tise, 1993, p.66) explained with the power of hindsight that 'The emphasis was on what we could do for them. There was little thought of encouraging people to do something for themselves'. Despite this, the dominant feature of the new approach was extension of support to families using conditional cash transfers and direct service provision, either free or subsidized. Arguably, such transfers were conceived as being more likely to maintain children in their families, reduce high costs associated with institutional care, allow families the dignity of choosing how to expend funds and position the family as a conduit through which children would ultimately benefit.

In 1981 a comparison of various CS INGOs recorded that ChildFund's 236,000 sponsors were assisting 251,000 children in 26 countries:

> ...through its strictly one-to-one sponsor-child program. No religious requirement is imposed or inducement offered. It still supports some orphanages, but most of its work is done through its family-helper and educational programs. Funded entirely through private donations, its sponsors pay $15 monthly (Livezey, 1981, p.9).

However, in the 1980s ChildFund transitioned further to community development initiatives funded through CS. Responding to a General Accounting Office study of five large children's charities (including Foster Parent's Plan and Save the Children) which cited evidence of poor fiscal management or misrepresentation of policies in a number of organizations, ChildFund phased out funding for numerous third party partners (many of whom were local missions and missionary organizations) to improve financial transparency with the result that 'Within a year or two, all funds were remitted directly to the bank account of each CCF project' (Tise, 1993, p.80).

A push towards projects and community initiatives delivered by ChildFund was justified by self-initiated audits between 1972 and 1981 that had inexorably led staff to conclude that '...you can't effectively help a child apart from the context of his or her family, community and nation...' (Tise, 1993, p.84). For readers well versed in ideals of community development, self-help and empowerment this may be self-evident however through the mid to late 1980s ChildFund increasingly prioritized primary healthcare, nutrition, safe drinking water, basic education, income generation, environment and broader rights in programmes. It is evident that while former activities continued, over time CS in ChildFund had transitioned away from the individual support of orphans in institutions, to the support of children and their families in Family Helper programmes, and then to pooled funding for broader community development projects with some continued benefits to individual children. This involved challenges for ChildFund and other INGOs in transition, one of which was the fact that 'When an agency moves into the arena of community development, yet continues to operate on a sponsorship basis, it is sometimes difficult for the potential donor to understand exactly how his funds will be spent' (Livezey, 1981, p.3).

In its early years Plan International (known formerly as Foster Parent's PLAN for War Children and referred to simply as Plan in the remainder of this chapter) was also devoted to the support of orphans and war-affected children. Sponsorship of individuals in children's colonies during the course of the Spanish Civil war provided places of refuge for children who had been orphaned, separated from parents or identified as at risk of harm. Plan also fundraised for children in Korea in the 1950s however its staff argued that there were already too many poorly run and poorly funded orphanages in Korea (about 595 in 1953) and that a more urgent need was assistance to children living with their families. Although PLAN enrolled a similar number of children from families as from institutions in Korea, it avoided establishment of new orphanages and '...after 1954, it consciously leaned towards family-based enrolments with a view to preserving the family' (Plan International, 1998, p.26). Like ChildFund, historic Plan support of children in 'safe havens' generally required that sponsorship funds be directed to third party care providers. However, its new emphasis on support to families required direct cash grants to family members and provision of social services or community-based health programmes (Plan International, 1998, p.28).

The shift away from orphan support to family support is referred to with some pride in Plan International publications with the claim that 'Alone among children's organizations in Korea, Plan began a programme of direct assistance to families with children, guided by social workers working intensively in the communities around Pusan'. Excitingly for the organization at that time, its staff developed the model programme adopted by the South Korean government to resettle numerous orphans in family care (Plan International, 1998, p.27). However, whilst working with poor Chinese immigrants in Hong Kong, Plan staff recognized that 'Simple cash grants and parcels were not enough to save these children. Nor was PLAN's usual staffing system of one social worker to every 360 families enough to provide consistent support...' (Plan International, 1998, p.35). Utilizing family payments as a key plank of sponsorship practice, Plan staff in Hong Kong enrolled disadvantaged families (many of whom had fled mainland China) in a simple health system, provided children with uniforms and books, funded summer camps for sponsored children, encouraged recreational activities to keep children out of trouble and eventually initiated vocational training programmes for some parents to help them escape poverty (Plan International, 1998, p.35).

Clearly, Plan's CS funded interventions were not uniform. CS funded activities in Vietnam between 1957 and the fall of Saigon in 1975 were characterized by 'direct subsidies for food, education, school supplies and uniforms to the very poorest families and helped to support and train staff at hospitals and clinics' (Plan International, 1998, p.34). In the case of one sponsored child named Thahn, a small monthly cash grant enabled his mother to '...buy a few bricks each month until she had enough to build a small store' (p.34). By way of contrast, the ill-fated Ethiopian programme that was terminated in 1977 faced strong government opposition in which 'The People's Revolutionary Government of Ethiopia agreed and said in no uncertain terms that cash grants to particular members of a community would perpetuate an economic class structure that they believed had no place in Ethiopian Society' (Molumphy, 1984 p.282). Plan adapted its CS programme accordingly, informing Canadian sponsors that 'Instead of giving a family a gift of ten dollars, for instance, Plan has found it to be more beneficial to the family if the gift is used for village improvements...the provision of such necessities as uncontaminated water and mass inoculations' (Molumphy, 1984, p.282). For Plan International it is difficult to pinpoint a date at which we can declare that sponsorship funds were predominantly focused on community development however in 1984 the Board of Plan International '...adopted a Program Policy Statement that focused on developing skills and institutions within each community that would persist long after PLAN's departure' (Plan International, 1998, p.51).

In answer to questions about what sponsorship looked like when criticism began to emerge in the 1970s and 1980s, it seems self-evident from these two brief case studies that as a fundraising technique CS involved the selection of individual beneficiaries, provision of their details to a donor, and ongoing communication about children, typically involving letters and cards from the child and sometimes with letters or gifts from the sponsors. In reviewing CS practice employed by ChildFund and Plan, it is equally evident that historic interventions tended to favour support of individual children in orphanages and institutions during the INGOs early years, subsidization of disadvantaged children's school fees and educational expenses (including books, uniforms and pencils), transition to direct assistance to family members in the form of cash transfers and, increasingly, small-scale community development projects or direct service provision in a community context.

Child welfare vs community development

Although they are still popular with some INGOs (especially smaller ones), the direct handouts and child welfare activities common in the period 1940 to 1980 are now viewed with high levels of cynicism in regards to their ability to address and impact complex causes of poverty. Although Figure 3.1 places development and welfare on an artificially flat plane and posits them in a binary relationship, it is useful for summarizing the prevailing contemporary 'wisdom' regarding legitimate poverty reduction interventions. Where development-oriented activities offer self-help, enhanced community capacity and sustainable, long-term change, welfare-oriented activities are said to be characterized by gifts and handouts leading to improvements in individual well-being and possibly, dependency evidenced in a loss of well-being when support is removed suddenly.

McIlwaine's (1998, p.651) observation that civil society is fractured and that civil society organizations may be in conflict with each other, applies here in the sense that many non-CS INGOs have criticized early CS interventions as being welfarist, unsustainable, prone to creation of dependency and oriented towards child welfare rather than the difficult task of grappling with underlying causes of child poverty. While the transfer of clothing, gifts and direct cash payments to beneficiaries was an important feature of CS programmes historically, leading CS INGOs have minimized or moved away from the practice. Plan Australia (2012) informs sponsors that 'Plan has a policy of no

Development Oriented---Welfare Oriented

Facilitates partnership and self-help	Facilitates paternalism, gift giving & service
Hand-up – teaches the beneficiary to fish	Hand-out – gives the beneficiary a fish
Promotes independence and self-sufficiency	Encourages dependence and reliance
Builds community capacity and cooperation	Improves individual wellbeing
Targets community – focuses on community	Targets beneficiaries – focuses on individuals
Seeks sustainable, long-term change	Seeks to meet individual needs
Addresses underlying causes of poverty	Addresses symptoms of poverty
Seeks collaboration, networking etc.	Avoids collaboration, networking
Advocates for systemic change	Advocates for charitable help
Improves local disaster management capacity	Provides disaster relief
Improves capacity for the poor as self-advocates	Markets the poor

Figure 3.1 The development vs welfare spectrum

cash gifts as this has proven to cause disharmony and problems within the family and community and may place children or their families at risk'. Such a stance is in keeping with MacAuslan and Riemenschneider's (2011, p.4) call for greater awareness of the relational impacts of cash transfers by INGOs and governments, rather than the economic benefits alone. For Plan in the mid-1970s, inoculation and service provision programmes in Ethiopia were based on the idea that '...they did see the disruptive and dependency-producing potential of direct injections of cash into what were essentially non-cash village economies' (Molumphy, 1984, p.282).

Welfare seems to be a troublesome word for many aid and development organizations though discussion is generally diplomatic. The Australian Agency for International Development (AusAID, 2012) asserts that 'Welfare is typically provided on an individual or family basis including home-based and institutional care programs, such as those provided by orphanages, homes for the elderly, hospices, support to the disabled, and the provision of food for those who are destitute...'. Australian INGOs providing such 'welfare' are typically not able to provide tax-deductibility for donations because they are not sufficiently developmental in their intervention approaches. This critical stance is informed by the precepts of sustainability, notably the idea that INGOs must work themselves out of a job and build the capacity of local government and NGOs as service providers while avoiding creation of long-term dependency. As such the emphasis is not so much on interventions with short-term functional accountability and individual impact, but on those with long-term strategic accountability for impact on other organizations and the wider environment (Avina, 1993).

For Sen and Muellbauer (1987) effective development emphasizes means rather than ends, and it values improved capabilities of people and groups, leading to greater 'individual' and 'collective' freedom for self-determination. Likewise, interventions that improve collective or organizational capacity have gained favour over those that rescue or empower individuals. The relatively new emphasis on community empowerment, capability and capacity-building, with an associated critical questioning of traditional, individual CS as a credible poverty alleviation tool, is evident in several Australian non-CS INGO websites. For example, the Caritas Australia website's (2012) frequently asked question 'Can I sponsor a child?' is answered with a caution that 'Caritas Australia does not believe focusing on individuals addresses the underlying causes of poverty. We are concerned that it may also isolate individuals from their own family and community. Sponsorship can also lead to families and communities becoming dependent on aid rather than developing enterprise and initiative....' Similarly, The DFID-funded *The Rough Guide to a Better World* (Wroe and Doney, n.d., p.86) generalizes that CS is expensive, creates dissatisfaction, reminds recipients of their dependence and ignores the root causes of poverty. In an unconscious appeal for a typology of CS activities, the authors remind readers that 'In most cases "child sponsorship" is a misnomer. It is community development by another name'.

The evolution of INGOs

A number of CS INGOs have adapted and changed over time, sometimes dramatically. Further, the change in some CS INGOs has been consistent with David Korten's (1987) observation that INGOs tend to evolve through stages. Korten broadly described the evolution of development oriented NGOs as following three stages or three distinct generations, with possibility of a fourth, as seen in Figure 3.2 Korten's Generations of INGO.

First generation NGO: emphasis on relief, welfare and rehabilitation activities.

Second generation NGO: emphasis on community development and localized poverty reduction.

Third generation NGO: emphasis on 'sustainable systems development' associated with broader programs, upscaling, and contribution to regional or national development programs.

Possible Fourth generation NGO: arguably characterized by strong People's or social Movements with emphasis on advocacy and rights.

Figure 3.2   Korten's generations of INGO
Adapted from de Senillosa (1998, pp.2–3)

Rather than identifying generational leaps as Korten did, Clark (2003, p.144) argues that 'NGOs tend to broaden from one activity to encompass new ones rather than abandon the old entirely and jump to the new'. Biggs and Neame (in Edwards and Hulme, 2002, pp.34–35) observe that some NGOs in the Philippines actually moved away from political mobilization and embraced relief and welfare activities as a rational response to militarization.

In keeping with Korten's observation, ActionAid's initial work in CS funded education, begun in 1972, collected short profiles and photos of poor children for school fees, uniforms and equipment. Archer (2010, p.612) comments that '...within a very short time, ActionAid's field workers expressed concerns that this approach was ineffective and unjust'. The conclusion made by ActionAid staff was that they were helping needy children, but ignoring brothers, sisters and neighbours. According to Archer (2010, p.612) 'It was random and inequitable – but also it was ineffective. ActionAid was helping lots of individual children to access schools, but doing nothing to help the schools themselves – which were often in an appalling state'. ActionAid responded by building better schools in the 1980s to benefit all children in the community, arguably beginning a transition from a first to second generation development oriented INGO.

Despite a shift towards better schools, internal evaluation of 16 years of ActionAid school-building in Kenya found much-improved school facilities yet little evidence of improved access for poor children or increased academic performance. Indeed it seemed that in some cases 'poor children were more systematically excluded, especially when schools with good infrastructure imposed fee hikes' (Archer, 2010, p.612). Ironically, those schools which had received the most help and improved their facilities greatly, sometimes became the more likely to exclude poor children. ActionAid's subsequent experiment with non-formal education in the 1990s, and provision of pro-poor community schools with flexible curriculum and hours, is best seen as part of an evolutionary approach that would culminate in rights-based interventions designed to 'enable communities to demand quality education as a basic right and to enable governments to effectively deliver quality services' (Archer, 2010, p.612). This may be seen loosely as progression towards Korten's third generation with a more recent emphasis on up-scaling and the establishment of people's movements (rights-holders) empowered to leverage change from institutions and government (duty-bearers).

Although he was not commenting on CS INGOs specifically, Clark (2003, pp.145–146) illustrates the shifting focus of INGO activities in Figure 3.3. He asserts, 'I am not suggesting that NGOs are all making the same linear thought progression and are simply at different stages, or that the earlier stages are less important...'. However, he is explicit in urging that they work with civil society at local and national levels to address social injustice, weak institutions, and poor governance. Although it is clear that INGOs do not always progress neatly through Korten's generations, the reality for many CS INGOs is the perception of critics that they have not 'matured' and are still targeting poor individuals through low-yield relief and welfare activities. The consequence is a sizeable question mark against their legitimacy within the aid agency and academia, if not within the broader public.

Towards a typology of child sponsorship INGOs

Many CS INGOs have already transitioned, or are in the process of transitioning away from the exclusive support of individual children and their families. It should be obvious that there are a variety of historic and current CS funded interventions and that the construction of a typology is necessary in order to move discussion beyond generic statements and criticisms. In constructing a simple typology it soon becomes evident that several CS INGOs have evolved beyond micro-projects and individual welfare to 'the battle of ideas' and what Sogge

Target ➡️ Strategy ⬇️	Poor Individuals	Poor communities	Poor societies
Objectives	Relief and Welfare	Self-help	Equity, building institutions for inclusion
Operation goals	Meeting basic needs	Participation, sustainable poverty reduction	Rights-based development, voice, and empowerment
Local partners	Charities, missionaries	Community-based organizations, local NGOs	Civil society, progressive people in power
Local bases	Orphanages, refugee camps, schools	Village- and slum-level institutions, co-ops	Civil society networks from local to global levels
Sources of problems	Nature, wars, ill-fortune	Local elites, resource poverty, etc.	Social justice, weak institutions, bad governance
Typical instruments	Needs assessment, cost-effective business plan	Participation - from project planning to implementation and evaluation	Advocacy to ensure civil society views are reflected in national development plans, 'scaling-up' innovations
Key allies	Local religious institutions	Community leaders, existing community organizations	National and international media, unions, progressive politicians
Key INGO strengths	Fund-raising, logistical skills	Local knowledge, listening skills	Persuasion, access to influence, linking skills (from bottom to top, North to South, academic to practitioner).

Figure 3.3 Shifting focus of INGO activities
From 'Worlds Apart' by J.D. Clark, Copyright © 2003 by Kumarian Press, a division of Lynne Rienner Publishers Inc. Used with permission of the publisher.

(2002, p.160) refers to as 'the larger contexts of their work'. ActionAid is a prime example of this though to what extent the battle is going well, and how CS can contribute seems unclear at the time of writing. Having said this, it is equally evident that many CS INGOs retain interventions congruent with Korten's first generation. Perhaps the most interesting question is whether there is a place for diversity in the CS

INGO sector and how the legitimacy of these diverse civil society organizations is best evaluated? Should all CS INGOs conform to a community development model or other paradigms regardless of their size, economies of scale, networking ability and experience?

Individual or institutional child sponsorship (IICS)

Brehm and Gale (2000, p.2) classify CS INGOs into two classes, those that support programmes targeted at development which benefits all children in a given community and those that 'focus on the individual child as the recipient of the sponsor's donation'. This is consistent with Livezey's broad classification (1981). The latter, individual or institutional child sponsorship model (IICS), is rooted in the individual and often individual institutional care of children. It forms the basis of the traditional approach, in which disadvantaged individuals such as orphans, children with disability, or poor children, are identified and supported in an institutional setting (including support to attend school). In some cases this may be a church or a secular school, depending on the underlying philosophy and religious world view of the CS INGO. Often the individual child's situation is documented, pictures are taken, and details are sent to a donor nation where they are distributed and used to solicit commitment from an individual donor for ongoing individual support (sponsorship) in return for personalized feedback, usually in the form of letters, school reports, photos, cards and drawings. A child sponsored in such a programme would often receive varying degrees of assistance including school fee help, uniforms, books, gifts and perhaps medical checks. Orphans, disabled children and boarding students may receive accommodation, cultural experiences, food, substitute parental care and a variety of other benefits. Generally, in IICS programmes a significant amount of the sponsorship dollar benefits an individual child rather than family members. In many instances sponsorship funds have been paid directly to the school or institution rather than the individual or child's family.

Historically the IICS model is the most enduring. Although it predates the emergence of community development imperatives, it elicits a high level of concern from INGO practitioners who abide by principles of community development. Variants of IICS are usually placed by critics at the welfare end of the welfare and development spectrum because individuals are perceived to be receiving assistance without addressing root causes of poverty or building the capacity of communities to meet their collective needs. In the words of one online critic who had worked for OXFAM, 'the idea that individual children could be targeted and given sustainable development assistance was never sound and for a long time hasn't been part of any kind of reputable development programming' (Elliot, 2010). To be fair to some CS INGOs that maintain IICS interventions, they do not claim that sponsorship is a highly effective method of community development, rather that sponsorship can change the life of a child. For an organization like SOS Kinderdorf, which predominantly sponsors orphans, legitimacy would therefore be assessed in terms of compliance with best practice in orphan care and child welfare rather than best practice in poverty reduction or community development. Generally speaking, SOS Kinderdorf prides itself on provision of high standards of childcare utilizing family-home care for only the neediest children.

Example of IICS – Asian Aid organization

The emphasis of Asian Aid Australia's programme is the selection of highly disadvantaged children and direct service provision to individuals through institutions such as orphanages, day-schools, boarding-schools and special education centres. In 2012 this small Australian CS INGO assisted a modest 8,400 children in this manner, representing the bulk of funding dispersed to three countries in Southern Asia. Contrary to common criticisms of individual sponsorship, Asian Aid Organization could be described as a cost efficient faith-based organization (typically retaining less than 10 per cent of donated funds for administrative and marketing overheads), an achievement attained by locating itself in a regional area in the donor country, sourcing child updates directly from schools rather than a large contingent of field staff or social workers, and by utilizing a low-cost marketing model through church presentations and newsletters. Sponsorship funds are paid directly to schools and institutions rather than individuals. Asian Aid Australia (2012) states on its website that it

> 'gives hope by fostering permanent positive change in the lives of disadvantaged children and their communities'. Sponsors may give $25 per month for day school education, $30 per month for day school expenses plus a mid-day meal, $40 per month for costs associated with boarding school education and accommodation or $50 per month for tertiary students or for children who are orphans, deaf, blind and have special needs.

The question for organizations like Asian Aid Australia is not whether individual sponsorship can benefit some very poor children. Internal research has confirmed that it can. Rather, it is whether the support of individual children, often in isolation from their families or communities, can be justified as an impactful, legitimate poverty reduction intervention in the prevailing climate of ideas. For Asian Aid Australia staff consensus has emerged that sponsorship dollars are best spent when individual children benefit from improved capacity of schools and the broader education system to meet the needs of children in the community.

Individual/family child sponsorship (IFCS)

Family Helper programmes run by Plan International and ChildFund in the 1970s identified needy children using a case work approach. Rather than automatically placing needy children in orphanages or boarding schools, CS funds were used to provide welfare services of benefit to the families and children and cash transfers or direct gift giving. Usually, children remained in their families and communities with some benefits to family members. Arguably, this model of intervention was pioneered by Save the Children Fund in the 1920s although at that time support for children was generally short term and consisted of food provision rather than cash. Like IICS, the emphasis of such programmes is on individual child development outcomes. However, unlike IICS, CS INGOs may identify a 'needy' community, select apparently needy children for sponsorship, and provide services within the community specifically targeting those children and others. In such programmes, the interventions offered by CS INGOs are aimed squarely at sponsored individual children or groups of sponsored children, and benefits are skewed towards these two groups rather than to community collaboration and empowerment at large.

Example of IFCS – Compassion International

Compassion Australia describes Compassion International as a 'holistic child development' organization rather than a community development specialist. When it was founded in 1954, Compassion's sponsorship programme also facilitated monthly support of children in Korean orphanages, providing 'Biblical lessons, food, clothing, shelter and medical aid on a regular basis...'. By 1968 however, a new Family Helper Plan had begun in India, Indonesia, Haiti and Singapore and

Compassion International also experimented with Special Care Centres from 1970, established to 'treat children with physical handicaps and medical illness, offering relief through surgery, training, physical therapy, adequate nourishment and special equipment'. Additionally, from 1974 sponsorship extended to children unlikely to receive an education through projects that '...pay for teachers' salaries, books, supplies, school uniforms, medical care and, in many instances, a hot, nutritious meal each school day' (Compassion, 2013). According to their website:

> Compassion's Child Sponsorship Program is comprehensive, holistic and unique. It's dedicated to helping children find a path out of poverty through the love of Jesus Christ. By working with local churches, the Child Sponsorship Program offers educational opportunities, health care and health-related instruction, nutrition, life-skills training, and opportunities to hear about and respond to the gospel (Compassion, 2012).

In the example above, Compassion indicates that it partners directly with Christian church groups in poor countries to deliver services to sponsored children through a community group (local church), within the context of their communities. To an extent this is building the capacity of local church to respond to needs in its own community and this may complicate its categorization somewhat. However, a Compassion child typically receives benefits from one-to-one sponsorship in the form of medical or dental care, food, clothing, primary education assistance or tutoring, secondary education/vocational training assistance and youth programmes offered through local churches. Rather than provide institutional care, the emphasis is on individuals and their families as beneficiaries, within the setting of their community.

Community development child sponsorship (CDCS)

CDCS is less oriented to the selection of very poor individual children for special benefits than to the transformation of the community surrounding disadvantaged children and their families. Brehm and Gale (2000, p.2) have observed that such funding models 'use the funds to support development programmes based in the community in which the sponsored child lives, to benefit all children in the community'. Rather than seeking to identify the most needy children in the community, in the pretense that they will exclusively benefit, contemporary CDCS positions sponsored children as ambassadors. Duly photographed and processed, the children or youth who will be used to solicit sponsorship donations function as a medium or conduit through which funding flows to the benefit of the whole community when the funds are pooled for interventions such as economic development (microcredit and loans), education (primary and secondary) and health projects (including nutrition, primary healthcare and risk reduction).

Example of CDCS – World Vision

The World Vision Australia website (2011) poignantly described the impact of CDCS on Levy, a four-year-old Zambian child sponsored by Kate, an Australian. According to World Vision Australia's marketing department Levy was 'small, and malnourished. Going to bed hungry was normal...the water Levy drank was dirty and it often made him sick. He barely had the energy to move...'. Through pooled sponsorship funds utilized in an Area Development Program (ADP)

> He had grown considerably and was healthier, stronger and had lots of energy to play with friends...Levy's family had developed a garden...and Levy was now eating two nutritious meals a day...now there was a borehole only 200m from their house that the whole community was benefiting from... The support...also helped Levy's community build a school and health clinic... He attends school regularly...

In marketing the CDCS model above, WV Australia effectively communicates the impact of interventions on individuals (thus maintaining the marketing advantages of individual CS) within the context of community development initiatives (aimed at strengthening the community around the child). The reality however is that this simplifies World Vision's development programming. In its Handbook for Development Programs (World Vision International, 2011, p.8) we read that the preferred role of World Vision is to 'serve as a catalyst and builder of the capacity of local partners and partnerships for child well-being'. The shift took place in 1979 when World Vision pledged to move 50 per cent of its childcare projects to development by 1984 when there would be over one million children sponsored (Watkins, 1998, p.5). Although World Vision Area Development Programs have emphasized community development and capacity building, the current Development Programming Approach emphasizes local partners and actors as primary stakeholders, prioritizes rights-based approaches and fosters some local advocacy. The Citizen Voice and Action component World Vision Area Development Programs (began in 2005) was present in 209 ADPs in 29 countries by 2011 (World Vision International, n.d., p.2) and is central to the Child Health Now campaign which educates citizens about their rights and explains how rights are articulated under local law.

> ...communities work collaboratively with government and service providers to compare reality against government's own commitments... Finally, communities work with other stakeholders to influence decision-makers to improve services, using a simple set of advocacy tools. As government services improve, so does the well-being of children (World Vision International, n.d., p.1).

Rights-based child sponsorship – RBCS

A rights-based CS (RBCS) model utilizes CS fundraising to promote the human rights of children and other community members, advocating for change and mobilizing local resources and communities in its pursuit. Reflecting on ActionAid's evolution over time, Archer (2010, pp.615–617) has observed that by 1997 ActionAid had articulated a new approach to education which involved moving 'from providing to enabling', a strategy justified by the belief that 'The challenge for the 2010s is to connect programme, policy and campaigning work at all levels'. Although there is often a gap between action and rhetoric, it is evident that ActionAid has made significant progress in building capacities of local communities and network partners to maintain pressure on governments and international institutions. While many INGOs currently use the issue of rights to justify and legitimate their interventions, it is argued here that few have, and are capable of making the painful transition away from service provider and advocate to genuine partner and facilitator of direct action and grass-roots advocacy.

Example of RBCS – Plan International

In a recent report, Plan International (2008) reiterated support for what it calls Child Centred Community Development (CCCD), adopted as a planning tool for use in developing countries to benefit all children in a community rather than just the sponsored ones. Vijfeijken (et al, 2009, p.78) acknowledge Plan International's long history as a needs-based change agent working at community level through individual sponsorship and direct service delivery, an emphasis still evident in many country offices despite the emergence of a rights-based approach (RBA). However, in assessing the recent strategic shift of Plan Guatemala, they note:

> The adoption of CCCD represents a significant departure from Plan's previous approach to development work, which was characterized by individual support to sponsored children, direct provision of goods and services, and a welfare-based model of NGO interventions. Under CCCD, Plan redefined its role and responsibility in development processes and moved towards a facilitating role in an effort to enhance the ability of local stakeholders, including state actors, communities, and domestic civil society organizations, to create the changes necessary for sustained development progress (Vijfeijken et al, 2011 p.5).

It is interesting that Plan International has considered the potential for its programmes to morph into an 'activist' model of sponsorship that 'anticipates children/communities/sponsors being involved in lobbying decision makers', a view consistent with ActionAid's emphasis on grassroots advocacy and the empowerment of local agency in the quest to hold duty bearers accountable. In seeking to facilitate strong bottom-up advocacy, running in parallel with community-based initiatives, there is some justification for coining the term RBCS. Arguably, there is a distinction between rights-based interventions (in which interventions are justified by ones' understanding of the rights of the beneficiaries/partners) and rights-based community empowerment evidenced by collaborative processes in which donor INGOs genuinely foster the ability of grassroots organizations and social movements to agitate and strategize for the fulfilment of their own rights, using their own resources. A critical question for such organizations is the extent to which individual sponsorship as a fundraising tool is adaptable to community empowerment and rights-based activism given the reality of a large gap between donor expectations and programmatic realities.

   Vijfeijken et al (2009, pp.76–77) argue that Plan International takes a bottom-up approach to rights-based development that differs from strategies of other rights-based development organizations. Unlike organizations such as ActionAid, Plan is not working to support local movements and grassroots organizations (GROs) to claim their rights but instead focuses on strengthening existing community structures as

IICS Individual/ Institutional	IFCS Individual/ Community	CDCS Community Development	RBCS Rights Based
Child Development oriented	Child Development oriented	Community development oriented	Social systems and advocacy oriented
Empowers/assists individuals	Empowers/assists individuals & family members	Empowers communities across a range of sectors	Empowers communities, disadvantaged groups and seeks 'justice'
Delivers via schools and institutions as partners	Delivers via institutions/local church and local community as partners	Delivers via dev orgs, southern NGOs government and community organizations as partners	Delivers via dev orgs, influential grassroots orgs and social movements, networks
Links donors to individuals assisted in an institution e.g. a school or orphanage	Links donors to individuals assisted in the context of their families	Links donors to individuals for service delivery to communities or integrated community development	Links donors to individuals and communities for community development, advocacy and rights-based mobilization
Targets individual beneficiaries for majority of assistance	Targets individuals, families and some groups of individuals for assistance	Targets whole communities for assistance, increasingly on a large scale	Targets whole communities and disadvantaged groups for advocacy and assistance
Promotes individual child improvement	Promotes child holistic development	Promotes sustainable community development	Promotes networking, systemic change and altered power relationships
Addresses impacts of poverty at an individual level for long-term impact	Addresses impacts of poverty at an individual level for long-term impact, often involved in local service delivery	Addresses underlying local/regional causes of poverty. Significant capacity	Addresses underlying local causes of poverty and systemic injustice
Seeks short-term and long-term individual impact	Seeks long-term individual impact and some community capacity improvement	Seeks long-term capacity building and community impact	Seeks long-term capacity building, mobilization of rights activists and empowerment of social movements
Evaluation top-down Reporting to donors Focus on outputs rather than impact Beneficiaries viewed as passive	Evaluation top-down Reporting to donors Focus on outputs rather than impact Emerging commitment to data and evaluation Heavy use of outside experts	Evalution participatory. Focus on outcomes Programmes increasingly data-driven. NGO becomes accountable to beneficiaries as well as donors. Beneficiaries viewed as partners and experts	Evaluation participatory. Focus on outcomes Genuine, bottom-up, collaborative evaluation. NGO accountable to beneficiaries and donors Declining Focus on reporting to donors

Figure 3.4   CS Intervention Comparison Table

democratic expressions of community life. Thus the focus of Plan International lies (so far) less on grassroots activism but instead on the practical exercise of human (and child) rights by local communities and their ability to participate in the local democratic process.

Questions and comments

Having proposed a typology of CS funded interventions, inevitable questions must be raised whilst keeping in mind that many CS INGOs may not neatly fit, or may fund other interventions using non-CS income. Nevertheless, we might ask, is this typology inclusive enough to adequately categorize most CS funded work past and present? If so, in the current climate in which INGO legitimacy is questioned, is it desirable, or possible for CS INGOs to transition to RBCS as ActionAid and Plan are seeking to do? Is it possible to be a legitimate, effective partner in poverty reduction at each level of the proposed typology, given the small size of some organizations and their limited capacity? And, to what extent is diversity in the CS INGO sector an asset? How might we measure success and benchmark good practice?

Despite some recent progress, the INGO sector at large is notorious in that 'Internal evaluations are rarely released, and what is released comes closer to propaganda than rigorous assessment' (Edwards and Hulme, 2002, p.6). Undoubtedly some CS INGOs are still stuck in what Van Rooy (in Eade and Ligteringen, 2001, p.37) refers to as the 'do now, think later mentality'. In fairness, however, many are stuck in a 'do now, research later because the need is great and funds are short mentality'. A prominent recent exception is work conducted by Wydick et al (2013, pp.425–426) on Compassion International's holistic child development programmes in five countries. They found (among other important indicators) that Compassion Sponsorship increases years of completed schooling by '1.03–1.46 years over a baseline of 10.19 years and increases the probability of primary school completion by 4.0–7.7 percentage points (baseline 88.7%), secondary school completion by 11.6–16.5 percentage points (baseline 44.9 percent)'. Such findings support the credibility of Compassion's CS programme as an IFCS intervention predicated on child development, however they cannot be used to assess the value of this form of CS as a catalyst for broad-based poverty reduction at a community level.

It is unfortunate that debate over CS has also been constrained by a frustratingly simplistic use of CS as a blanket term and disregard for diversity in the sector. In the absence of simple answers for several of the difficult questions above, three key points may be made. First, when critiquing CS it is wise to consider the evolution of the organization's work and perhaps to benchmark CS INGOs against others with similar intervention strategies as a first step. As a rule, we should compare apples to apples as well as consider the merits of oranges as alternatives. Second, just as Clark (2003) suggested that INGOs tend to morph into new activities while retaining aspects of previous work, CS INGOs may be similarly likely to utilize the same fundraising tool for different interventions, especially where network partners have differing ideologies. This may explain growing preference for rights-based initiatives in Latin America with its history of dependency theory and structuralism (MacAuslan and Riemenschneider, 2011, p.5), and in the same network but different geographical context, a community-oriented sponsorship programme informed by a utilitarian needs-first view. Third, it would seem that while many CS INGOs have embraced various codes of conduct, they could be more active in evaluating their activities, disseminating the results and sharing the lessons learned. To some extent this is needed across the INGO sector!

Lingan et al (2009, p.1) observe that INGOs have made, and continue to make, ambitious claims about the impact and influence of their activities. However, the claim that a small donation each month can change the life of a child, or the capacity of the community surrounding the child, is best judged by placing CS INGO activity in a typology which facilitates informed discussion by INGO staff and the beneficiaries whose voices are strikingly absent in the debate over legitimacy. Lister (2003, p.16) reminds us that legitimacy goes beyond questions of accountability, representation and performance to ask legitimate for whom and 'does some legitimacy matter more than other legitimacy?'

Bibliography

Archer, D. (2010) 'The evolution of NGO-government relations in education: ActionAid 1972–2009', *Development in Practice*, 20, 4–5, 611–618.

Asian Aid Australia (2012) *The Joy of Sponsorship*, http://www.asianaid.org.au/ Newsroom/joy-of-sponsorship.aspx, date accessed 21 May 2012.

AusAID (2012) *AusAID – NGO Cooperation Program (ANCP) Guidelines*, http://www.ausaid.gov.au/ngos/Documents/ancp_guidelines.pdf, date accessed 6 May 2012.

Avina, J. (1993) 'The evolutionary life cycles of non-governmental development organisations', *Public Administration and Development*, 13, 5, 453–474.

BOND (2006) *A BOND Approach to Quality in Non-Governmental Organisations: Putting Beneficiaries First*, a report by Keystone and AccountAbility for the British Overseas NGOs for Development (London: BOND).

Brehm, V. and Gale, J. (2000) 'Child sponsorship: A funding tool for sustainable development?' *informed: NGO Funding and Policy Bulletin – NGO Sector Analysis Programme Bulletin* no.3, November 2000, pp.2–6.

Caritas Australia (2012) *Frequently Asked Questions*, http://www.caritas.org.au/about/faqs, date accessed 8 May 2012.

Clark, J. (2003) *Worlds Apart: Civil Society and the Battle for Ethical Globalization* (Bloomfield, CT: Kumarian Press).

Compassion (2012) *Compassion's Holistic Child Development Model*, http://www.compassionmodel.org/child-sponsorship.php, date accessed 22 May 2012.

Compassion (2013) *Compassion's History – 1970s*, http://www.compassion.com/about/history/1970s/default.htm, date accessed 13 September 2013.

de Senillosa, I. (1998) 'A New Age of social movements: A fifth generation of non-governmental development organisations in the making?' *Development in Practice*, 8, 1, 40–53.

Eade, D. and Ligteringen, E. (eds) (2001) *Debating Development* (Oxford: Oxfam).

Edwards, M. and Hulme, D. (2002) *Non-Governmental Organisations – Performance and Accountability Beyond the Magic Bullet* (London: Earthscan).

Elliot, M. (2010) *Child Sponsorships: Are they Effective Aid?* http://marianne-elliott.com/2010/05/child-sponsorships-are-they-effective-aid/, date accessed 8 May 2012.

Fowler, A. (2000) *The Virtuous Spiral: A Guide to Sustainability for NGOs in International Development* (London: Earthscan).

Klein, C. (2003) *Cold War Orientalism: Asia in the Middlebrow Imagination, 1945–1961* (Berkeley: University of California Press).

Korten, D. (1987) 'Third generation NGO strategies: A key to people-centered development', *World Development*, 15, supplement, 145–159.

Lingan, J., Cavender, R.L. and Gwynne, B. (2009) 'Responding to NGO development effectiveness initiatives', *One World Trust/World Vision Briefing Paper* No. 122, November.

Lister, S. (2003) 'NGO legitimacy: Technical issue or social construct?' *Critique of Anthropology*, 23, 2, 175–192.

Livezey, E.T. (1981) 'Child sponsorship dollars: How much goes to him? *The Christian Science Monitor*, 6 August 1981, http://www.csmonitor.com/layout/set/print/1981/0806/080657.html, date accessed 27 March 2013.

MacAuslan, I. and Riemenschneider, N. (2011) *'Richer but Resented: What Do Cash Transfers Do To Social Relations and Does It Matter?'*, Paper presented at international conference 'Social Protection for Social Justice', Institute of Development Studies, UK 13–15 April.

McIlwaine, C. (1998) 'Contesting civil society: Reflections from El Salvador', *Third World Quarterly*, 19, 4, 651–672.

McKenzie, R.B. (ed.) (1999) *Rethinking Orphanages for the 21st Century* (Thousand Oaks, CA: Sage Publications).

Molumphy, H.D. (1984) *For Common Decency: The History of Foster Parents Plan, 1937–1983* (Warwick, RI: Plan International).

Plan Australia (2012) *Communicating with Your Sponsored Child*, http://www.plan.org.au/myplan/faq/childsponsorship/letters, date accessed 6 May 2012.

Plan International (1998) *A Journey of Hope – The History of Plan International 1937–1998* (London: Plan International).

Plan International (2008) *The Development Impact of Child Sponsorship: Exploring Plan International's Sponsorship-Related Processes and Materials, Their Effects, and Their Potential Evolution* (London: Plan International).

Riddell, R.C. (2008) *Does Foreign Aid Really Work?* (Oxford: Oxford University Press).

Sen, A. and Muellbauer, J. (1987) *The Standard of Living* (New York: Cambridge University Press).

Sogge, D. (2002) *Give and Take: What's the Matter with Foreign Aid?* (New York: Zed Books).

Tise, L.E. (1993) *A Book about Children: The World of Christian Children's Fund 1938–1991* (Falls Church, VA: Hartland Publishing).

Vijfeijken, T.B., Gneiting, U. and Schmitz, H.P. (2011) *How Does CCCD Affect Program Effectiveness and Sustainability? A Meta Review of Plan's Evaluations* Transnational NGO Initiative, Moynihan Institute of Global Affairs, http://www.maxwell.syr.edu/moynihan/tngo/Publications/, date accessed 13 May 2012.

Vijfeijken, T.B., Gneiting, U., Schmitz, H.P. and Valle, O. (2009) *Rights-based Approach to Development: Learning from Plan Guatemala* Transnational NGO Initiative – Moynihan Institute of Global Affairs Syracuse University, http://www.maxwell.syr.edu/uploadedFiles/moynihan/tngo/PLAN_guatemala _strategy_evaluation.pdf, date accessed 13 September 2013.

Watkins, S. (ed.) (1998) *Understanding Child Sponsorship: A Historical Perspective*, 20 March 1998 (WVUSA Archives).

World Vision Australia (2011) *Transforming Lives and Child Sponsorship: Who is it Happening To?* http://www.worldvision.com.au/issues/Transforming_Lives __Child_Sponsorship/Who_is_it_happening_to_.aspx, date accessed 22 May 2012.

World Vision International (2011) *The Handbook for Development Programs: The Essentials* (Monrovia, CA: World Vision International).

World Vision International (n.d.) *Citizen Voice and Action – Helping Communities Discover the Power Within*, World Vision internal documentation.

Wroe, M. and Doney, M. (n.d.) The *Rough Guide To a Better World and How You Can Make a Difference*, http://www.roughguide-betterworld.com/better-world.pdf, date accessed 8 May 2012.

Wydick, B., Glewwe, P. and Rutledge, L. (2013) 'Does international child sponsorship work? Six-country study of impacts on adult life outcomes', *Journal of Political Economy*, 121, 2, 393 436.

4
Issues in Historic Child Sponsorship

Brad Watson, Harwood Lockton and Manohar Pawar

Introduction

Arguing that children serve the international humanitarian community as 'embodiments of a basic goodness' and 'symbols of world harmony', Malkki (1997) and Bornstein (2005) warn that in Child Sponsorship (CS) children are not just 'ambassadors of hope', they take centre stage as symbols in 'explosive moral terrain'. Peter Stalker's 1982 article in the *New Internationalist* epitomizes the tension that emerged in the 1980s and 1990s over CS-funded interventions. Although Stalker (1982, p.1) referred to sponsorship of one million children by international 'foster parents' as an extraordinary international exchange, he parodied CS INGOs and their advertising, featuring a picture of a small child and the header 'Please do not sponsor this child'. Stalker (1982, p.2) was explicit in his critique, bluntly asserting that '...in almost every other way in which the donor is better off through a sponsorship scheme, the sponsored child or family is correspondingly worse off'.

The negative portrayal of CS by Stalker and other *New Internationalist* journalists in the 1980s was embraced by critics in non-CS INGOs and is understandable given that the publication was co-founded by Oxfam, a leading advocate for poverty reduction through community development. In 1985 the *New Internationalist* informed readers that 'doubts about the principle of singling out individual children for special children had been circulating for years among the voluntary agencies' (*New Internationalist*, 1985, p.4). For CS INGOs the critique cut deeply, not because they were unaware of the pitfalls of traditional forms of CS, but because it portrayed them as unethical, irresponsible and ineffective at a time when they were riding a wave of unprecedented public support. Strident critique of CS INGOs reached a crescendo in 1998 with a *Chicago Tribune* 'Special report' titled 'The Miracle Merchants: The Myths of Child Sponsorship'. The Tribune's journalists featured sensational accounts of alleged organizational ineptitude. The special report – fairly or not – depicted Save the Children USA, Childreach, Children International and Christian Children's Fund as collectively lacking accountability, transparency and efficacy. Having assumed a vital role of 'child saving', with children as 'deserving victims' CS INGOs found themselves cast in a new role, that of 'villains' (see Mahood and Satzewich, 2009, pp.55–58 for a fuller discussion of social problems and claims making).

Unfortunately, the task of revisiting earlier critique of CS is complicated by several factors. Firstly, although media accounts and exposes have had undue influence in swaying perceptions of CS, they are typically limited by reference to a small number of CS INGOs and reliance on opinion and anecdotal accounts at particular points in time. Secondly, much of the historic critique of CS-funded interventions refers to the sponsorship of individual children or families through direct service provision, cash transfers and gift-giving. Referred to in Chapter 3 of this book, such activities may be loosely described as welfare provision and may be classified in a typology as IICS (Individual/Institutional Child Sponsorship) or IFCS (Individual/Family Child Sponsorship). These forms of assistance should not be confused with CDCS (Community Development Child Sponsorship) which involved a paradigm shift away from individual welfare to community development, community empowerment and poverty reduction for whole communities. Thirdly, an abundance of anecdotal evidence used to condemn historic CS INGO activity is still largely matched by '...a scarcity of empirical research-based evidence about the impact of child sponsorship on recipient families and communities' (Brehm and Gale, 2000, p.1).

In documenting critique of past sponsorship practice it must be noted that that many large CS INGOs have evolved over time. For example, one history of Plan International observes that between 1937 and 1983 Plan International was involved in a '...transition from child welfare to child, family, and community development ...' (Molumphy, 1984, p.302). A similar trajectory has been evident with World Vision which, in the mid-1970s moved beyond support of individual children in orphanages and home environments, to a 'family-to-family' model in which sponsorship funded benefits became more family focused (Watkins, 1998, p.3), and then to community development initiatives by the 1980s.

Mindful of the caveats above, and the anecdotal nature of much of the evidence used to bolster critique, this chapter discusses a range of historic criticisms of CS as they relate to IICS and IFCS to the 1990s. The manner in which leading CS INGOs have proactively changed, responded to critique and set new benchmarks for best practice are discussed in the final chapter of this book (see Chapter 15).

Issues for historic CS funded orphan care (IICS)

A concern for CS INGOs involved in historic provision of orphan care in the global South in the 1950s and 1960s was the steady decline of traditional orphanages in Northern countries throughout the twentieth century. Shughart and Chappell (in McKenzie, 1999, p.153) have observed that in 1933 approximately 144,000 children were cared for in orphanages in the USA. However, 'by 1977, only 43,000 children were living in orphanages. And by 1980, the orphanage had for all practical purposes ceased to exist'. Shughart and Chappell point out that by the 1960s the financial cost of family-based foster care in America was approximately half that of support in an institution, however the shift was also due to the activism of social workers and researchers who had concluded – based more on selected clinical research than comparative evaluations – that institutions were often unable to meet children's social and developmental needs. Thus, over the course of the twentieth century a bleak and rarely contested view of orphanages developed, based on the presumption that 'Any amount of orphanage experience is harmful. The damage is greatest during the first years of life and increases dramatically with length of stay in an institution' (McCall in McKenzie, 1999, pp.129–130).

The impact of institutional life funded by CS INGOs has been called into question, especially where children with families or supportive relationships were funneled into dormitory style orphanages. Dr. Chun Wai Chan, an ex-resident of Faith Love Home in Hong Kong writes:

> It was a very regimented and totally insulated environment... We were stigmatized...and treated like aliens... We had gates right in front of the school, with a sign saying 'ORPHANS HOME'. There was barbed wire – it was more or less like a correctional institution.... Each time I returned home, I felt less and less like I belonged there... Little by little, I noticed how different I was becoming from the rest of my family... (in Tise, 1993, pp.45–46).

Clearly, not all orphanages were run in this way, and Chan's account represents one negative story, in one cultural context with a very positive eventual outcome in which Chan eventually became a cardiologist in the USA and served as a director of Christian Children's Fund (CCF). Although they maintained that orphanages could transform the lives of some children, CS INGO staff increasingly suggested throughout the 1960s and 1970s that as a welfare measure, placement of children in orphanages was costly, prone to manipulation, potentially harmful to some children and more importantly, did little to address the underlying conditions that perpetuated poverty. In the case of the Shanghai Canaan home, segregation of children from the broader society meant that:

> We had lots of problems with those kids... They had been isolated from the community, and they couldn't adjust to being outside. They stopped going to church, they found it difficult to find jobs, they didn't know the outside customs, they were maladjusted (Mills in Tise, 1993, pp.23–24).

A practical problem for CS INGOs engaged in offering direct benefits to children was the unintended side-effect of enormously successful advertising necessitating rapid recruitment of children. Tise (1993, p.66) explains that The Korean Association of Voluntary Agencies conducted a study in 1960 for CCF (known now as ChildFund) to ascertain the origins of children in its funded institutions, length of stay and proportion who returned to the family. 'The findings were unequivocal. A large proportion of these children had been transformed into 'orphans' by their families'. CCF was not alone in experiencing this phenomenon. For impoverished families, offers of free food, shelter and schooling provided significant incentive to place children in institutions.

To its credit, staff at CCF recognized and responded to its self-imposed discovery that it had been inadvertently contributing to the manufacture of an artificial orphan crisis in the 1950s insofar as 'Parents would go through all sorts of shenanigans to get their child into an orphanage so that he could get an education' (Tise, 1993, p.66). However, direct benefits to poor families and poor children outside orphanages could also be problematic. Referring to Save the Children USA's domestic CS programme in the 1980s and 1990s, Maren (1997, p.150) quoted a staff member who described one programme in which 'The pressure is on from headquarters; we're given a month to sign up so many children or our budgets will be cut. So we signed up anyone who came through the door'. Although this anecdotal account of child recruitment cannot be used to imply systemic issues in world-wide recruitment for Save the Children, it is not unfair to say that numerous CS INGOs found it difficult to balance rapid growth with effective recruiting based on adequate screening of sponsored children prior to enrolment and throughout the duration of programmes. Perhaps alluding to this dynamic Herrell (1974, p.691) observed 'A sponsorship program should be used for finding sponsors to provide for identified needs of priority-risk children, rather than "for finding children for sponsors"'.

Herrell (1974, p.685) conceded in the 1970s that '...an occasional sponsor may have a desire to shape other person's values according to his own religion or ideology....' In the broader context of religious CS INGOs, this concession flagged an emerging debate about the role of religion in foreign aid. Staff at the *New Internationalist* (1989b, p.3) were blunt, stating 'In order for a child to qualify its parents may have to cease certain forms of political or religious activity – or the child may be pressured to take up activities like reading the Bible'. A cartoon accompanied the text and is shown below in Figure 4.1. This was espe-

Figure 4.1   New Internationalist cartoon – Sponsored children as political pawns (New Internationalist, 1989b, p.1)

cially true of orphan care programmes funded by large, religious CS INGOs partnering directly with missions and church groups, and led to concerns over coerced participation of children in religious activity.

Writing over 30 years ago, Livezey (1981, p.10) praised Compassion International for its transparency and forthright declaration at the time that '...a child needs to know about God's love for him as much as he needs food and clothing'. However, the rise of secularism, post-modernism and material definitions of poverty in the Global North have, by and large combined to alter perceptions of the legitimacy of CS INGOs formerly involved in direct evangelism. For most large CS INGOs, religious or otherwise, coerced participation in religious activity is now contrary to their humanitarian charter and various NGO codes of conduct. Having said this, of interest is the growing disconnect between secular aid agencies wary of religion as potentially divisive, and Southern beneficiaries for whom voluntary participation in religious activity is highly valued and central to life. Though not specifically referring to CS, in Ver Beek's (2000, p.31) opinion 'This avoidance results in inferior research and less effective programs, and ultimately fails to provide participants with opportunities to reflect on how their development and their spirituality will and should shape each other'.

It is noteworthy that in its transition to a secular INGO, CCF was criticized for retaining a religious name (see *Christianity Today* articles circa 1994) when it had functioned as a secular INGO for some time. This tension was referred to by Lissner (1977, p.229) when he observed that many INGOs at that time displayed a Christian name and religious affiliation when appealing to constituents, 'while their "modus operandi" vis-a-vis government at home and overseas is distinctly non-sectarian/humanitarian in character...'. While it is a truism that through sponsorship Christians can '...find a way to actively enact their faith' (Yuen, 2008, p.46), a related issue for CS INGOs that have distanced themselves from evangelism is the perception of some sponsors that this has compromised their level of care rather than enhanced it.

Given the emergence of a pervasive narrative that any amount of institutional care is harmful, and the serious issues that arose in orphan care programmes funded by CS INGOs in the 1950s–1970s, it is not surprising that most CS INGOs have transitioned to new forms of sponsorship-funded activity. Ethically-attuned CS INGOs engaged in orphan care emphasize the importance for children of cultural integration, religious freedom, social connectedness, high levels of adult care

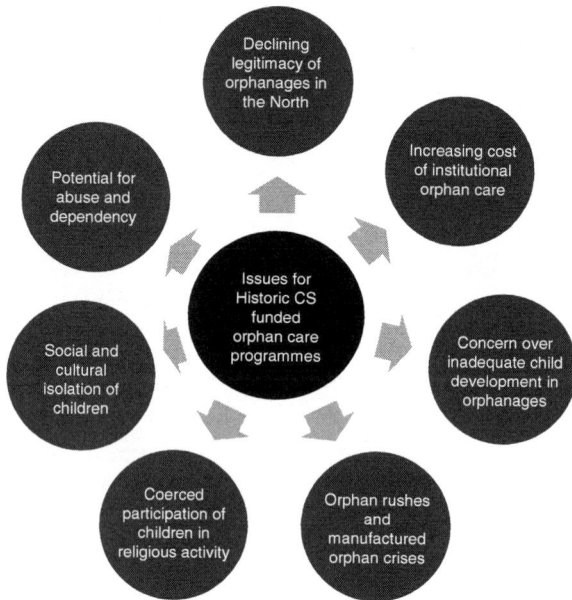

Figure 4.2   Summary of key issues for historic CS funded orphan care programmes

in family homes and selection processes designed to ensure that only the neediest children are admitted.

Issues in CS funded direct transfers to children and families (IFCS)

Leading CS INGOs transitioned from sponsorship of orphans in institutions to Family Helper and similar programmes in the 1960s and 1970s (see Chapter 2). The logic of these and similar interventions was simple: small cash transfers to families or children, or various gifts (such as uniforms and books or food) could, it was thought, boost individual or family well-being (and sometimes nutrition), improve school retention and help children in the context of their communities. Diversity was evident. Commenting on the Save the Children UK domestic CS programme in post-World War Two Britain when government welfare services had improved, Freeman (1965, p.119) proudly asserted that sponsored children were not starving or destitute but chosen specifically to benefit from '...the personal interest taken by the sponsor...' and grants 'spent quarterly by an administrator on the spot on food, clothing or school needs'.

At a very basic level some individual and family oriented cash transfers offered by several CS INGOs in the 1960s and 1970s were not dissimilar to Mexico's current and much lauded anti-poverty cash-transfer programme Oportunidades, praised as an effective innovation benefiting up to four million Mexican families since 2002 (World Bank, 2013) in regards to improved education, health and nutrition. However, unlike Oportunidades with its formidable resources, national presence, rigorous selection procedure using household surveys, comprehensive analysis of socio-economic information, and targeted support to females, CS-funded family helper programmes utilized by CS INGOs in the 1970s and 1980s were often localized, delivered through inexperienced partners, offered in isolation from government services and sometimes exclusive. CS INGOs historically funded only one child or perhaps a small number per family.

Problematically, there is a dearth of historic impact studies investigating the impact of the INGO cash transfers referred to above and it is unclear how effective they may have been. McDonnal and McDonnal (1994, pp.199–204) randomly sampled 5 per cent of Children International's sponsored children in 1993, comparing 4,764 beneficiaries to 627 children who had applied for sponsorship but had not yet received assistance. It is not clear how significant cash transfers were in programming, however of 16 projects analysed the authors claimed that 11 displayed significant improvements in the lives of sponsored children with 'The most dramatic effects...seen on education and physical health...'. Taking a negative view, Stalker (1982, p.2) warned readers that helping individuals was divisive and damaging in societies already sharply divided, and led to family rifts where one child received preferential treatment. In 1989 the *New Internationalist* deepened its critique, declaring that:

> The chosen few may receive extra food, education, clothes, medical treatment and gifts which others do not. Brothers, sisters or other families become jealous. And parents can feel humiliated... (*New Internationalist*, 1989b, p.1).

Although such claims have rarely been tested in a scholarly manner, there is consensus among leading CS INGOs that direct benefits were prone to divisiveness and may have been conducive to corruption, expressed more nicely as 'favouritism' in which '...family, tribal and

Figure 4.3   New Internationalist cartoon – Family rifts
(New Internationalist, 1989b, p.1)

other loyalties impact on the selection of children' (van Eekelen, 2013, p.476). A World Vision discussion paper (World Vision, 2006, pp.7–8) suggests that singling out individual children '...creates two classes of children', 'often creates jealousy', 'creates welfare expectations', establishes patterns of 'transactional participation', 'can create dependence', 'can divert resources from development' and can send mixed messages to the community about the role of INGOs.

In a candid assessment of CCF's experimentation with early Family Helper projects CCF staff member James Hoestetler explained that:

> The emphasis was on what we could do for them. There was little thought of encouraging people to do something for themselves... They were capable of doing that, but somehow we saw them as cases. We had caseworkers... They would go out and deliver money to the families. There was very little interaction between the families (Hoestetler in Tise, 1993, p.66).

Reflecting on 25 years of work with CS INGOs, McPeak (2013) addresses the claim that singling out individual children and families for cash payments, gifts such as bicycles, scholarships, and house repairs did divide families, '...inadvertently causing resentment and jealousy'. Further, gift-giving was often difficult to manage at a procurement and distribution level, complex to administer, prone to corruption, hard to evaluate and cash grants were often associated with increased levels of dependency when provided over long periods of time. Although some leading CS INGOs have retained tokenistic gift-giving, and this can be appreciated by child recipients, the usefulness of such gifts is also problematic. McDonic (2004, p.92) describes the exasperation of the mother of a West African child who had been sent coloured pencils, letters, stickers and photographs, concluding:

> Why should I care about these things? They are of no use to me...I need a hoe. That is what I need. I do not need these things. I think I should take my picture back...

Direct correspondence has been identified as problematic for several reasons. Plan International's executive director in the 1950s, Gloria Matthews, defended letter writing, stating that 'person-to-person contact is a good influence. It's a hopeful thing! ... And what's wrong with a kid saying "thank you"?' (Plan International, 1998, p.24). Nonplussed by the presumed impact of a simple thank-you, Stalker wrote in the *New Internationalist* in 1982, 'there's nothing like writing a regular thank-you letter to keep you in your place' (Stalker, 1982, p.2). A follow-up article by the *New Internationalist* (1985, p.4) posited that Bolivian children and their families:

> ...may be permanently marked by psychological and material dependence on their 'padrino' from the North. However well-intentioned such aid may be, the kernel is the creation of a paternalistic relationship which is unnecessary and potentially harmful.

Others, relying on opinion and anecdotal evidence, have pointed to potential shame experienced by parents reliant on handouts to support their children. Yuen (2008, p.49) asserts that fathers in Ghana '...are led to believe that their authority is being undermined by the gifts, attention, and correspondence lavished on their children'. However, the absence of robust studies makes it especially difficult to ascertain the degree to which these and similar criticisms were and are justified across various historic CS INGO programmes.

The nature of sponsor and sponsored child communication and non-communication has been an ongoing issue for CS INGOs. Referring to his sponsorship in a 1950s Hong Kong CCF orphanage, Dr. Chun Wai Chan noted how happy children would feel when they received letters or gifts yet observed that 'About a third of the children at Faith Love Home never heard from their sponsors' (in Tise, 1993, p.47). In contrast, a more recent study conducted by an assessment team from the Institute of Development Studies (Sussex) on behalf of Plan International (2008, p.3) found that 'Only 30–35% of sponsored children receive letters and gifts from sponsors, creating jealousy and disappointment...'. Further, 'claims of positive effects on children's growth, self-esteem and ability to communicate...can't be substantiated enough to advertise them'. This is not to say benefits do not exist for those children who do receive letters, rather, it is a reminder that positive claims should be based on solid research and an understanding of impact on those who miss out.

Critically, sponsor participation rates in communication vary across CS INGOs and the facilitation of meaningful cross-cultural communication is highly problematic, especially where sponsorship transitions from support of children in orphanages or schools (where it is much easier to facilitate communication) to support of children in their communities where language, literacy and cultural differences are more obvious. In the case of Plan International:

> What had been simple for a Spanish child in 1937 could be very hard for a child in Mali in 1987. Plan now worked where literacy was low, education was poor and letter-writing uncommon (Plan International, 1998, p.54).

Pragmatic challenges inherent to facilitating meaningful communication between sponsors and sponsored children include difficulty in bridging cultural or age gaps, necessity of costly translation services, accessing remote areas, protecting sponsors from additional requests for help, protecting children from predators and guaranteeing cultural sensitivity in the exchange of images. Filtering and censoring of correspondence can be difficult and in some cases leads to dictation of letters to children and provision of samples.

The disappointment of some children who receive no contact from a sponsor is evident in the following letter from a youth in India sponsored through the programme of a small Australian CS INGO. When asked by one of the authors of this chapter to write a sincere letter to her sponsor in 2011 the sponsored girl wrote:

> Dear Sponsor, I write so many letters but there is no reply from you. I feel very bad...I have not received any gifts or letter from you...still you help me. By so many ways you are really good. I thank you for everything... please can you send me any gift or a letter... I would at least feel like you are talking to me, please don't mistake me if I have written anything wrong it is because I wanted to see you. Yours obediently and loving... (Personal Correspondence).

Such letters recognize the willingness of some sponsored children to communicate meaningfully with their sponsors, while also questioning the ethics of a communication strategy that historically prioritized donors and guaranteed correspondence from a child without a commitment from a sponsor to write in return. Sponsorship can be intimate, and letter writing important, although there is some controversy as the degree to which this intimacy is self-constructed and mutually shared. It is noteworthy that Plan International began to emphasize dialogue rather than friendship from 1983, reducing the number of letters required of Foster Children from six per year to one, with an annual report facilitated by Plan International staff (Plan International, 1998, p.54).

Prevalent in early CS critique was the widespread notion that sponsorship of children to attend schools, especially boarding schools, was harmful and that communication with donors created empty aspirations. In one 1989 article (*New Internationalist*, 1989b, p.1) journalists suggested that provision of Christmas cards to non-Christian children was equivalent to Western children receiving a copy of the Koran. Further the authors claimed that programmes which provided education of individual children ensured that:

> They are educated to uselessness, unable to obtain well-paid white-collar work in their own towns or villages and unwilling to do low paid 'menial' labour. As adults they either remain at home dissatisfied, or take their skills further afield, away from the community that needs them.

Given the reality of current rural-urban migration patterns in the Global South, and the Millennium Development goals relating to education, such critique now seems questionable. Other lesser criticisms may have underestimated the ability of children to contextualize communication from donors. For example, it was speculated that 'a child who learns of a sponsor's large house and reads about their skiing holidays or big cars can become dissatisfied with his or her own community...' (*New Internationalist*, 1989b, p.2). Writing several years earlier Stalker cited one case of a 16 year old girl who 'honestly believed that someday her sponsor, who lived in Toronto, was going to invite her to go and live there' (Stalker, 1982, p.2). He referred to this as creating 'empty aspiration'. However for the most part, these and other claims have remained untested and unstudied in organizations that retain direct benefits to children or families.

It is evident that by the 1980s child welfare activities were increasingly out of favour. As community development and community empowerment ideology became pervasive in the 1980s, INGOs devoted to orphan care, direct handouts and direct service delivery were increasingly motivated to transition sponsorship to a funding tool for community development and poverty reduction. Weaning recipients off direct benefits was often difficult and CS INGOs sometimes found it easier to close their programmes entirely and relocate rather than remain and transition the expectations of former beneficiaries. The cutting of direct cash transfers to families was especially difficult. In 1985 the *New Internationalist* could report that according to a Plan worker in Bolivia:

> We don't want to be paternalistic, so, we're making the families work in local groups, and the contributions are going more to those projects now, and we're cutting down the aid to individual families. A lot of them don't like it. They're writing letters asking their sponsors not to send donations for the groups because they're afraid of losing their money (*New Internationalist*, 1985, p.3).

By the 1980s, community development programmes involving preventative health, women's literacy, primary and vocational education, improved farming practice, local infrastructure and micro-enterprise (see Korten, 1987, p.148) were upheld as having greater potential to reduce poverty and catalyse sustainable change than child welfare activities and handouts linked to direct service delivery, educational support and cash transfers over long periods of time. While this chapter does not discuss issues in CDCS (Community Development Child Sponsorship) it is noteworthy that the transition was often difficult and ironically, would lead to significant criticism that CS

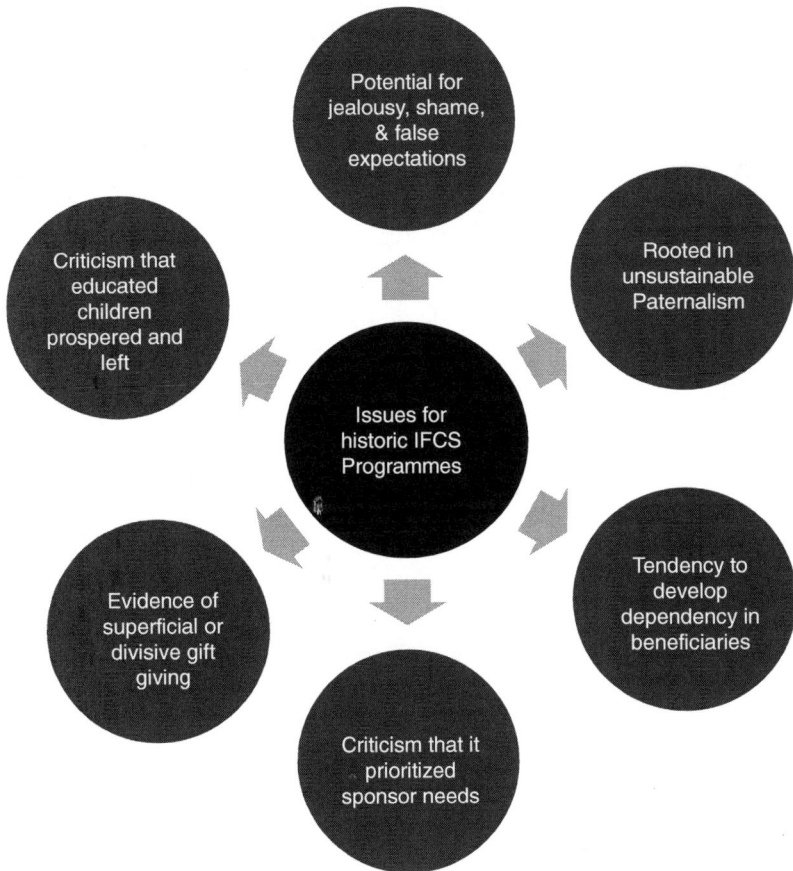

Figure 4.4 Summary of key issues for historic CS programmes involving individual support and direct benefits to families (IFCS)

INGOs were fundraising using a paradigm of individual child welfare while delivering programmes based on pooled funding for community development. Investigated by journalists, this would lead to damaging claims in the 1990s that CS INGOs lacked transparency.

Impact of CS on sponsors and the public in the North

Manzo (2008, p.652) draws parallels between the images frequently used by CS INGOs and historic missionary work, arguing that the iconography of childhood has functioned for INGOs similarly to missionary iconography utilized in the colonial era. Manzo argues that '...the same image (such as the much critiqued "starving baby" image still featured in many INGO emergency appeals) can faithfully represent a shared value such as the principle of humanity while representing one part of the world as infantile, helpless, and inferior'. In similar vein Jefferess (2002, p.1) argues that 'World Vision Canada's television fundraising appeals construct Canadian sponsor identity in relation to a "needy" "Third World" other. The programmes utilize structures of identification reminiscent of earlier forms of colonial discourse and are dependent on discourses of consumer capital'. A common concern is that CS advertising has contributed to '...creation and solidification of stereotypes', including that of an African continent dominated by disease, dependence, poverty, hunger and helplessness (Mittelman and Neilson, 2009, p.66).

Children were, according to some critics (*New Internationalist*, 1989a) prone to being commodified and 'sold' through marketing activities that presented the child as a product to consumers. Photographed as the passive victims of helpless parents, the children presented to sponsors have been associated with a distorted image of the 'Third World', bereft of context and real understanding of causes of poverty, if not outright racism. Concern over the commodification of children, at the expense of truthful representation, is seen below in Figure 4.5. In the late 1980s Burton, director of Save the Children Bolivia hinted at the difficulty in catching a donor's eye, stating:

> We're trying all different ways of making the children come out more attractive. They don't look good against a plain background or wall. Now we're doing them against natural landscapes or colored weavings. Even some quite ugly children have been sponsored... (*New Internationalist*, 1989a, p.2).

Interestingly for CS INGOs, Yuen (2008, p.49) describes the presence of money in a love-based relationship as problematic while McDonic (2004, p.77) suggests that money invalidates relationships between the children and sponsors. While the cliché that 'love can't buy friendship' is true for many sponsors, and symbolizes western ideals of relationships based on emotion, the extent to which donors view sponsorship as an act of consumerism, and the extent to which sponsored children view financial assistance as irreconcilable with friendship, may be overstated and requires further investigation (see Chapter 13 by Frances Rabbitts).

Figure 4.5   New Internationalist cartoon – Fostering racism
(New Internationalist, 1989b, p.1)

Arguing that many historic CS INGOs were doing little to address factors that had rendered children destitute in the first place, Small (1997, p.586) describes CS as the epitome of a donor-oriented programme which '...not only failed to challenge the misunderstanding of donors but it actively pandered to them, packaging the problem into a saleable commodity...'. Small argued that NGOs were often torn between the choice of being wealthy and pragmatic (by commodifying children if necessary and perpetuating a false understanding of causes of poverty) or poor and principled (rejecting sponsorship).

Through trial and error INGOs have discovered what works in eliciting response. Burman (1994, p.2) points out that the 1950s and 1960s were '...the heyday of the hungry child images...' and as a heavy user of child images Oxfam's income peaked in the 1960s with each Pound spent on advertising yielding an enviable 31 Pounds raised. ActionAid UK began mass marketing of CS in the mid-1970s with pre-trialed, enormously successful 'postal parents' advertisements, often in the form of off-the-press advertising and loose leaf inserts. Conceived by Harold Sumpton, the advertisements featured close-up black and white images of children and statements such as 'Won't you be my "Postal parent" for £4.33 a month?' SOFII (2010) states that 'for press advertising off-the-page they were masterful examples of how to use a small space effectively, with not a millimeter of wasted space'. ActionAid learned that head and shoulder shots were more effective, that four head and shoulder shots worked better than one, and so on.

Implicit in much sponsor recruiting but explicit in World Vision Canada's tagline was the concept of 'Change a life. Change your own'. (cited in Yuen, 2008, p.50). The very idea that a small monthly donation could significantly change the life of a child and the life of a giver has been ridiculed however a more valid criticism is that CS INGOs were slow to communicate the reality of pooled funding for community development. Early 1980s experimentation with advertising for Childcare Partners by World Vision USA, Canada and Australia was consistent with a 1979 plan to move 50 per cent of programmes to a community development model, a shift that would promote self-sufficiency and the Area Development Program (ADP) which became a standardized approach to World Vision's CS in the late 1980s and 1990s (Pratten et al, 2007, p.1).

World Vision's Childcare Partners provided donors with folders containing information about representative children in a community, and sought to move beyond individual sponsorship. Unfortunately, by 1985 the two year trial revealed 'a substantial reduction in their sponsor fulfillment rates', mandating a return to use of specific, named children (Watkins, 1998, p.5). When Save the Children Canada terminated its individual CS programme in the early 1980s and replaced it with community sponsorship it lost 3,000 of its 8,500 sponsors (*New Internationalist*, 1985, p.4). A comment from Robert Brooks, National Director of CCF in Australia in the early 1990s illustrates the tension within CS INGOs well:

> Community development is a better way of helping people...but that's not something people are moved to give money for; it doesn't give them an emotional reward. Whereas they are rewarded emotionally by helping an individual child (Tise, 1993, p.73).

Appeals from INGOs to their constituents to sponsor villages or communities have frequently failed to result in the same enthusiastic response as for individual CS. CS INGOs therefore have tended to continue to offer individual sponsorship while transitioning to development work. For Plan Netherlands (Foundation Foster Plan Nederland), a board decision in the mid-1990s to move away from individual support of sponsored children resulted in heated constituent reaction. Hondius (2002) states that 'To outside observers, the violence of the conflict was puzzling'. Publicized accounts of sponsorship of children who had died or relocated, and allegations that only approximately 50 per cent of donations reached children (van Krimpen, 2012, p.15), combined with concern over a shift away from individual support, resulting in a stream of negative publicity and a series of legal challenges. Plan Netherland's success in promoting CS to Dutch citizens

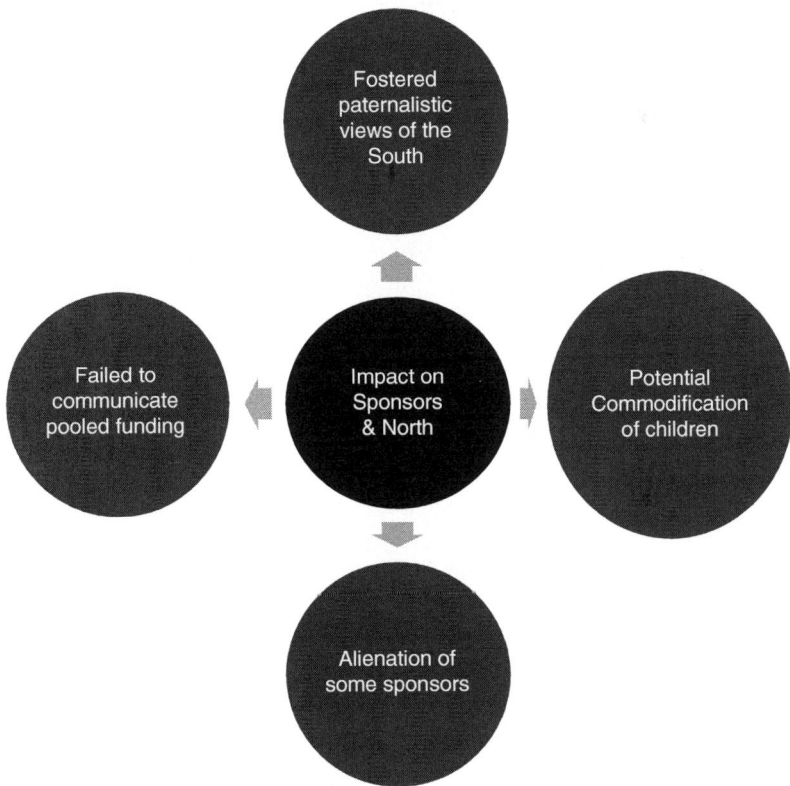

Figure 4.6 Summary of key issues for historic CS programmes relating to impact on sponsors in the North

had been phenomenal to that point insofar as 'By 1994, almost 40 per cent of Plan's worldwide child sponsorships were being financed from Holland alone' (Smillie, 1995, p.200).

Negative impacts on CS INGOs

CS has been identified as an impediment to radical change due to its relational nature. In listing several dangers and drawbacks of traditional forms of CS, Herrell (1974, pp.685–686) expressed concern that the sponsor:

> ...wants a long-term relationship with the child. He wants to watch a child grow up so that he can feel pride in having nurtured the child along as much of the way as possible from infancy to childhood. This may, unfortunately, inhibit the agency from shifting its support from one program to another, for fear of terminating a child-sponsor link.

Herrell also noted that interest in one child could, for sponsors, eclipse their recognition of the need to assist non-sponsored children or the community surrounding the child. Writing a decade later, he argued that when sponsorship funds were provided to the bank account of a community association it had '...major power to mobilize community participation...' and was one of the '...least expensive ways to raise funds for programs serving children' (Herrell, 1986, p.239). Writing in the mid-1990s Smillie (1995, p.136) posited that 'although most child sponsorship agencies now target communities in their field work as much as the child, the child remains the publicity anchor, and projects are therefore smaller, more parochial and are often less cost-effective than others'. A common perception within the INGO sector at large is that the CS fundraising mechanism may have slowed the progress of many CS INGOs in their transition away from individual child welfare activities, to community empowerment and development.

The very rapid growth of a small number of early CS INGOs created significant tension within the INGO sector in the 1980s. Issues of overhead expenses and administration costs have long been politicized by some voluntary agencies keen to position their organizations as more efficient, and consequently, more deserving of public support than government agencies (Lissner, 1977, p.231). From the 1970s this extended to comparisons between INGOs with little consideration for the age of the organizations, quality of programmes, competency of staff or programmatic outcomes. Concerned about prominent CCF advertising in Lutheran publications, leading to as much as one million dollars per year in income for CCF, a Lutheran INGO, Lutheran World Action (LWA), attempted to politicize administration costs, informing readers that '...the overhead in many such organizations runs from 30 to 50 per cent or more, so that sometimes less than half of what you give usually gets to that child. This is a very expensive business, when mass needs are met on an individual case basis' (Empie in Lissner, 1977, p.233). Although sweeping claims that CS organizations were expensive to run were rarely made with hard comparisons to other INGOs or government agencies, the mud stuck!

Smillie (1995, p.153) identified 'dramatic subterfuge' used by World Vision Germany in the late 1980s in which the organization declared that 80 per cent of donations went overseas without informing donors that money went through several World Vision offices, each responsible for taking a cut, and eventually, 'a hefty proportion was transferred back to Germany, to a marketing company...'. Though CS INGOs of that era went to significant lengths to be seen as good financial stewards, speculation had grown that expensive marketing campaigns, large donor-relations teams and considerable cost in facilitating individual communication and individual benefits ensured that too little money reached developing countries. For the *New Internationalist* staff (1985, p.4) there were better ways to help and 'The money that is spent on sponsoring a single child for one year could immunize 31 children against the six major child-killer diseases...'. Daniel Borochoff, from the American Institute of Philanthropy, was blunt in his assessment of overhead costs associated with linking individuals, stating 'Just think of the savings if the charity didn't have to do this charade of matching up an individual with a kid' (cited in Moore, 1998, p.16). The issue was arguably more complex than Borochoff implied. In reality the administrative expenses of INGOs in Northern countries were also impacted by start-up costs, advertising costs required to establish a donor base and contributions to parent bodies.

Referring to a 1970s USA General Accounting Office study of five large children's charities (including Plan and Save the Children) which cited evidence of poor fiscal management or misrepresentation of policies, columnist Jack Anderson wrote,

> The renowned Christian Children's Fund, like the old lady who lived in the shoe, has so many children it doesn't know what to do. Worse, it doesn't know what it did with $25 million, which was

raised to feed, clothe, and educate needy children around the world (in Tise, 1993, p.79).

Although CCF largely denied the allegations, sporadic accusations of mismanagement or high cost structures have dogged CCF and other leading CS INGOs for decades. For example, former CCF board member Professor Thomas Naylor's 1994 report triggered 14 front-page articles in the *Richmond Times-Dispatch* (later picked up the *Washington Post, Chicago Tribune, Christianity Today* and *NBC News*) alleging, among other issues, lavish spending by executives, and a creative accounting system which indicated that 80 per cent of donations benefited children directly when in fact the figure was closer to 50 per cent (Naylor, 2011, pp.1–2). In his expose of Save the Children USA's domestic sponsorship programme, Maren (1997, p.152) charged that the organization misled USA sponsors of the domestic programme by claiming it used 80–85 per cent of income for programme services. Maren countered that on average only US$35.29 of US$240.00 raised annually through sponsorship was disbursed to the direct benefit of each child in the United States. By inference, many CS INGOs were portrayed in media exposés as opportunistic fundraisers. In Lissner's (1977, p.228) view many INGOs, not just CS ones, have followed a zigzag course between income maximization and adherence to agency conviction. Critically for CS INGOs, the combination of their child-centredness, links to individual children, and significant claims about impact have done little to communicate to sponsors the real costs of 'doing business'.

The real cost of CS interventions versus administrative overheads has been frequently queried. Reasons cited for high costs in traditional CS interventions in Southern countries are varied. Singling out CS INGOs for mention, the 1993 *Human Development Report* (UNDP, 1993, p.89) noted that 'Agencies that receive money from child sponsorship organizations, for example, have to spend much of their time collecting copious quantities of personal information about the sponsored children – and employ large teams of 'social workers' for this'. Van Eekelen (2013, p.475) cites high costs in identifying children, monitoring their progress, writing reports, communicating with sponsors, facilitating sponsor visits and following up on difficult cases. In its 1989 article entitled 'Letters to a god', *New Internationalist* (1989a, p.1) staff quoted the head of Save the Children Bolivia:

> Sometimes a sponsor will contact head office in the US asking for a photo. They don't realize how much time expense that means. We

reckon it costs $19 a photo with all the administration, work and materials. That's equivalent to a month's sponsorship.

The high cost of maintaining large donor-support teams has also been cited as a reason for significant overheads in traditional sponsorship programmes, as has high levels of engagement with celebrity advocates and mass media.

Strident debate over public fundraising for INGO work has centred on CS as a marketing tool, especially in relation to their depiction of children/beneficiaries, their truthfulness and the impact on donors. According to Mittelman and Neilson (2009, p.63) 'The marketing of child sponsorship programs has been laden with accusations of deceitfulness and disrespect towards the dignity of the children they purport to help'. Lissner's 1977 thesis *The Politics of Altruism* questioned images used by humanitarian organizations for fundraising. Concerned that northern NGOs often misrepresented the South via fundraising strategies laden with unrepresentative images of malnourished children, Lissner (1981, p.1) concluded that:

The public display of an African child with a bloated Kwashiorkor-ridden stomach in advertisements is pornographic, because it exposes something in life that is as delicate and deeply personal as sexuality...

The unpleasant phrase 'pornography of poverty' has become widespread as 'a term used by development practitioners in the North and in the South to describe the worst of the images that exploit the poor for little more than voyeuristic ends and where people are portrayed as helpless, passive objects' (Plewes and Stuart, 2007, p.23). CS INGOs in particular have been identified as frequent past users (by non-CS INGOs and others) of emotionally manipulative imagery, which humiliated, demeaned and inadvertently misrepresented reality in the South. Plewes and Stuart (2007, p.23) go so far as to say that CS INGOs have been '...demonstrably the biggest users of pornography of poverty images, whether for sponsorship or for fund-raising for humanitarian emergencies'. For Holland (1992, p.154) it can position children and their communities in '...a dangerous area between sympathy, guilt and disgust'. Repetitive use by Save the Children of Kevin Carter's Pulitzer-prize winning picture of an emaciated Sudanese child with a vulture waiting nearby, is perhaps the most infamous example of this.

The tensions inherent in mobilizing public support from a complacent public for humanitarian aid are evident as early as the 1920s when Save the Children Fund UK was criticized for exaggerating levels of need and manipulating emotions. Save responded then by saying 'It has been said – and generally with derogatory intention – that the Save the Children Fund has made capital of our popular emotion. That is exactly what it set out to do' (S.C.F., 1922, p.142). At a time when humanitarian fundraising was in its infancy, Save the Children justified its emotional appeals and imagery as a necessary attempt by a few people to 'open the eyes and stimulate the emotions of their fellows'. Unfortunately, CS advertising in the 1980s frequently featured starving or malnourished children, while the reality of most CS interventions involved school support and programmes in non-famine areas. One explanation for this is the rapid growth of CS INGOS and their employment of senior administrators and specialist marketers with little or no experience of programmes and no mandate to engage in development education. Herrell (1974, p.687) cautioned that:

> Some sponsors may not understand the broad international economic and social forces that have placed certain countries and cultures at a disadvantage in economic development. Instead these sponsors may take a condescending view toward the country, culture and even the family of the child. Sponsorship agencies must resist the temptation to pander to this tendency.

Problematically, the absence of effective development education was not isolated to CS INGOs in the 1950s–1980s.

CS marketing has frequently been identified as an impediment to effective development education. Interestingly, as early as 1920 Save the Children Fund in Britain had already been criticized for not being '...sufficiently educational and constructive' (S.C.F., 1920, p.21). To its credit, in 1925 Save the Children Fund urged readers to consider the importance of not just feeding the hungry (a key aim of the child sponsorship programme) but making hunger impossible. Quoting *My Life and Work* by Henry Ford, the editor of the Save the Children Fund's publication (S.C.F., 1925, p.39) began with the warning that 'It is easy to give; it is harder to make giving unnecessary. To make the giving unnecessary we must look beyond the individual to the cause of his misery...'. The advice was excellent and at first glance provides a sharp rebuke to many historic CS programmes although CS INGOs emphasizing literacy, numeracy and education tended to view their work as a pre-emptive strike against causes of misery.

Commenting on the daunting logistical challenges evident in serving CCF's 400,000 sponsors and 533,000 children in the early 1990s, CCF's Sponsor Services Director noted 25,000 outgoing phone calls and letters to sponsors in one month alone and enthused that each communication was an:

> opportunity to educate the sponsors about what life is like in other parts of the world. When a sponsor learns that the reason letters take so long in Sierra Leone is that there's no reliable postal system, he or she is being educated (Tise, 1993, p.99).

Unfortunately, the reality is that CS marketing practices have been designed to trigger giving rather than develop understanding. A challenge for contemporary CS INGOs is to do development education much better. This applies to many non-CS INGOs as well. In his review of development education in New Zealand, Small (1997, pp.585–586) notes the proliferation of NZ NGOs since the 1980s and widespread use of messages and images that '...exoticizes world poverty and powerlessness and thereby undermines the international solidarity that is needed to fulfill the dual tasks of tackling the causes of the growing inequalities in wealth and power, and building sustainable people-centered alternatives'. Similar sentiment is expressed by Dogra whose interest in dominant themes of 'difference' and 'distance' in INGO messaging leads to the conclusion that INGOs in general resort to discursive strategies of infantilization and feminization that reinforce colonial ways of seeing things (Dogra, 2012, p.31). Whether there is any difference for CS INGOs is a question requiring further consideration.

A significant criticism – which peaked in intensity in the 1990s – leveled against several large CS INGOs related to the obvious failure of some children to receive direct benefits and lax or blatantly misleading communication between CS INGOs and their sponsors. *The Chicago Tribune* 'bombshells' of 1998, later published by *The New York Times* embarrassed Save the Children, Childreach, CCF and Children International. Singling out the largest CS INGOs for which negative findings would be more newsworthy, journalists attempted to visit 12 children whom they had sponsored over two years. One, a child in Mali named Korotoumou Kone, had died despite sponsorship and letters continuing for two years. Another child, Wagner Villafuerte from Guatemala, had been used to solicit a US$25 birthday gift for a jogging suit and festive birthday party however received a sweat suit, cup of juice and a packet of cookies. In another case, after US$500 in sponsorship over two years, a child had benefited through five visits to a clinic and US$53 of training for the mother as a rug maker.

Read as case studies, the anecdotal accounts reported above painted CS INGOs as unable to track individual benefits to children at best, and manipulative or dishonest at worst. For the purpose of this chapter it is notable that the cases revealed tension between the oftentimes historic promise of tangible child benefits and the complex reality of monitoring children in often remote locations during a transition to community development initiatives using pooled funding. World Vision has noted that the selection of neediest children in a community is

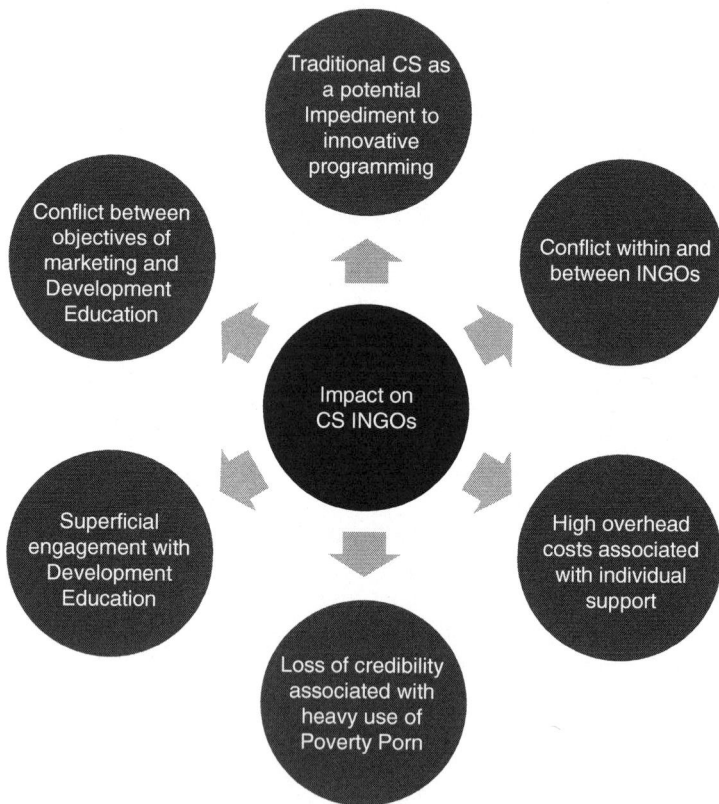

Figure 4.7   Summary of criticisms of CS in relation to INGOs themselves

complicated by high migration and dropout levels, and in some cases, diversion of funds from 'longer term, community-based, sustainable interventions' (World Vision, 2006, p.7).

Nevertheless, for the select group of CS INGOs featured, much work would be required to ensure that marketing messages reflected the reality of programmatic imperatives and information about specific children aligned with reality. The cumulative impact of media exposes was to undermine the pubic legitimacy of CS INGOs, generate disillusionment and perpetuate controversy. Ironically, this occurred as the majority of the large CS INGOs involved were transitioning towards more impactful programmes! A consequence within CS INGOs has been ongoing tension between programming staff and marketing staff as they deal with the reality that 'Every organization walks the fine line between presenting its most appealing program what will generate support, and honestly saying what they are, in fact, doing' (Livezey, 1981, p.4).

Conclusion

Readers who expect sweeping condemnation of all things related to CS are likely to be disappointed with the conclusion to this chapter. As authors we resonate with Theodore Roosevelt's 1910 speech at the Sorbonne, Paris, in which he famously said:

> It is not the critic who counts; not the man who points out how the strong man stumbles, or where the doer of deeds could have done them better. The credit belongs to the man who is actually in the arena, whose face is marred by dust and sweat and blood, who strives valiantly; who errs and comes short again and again... (Roosevelt, 1910).

Recognizing the overwhelmingly negative portrayal of historic CS by some journalists and various critics, we acknowledge the many staff in various CS INGOs who have, since the 1920s, facilitated programmatic improvements. It is noteworthy that programmes staff in leading CS INGOs have been instrumental in moving CS interventions from orphan care, to family helper programmes and beyond to pooled funding for service provision, holistic child development, community development activities and advocacy. To imply that the push for change came exclusively from outside CS INGOs would be a grave injustice and it may be fairer to say that most CS INGOs have improved again and again rather than come short again and again. However, also we acknowledge those critics who have been motivated by the compelling logic behind Winston Churchill's reminder that criticism is necessary to correct an unhealthy state of things.

Having discussed a range of historic criticisms of CS as they relate to the individual sponsorship of children in institutions (IICS) and the support of children in the context of their families and home communities (IFCS), it should be evident that much critique needs to be grounded in its historical context. Importantly, challenges inherent to pooled funding for community development (CDCS) and rights-based child sponsorship have not been discussed here. The manner in which leading CS INGOs have proactively changed, responded to critique and set new benchmarks for best practice are discussed in the final chapter of this book (see Chapter 15).

Bibliography

Bornstein, E. (2001) 'Child sponsorship, evangelism, and belonging in the work of World Vision Zimbabwe', *American Ethnologist*, 28, 3, 595–622.
Bornstein, E. (2005) *The Spirit of Development: Protestant NGOs, Morality and Economics in Zimbabwe* (Stanford CA: Stanford University Press).
Brehm, V. and Gale, J. (2000) 'Child sponsorship: A funding tool for sustainable development?' *Informed* (no.3, November) 2–6.
Burman, E. (1994) 'Poor children: Charity appeals and ideologies of childhood', *International Journal of Psychology and Psychotherapy*, 12, 1, 29–36.
Dogra, N. (2012) *Representations of Global Poverty: Aid, Development and International NGOs* (London: I.B. Tauris).
Freeman, K. (1965) *If Any Man Build: The History of Save the Children Fund* (London: Hodder and Stoughton).
Herrell, D.J. (1974) 'The effects of sponsorship on child welfare', *Child Welfare*, LIV 10, 684–691.
Herrell, D.J. (1986) 'Effective social services through international child sponsorship programmes', *International Social Work*, 29, 237–245.
Holland, P. (1992) *What is a Child? Popular Images of Childhood* (London: Pandora Press).
Hondius, F. (2002) 'Mid-life crisis of "Plan": A Dutch case study', *The International Journal of Not-for-Profit Law*, 5, 1, September, http://www.icnl.org/research/journal/vol5iss1/cn_6.htm, date accessed 16 September 2013.
Jefferess, D. (2002) 'For sale – Peace of mind: (Neo-) colonial discourse and the commodification of third world poverty in World Vision's "telethons"', *Critical Arts*, 16, 1, 1–21.
Korten, D.C. (1987) 'Third generation NGO strategies: A key to people-centered development', *World Development*, 15, 145–159.
Lissner, J. (1977) *The Politics of Altruism: A Study of the Political Behaviour of Voluntary Development Agencies* (Geneva: Lutheran World Federation).

Lissner, J. (1981) 'Merchants of misery', *New Internationalist*, 100, June, http://newint.org/features/1981/06/01/merchants-of-misery/, date accessed 16 September 2013.

Livezey, E.T. (1981) 'Child sponsorship dollars: How much goes to him?' *The Christian Science Monitor*, 6 August, http://www.csmonitor.com/layout/set/print/1981/0806/080657.html, date accessed 27 March 2013.

Mahood, L. and Satzewich, V. (2009) 'The Save the Children Fund and the Russian famine of 1921–23: Claims and counter-claims about feeding "Bolshevik" children', *Journal of Historical Sociology*, 22, 1, 55–83.

Malkki, L.H. (1997) 'Children, futures, and the domestication of hope'. Paper presented at the University of California Humanities Research Institute, group convened by Susan Harding, 'Histories of the Future', University of California.

Manzo, K. (2008) 'Imaging humanitarianism: NGO identity and the iconography of childhood', *Antipode*, 40, 4 632–657.

Maren, M. (1997) *The Road to Hell: The Ravaging Effects of Foreign Aid and International Charity* (New York: The Free Press).

McDonic, S.M. (2004) *Witnessing, Work and Worship: World Vision and the Negotiation of Faith, Development and Culture*, Dissertation, Graduate School of Duke University.

McDonnal, W.A. and McDonnal, T.P. (1994) 'Quality evaluation in the management of child sponsorship', *Journal of Tropical Medicine and Hygiene*, 97, 199–204.

McKenzie, R.B. (ed.) (1999) *Rethinking Orphanages for the 21st Century* (Thousand Oaks, CA: Sage Publications Inc).

McPeak, M. (2013) *Some Thoughts on Child Sponsorship*, http://markmcpeak. wordpress.com/2013/01/24/some-thoughts-on-child-sponsorship/, date accessed 9 April 2013.

Mittelman, R. and Neilson, L. (2009) 'I saw a picture of a child living on 14¢ a day and I nearly choked on my $12 Scotch', Plan Canada's marketing of child sponsorship programs: A content analysis of print advertisements from the 1970s and 1980s, in Witkowski, T.H. (ed.) *Rethinking Marketing in a Global Economy: Proceedings of the 34th Annual Macromarketing Conference*, Kristiansand, Norway, pp.370–401.

Molumphy, H.D. (1984) *For Common Decency: The History of Foster Parents Plan 1937–1983* (Warwick, RI: Foster Parents Plan International).

Moore, A. (1998) 'The myth of the needy child?' *Christianity Today*, 42, 6, 16.

Naylor, T.H. (2011) 'The 1994 Christian Children's Fund scandal', *Counterpunch*, http://www.counterpunch.org/2011/11/15/the-1994-christian-children..., date accessed 22 August 2013.

New York Times (1998) 'Donations from the heart, greetings from the grave', *New York Times* (Late edition, East Coast), April 5, http://www.nytimes. com/1998/04/05/weekinreview/word-for-word-sponsoring-child-donations-heart-greetings-grave.html?pagewanted=all&src=pm, date accessed 6 October 2013.

New Internationalist (1985) One Child at a Time. Issue 148, June, http://newint. org/features/1985/06/05/one/, date accessed 3 June 2013.

New Internationalist (1989a) Letters to a God. Issue 194, April, http://newint. org/features/1989/04/05/god/, date accessed 4 October 2013.

New Internationalist (1989b) Simply...Why You Should Not Sponsor a Child. Issue 194, April, http://newint.org/features/1989/04/05/simply/, date accessed 3 June 2013.

Plan International (1998) *A Journey of Hope – The History of Plan International 1937–1998* (Woking UK: Plan International).

Plan International (2008) *The Development Impact of Child Sponsorship: Exploring Plan International's Sponsorship-Related Processes and Materials, Their Effects, and Their Potential Evolution* (Surrey, UK: Plan International).

Plewes, B. and Stuart, R. (2007) 'The pornography of poverty: A cautionary fundraising tale', in D.A. Bell and J.M. Coicaud (eds) *Ethics in Action. The Ethical Challenges of International Human Rights Nongovernmental Organisations* (Cambridge: Cambridge University Press), pp. 23–37.

Pratten, B., Granada, J.C., Torres, J. and Pierce, B. (2007) 'Refocussing the sponsorship model. Pilahuin & Lamay: Reflection on effectiveness from Peru and Ecuador', *Responses to Poverty*. World Vision International.

Roosevelt, F. (1910) Excerpt from the speech 'Citizenship in a Republic', http://www.theodore-roosevelt.com/trsorbonnespeech.html, date accessed 10 February 2014.

S.C.F. (1920) 'The S.C.F. at Home', *THE RECORD of the SAVE THE CHILDREN FUND*, 1, 2, November 1920, pp.17–32, SCF Box A670.

S.C.F. (1922) 'The new charity', *The World's Children: A Quarterly Journal of Child Care and Protection Considered from an International Viewpoint*, 2, 9, 135–150.

S.C.F. (1925) *The World's Children: Journal of Child Care and Protection Considered from an International Viewpoint*, 5, 3–4, December–January 1925, pp. 39–68, SCF Box A670.

Small, D. (1997) 'Development education revisited: The New Zealand experience', *International Review of Education*, 43, 5/6, 581–594.

Smillie, I. (1995) *The Alms Bazaar: Altruism Under Fire – Non-Profit Organisations and International Development* (London: IT Publications).

SOFII (2010) SOFII showcase of fundraising innovation and inspiration. ActionAid: The 'postal parent' advert, http://www.sofii.org/node/239, date accessed 20 June 2013.

Stalker, P. (1982) 'Please do not sponsor this child', *New Internationalist*, Issue 111, 7–9, http://newint.org/features/1982/05/01/keynote/, date accessed 3 June 2013.

Tise, L.E. (1993) *A Book About Children: The World of Christian Children's Fund 1938–1991* (Falls Church, VA: Hartland Publishing).

UNDP (1993) *Human Development Report 1993* (New York: Oxford University Press).

van Eekelen, W. (2013) 'Revisiting child sponsorship programmes', *Development in Practice*, 23, 4, 468–480.

van Krimpen, R.S. (2012) The influences of cause brand concepts on consumer responses to charity brands. Thesis for Master of Business Studies, Universiteit van Amsterdam.

Ver Beek, K. A. (2000) 'Spirituality: A development taboo', *Development in Practice*, 10, 1, 31–43.

Watkins, S. (ed.) (1998) 'Understanding child sponsorship: A historical perspective', Internal discussion paper, 20 March 1998 (World Vision USA Archives).

World Bank (2013) Shanghai poverty Conference: Case Study Summary Mexico's Oportunidades Program, http://info.worldbank.org/etools/docs/reducingpoverty/case/119/summary/Mexico-Oportunidades%20Summary.pdf, date accessed 3 July 2013.

World Vision (2006) *Contemporary Approaches to Child Sponsorship: A Discussion Reflecting Contemporary Approaches to Child Sponsorship within the World Vision Partnership* (Melbourne: World Vision Australia).

Yuen, P. (2008) "Things that break the heart of God": Child sponsorship program and World Vision International', *Totem: The University of Western Ontario Journal of Anthropology*, 16, 1, 39–51.

5
Excellence or Exit: Transforming Save the Children's Child Sponsorship Programming

Amy Jo Dowd, Céline Gustavson and Earl Moran

Introduction

Save the Children is the world's oldest and largest independent child rights organization. In 2012 the 30 members of the global movement collectively funded programmes in 120 countries, touching the lives of more than 125 million children worldwide and directly reaching 45 million children (Save the Children International, 2013). Combined 2012 annual revenues approaching US$1.6 billion have, among other key areas, been used to fund programming in core competencies of health and nutrition, education, child protection and child rights governance. Since its inception in 1919, Save the Children has been committed to improving the lives of children through sustainable change by continuously highlighting the needs of children and inspiring breakthroughs in the way their rights are expressed and fulfilled. This commitment continues as Save the Children seeks to be innovative (developing evidence-based, replicable solutions), achieve results at scale (supporting best practices, programmes and policies) enhance the voice of children (advocating and campaigning with and on their behalf) and build partnerships with children, civil society, governments and the private sector.

Although it has declined in proportional terms of overall revenue, child sponsorship (CS) has been an important part of Save the Children since 1919 when the pioneering Save the Children Fund in the United Kingdom (UK) initiated international sponsorships by connecting caring individuals in the UK and elsewhere with needy children in European countries including Austria, Germany and France. Initially funds raised through sponsorship were used to purchase and provide food for needy children affected in the post-war blockades.

Even then direct food aid to children was a far larger component of historic Save the Children work, with 300,000 children fed daily in 1922 via 1,450 kitchens in the Russian province of Saratov alone (Mahood and Satzewich, 2009, p.56). In 1932 the Save the Children Federation was established in the United States of America (USA) to help children in the Appalachian Mountains during the Great Depression.

As an economically depressed area, conditions in the region encompassing the Southern Tier of New York state to northern Alabama, Mississippi and Georgia, were similar to those experienced by the Welsh coalminers assisted by early sponsors in the UK during the 1920s. Using a similar model employed by Save the Children Fund in England, where funds provided necessities to children such as milk, staff in the independent USA organization began to recruit sponsors in America to help disadvantaged children in Appalachia. Beginning in 1938 this enabled very poor children to receive hot lunches cooked in school kitchens built by the community and paid for by sponsor's donations. By the 1970s CS had grown to represent 75 per cent of Save the Children USA's revenue and supported programmes in the USA and internationally in the developing world. From the 1950s to the

Figure 5.1 Children in Appalachia
Save the Children supported children, Appalachian region, circa 1930s

mid-2000s, Save the Children USA was the primary Save the Children member implementing CS. Save the Children USA will be referred to specifically, where appropriate in this chapter (i.e. in topics related to the period before the mid-2000s). Otherwise, the name Save the Children will be used.

As with many of the other CS international non-governmental organizations (INGOs), Save the Children's approach to CS has evolved over the many decades since its inception, with some of the most significant changes made in the past 15 years. During this time, Save the Children has sought to address head-on some of the criticisms aimed at it and other CS organizations, especially in the 1980s and 1990s. This has led to many changes in the way that Save the Children manages CS. This chapter will focus specifically on the evolution of Save the Children USA's approach to the use of CS funds to implement development programmes, and on a description of the approach itself. This approach was overhauled in the early 2000s to ensure that the programmes funded through sponsors' generous donations were not based on an anachronistic model of development (e.g. handouts). Rather, the new approach was designed to achieve meaningful results for children and to support sustainable development in partnership with them, their communities and local government.

The evolution of CS at Save the Children USA began in the mid-1970s when it was realized that sending sponsorship donations directly to children and their families might not be the most effective way to improve their lives. By the late 1970s and 1980s funding was pooled to reach more children with community-based programmes such as school-building, health clinics, teacher training and small projects. This was communicated to sponsors and follow-up interviews and focus groups showed sponsor support and understanding about the advantages of pooling funding in reaching more children and achieving more sustainable results. The move to pooled funding also required operational changes to ensure that sponsored children were benefiting from programmes and the relationships between sponsors and children were well supported.

During the 1990s CS revenue growth slowed, due largely to a strategic decision within Save the Children USA to grow grant revenue from the United States Agency for International Development (USAID) and other donors. By the late 1990s, CS was less than 25 per cent of the organization's revenue base. Public scrutiny had identified gaps in communication of the status of individual children and highlighted the need for stronger monitoring systems to quickly and accurately track the status of these children across the globe. At the same time, staff members began to debate whether CS had kept pace with the programme approaches and innovations that the organization had learned were essential in making the greatest impact on children's lives.

Spurred by a mandate from Save the Children USA's Board of Directors to address operational issues and pursue excellence in all areas of CS, an initiative titled 'Excellence or Exit' was undertaken in the late 1990s to rework sponsorship within a framework that started with the needs of children in country offices, developed evidence-based responses and drove changes up through the organization. Initially this meant that Save the Children USA focused on redesigning the operations that supported CS, reviewing organizational structures, and developing cross-functional teams to support all aspects of CS internationally and in the United States. New technology and continuous improvement strategies were employed. A new database allowed staff to exchange information about children and sponsors digitally, instead of by mailing paper and physical photos back and forth. In this way CS became much more efficient while ensuring that Save the Children USA's sponsors were better connected with the children they supported.

Up until this point, Save the Children USA's sponsorship-funded programmes had consisted of a wide variety of activities that were strongly focused on building the connection between the sponsor and the sponsored child, for example, by providing school supplies to individual children. Although direct assistance to individuals often resulted in inspiring stories that were shared with sponsors, there was limited evidence of the lasting impact of these activities. In order to deliver more effective and long-term results for children Save the Children USA staff knew that they needed to develop a new programme approach for Save the Children's CS funds. Organizational learning suggested strongly that the best outcomes for children occurred when Save the Children advocated for child rights and partnered in programmes that emphasized capacity building of communities and service providers. For example, instead of focusing on handing out school supplies only to the sponsored children, as Save the Children USA's CS programme had done in the past, the new programmes sought to address the critical issues that were preventing all children from accessing education and succeeding in school, in partnership with local governments and communities.

The new programme approach also required close collaboration with Save the Children's country office staff and technical programme experts based in the headquarters and regional offices, many of whom had never engaged in CS programmes before. The new approach drew heavily on Save the Children's experience with grant-funded programming, as well as the prevailing international development paradigms. It was named 'The Common Approach to Sponsorship-funded Programming' (henceforth referred to as 'The Common Approach') and sought to provide a more focused, systematic program approach for the use of CS resources, while still allowing enough flexibility to respond to local contexts and needs. The objective of developing and implementing this framework globally was to ensure that programmes implemented with CS funds would be of consistent and high quality and would meaningfully address the needs of children. Significantly, the approach also mandated that sponsorship-funded programmes must be accessible to all children of the appropriate age in the sponsorship communities, not just those children who were sponsored. This was a significant shift from previous practice, and also a point of difference between CS as implemented by Save the Children and the model used by many of its peer CS organizations at the time.

The Common Approach has added significant programmatic value to the organization and forms the backbone of the education portfolio in each country office with CS resources. Significantly, over the past ten years sponsorship-funded programmes have also become an 'incubator' for programme innovation within the organization, particularly in the area of education where the majority of Save the Children's CS resources are invested. Further, evidence and results generated at the country office level ensure that CS continues to play an important role in Save the Children's global education strategy. The following section will outline the core elements of the Common Approach that help explain how it has achieved this success.

Seeking excellence through the Common Approach to Sponsorship-funded Programming

The success of the Common Approach framework is largely predicated on its programme focus, and the supporting systems in place that allow for continuous improvement. The five main components of the approach are heavily influenced by Save the Children's overall approach to quality programming and include a focus on education, adherence to a seven-step programme cycle, commitment to best practice in country office teams, provision of appropriate technical assistance, and commitment to accountability and learning mechanisms.

CS funded interventions typically focus on four 'core' programmes areas (largely in the area of education): Early Childhood Care and Development (ECCD); Basic Education (BE); School Health and Nutrition (SHN); and Adolescent Development (AD). These programmes areas were chosen because Save the Children has extensive experience and expertise in them, and together they enable continuous participation by children from their early years through to age 18. Focusing the majority of CS funded resources on this limited number of important programme areas has been a strength of the approach.

Adherence to a common programme cycle consisting of seven steps is now fundamental to CS funded interventions at Save the Children. This requires situational analysis; programme design; monitoring and evaluation plan design; baseline; implementation and monitoring; evaluation (mid-term and end-line); and lessons learned. The programme cycle provides a standard process for designing, implementing, monitoring and improving sponsorship-funded programmes. It is the same approach typically used by Save the Children's grant-funded programmes. The recommended programme approach (based on Save the Children's experience) for each of the four core programmes is documented in 'Program Modules'. These modules guide field staff in programme design and implementation. The modules are 'evidence-based' – meaning the strategies recommended in the guidance reflect proven solutions to the challenges facing children – and are intended to be adapted to respond to the local contexts and needs of each country. For example, the evidence has shown that it is not enough for a child to have access to a school in order to learn; the teachers must also be well trained in order for that child to succeed in school.

Ensuring the implementation of quality CS-funded programmes

A key objective of the Common Approach is to ensure programme quality at the field level. This begins with strong country office leadership and programme teams supported by global-level programme experts. As experts in their field, these technical assistance providers guide and support country offices with programme design, implementation, monitoring and evaluation, planning, and reporting. They also facilitate information sharing and learning across offices and programmes. Support is provided both remotely and in-country. In addition, a number of quality improvement and accountability mechanisms are utilized at the field level, which enable Save the Children to learn from experience to make programme, and other improvements. These include periodic analysis of programme data, making time to reflect on lessons learned, and conducting regular self-assessments, which include receiving and responding to beneficiary feedback, including children. In addition, all aspects of CS are regularly reviewed by a team external to the country office, and recommendations for improvement are made and followed through to implementation.

In addition, Save the Children has articulated principles to guide programming. These draw on the *Convention on the Rights of the Child* (CRC), and are informed by Save the Children's wider development experience. They state that sponsorship-funded programmes:

1. *Are participatory*. Sponsorship-funded programs promote the meaningful participation of children and communities. Programs are child-centred and family-focused, working to enable parents to support their children's rights.
2. *Are gender-sensitive and inclusive of all children*. Sponsorship-funded programs do not exclude or discriminate on the basis of difference. Instead, all children are welcomed, treated equitably and given equal opportunities.
3. *Are safe and protective of children*. Programs promote the healthy physical, social and emotional development of children in environments that are free from abuse, corporal punishment and harassment.
4. *Mobilize communities*. Sponsorship-funded programs seek to mobilize communities to organize for action; explore the development issues and set priorities; as well as plan, act, and evaluate together through the application of a proven community mobilization approach.
5. *Are accountable for results*. Through regular assessment and monitoring and evaluation, programs demonstrate how investments and interventions are contributing to improvements in program outcomes.
6. *Test and document innovative approaches*. Programs develop, test and refine new and/or better ways to address the key educational, health and developmental needs of children. Investing in innovation and documentation is critical to achieving positive, lasting change.
7. *Collaborate and partner*. Programs work with governments and other stakeholders to ensure that they complement and strengthen the government system and are not offered merely as substitutes.

8. *Are sustainable.* It is critical that local governments, communities and other stakeholders continue to maintain and expand sponsorship-funded programs and/or outcomes beyond Save the Children's eight to ten year presence in an area. From the beginning, programs are developed in line with government standards and norms. Programs are designed with time and resource limits, and develop strategies to ensure that communities and institutions do not become exclusively dependent on Save the Children and its resources.

9. *Are cost effective.* Programs should seek to identify and prioritize those interventions that produce the greatest impact for the least amount of resources. In addition, programs ensure that each core program area receives enough resources to implement a comprehensive program, while minimizing expenditures on operations and management.

10. *Are flexible, relevant and appropriate.* While the state-of-the-art is documented in the Common Approach Program Modules, programs are flexible and should be adjusted to ensure they are relevant to children's needs and country contexts, now and for the future. This involves identifying successful practices and determining acceptable ways to introduce new activities and practices.

11. *Are integrated across sectors.* None of the sponsorship-funded programs should be implemented in isolation. They must be linked to each other (for example, ECCD programming must be linked to Basic Education programming), as well as to other relevant non-sponsorship-funded programs (for example, a grant-funded education project), as appropriate. In addition, collaboration between the people involved in program implementation and those who work on maintaining the connection between sponsors and the children they support (for example, through letter writing) is critical.

Taken together, the Common Approach framework and guiding principles provide a clear roadmap for programme design, implementation and monitoring. They have enabled the experience and programme evidence generated by CS resources to be harnessed by the organization as a whole. This is evident in the contribution of sponsorship-funded programmes to the innovations developed through Save the Children's Theory of Change. Significantly, sponsors have reacted positively to this approach over the last decade. The vast majority have supported the effort to improve programme quality by implementing comprehensive programmes that not only benefit their sponsored child but that seek to address the development challenges faced by all of the children in the community.

Child sponsorship and Save the Children's theory of change

In 2008, Save the Children rolled out a new five-year global strategy. This strategy introduced a Theory of Change that articulates how the organization can be most effective. It states that Save the Children is able to create lasting impact for children when it innovates and proves evidence-based, replicable breakthrough solutions to problems facing children; advocates effectively for child rights based on this evidence; builds meaningful partnerships at all levels; and implements best-practice programmes at scale.

By 2008, all country offices with CS funding had adopted the Common Approach and were in a position to drive this Theory of Change. While CS has contributed to all aspects of the Theory of Change, the strong programmatic focus of the Common Approach, and the emphasis on the development, documentation and utilization of evidenced-based programming has led sponsorship to play a catalytic role in the 'Be the Innovator' component. Spurred by the adoption of the Theory of Change, CS resources have been intentionally invested in finding more effective and efficient approaches to achieving results for children since 2009. This has been done in addition to the continued implementation of the existing evidenced-based core programme interventions. One significant example of this is sponsorship's early support for 'Literacy Boost', an approach to improving learning among school-age children in the developing world. Literacy Boost holistically pursues the goal of literacy by: using assessments to identify gaps and measure improvements in the five core reading skills; training teachers to teach national curriculum with an emphasis on reading skills; and mobilizing communities to support children's reading. Literacy Boost began as an innovative idea that has since been taken up by other members of Save the Children, a number of external donors such as USAID and AusAID, as well as partner organizations. A case study of this innovation funded by CS is presented in the next section.

Case study: Child sponsorship, innovation and 'Literacy Boost'

In 2000, the Millennium Development Goals renewed the already decade-old 1990 call for 'Education for All' with 'Goal 2: that all children complete a full cycle of primary education'. Hopes were high that this could be achieved by 2015, but by 2005 the assumption behind the statement (that children who completed primary school had basic skills for a lifetime of learning and productivity) was proving to be flawed. Primary school enrolment reached 90 per cent in 2010 for children in developing regions (United Nations, 2013), but assessments employed in country after country show that enrolment in school does not necessarily translate to quality learning (Hewlett Foundation, 2011). In fact, a recent study found that 30 per cent of 15–19 year olds who completed six years of schooling in Mali could not read a simple sentence, and the same was true of 50 per cent of Kenyan adolescents (World Bank, 2011). The Brookings Institute (2012) further reports stagnant learning and high probabilities of illiteracy among children reaching grade five in sub-Saharan Africa, warning that the lack of effective teaching and learning in countries with increased enrolment in the past ten years threatens to reverse progress made in educational access. Retention of children in schools without adequate support for effective learning risks systemic wasting of resources, children wasting their time and families wasting opportunities.

The problem of inadequate learning was documented in many Save the Children basic education programmes where the situation was just as dire, as evidenced by reading studies in CS programmes in Haiti, Nepal, Ethiopia and Guatemala in 2007–2008. Findings showed that between four and 42 per cent of third graders were unable to read a single word of grade-level text, and children who could read demonstrated limited comprehension. Such findings were later confirmed in other non-sponsorship sites. Save the Children staff, as well as multiple ministry and non-governmental organization (NGO) partners on the ground, came to the conclusion that many children in education programmes were reaching grade five without demonstrable skills, including the ability to read. Save the Children set its sights on a new, flexible, cross-country solution to ensure that children in basic education programmes were not only able to go to school and complete a full cycle of primary education, but learned basic skills while there.

Save the Children's first step was to review the research on reading. Questions included: What are the key reading skills? How do they develop? How do teachers/parents/peers support them? How does their development relate to life, motivation, school, play and fun? This review led to potential solutions for consideration in programmatic contexts, and laid the foundation to innovate with the development of a two-sided intervention emphasizing teacher training (using participatory methods to teach the five key reading skills) and encouragement of reading outside of school with family, friends and community members. The second step was to review Save the Children practice in teacher training and community reading promotion across the sponsorship and non-sponsorship programme portfolio. This revealed strengths to build on, such as the tried and tested use of reading buddies in Bangladesh and strong participatory teacher training materials in Malawi. It also identified gaps to fill such as local language materials, teacher training focused on reading skills development, and reading in groups to spread across whole villages scarce reading resources. After reviewing international best practice Save the Children sought proven solutions and opportunities for impactful change that were realistic given the resources at Save the Children's disposal, operational constraints and the drive for sustainable impact through systems change.

The 'Literacy Boost Toolkit' (completed in 2008), provides guidance in three interrelated components: assessment, teacher training and community action. Literacy Boost uses assessments to identify gaps in the five core reading skills (letter knowledge, phonemic awareness, vocabulary, reading fluency and comprehension (Snow et al, 1998)), trains teachers to teach national curriculum with an emphasis on these skills, and mobilizes communities to lead reading camps, be reading buddies and participate in reading awareness workshops. Core to Literacy Boost is Save the Children's belief in relevance for effective learning: more children will learn to read with comprehension if teacher training, materials and opportunities to practice are combined with the use of reading skills in daily life that elicits both motivation and enjoyment. Beginning in 2009, CS provided the funding and the programme platform through which Save the Children could begin testing our innovation hypothesis: 'If we intervene with teachers to improve reading instruction and with communities to extend the literacy environment and habits, then we can demonstrate impact on children's learning.'

With long-term sponsorship commitments in a core of communities, the Malawi and Nepal country offices became the first two field test sites for the Literacy Boost innovation. Nepal had been a site of study in 2008 and the team was anxious to address the findings, while Malawi had a long history of assessments and testing ideas to address dire reading results. CS funding enabled education staff at the country office level to work with headquarters-based technical assistance providers to adapt the Literacy Boost Toolkit and put together both teacher training and community reading interventions. To evaluate impact, staff developed skill assessments of letters, words, fluency and accuracy of reading text and comprehension for use with ten girls and ten boys in project and non-project schools, enabling a comparison of impact after a full school year.

Programmatic changes included reconsidering existing program interventions in light of a new focus on skills, as well as several new activities such as book banks, which are collections of locally relevant children's reading materials. This was done in Nepal by gathering part-ners involved in the creation of such resources and translating them, and in Malawi by contracting additional short-term staff to develop local language texts. While both offices had teacher training, neither had engaged in it on a monthly basis, or with a focus on specific skills. This required flexibility on the part of the sponsorship programme teams and a willingness to redesign the programme to support a new focus on literacy and learning. Building on the success of these two pilots the innovation was quickly expanded to sites in other countries where Save the Children had a presence through CS.

In the two initial sites as well as in the later ones, sponsorship funding also supported research fellows to work alongside the imple-menting teams to demonstrate the innovation's significant impact in the short and long term.

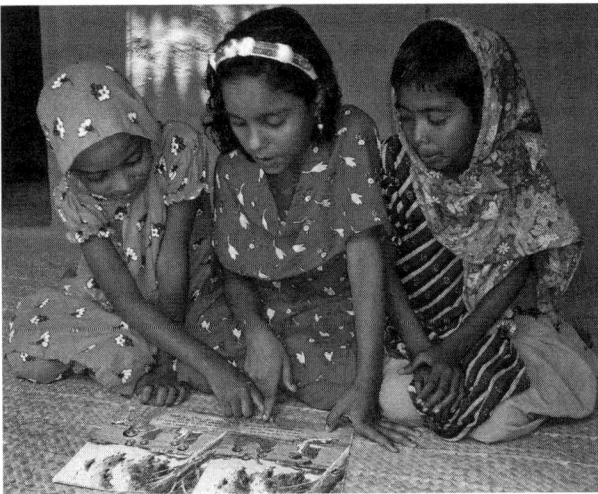

Figure 5.2 Delwara and her friends, reading a book from the Literacy Boost supported school 'book bank' in Meherpur, Bangladesh
Photo by Susan Warner

Literacy Boost interventions funded by CS have demonstrable impacts. After three months Ethiopian students demonstrated greater learning of letters and words (Cao et al, 2011). In Nepal, significant learning across many more reading skills (letters and words as well as fluency and accuracy), and in math was evident one school year later (Pinto, 2010). In Mozambique, third grade children's reading skills in Portuguese improved after two years' intervention (Mungoi et al, 2011). Importantly, analysis of these impacts by target group shows that through Literacy Boost we are reaching the children often struggling most to learn – girls, the poorest and children from homes with little literacy materials or practice (Friedlander et al, 2012a and Friedlander et al, 2012b). Further, when Malawian children borrowed books, they demonstrated significantly greater vocabulary gains (31.8 percentage points) than those in the same schools who did not (Wiener, 2010). In Ethiopia, very poor students with a reading buddy gained 22.3 percentage points in reading single words, while the poorest children who did not read with buddies gained 0.4 percentage points (Pisani and Diyana, 2013). Finally, in Figure 5.3, grade 1 children in Mozambique who reported a change in the presence of reading

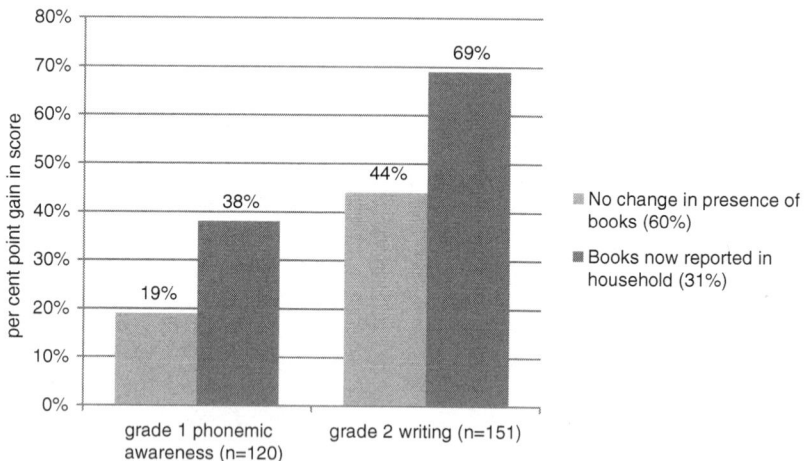

Figure 5.3   Mozambique: Percentage point reading skill gains by change in home literacy environment
(Guajardo and Ochoa, 2012)

materials in their home from baseline to end-line (two years later) made double the phonemic awareness gain and grade 2 students made 1.5 times the gain in writing skills when compared to those with no change in home materials (Mungoi et al, 2011).

Although Literacy Boost continues to be tested and implemented in new areas and countries, field test results such as those above have been presented at professional and academic gatherings since the results from the first sponsorship sites were available in March 2010. Each country and year offers further insight and evidence for impact, equity and effectiveness. These results generate interest across borders and lead to more countries utilizing the Literacy Boost Toolkit. As of 2013, Literacy Boost is being implemented in Afghanistan, Bangladesh, Burundi, El Salvador, Ethiopia, Guatemala, Indonesia, Kenya, Malawi, Mali, Mozambique, Nepal, Pakistan, Peru, South Africa, Sri Lanka, the Philippines, Uganda, Zimbabwe, Rwanda, and planning is underway in Zambia and Laos. Half of these sites – and the bulk of the early adopters – are CS programmes. The other half of these sites are funded

Figure 5.4   Rupmati Dangaura leads a Literacy Boost reading camp in front of her father's home in Katatulsipur, Nepal
Photo by Susan Warner

by private donors, foundations, bilateral agencies (AusAID, DFID, USAID) and partner NGOs such as World Vision who with Save the Children's technical assistance is implementing Literacy Boost in four sites in Africa, building its capacity to focus on learning and ensuring more effective sponsorship results.

Literacy Boost's focus on learning outcomes is now the strategic objective of all basic education programming supported by Save the Children. In Nepal, for example, this has led not just to new investment in basic education, but to rethinking how existing sponsorship and other funding opportunities might be better invested to support learning. A staff member working in this site for several years reflected that the first year of Literacy Boost implementation was the first year he felt he had made a real difference for children's learning. And in the context of the educational crisis across the development industry, international NGOs and donors, such as the Millennium Villages Project and the Children's Investment Foundation Fund, have approached Save the Children to access this experience and expertise and learn how to better ensure more children achieve positive learning outcomes and leave primary school able to read to learn. Given CS's crucial support in the early testing of the innovation, and the prominence of sponsorship sites in the group of programmes implementing Literacy Boost, it is no exaggeration to state that the success of Literacy Boost would not have been possible without CS support.

Significantly, the evidence generated through Literacy Boost (first through CS-funded programmes and then through additional grant-funded projects) is of increasing interest to many inside and outside of Save the Children as the international policy debate moves beyond enrolment and completion to focus on learning. For example, Save the Children's global education strategy for 2012–2015 includes the pursuit of two global 'breakthroughs' (defined as a remarkable shift from current practice and a sustainable change in the way the world treats children) one of which is 'improving literacy for all children and young people'.

As an evidence-based intervention for ensuring learning, Literacy Boost has led to the recognition of additional challenges related to supporting learning. Since 2010, Save the Children has been developing and testing Emergent Literacy and Math (ELM) resources to support field staff and programmes in early childhood care and development to more systematically understand and promote emergent skills in age-appropriate ways. Testing is under way in Bangladesh, Ethiopia and

Pakistan. Building Save the Children capacity and effectiveness in these early interventions will further increase impact for learning in primary schools. In collaboration with colleagues in the School Health and Nutrition team, Save the Children has also been augmenting research tools to include indicators that will enable the investigation of the influence of health status on learning in Literacy Boost sites. Finally, although the Literacy Boost data has shown some impact on math skills, work has begun to tackle math learning head on with 'Numeracy Boost,' now being field tested in sponsorship sites in Bangladesh and Malawi. In fact, in all of these cases (with the exception of Pakistan, which does not currently receive CS resources), learning innovations are tested through Save the Children's CS programmes in each country.

Conclusion

Since the 'Excellence or Exit' initiative, CS at Save the Children has enabled innovation and testing of new solutions for children within a new Theory of Change. Literacy Boost is a prime example of this and represents a pursuit of excellence that led Save the Children to develop a new approach to programming drawing heavily on its extensive non-sponsorship development experience. CS funded programmes now deliver measurable results for children, build a growing evidence base, and provide a multi-country platform for programme delivery and innovation. This is achieved through an approach that provides a package of best practice guidance, as well as programme technical support and continuous improvement mechanisms to help ensure programme quality, including the potential for replication and scale-up. The programmes are designed to achieve clearly articulated results, not just for sponsored children, but for all children in the sponsorship communities and beyond. Further, despite the fact that CS now represents a much smaller percentage of Save the Children's total revenue than it did historically, sponsorship-funded programming has added significant value – well beyond its actual size – to the organization and to the broader development agenda for children, in particular in the area of programme innovation and as a long-term, consistent source of funding for country offices. As in all development programmes, challenges remain but Save the Children has created a framework and approach that fosters sustainable improvements in the lives of children through the implementation of quality programmes.

Bibliography

Brookings Institute (2012) *A Global Compact on Learning Taking Action on Education in Developing Countries* (Washington, DC: Brookings).

Cao, Y., Dowd, A.J., Mohammed, O., Hassen, S., Hordofa, T., Diyana, F. and Ochoa, C. (2011) *Literacy Boost Dendi, Ethiopia: Three-month Report* (Washington, DC: Save the Children).

Friedlander, E., Hordofa, T., Diyana, F., Hassen, S., Mohammed, O. and Dowd, A. J. (2012a) Literacy Boost Dendi, Ethiopia Endline II (Washington, DC: Save the Children).

Friedlander, E., Dowd, A.J., Borisova, I. and Guajardo, J. (2012b) *Life-Wide Learning: Supporting All Children to Enjoy Quality Education* (NY: UN Women & UNICEF). Available at http://www.worldwewant2015.org/node/283236, date accessed 14 October 2013.

Guajardo, J. and Ochoa, C. (2012) Literacy Boost: Lessons from Assessment and Community Presentation to the Global Partnership for Education All Children Reading Workshop, Washington, DC, http://www.global partnership.org/media/cop%20meeting/Save%20the%20Children_Jarret%20 Guajardo_ERG%20COP%20Presentation_July%2024,%202012.pdf, date accessed 14 October 2013.

Hewlett Foundation (2011) Quality Education in Developing Countries, http://www.hewlett.org/programs/global-development-program/quality-education-in-developing-countries, date accessed 14 October 2013.

Mahood, L. and Satzewich, V. (2009) 'The Save the Children fund and the Russian famine of 1921–23: Claims and counter-claims about feeding "Bolshevik" children', *Journal of Historical Sociology*, 22, 1.

Mungoi, D., Mandlante, N., Nhatuve, I., Mahangue, D., Fonseca, J. and Dowd, A.J. (2011) *Endline Report of Early Literacy among Pre-school and Primary School Children in Elma-Supported Schools Gaza Province, Mozambique* (Maputo, Mozambique: Save the Children).

Pinto, C. (2010) *Impact of Literacy Boost in Kailali, Nepal 2009–2010: Year 1 Report* (Washington, DC: Save the Children).

Pisani, L. and Diyana, F. (2013) *Ethiopia Literacy Boost Midline Report* (Washington, DC: Save the Children).

Save the Children International (2013) *2012 Annual Report*, http://www. savethechildren.net/about-us/our-finances, date accessed 15 August 2013.

Snow, C.E., Burns, S.M. and Griffin, P. (1998) *Preventing Reading Difficulties in Young Children* (Washington, DC: National Academy Press).

United Nations (2013) *Millennium Development Goals and Beyond 2015 – Goal 2 Achieve Universal Primary Education*, http://www.un.org/millenniumgoals/education.shtml, accessed 24 May 2013.

Wiener, K. (2010) *Literacy Boost: Malawi Household Literacy Environment Follow-Up Report* (Washington, DC: Save the Children).

World Bank (2011) *Learning for All: Investing in People's Knowledge and Skills to Promote Development* (World Bank Group Education Strategy) (Washington, DC: World Bank Group).

6
Child Sponsorship and Rights-Based Interventions at Plan: Tensions and Synergies

Han Dijsselbloem, Justin Fugle and Uwe Gneiting

Introduction

Plan International is one of the oldest, largest and most geographically diverse children's development and child rights organizations. In 2013, it impacted 78 million children in 90,229 communities throughout developing countries in Africa, Asia and the Americas (Plan International, 2013). Plan is independent, with no religious, political or governmental affiliations. Child sponsorship (CS) funded interventions have been an integral part of Plan's work since inception during the 1936–1939 Spanish Civil War and CS remains important as a significant source of funding for innovative programming which includes rights-based advocacy for poverty reduction. In 2013 there were just over 1.5 million children sponsored by Plan globally. Although Plan's commitment to children remains unchanged, the methods used to protect, nurture and empower children have evolved considerably, moving from the historic provision of safe havens for war affected children to the current rights-based interventions.

Plan, children's colonies and orphan care

Plan's origins are found in attempts to protect children adversely affected by the Spanish Civil War. In July 1936 nationalist rebels led by General Francisco Franco launched an attack to overthrow the legitimately elected Spanish Republican Government. A decisive moment in three years of brutal war came on April 26, 1937, when the German Luftwaffe bombarded and almost completely destroyed the town of Guernica, some 20 miles from Bilbao. This widely publicized case of terror bombing of a civilian target had a deep impact on members of the public in England and the USA with pictures of rows of children's bodies published internationally. In the immediate aftermath of the Guernica massacre, 3,840 children, 120 helpers, 80 teachers and 15 Catholic priests were evacuated to England on the steamship Habana (Basquechildren.org, 2013) particularly due to the work of the Duchess of Atholl, chairwoman of both the British National Joint Committee (NJC) for Spanish Relief and Basque Children's Committee, Edith Pye of the Society of Friends and Leah Manning of Spanish Medical Aid. After their safe arrival in the UK the children initially camped at three fields in Eastleigh, however they were then placed in British children's colonies or put in home care.

As a Conservative Member of Parliament, outspoken critic of Chamberlain's non-intervention policy, and eventual author of best-selling *Searchlight on Spain*, Katherine Marjory Stewart-Murray (Duchess of Atholl) was a prominent public advocate for children. In 1937 she was trying to establish children's colonies in Spain (Molumphy, 1984, p.29). Plan founder John Langdon-Davies shared her dismay over the official policy of non-intervention and her concern for children. He was a self-proclaimed aficionado of Spain, where he had lived for several years and in 1936 had returned as Special Correspondent for London's *News Chronicle*. Langdon-Davies had formed the opinion that '...Europe is divided into two halves, the Fascist International and the Anti-fascist International, and (the British) government has done all it can to give comfort to the first and to embarrass the second' (Langdon-Davies, 1937, p.268). As an eye-witness to horrific casualties he wrote 'I am obsessed with the disintegration of human nature that comes with the greatest atrocity of all, civil war' (Langdon-Davies, 1937, p.vii).

Similar sentiment was shared by Plan co-founder Eric Muggeridge, a 30 year old travel clerk who made his way to Spain in 1936 after the Duchess of Atholl called for volunteers to deliver a convoy of trucks. Unlike many thousands of other young reformers and revolutionaries who joined the International Brigades to fight alongside Spanish Republican forces, he found work as a volunteer lorry driver, completing 57 trips (over 35,000 km) from Valencia to Spain in his first 18 months, taking food in and picking up 'refugees from the road out of Malaga, children injured and dying, children who had left parents and relatives dead on the roadside...' (Molumphy, 1984, p.29). He reminisced 'I went because I knew that help was required to meet the emergency in civilization. I went because the Duchess of Atholl appealed for volunteers. I was single and with no real responsibilities. I went because I was given six weeks leave of absence from my job in London' (Muggeridge, 1939).

It may have been on one of his many trips into Spain that Muggeridge first met another National Joint Committee truck driver, 22 year old American Barton Carter. Carter came from a prominent family in Massachusetts and New Hampshire where his father was president of the Nashua Gummed and Coated Paper Company. Following a broken engagement Carter had also travelled to Spain where, like Muggeridge, he volunteered to transport food and refugees. His presence was fortuitous for Langdon-Davies. With support from the Duchess of Atholl, the Foster Parent's Scheme for Children in Spain was formally established in early 1937 as an affiliate of the NJC to establish children's colonies, collectively known as the Children's Republic. Langdon-Davies proposed to fund the support of children by 'establishing a lasting personal relationship between an orphaned or refugee Spanish child and a foreign sponsor' (Molumphy, 1984, p.29). In the interim the NJC agreed to provide office space at its headquarters and pay salaries and operating costs of newly established children's colonies (Plan International, 1998, p.5). Provision was made for children's colonies in Caldetas, outside Barcelona, and in Puigcerdà, a village high in the Pyrenees near the French Border. A new lorry provided by the NJC allowed purchase and transport of food and supplies in England, France and Spain, making Plan staff responsible for '…buying everything instead of paying your money to the Spanish authorities' (Langdon-Davies, 1938, p.3).

A fourth key person arrived in Spain in 1937 and was tasked with co-administering the children's colonies. Esme Odgers was young, spirited and active in her local Communist Party chapter in Cessnock, a small coal-mining town in Australia. Langdon-Davies acknowledged her role after a 1937 visit to the children's colony near Puigcerdà, right on the Spanish-French border. Commenting on Carter's ability to procure food from England and France, as well as 'nose out good bargains' locally, he added: 'He and Esme Odgers are not only very efficient but very popular with the children and the local authorities. Wherever you go, you hear shouts of "Nick!" and "Esmé!" from children,[1] many of whom were evacuated from Madrid by Carter in the first place' (Langdon-Davies, 1938, p.3).

One of the first Plan children supported was José. Although the story has been told and retold with slight variation many times, and attributed to Langdon-Davies, it was Carter who first met the child. In his Spain Today Speech, delivered on December 2, 1937, Carter said:

I was mixing with some refugees…who had just come in from France. I came across a little child of about five years. He was a cute little youngster, but I found him shy and hard to draw into conversation. Then, one of the older refugee women came over to me and gave me a note that she said she had found on him during the journey. It read like this. ('I know that I shall be killed when they capture Santander, and I beg that whoever reads this will take care of my child for me.') We took the child but at the same time had to turn down 90 orphan children... (Carter, 1937, p.5).

The scale of need was certainly overwhelming. An estimated one million refugees from Asturias, the Basque Country, Madrid and Malaga fled into Catalonia, ahead of the advancing rebels. Painful choices and dilemmas were inevitable for the Plan staff. In the *New York Post* (Cameron, 1938) Langdon-Davies described the dilemma of being confronted with a thousand children, some as young as three or four, dumped late at night at a lonely railway station, cold, hungry and partly clothed. He said '...suppose, further, that you could provide for only twenty of them. You'd just have to be tough. But you wouldn't forget the kids you had left behind to spend the night in a movie house and to be sent from there into concentration camps'.[2]

The idea of Children's colonies was not unique to Plan staff. In December 1937 Carter explained that throughout Spain 30,000 children of the 900,000 children who needed help were being assisted in colonies (Carter, 1937, p.4). In the case of Plan, the first colonies harbored up to 300 children and were established with help from Asistencia Infantil, a Spanish agency (Plan International, 1998, p.6). A shilling a day (Carter estimated 25 cents per day or approximately US$100 per year) guaranteed support of a child in a process described as follows:

On receipt of the first payment, a child was chosen from among the thousands of homeless children and, in due course, the Foster Parent was sent the name, age, a brief history, and a photograph of the child. The children were told how and by whom they were being provided for, and encouraged to write letters to the Foster Parent. The Foster Parent also received a monthly bulletin from Spain and news, letters, and drawings from the Foster Child. The Foster Parents were asked to send photographs, letters, small personal gifts, and clothing to the Foster Children (Molumphy, 1984, p.30).

Although the selection of individual children was distressing, the idea was not just to cater to immediate physical needs. In one of many fundraising speeches Muggeridge would make, he explained the purpose of Plan's fundraising was not just to provide food, shelter and clothing. It was also to '...give the Spanish people the feeling they are not deserted...[and] break down official governmental resistance to doing the right thing for these fine Spanish people'[3] (Muggeridge, 1939). For Langdon-Davies and Muggeridge, the rescue of individual children was clearly a form of advocacy and an act of solidarity. However, the personal touch was also valued. In the words of a 1937 English appeal 'Children who have lost all personal ties are encouraged to feel the existence of a personal friend rather than a vague dispenser of charity. This is the essence of the Foster Parent's Scheme' (Molumphy, 1984, p.30).

Odgers acknowledged the importance of personal bonds between Foster Parents and war-affected children when she wrote 'The terrific "personalness" of the Plan is very exacting. But what else is there in life? – to help our comrades in distress with warmth and understanding, not with cold charity' (Plan International, 1998, p.5). Writing after a visit to Colonia Inglaterra (referred to as the England Colony) Langdon-Davies observed fondly that although the house itself was '...a gloomy great monster of the sort in which rich Catalans loved to incarcerate themselves...' he had attended a puppet show and play where he 'was amazed at the "professional" way in which the small boy and girl gave the performance' (Langdon-Davies, 1938, p.4). The positive effects of letters from sponsors on the children's morale were also recognized by Langdon-Davies. At about the same time he wrote that he had many proofs of the vital reality of the Foster Parent idea to children, having fielded many questions from the children about the sponsors he knew personally. Referring to a week of inspections in late 1937 he explained:

> We have a splendid girl from Madrid, named Henriquetta, who translates every letter and gives a typed translation with the letter to each child who gets one. Perhaps the pleasantest surprise was when a small boy of about twelve vigorously protested that he wanted to hear from his foster father. 'Haven't you had anything from him?' I asked. 'Yes, he sent me a present, but what I want is a letter, that's more important' and a chorus added: 'Yes, we want letters so that we can know about our Foster Parents.' Photographs and postcards

are cherished. May I ask any Foster Parent who has not yet done so to send their photo and also a chatty letter? You may be certain of it really being appreciated (Langdon-Davies, 1938, pp.4–5).

In November 1937, Langdon-Davies, Muggeridge and Carter embarked on a journey to the USA to garner support for Plan. They crafted a fundraising strategy hinging on a speech titled *Spain Today*. The first use on record was by Barton Carter at his father's Exchange Club in Boston on Thursday, December 2, 1937. There he described in graphic detail the plight of the hundreds of thousands of refugees and harsh conditions in 'concentration camps'. He described Plan's work as 'a small oasis in a desert of human misery' and informed his audience that 'Twenty five cents a day or approximately $100 provides for one Spanish child for one whole year.' Carter explained that 300 children were being cared for in two children's colonies, and added, '...high up in the Pyrenees, we have watched 200 children gradually forget the horrors of war and start to live in a normal way... I have seen these children grow from tired unfed-looking urchins into happy and eager children' (Carter, 1937, pp.4–6).

Plan has recognized that other organizations in Spain with vastly greater funds 'saved thousands of children by providing food, blankets, and shoes on a massive scale' (Plan International, 1998, pp.9–10). However, in identifying a unique role in Spain for itself, it has been suggested that 'But a fortunate few hundred Foster Children in Spain and France received healing and care for their minds and spirits as well as their bodies' (Plan International, 1998, pp.9–10). Despite this, the tide of conflict made it difficult to continue to provide individual care to children in Spain. The La Rigolisa Colony (located near Puigcerdà with 200 children) was considered relatively safe until January 1938 when Italian planes bombed the unprepared town. An apparently distraught Carter quietly resigned from Plan soon after and enlisted in the British Battalion of the International Brigades where he received training as a paramedic. Although his exact fate remains unclear, it seems that his unit was ambushed by an Italian tank column on March 31 after which he was recorded as one of 141 missing men. A proxy death certificate was issued in Barcelona in 1939. An excerpt from one of Carter's letters home survives on a bronze plaque at his childhood home in Nashua, New Hampshire, USA. It states 'I shall always feel those Puigcerdà children are mine – they had already started writing to me as their "padre" – anything I do for Spain, in whatever way, I do for the ideals I believe in, and more directly for these "niños" of mine'.

Muggeridge remained in the United States during 1938, making more than 400 fundraising speeches. At the PS3 Elementary School in Forest Hill on Long Island he met Edna Blue, a parent who became the driving force behind Plan's rapid growth in the USA. Blue wrote that she had been distressed by a newspaper picture of rows and rows of children's bodies piled up neatly in a street in Spain and had asked herself, 'What's wrong? Why don't I concern myself with this?' (Blue, circa 1948, p.1). After meeting Muggeridge, Blue volunteered to help establish Plan in the USA, recalling 'I worked day and night till my portable typewriter nearly fell into pieces. I had found a way to help – and I knew there were thousands of Americans like myself who needed only to be reached, who would want to help also' (Blue, circa 1948, p.3). Operating from rent-free hotel suites at Hotel Bedford, and using donated stationery the volunteers struggled to recruit new Foster Parents.

Blue sought powerful advocates for Plan's work in Spain and began writing to Walter Winchell, a popular radio host. 'I wrote at least twice a week for months and months. One day it happened on the radio. By the way the phone rang next day I knew I had succeeded – or I should say Winchell had succeeded for us. Letters of inquiry began coming in and, in about one week, checks!' (Blue, circa 1948, p.7) Ambitiously, Blue also began writing to First Lady Eleanor Roosevelt, who became a foster parent in April 1939 (Plan International, 1998, p.9). Jubilant at the outcome Blue said:

> I think I wrote for exactly one year – then one day it happened. Mrs. Roosevelt mailed us her application to become a Foster Parent with her first month's check. At that time we had about 35 Foster Parents. We had the photo of her child and its case history published in all the papers, and that did it. In less than two months we had 200 Foster Parents – we were now on the map! (Blue, circa 1948, p.8)

By January 1939, the war in Spain was almost over. Barely ahead of the advancing rebels, Odgers and Muggeridge (who had hastily returned from America), began the arduous and dangerous task of evacuating 475 Foster children to Biarritz, France. Muggeridge arrived with crucial stocks of gasoline just in time to move 150 children across the border (Plan International, 1998, p.9) making three more perilous forays to rescue another 202 children when the border was still officially closed to refugees. Referring to their efforts (Molumphy, 1984, p.40) describes

Figure 6.1   Eleanor Roosevelt with her sponsored children in 1942
Mrs Eleanor Roosevelt became a Plan sponsor in 1939 before World War Two began and continued her support for many years. In 1942 she visited Barnet colony to see her three foster children. The children presented Mrs. Roosevelt with a group portrait of themselves during her visit to the Barnet Colony in England.

the joy and excitement of finding 43 of the children who had '...been stranded in the snow for two days without food. Some of them were barefoot, others had only light clothing. All of them coughed.' The situation of the children Plan staff rescued from refugee camps was also dire. Odgers described one group of 70 orphans as thin, filthy and frightened, pointing out that:

> I do want you to see that we are doing a work not of giving a little food and some beds to children living in wretched barns, prisons and stables, but taking them into healthy surroundings, educating them, giving them a chance to face life with courage and understanding (in Molumphy, 1984, pp.49–50).

Plan's early work in France grew rapidly with the onset of World War Two in September 1939, resulting in the care of 900 children primarily from Spain, Poland, Belgium, Holland and France itself. This required two name changes in rapid succession, resulting eventually in 'Foster

Parent's Plan for War Children'. Distancing itself from political or propagandist interests, the intent described in the charter was to provide for the care, maintenance, education, training and well-being of children, orphaned and distressed as a result of the ravages of war. By August 1939 Plan was supporting children in 8 hostels in and around Biarritz, with the number of children increasing to 1,200 by 1940. Odgers wrote:

> Never have we worked so hard to get a colony organized as with this last lot from the concentration centers... All of them are covered with scabies from head to toe... Once the children are well enough to leave their beds, we shall begin taking them on picnics and reading to them (in Molumphy, 1984, p.4).

Odgers praised the impact of Plan work with children, writing that for six months she had been able to implement her childcare ideals and had seen '...growing under our care a new type of child – a child that is free and independent, winning back health, being carefully educated to make him or her a useful member of society...' (Plan International, 1998, p.10). Nevertheless, Germany's invasion of France in May 1940 resulted in frantic efforts to repatriate as many Spanish children to Spain as possible and return French foster children to French families. On June 24, 1940 45 Spanish children were left at Biarritz for care by the Red Cross. Distraught, Muggeridge and Odgers were forced to leave 33 Polish foster children and their mothers at the port of St Jean de Luz when 'At midnight, soldiers pushed the two heartbroken Plan staff members onto a boat sailing for England' (Plan International, 1998, pp.14–15).

When Muggeridge proposed establishing colonies in England for refugee children from continental Europe as well as English children who for a variety of reasons required shelter and protection, the idea was welcomed. Replicating what had happened in Spain, a large house was found. With help from the English Committee '...the Sanctuary colony was established at Woodbury Down, an estate of several buildings in the London suburb of Stoke Newington. A second was soon set up at Melton Mowgray...' (Plan International, 1998, p.15). Odgers was excited when she wrote to Blue:

> And now we are in business all over again! Tomorrow we start with our new colony and hope to have children in it at the end of the week. It has really been difficult to obtain a house (but) the

tremendous advantage of the place we have taken is its excellent state of repair and the fact that there are three houses alongside – just waiting to be occupied as we grow again! (in Molumphy, 1984, p.60)

Although Langdon-Davies resigned in 1940 to serve as a war correspondent and Odgers departed in 1941, followed by Muggeridge in 1944 when he was pressed into military service, Plan expanded, eventually operating 25 colonies in England with more than 1,000 children of different nationalities. Many of the staff who worked at the Plan colonies were refugees themselves, receiving room, board and some pocket money.

Although sponsorship of children in colonies was prioritized, the unusual circumstances of war demanded flexibility. A 1941 newsletter apologetically stated that 'we have been asked to depart in some ways from just helping children' (Foster Parents Plan, n.d., p.1), and was followed by a list of projects being operated in England, including a Nurse's rest home, a home for aged people bombed out of their residences, recuperation centre for mothers and children, farm colony for children too old to remain in children's colonies and the Hampstead Nurseries managed by Drs Anna Freud and Dorothy Burlingham. Plan also began sponsoring children in families from which one or both parents had been mobilized for the war. Additionally, it began to sponsor children who were injured or living in crowded quarters in the aftermath of the Blitz which had destroyed hundreds of thousands of dwellings. American Foster Parents also sponsored children at children's colonies of various other organizations, which were supported with equipment, food, some operating expenses and sometimes staff. Plan also provided 'innovative programs for as many as 4,000 children in total, including day-care, emergency shelter and rest and recuperation for injured and war-shocked children' (Plan International, 1998, p.16). Further, Plan's support of Hampstead nurseries between 1940 and 1957, directed by pioneering child psychologist Anna Freud, facilitated her technique of developing artificial families consisting of staff and children, '...a breakthrough in child care at the time' (Plan International, 1998, p.16).

After the war Plan established programmes in Europe, including Malta, Belgium, France, Czechoslovakia, the Netherlands, Poland, Italy, Germany and later, Greece. By 1950 the number of children registered worldwide was 5,706 and 'More than 60,000 children had been helped...' (Plan International, 1998, p.22). With a continuing emphasis on the care of orphans in children's colonies and institutions, Plan increasingly experimented with direct gifts and cash subsidies to families of needy children. In post-war years, Plan advertising prominently featured the plight of thousands of children who had been maimed, even though the number of such children actually sponsored through Plan was rather small. But from a fundraising and public relations perspective the formula of disabled children and celebrity sponsors was especially effective in drawing attention to its work with children. Barbara Nikoli, the first Plan child in Greece, was sponsored by Tallulah Bankhead, then a famous American actress. Disabled by a mortar shell, the girl had lost one eye and could barely see with the other. She underwent several surgeries in the US and participated in numerous public appearances with her celebrity sponsor, particularly in the New York area.

Funds continued to be raised primarily in the United States where Plan grew steadily. When Blue suffered a stroke and became incapacitated in 1950, her New York staff initially chose not to inform Plan's overseas staff, but ultimately had no choice when she passed away in 1951. In her place the Board appointed Gloria Matthews, Blue's right hand. In 1955, the Plan office in New York received letters from the British Consulate in that city, asking that Plan refrain from publicizing that it was working in England. It was a clear sign that England, and the rest of Europe, was recuperating from the war and increasingly capable of caring for its own people and for refugees seeking resettlement. As a consequence, Plan's Lea colony in England closed in 1957 when its Polish and Ukrainian children reached adulthood. Support for children in Italy and Greece ceased in 1968 and 1974 respectively.

The shift to disabled children and direct family assistance

Although the support of children in children's colonies and hostels remained a feature of Plan work in post-World War Two Europe, the sponsorship of disabled children in institutional care and within families was also important. Writing in 1949 Blue recounted her visit to blind and maimed children in Italy, noting that 37 per cent of all children directly supported by Plan sponsorship or Plan assistance to institutions, '...needed artificial limbs, plastic surgery, or glass eyes' (in Molumphy, 1984, pp.79–80). In 1960, 3,450 Italian Foster children were receiving 'monthly cash grants and parcels of food and clothing from Foster Parents in the United States and Canada' (Molumphy, 1984, p.82). In France up to 50 per cent of Plan assisted children were in institutional care, a setting that required all children benefit rather than just the ones sponsored (Molumphy, 1984, p.85). In the Netherlands Plan focused on sponsorship of maimed children, resulting in medical care, goods-in-kind and educational support however in Greece 'PLAN's services were largely limited to cash, educational support, and gift parcels' delivered through 63 government-run social welfare centres (Molumphy, 1984, p.93).

As Plan wound down its operations in Europe it expanded to Asia. In 1953 Plan started a programme in Korea. Initially children were supported in orphanages however Plan eventually prioritized provision of household items, clothing and cash transfers to families. This shift to family support is referred to with some pride in Plan because 'Alone among children's organisations in Korea, Plan began a program of direct assistance to families with children, guided by social workers working intensively in the communities around Pusan. Eventually, Plan developed the model program that Korea's government adopted to systemically resettle Korea's orphans in family care' (Plan International, 1998, p.27). Direct financial assistance, food and household items, used clothes, as well as rehabilitation services were common features. Non-institutionalized children and their families were required to come to a Plan office because they were often not easily accessible and 'the enrolment process, the interviews and investigations, the taking of photographs, the filing out of forms, and the delivery of cash gift parcels and cash payments all took much longer...' (Molumphy, 1984, p.113).

Emerging country programmes were strongly impacted by the experiences and insights of diverse Plan country directors. In 1961, Plan Hong Kong began providing services to Foster Families in lieu of (part of) the cash or purchased goods given elsewhere. Director George Ross made flat monthly-fee arrangements with private physicians, including an eye doctor and three dentists, to provide regular services to a number of families, with the funds deducted from each child's monthly purchase allotment.[4] Ross felt that the benefit for the child and family was much greater this way. Some families had started wondering about the usefulness of monthly cash transfers, especially if they had to travel a large distance from their homes to receive the relatively small amount. The same issue emerged elsewhere. For example, in Colombia in 1973 Assistant Director Charles Winkler was approached by a sponsored family and asked why money couldn't be saved for a major family need or for a project benefiting several enrolled families.

Transitioning to community development and rights-based approaches

The tension between direct benefits to children or families, and need for innovation was ongoing in the 1960s. When designing its first Latin-American programme in Bogota, the Plan director dutifully included direct financial assistance, despite concern that:

> The Minister had no objections to our proposed agreement but he believed it would be wrong to give monthly cash payments to Colombian children. Because of social conditions, the Minister expressed the opinion that such money would be used by the parents for the purchase of beer instead of meeting the needs of the children. He suggested instead that the $8 monthly cash grant be accumulated and given to a specific school or other institutions devoted to child welfare, thus ensuring a definite benefit to certain selected children (Turner, 1962, p.1).

Staff at Plan headquarters in the USA felt that success in Europe, where cash assistance had been key in helping people get on their feet again, more than justified a similar approach elsewhere. However, awareness was growing within Plan that cash transfers and family support was problematic in communities where poverty was endemic and linked to ongoing socio-economic causes. When opening Plan's first African programme in Ethiopia in 1974, Lloyd Feinberg was keenly aware that while direct cash assistance had seemed to be the perfectly sensible thing to offer destitute families in post-war European settings, it might not be appropriate in Africa. He raised his concerns in correspondence with Plan International headquarters, writing:

> The absolute poverty of just about everybody and the record of failures of the drought relief grant programs, seem to indicate that that we should not give any cash grants or, if we do, to keep them at an absolute minimum. People warn that if we do give money to individual families, incredible demands will be made upon them, which they will not be able to refuse, and which may place them in a position much worse-off than they are now. I'd like to present three faint beginnings of ideas which I'm toying with: (1) a credit cooperative; (2) injecting money into the community via wages, or in-kind payment, for work in community projects or (3) a combination of all three (Feinberg, 1974, p.3).

Don Roose, Plan's Director in Bolivia in 1970 noted the shift to community development ideology, stating: '...an increasingly important debate is taking place within our organization in terms of "community development"... I'd like to begin a dialogue within Plan on this vital subject...' (Roose, 1970, p.1). Defining Community Development (CD) as 'approaches and projects which promote the visible or non-visible growth of the general community...' he became an early advocate for CD in Plan. Recalling an experience at this time in Plan's history he stated:

> I'll always remember our very first community development project. There was this one classroom school and they said: 'You know, we don't have a meeting place – if we only had some light'... So, our very first community development project was a $75 electricity project, rolling out wires from the main to the schoolhouse, a single, powerful light bulb hanging right in the center of the room, a fuse, a switch, and that was it! And, oh-my-God, if you saw the faces of those people! They knew in the evening that room was theirs! They strengthened their community development association and became much more active. Before too long they organized evening adult literacy classes. It sounds simple now, but back then this was a huge change (Roose, 2006).

In 1974, Plan's Headquarters relocated from New York to Warwick, Rhode Island and Plan International was established. In 1975 National Organizations with their own board of directors existed in the United States, Australia and the Netherlands with one quarter of all foster parents residing in Canada by 1970 (Plan International, 1998, p.40). The national organizations were tasked with raising funds for Plan's overseas programmes, managed by International Headquarters which had its own board of directors representing all national organizations. This new international structure provided the impetus for change. The Dutch, Canadian and Australian members in particular were generally more sympathetic towards a CD approach. However, a 1977 letter from the Chairman of the US National Board of Directors to his fellow chairmen reveals concern that 'a change to the Community Approach is a 180-degree reversal in Foster Parents Plan's philosophy and traditional program'. The writer was clearly worried that 'the Foster Parents Plan program has changed, whether the National Companies and their subscribers desired it or not...'. Critically, USA marketing staff anticipated that the further they went in the direction of community development

Figure 6.2 Plan community development activities, Upper Volta (Burkina Faso), 1981
Plan enrolled children from the Mossi tribe whose families lived together with their livestock in family compounds. Community development activities included provision of water wells.

'...the more difficult it is going to be to promote this whole program' (Hoberman, 1977, pp.4–13).

Despite continuing concern, the transition towards CS-funded community development interventions continued. In August 1980, under the watchful eye of the new International Chairman, Dutchman, Jaap van Arkel, International Executive Director, George W. Ross opened Plan's second worldwide conference at Bryant College (now Bryant University) in Rhode Island declaring that the programme innovation driven by Plan Directors in developing countries was desirable, especially when various projects supported each other and were designed to match host government development plans. Throughout the 1980s and 1990s, Plan was increasingly influenced by the values of community participation, community empowerment and sustainability through partnership with the local government. There was growing awareness that poverty was not as much about people lacking certain things, but rather being unable to make change for themselves.

There was neither a linear progression nor an agreed institutional mandate for the innovation that occurred in Plan. Under Plan's decentralized structure, the emerging approach was adapted by each Director to the local context and available opportunities. For example, in Meru, Kenya Plan staff provided the funding and technical expertise for a water pipeline while the communities organized themselves into committees to dig the trenches for the pipeline and collect funds for maintenance and recurrent costs. The Kenyan Ministry of Water Development approved the plans and oversaw the project. During a visit of the Vice-President of the Board, community and government leaders expressed overwhelming enthusiasm for this new approach and challenged Plan staff to adopt this approach more widely in the interests of improved long-term outcomes for the community. The Director of Plan in Kenya concluded:

> The subsequent labelling of this new approach evolved over time. 'Integrated community development' was the catchphrase of the 1980s. 'Child-focused community development programs' emerged in the 1990s and 'Child-Centred Community Development' more recently, but it was that interaction in rural Kenya that was groundbreaking (Keane, 2012, p.11).

While some Plan Directors and Communities embraced the new three-sided partnership model, others found coordination with the local government to be discouraging and disappointing. This led some Plan offices to continue with joint partnerships between Plan and the communities, while minimizing coordination with government. This variability continued into the mid-1990s when Plan's International Board mandated the creation of Country Offices in the national capitals and appointment of country directors. Long-time Plan Country Director, Bell'Aube Houinato, recalls that in Benin:

> [In 1995], Plan was working with the communities but not connecting enough with the state or other development organizations. People could live their whole lives with no interaction with the state – no birth certificate, no school, never going to a health centre. The state was not a reality to them and they did not take advantage of

their societies because they did not understand how (Bell'Aube in Anon, 2012, p.12).

For Plan, deeper engagement with communities brought greater realization that there were systemic factors creating and re-creating the conditions of poverty that required a strategic approach. Instead of repeatedly addressing the symptoms of poverty, exclusion and marginalization, Plan would need to seek out and impact the root causes of injustice. To do so, Plan's role would have to change. Bell'Aube summarizes the logic behind the shift as follows: '[In 1995], Plan's approach did not enable children, families and communities to demand their rights from the government. Instead, it created the illusion that Plan had all the answers, but this was not sustainable' (Bell'Aube in Anon, 2012, p.12). The challenge for Plan came down to questions of how it could go beyond service provision and community development, to improving dynamics between the state and marginalized or poor people.

A further issue for Plan was its level of engagement with youth and children. The Plan office in Quito, Ecuador developed a method called Community Planning for Children's Development (Planificacion Comunitaria para el Desarrollo del Nino), which Plan Ecuador and then Plan's South America Regional Office further developed into 'SASito'. This was a comprehensive method for involving children and youth in all phases of the Programme Cycle. Children and Youth were trained by Plan to analyse their context, identify their most critical issues, develop proposals for solutions, implement programmes and monitor the results. These processes led to a broader recognition of the value of the child and youth perspectives as they assumed their role as key resources in their own development and in the progress of their communities. Programmes like Child Media demonstrated that youth could become influential actors in their communities and nations by hosting radio programmes that presented their viewpoints and agendas.

Plan Bangladesh would ultimately provide the basis for a strategy that could unify Plan's commitment to children, poverty reduction, community empowerment and sustainable partnership. Under the leadership of Edward 'Mac' Abbey, Plan Bangladesh developed the 'Child Centred Community Development Approach (CCCDA)' between 1997 and 2004. CCCDA drew on Mac's many years of experience, the highly skilled staff of Plan Bangladesh, the writings of Robert Chambers and others to fuse many of Plan's strengths into a coherent whole. Subsequently, Plan institutionalized CCCD as an approach that could be utilized throughout the organization. After 2003, all new Country Strategic Plans and other key Plan documents were heavily influenced by the principles and strategies of CCCD and in 2010 the International Board decided to deepen and strengthen CCCD across all of Plan.

Plan's Programme Framework describes CCCD as addressing injustice and power imbalances that underlie child poverty. It is informed by previous findings that '...resource transfer to alleviate child poverty is not empowering or sustainable if it only addresses the symptoms and not the causes of poverty' (Plan International, 2007, pp.11–12). Positioning children, families and communities as leading participants in their own development, CCCD emphasizes initiatives to empower them, allow their voices to be heard, and bring about structural change at the district, national and regional levels. Advocacy activities include Plan interaction with government and duty bearers, others where Plan brings youth and other community members to major forums to speak for themselves, and instances where Plan builds citizen and local government capacity to more effectively engage with each other.

The CCCD Programme Guide states:

> CCCD is a rights-based approach.... It relies on the collective action of civil society to generate the empowerment of children to realize their potential, and on the actions of states to live up to their obligations under the UN Convention on the Rights of the Child... The CCCD focus on the structural causes of poverty, gaps and violations of child rights requires a strategy with a long horizon. The expected outcomes in terms of changes in policy, political will, public attitudes and systemic changes in service delivery require a long and steady engagement (Plan International, 2010, p.17).

In 2011, Plan International USA commissioned a meta-analysis of the programme effectiveness and sustainability of CCCD. This research was conducted by the Transnational NGO Initiative at the Moynihan Institute of Global Affairs at the Maxwell School of Syracuse University. There were a number of lessons learned, but the report made generally positive conclusions on the effectiveness of CCCD. The evaluators concluded that Plan has been able to draw on its traditional strengths in community development to inform its new work on the national and global scale (Vijfeijken et al, 2011, p.44). At the same time, the authors found that child sponsorship continues to anchor Plan in the communities and to provide the long-term funding essential for sustainable community development. Thus, 'Plan's long-term presence in communities through sponsorship activities allows the organization to support the continuous participation of community-based groups even after a particular project ends' (Vijfeijken et al, 2011, p.30).

In the next section, we will explore these results more extensively through a case study from Plan Guatemala.

Case study – Plan Guatemala

Although Guatemala leads other Latin American countries in per capita gross domestic product (GDP), the country lags well behind in terms of average human development index (HDI) scores. According to the UNDP 'Between 1980 and 2012 Guatemala's HDI rose by 0.7 per cent annually from 0.432 per cent to 0.581 per cent today, which gives the country a rank of 133 out of 187 countries with comparable data.' However, this still leaves it below the regional average (UNDP, 2012). Inequality in the Guatemalan context is closely linked to issues of discrimination and exclusion, in particular of rural and indigenous population groups, which for centuries have been discriminated against. Plan Guatemala moved to a rights-based approach and CCCD in 2005 after critically investigating two decades of achievements through the lens of sustainability and impact. Crucially, Vijfeijken (et al, 2009, pp.76–77) notes that Plan's approach to rights-based development differs from strategies of some other rights-based development organizations. The focus of Plan lies (so far) not on grassroots activism but instead on the practical exercise of human (and child) rights by local communities and their ability to participate in local democratic process.

Under CCCD, Plan Guatemala's work with local communities shifted from technical, project-focused interactions and direct service delivery towards cooperative partnerships geared towards enabling citizen participation in local political processes. Plan recognized that it needed to work effectively with multiple stakeholders, including state actors, communities and domestic civil society organizations, to strengthen the democratic system and encourage equitable resource distribution and provision of government services. Plan staff argued that this was likely to be a more effective and sustainable way to achieve long-term improvements for children and was necessary despite friction resulting when some communities experienced a sudden decrease of short-term material benefits. Although the provision of some services to communities continued under CCCD, service provision was no longer viewed an end in itself but a means to support communities to achieve the exercise of their human rights.

Evaluating the credibility of RBA and CCCD

In 2009, Plan commissioned the Transnational NGO Initiative of the Moynihan Institute of Global Affairs at Syracuse University to evaluate its CCCD approach in Guatemala (see Vijfeijken et al, 2009). In 2011 another project was launched to assess the relationship between CCCD and Plan's programmatic effectiveness and sustainability based on a review of programme evaluations on a global scale (see Vijfeijken et al, 2011). The findings from these projects provided Plan with the independent confirmation that the principles and strategies behind its CCCD approach were to a large degree congruent with internationally-recognized standards for rights-based approaches including a greater analytical focus on the root causes of persistent rural poverty, greater attention on the role of the state in local development processes and the elevation of political advocacy as development strategy.

A number of benefits were noted in the independent 2009 qualitative study investigating Plan Guatemala's transition to the CCCD approach. Though early friction was evident, Plan was able to transform its community relationships and the organization started to see encouraging results of supporting excluded and powerless communities to find their voice and become political agents of their own right. This transition ultimately also increased overall staff motivation as local Plan personnel could identify with their role in contributing to the larger development process within their country. Plan has established cooperative relationships with a variety of government institutions in order to increase their ability to fulfil their human rights obligations to communities. One example of this strategy consisted of supporting the Ministry of Health in expanding basic health services to more than 600 communities. On a local level, Plan Guatemala was influential in the passage of child-centred public policies, which are the basis for greater involvement of the municipal government in child-related issues.

A number of challenges have also emerged. New forms of dependency have evolved, such as citizens relying on Plan to organize communities and to facilitate their interactions with state institutions. Other factors impacting the sustainability of Plan's work include the frequent change of political leadership and the inherent lack of public

Figure 6.3 Child speaking at the 8th Child Parliament session in Dhaka
After claims that 75 per cent of teachers used mobile phones in class the education ministry banned mobiles during classes and exams.

resources that many government institutions faced at time of research. As in many other countries that Plan works in, Guatemala's fragile political context greatly influences the design and performance of government institutions, which play a significant role in alleviating poverty. In turn, unresponsive government institutions can pose a challenge to sustaining community mobilization as it can contribute to 'participation fatigue' of communities as a result of repeatedly unanswered claims and inquiries. On a national level, Plan's political engagement in the form of national-level advocacy campaigns has been less pronounced as Plan has been limited in its ability to employ political tactics without losing its politically neutral mandate as an international development NGO.

Synergies and tensions of RBA and child sponsorship

While child sponsorship ties Plan and its activities to specific geographic locations, it is generally unconditional with regards to programmatic allocation of funds due to the large number of individual sponsors. As a result, CS has allowed Plan to preserve a relatively high degree of organizational autonomy with regards to programmatic planning compared to other funding sources, such as bilateral government donors (Plan International, 2008, p.1). Sponsorship has helped prevent Plan from becoming co-opted by the political agendas of government, allowing it to act as an independent advocate for children's rights and design its country-level strategies based on community input and in accordance with context-specific requirements and priorities. Secondly, the relative stability of CS income enables long-term change processes within communities. Although Plan's long-term community presence could translate into community dependency under a traditional sponsorship model, CCCD shifts Plan's community presence towards accompanying communities in their adoption and institutionalization of practices and organizational structures that can deepen community capacity and mobilization. Finally, child sponsorship links Plan with millions of children around the world and positions Plan as an informed advocate for children and their rights.

CCCD represents Plan's interpretation of how to incorporate a child rights perspective within its existing child sponsorship model. Several tensions are evident as Plan seeks to harmonize Child Sponsorship with RBA. First, there continues to be a risk for an organizational disconnect between sponsorship communication in fundraising offices and RBA practice in programme or field offices. In many instances, the fundamental shift in programmatic strategy has gone unaccompanied by an equally fundamental shift in the organization's approach to fundraising and sponsorship. In the practice of country offices, sponsorship and RBA exist in organizationally separate domains that primarily come together through sponsorship organizations' engagement at the community level. Part of explaining this prevailing disconnect is the fact that the success of child sponsorship as fundraising model has been built on donors' motivation to establish a direct relationship with individual children in order to impact their lives. Changing the fundraising narrative from service delivery and direct material impact to shared responsibility and social justice is a challenging endeavor for any sponsorship organization. In the light of the potential for organizational resistance towards changing donor communication, RBA as a new organizational approach runs the risk of being applied superficially, functioning merely as an add-on to existing organizational structures and procedures.

A related tension linked to CS and Plan's commitment to RBA concerns the organizational definition, measurement, and communication of success. As NGOs are increasingly faced with public demands to demonstrate their accountability and effectiveness, organizational communication has become increasingly results-oriented. Historically, individual CS with its tracking of individual children provided assurance of impact. However, besides aggregate measures to demonstrate their responsible management of donor funds (e.g. programme vs. overhead costs), NGOs also are pushed towards demonstrating their contributions to tangible outcomes as a primary indicator for their organizational effectiveness in broader poverty reduction. This tendency belies the complexity of measuring the effectiveness of rights-based strategies associated with broader social, political and cultural changes at different intervention scales (i.e. individual, household, community, regional, national, international). Simply speaking, measuring and communicating NGO impact is far easier with direct service delivery but much more difficult where the NGO acts as a facilitator of local change processes. The development of innovative and dynamic monitoring and evaluation mechanisms are required to integrate progress-oriented goals with process-oriented indicators. Problematically, 'sponsorship is challenging for children who are "...mobile, transient, displaced, working or not attending school"' (Plan International, 2008, p.9).

Third, sponsorship and RBA can pose conflictive demands on local implementation practices. While sponsorship prompts NGOs to maintain direct community presence in order to establish and maintain linkages and communication between donors and children, RBA places emphasis on the role of domestic civil society actors as advocates for local social and political change. The presence of international NGOs at a community level can facilitate empowerment of community-based groups within local development processes; however it leaves the question sidelined of how communities can increase their bargaining power and organize collectively in the absence of international NGOs. A tension exists between sponsorship organizations' need to retain control over programme activities to ensure its accountability towards donors and its desire to contribute to longer-term political and social transformation processes that require the collective agency of local civil society actors.

Conclusion

Over a period of several decades Plan has transitioned from individual support of war-affected children and orphans, to poverty relief through cash transfers, to poverty reduction through community development initiatives and now, to a rights-based approach delivered through CCCD. In 2013 Plan's programme approach emphasized four 'pillars' of rights for children: Survival – through the provision of adequate food, shelter, clean water and primary healthcare; Development – in a safe environment, through the provision of formal education, constructive play and advanced healthcare; Protection – from abuse, neglect and exploitation, including the right to special protection in times of war; Participation – the opportunity to participate in social, economic, cultural, religious and political life, free from discrimination (Plan International, 2007, p.13).

The transition from a needs-based activity to a rights-based agenda is a profound process of transformation that affects all parts of Plan International's work. The historic needs-based approach involved charity, material assistance and the satisfaction of immediate needs, initially for children in conflict situations and then children, their families and communities affected by poverty. In contrast, a rights-based approach views poverty as a systematic violation of human rights and shifts away from direct alleviation of symptoms towards addressing the underlying root causes of poverty, utilizing advocacy and upholding the accountability of duty bearers. Success can be reliant on the goodwill of duty bearers and engagement of communities over long periods of time. International organizations embracing rights-based approaches no longer act solely as providers of goods and services but instead become political participants and advocates in struggles for justice, becoming less visible as service providers but more effective in their work with robust communities and accountable government service providers. CS continues to play an important role in this transition, necessitating new roles for sponsors as partners in systemic change rather than sources of individual charity. Plan remains committed to children and child sponsorship will continue to play an important role into the future.

Notes

1 Just how popular Esme and Nick were, is illustrated by the fact that the children themselves decided to christen one of their first two small colonies '*Torre Esménick*' (Esménick Tower). This colony later merged with *Torre Remey* into *La Rigolisa*.
2 At the time, the term Concentration Camp simply meant internment camp or detention facility. It did not yet carry the connotation of 'Extermination Camp' that it acquired in Nazi Germany.
3 Even though Plan's basic purpose has been articulated in a number of different ways during the past 75 years, these three elements have always been present: meeting basic needs, international solidarity and global advocacy.
4 A purchase allotment was the sum set aside by Plan staff for purchases anticipated by each individual.

Bibliography

Anon (2012) 'Change in thinking', Plan International *News and Views* – 75th Anniversary Edition, May, p.12.

Basquechildren.org (2013) *History of the Colonies*, http://www.basquechildren. org/colonies/history, date accessed 29 September 2013.

Blue, E. (circa 1948) Unpublished personal memoirs of Edna Blue, Chapter 1, *The Beginning*. Personal files of Alice Blue, Delray Beach, Florida, pp.1–8.

Cameron, M. (1938) 'Author! Author! John Langdon-Davies pleads for "adoption" of Spanish children', *New York Post*, 29 January.

Carter, B. (1937) Unpublished *Spain Today:* address delivered at the exchange club, 2 December by Barton Carter. Copy from Barton Carter's personal papers, in the possession of his niece, Ms. Nancy Clough, New Hampshire, pp.1–6.

Feinberg, L. (1974) Plan inter-office memo from Lloyd Feinberg to George W. Ross, 24 November, pp.1–3.

Foster Parents Plan (n.d.) *Foster Parents' Plan for War Children, Inc.* Undated Newsletter pp.1–2 (New York: Foster Parents Plan).

Hoberman, S. (1977) *The Community Approach or the Family Approach* – Comments by Solomon Hoberman, Chairman of the Board, Foster Parents Plan, U.S.A., August 1977, pp.1–13.

Keane, D. (2012) 'Title gets lost in translation', *News and Views* – 75th Anniversary Edition, May 2012, pp.10–11, Plan International.

Langdon-Davies, J. (1937) *Behind the Spanish Barricades* (New York: Robert McBride & Company).

Langdon-Davies, J. (1938) *A Visit to Foster Parents' Homes for Spanish Children*, University of Rhode Island Library, Special Collections and Archives. Guide to the Records of Foster Parents Plan International, Volume 2, 1937–1982. Sub Series, The London Committee 1937–1945, Box 84, Folder 63, 1938.

Molumphy, H.D. (1984) *For Common Decency: The History of Foster Parents Plan, 1937–1983* (Warwick, RI: Foster Parents Plan International).

Muggeridge, E.G. (1939) Mimeographed article *Spain Today and Yesterday*, University of Rhode Island Library, Special Collections and Archives Guide to the Records of Foster Parents Plan International, Volume 2, 1937–1982, Sub Series Biarritz, 1937–1945, Box 81, Folder 12.

Plan International (1998) *A Journey of Hope – The History of Plan International 1937–1998* (Surrey, UK: Plan International).

Plan International (2007) *The Effectiveness of Plan's Child-Centred Community Development – Internal Plan Program Review* (2003 to 2006) May.

Plan International (2008) *The Development Impact of Child Sponsorship: Exploring Plan International's Sponsorship-Related Processes and Materials, Their Effects, and Their Potential Evolution* (Surrey, UK: Plan International).

Plan International (2010) *Promoting Child Rights to End Child Poverty: Achieving Lasting Change through Child-Centred Community Development* (Surrey, UK: Plan International).

Plan International (2013) *PLAN Worldwide Annual Review and Combined Financial Statements 2013*, http://plan-international.org/files/global/publications/about-plan/annual-review-2013-english.pdf, date accessed 7 March 2014.

Roose, D. (1970) *Quarterly Report – Bolivia, April, May, June 1970*, dated 9 July 1970, p.1.

Roose, D. (2006) Unpublished interview with Han Dijsselbloem, 4 October 2006.

Turner, K. (1962) Plan inter-office memo from Keith R. Turner to Gloria C. Matthews, 28 February 1962, p.1.

UNDP (2012) *Guatemala Country Profile: Human Development Indicators*, http://hdrstats.undp.org/en/countries/profiles/GTM.html, date accessed 29 September 2013.

Vijfeijken, T.B., Gneiting, U. and Schmitz, H.P. (2011) *How Does CCCD Affect Program Effectiveness and Sustainability? A Meta Review of Plan's Evaluations. Transnational NGO Initiative*, Moynihan Institute of Global Affairs. http://www.maxwell.syr.edu/moynihan/tngo/Publications/, date accessed 29 September 2013.

Vijfeijken, T.B., Gneiting, U., Schmitz, H.P. and Valle, O. (2009) *Rights-based Approach to Development: Learning from Plan Guatemala*, http://www. maxwell.syr.edu/uploadedFiles/moynihan/tngo/PLAN_guatemala_strategy_ evaluation.pdf, date accessed 13 September 2013.

7
World Vision – Moving Sponsorship Along the Development Continuum

Brett Pierce and Christabel Kalaiselvi

Introduction

World Vision International is the world's largest child sponsorship (CS) organization, with close to half of all sponsored children from among the major international sponsorship agencies. As of December 2012, 4.2 million children were registered for CS in World Vision programmes globally (World Vision International, 2013). This direct support for children has been an integral part of World Vision since its founding by Bob Pierce in 1950 and the first World Vision CS programme for orphans in 1953. Since then, the success of CS fundraising has enabled dynamic organizational growth, diversification and long-term commitment to disadvantaged children and their communities. Although there has been change in the way sponsors are linked to children, the most significant changes in World Vision's CS activities have occurred in the area of programmatic strategy where organizational learning has led to new approaches to development, community engagement and advocacy. A review of these learnings and changes within World Vision illustrates how sponsorship practice can be adapted to support strong development outcomes with higher levels of sustained impact on children, their families and broader communities.

The gap between World Vision's early use of CS to fund orphan care in institutions, and its current programming based on community development, capacity building and poverty reduction, is evident in Chile, where government funding levels for child protection have been barely adequate. In San Carlos, the municipality Child Protection Office found itself mostly involved in the case management of the worst instances of abuse. In consultation with World Vision, staff reported that capacity for early detection of child abuse, prevention and promotion of child rights was low. The situational analysis also revealed that community engagement in the identification of abuse and its prevention was an area that could be strengthened to the benefit of children and their communities. Facilitating a partnership between the child protection office and the local community, World Vision has been able to help municipality staff to ensure that the office now functions at a high level, with a focus on early detection, prevention and the promotion of awareness and child rights.

Improved capacity of the San Carlos municipality Child Protection Office has been catalysed by World Vision sponsorship of children and enabled by a community child protection network associated with World Vision's partners and staff. According to Gloria Contreras, a staff member in the Child Protection Office, 'We can finally fulfill our role because of this monitoring mechanism'. Significantly, the community network is run entirely by passionate volunteers from local organizations. None of them report directly to World Vision. This CS community-based monitoring of children in Chile through a community network gives Gloria's office a powerful reach into households, identifying risk and reinforcing the application of skills by parents.

> It's the only way to know if our interventions are going to be successful. It provides a feedback loop. If I was transferred to another community, even if World Vision wasn't present, I would have to take this mechanism with us to be so effective (Pierce, 2012, p.5).

As a capacity building process this example of World Vision's engagement with government departments and community groups reveals a commitment in programming to partnership and collaboration. This example demonstrates one way in which contemporary CS can build and encourage community-based care and protection to promote the sustained well-being of children within families and their community.

With World Vision CS-funded projects, it can be difficult to immediately identify which children are sponsored, because all children can benefit and participate. Sponsorship now promotes children's participation, life skills and voice. The overflow of this participation is that children's voices are shared with their community as part of their advocacy efforts and, for those children who have a sponsor, this can form the basis of sponsor communications. This current sponsorship approach shows that not only has development programming shifted significantly to empower local actors and children in promoting children's well-being and rights, but also that specific sponsorship practices have been completely rethought to promote sustainable change. Activities such as child monitoring and correspondence with sponsors have transitioned into community tools. This is a new sponsorship paradigm, and in some ways a new leg in a journey that is incomplete. This chapter reviews the journey to date and will be helpful for readers who seek to understand why it is that World Vision now uses CS to empower communities to improve the well-being of their children.

Learnings from early approaches

For World Vision, CS began in 1953 as direct support for children in institutions associated with childcare during the Korean War, and subsequently as similar support in other countries. Often focusing on orphanages as partners, this form of intervention occurred at a time when welfare-based, institutional support of children was common in most developed countries. World Vision linked individual donors to individual orphans, and funded costs of direct care such as food, clothing, boarding and instruction. While this model of intervention clearly benefited orphans, it did not bring tangible benefits to communities,

Figure 7.1 Bob Pierce with Korean children
Bob Pierce maintained enormous enthusiasm for orphan care. Here he is pictured in the middle of a large group of Asian children, probably orphans, in about 1954

or result in cost-effective, sustainable outcomes in which local capacity for long-term child poverty reduction was evident.

In the 1970s and 1980s World Vision was increasingly involved in family welfare support, where assistance was given directly to individual children within poor families and communities. This began to include community development activities in the form of small projects. In some cases, children at a village or local level received direct support in the form of cash transfer payments for necessities such as clothing and school supplies, while also benefiting from community development initiatives such as water, hygiene and health. By the 1980s there were strong experimental links between World Vision CS and small community development projects, typically at the village level. Many children were given a good start in life and many projects showed signs of sustainable outcomes. Yet on the whole, by the late 1980s, it was clear that this mix of welfare and development did not deliver the kinds of sustainable change that were desired by World Vision and increasingly discussed in emerging literature about poverty reduction. There was something inherently problematic in bringing a welfare approach – the way sponsorship was practiced at the time – into development, with differences in approach evident in Figure 7.2 below. Also, the small-scale projects neglected strong links with the macro economy and opportunities for advocacy.

The transition to area development programmes

In keeping with a push for higher-impact, sustainable development initiatives, World Vision's Area Development Programs (ADPs) were developed in the early 1990s. These were long-term, multi-sectoral development programmes on a much larger scale (Christian, 2001) that included strong commitment to local capacity building. Funding was often mixed, although child sponsors were typically the primary supporters.

CS proved to be a useful base for development programmes in terms of flexibility and longevity, as it is not tied to specific funding windows, sectors or timeframes. The planned duration of ADPs is typically ten to 15 years, representing two to three five-year cycles of design, implementation and evaluation. Not being linked to a specific funding sector allowed programmes to begin with community priorities for needs and targeting. Sponsorship provided up-front funding for a 12- to 18-month preparatory phase for ADPs, which involved building relationships with community stakeholders, recruiting and training staff, and developing a design based on participatory processes

Early approaches: Trends and Learnings in World Vision CS		
Timeline	Sponsorship approach and beneficiaries	World Vision learnings
1950–60s	**Institutional child welfare** One sponsor/one child beneficiary Assistance to orphans in institutions	Succeeded in providing long-term care for orphans Not community-based – few family or community benefits Not sustainable – institutions required ongoing funding
1970s	**Community-based child welfare** One sponsor/one child or family beneficiary Assistance to individual children and their families in poor communities, often for schooling	Succeeded in improving education wellbeing of very poor children Not sustainable. Didn't address root causes of poverty Tendency towards welfare dependency, jealousy and undermined parental role/dignity Paternalism rather than partnership
1980s	**Community-based child welfare and community development (community focus)** One sponsor/one child or one community beneficiary Assistance to individual children and their families, increasingly linked to small community development projects (typically a 'village') with focus almost exclusively on sponsored children	Succeeded in pioneering better community support Some processes could be seen to undermine parental role/dignity and led to jealousy if applied without equity Limited sustainability and low impact on underlying causes of poverty More service delivery and less community empowerment

Figure 7.2   Early approaches: Trends and learnings in World Vision CS

(Christian, 2001). This greatly strengthened community participation and ownership of the design and development processes.

The shift to ADPs – features of which are shown in Figure 7.3 below – increased the effectiveness of CS to change children's lives: there was a new level of attention to the root causes of poverty, stronger community mobilization and ownership of the process, greater reach of advocacy and opportunities for sustainable change. The individual accountability continued to influence World Vision's focus, ensuring that macro-level programming remained accountable to individual children. The multi-sectoral programme approach addressed issues that affected the whole community, so now all children could benefit from the shared outcomes of projects. The fundraising emphasis remained on the individual child, but now needed to tell the story about how the funding addressed issues in the broader community: to change a child's life, by changing a child's world.

Sponsorship practice in communities varied from country to country, reflecting the richness of autonomy in affiliated national office partners. In many instances there were some added direct benefits for only the sponsored children, such as school supplies, whilst in others this was purposefully avoided (World Vision International, 2008).

From 2006 to 2007, World Vision commissioned a formal research and development process to review the ADPs. This study found many strengths with the ADP approach, along with some clear learnings. ADPs delivered strong development outcomes in a variety of contexts. One of the consistent challenges was that whilst the ADPs were community-based, they often lacked a clear and consistent definition of child-focused outcomes. It was clear that certain activities helped children, but it was sometimes difficult to identify that the other activities – indirect inputs of community development – were doing so. Greater clarity in targeting and measuring was required. Also, programmes worked to bring shared changes for vulnerable children in the community: water, sanitation, hygiene, nutrition, food security, clinics and other responses. Yet most local programmes continued to bring some benefits to only sponsored children, such as paying school fees or annual health checks, and in some contexts this was problematic (World Vision International, 2008).

Moving on to the development programming approach

A number of learnings and opportunities from the ADP review led to the creation of World Vision's Development Programming Approach (DPA). Since 2011, CS has been enabled through DPA, which has further refined the multi-sectoral programme approach of the ADPs. DPA aims to equip local-level staff to work effectively with partners

World Vision's Area Development Plan Approach 1990–2000		
Timeline	**Sponsorship approach and beneficiaries**	**World Vision learnings**
1990–2000s Area Development Programs (ADPs)	**Child and community development – change a child's life by changing a child's world** One sponsor/one child but funding pooled for multi-sectoral programs Children benefit through both direct and indirect inputs Micro/macro development Large area development – 10,000 to 150,000 beneficiaries Flexible, long-term funding, driven by community-based priorities rather than donor agendas Address root causes	Succeeded in transitioning most donor offices from welfare mindset to integrated development Strong foundation for long-term local capacity building and advocacy Better development processes and results Community-based organizations formed by World Vision often not sustainable Lack of consistent definition of child-focused outcomes across programs Growing tension between sponsorship as a fundraising tool and sponsorship as a programmatic tool Some sponsored children received special benefits not available to other children in the community (such as school fees and health checks to assure their participation), sometimes resulting in welfare expectations or jealousy/stigma Some ADPs too geographically large to assure results

Figure 7.3 World Vision's area development plan approach 1990–2000

towards the sustained well-being of children (especially the most vulnerable) within families and communities. It integrates and contextualizes child-focused development, advocacy, disaster management, and critical aspects of partnering and supporter engagement, building on local assets and existing community efforts towards child well-being (World Vision International, 2011).

Figure 7.4   Children celebrate the arrival of clean drinking water in Kenya
In the Wema ADP, Kenya, school children depended on water with high saline.
Before the project was initiated, children depended on water with high saline
from a lake near their school. Access to safe water is often the top priority
identified by rural communities. Photo by Kenneth Kibet/World Vision

Two of the definitive aspects of the DPA are World Vision's approach
to working with communities and local partners, and the focus on outcomes for child well-being. World Vision recognizes and seeks to
empower a wide variety of existing community groups that contribute
to the sustained well-being of children in any context, from small
informal community groups (including children and youth, where
appropriate), non-government organizations, local businesses, faith-
based organizations...right through to government at local and higher
levels (World Vision International, 2011, p.14).

World Vision's child focus is defined as 'prioritizing children, especially the poorest and most vulnerable, and empowering them together
with their families and communities to improve their well-being'

World Vision's Development Programming Approach since 2011		
Timeline	Sponsorship approach and beneficiaries	World Vision learnings
2011–present Development Program Approach (DPA)	**Development focused on child well-being outcomes – communities 'for' child well-being** Builds on strengths of ADPs (above) Sponsors' role as partners with the community sharing the journey of change for children's well-being Outcome-focused to catalyze community and partners for children's well-being Strengthen community capacity to care for children Focus on children's participation and voices Geographic focus, with higher percentage of sponsorship among the target population	Child-focused programs, working effectively with local actors/partners CS can be integrated with – and promote – local efforts CS used by community strengthens care and protection mechanisms, leads to stronger community ownership and enhances volunteerism Re-designed CS activities to enhance children's participation and voice, and ensure equitable participation among children, whether sponsored or not sponsored

Figure 7.5   World Vision's development programming approach since 2011

(World Vision International, 2012, p.9). DPA builds on and extends rights-based approaches through a holistic definition of child well-being (World Vision International, 2012, p.3).

Children are a barometer of poverty and childhood poverty can have lifelong consequences. 'Investment in children at an early age can generate huge returns to society' (World Vision International, 2012, p.2). Emerging research suggests that a focus on children contributes to better outcomes for development: when groups work with the most vulnerable children they sustain their actions over longer periods of time compared to community development focused mainly on economic or social concerns. Also, concern for children appears to unite communities to work together in ways that other issues rarely achieve. Children can be the social glue which sustains community involvement (World Vision International, 2012, p.2).

Outcomes for the sustained well-being of children

World Vision's theory of change looks beyond children alone; 'the sustained well-being of children depends on approaches that contribute to empowering children and interdependent communities, caring and transformed relationships, resilient and secure households and communities, and just systems and structures' (World Vision International, 2012, p.4). Child well-being outcomes are World Vision's way of describing a holistic picture of child well-being, recognizing the many interrelated factors that affect child development. These outcomes are an interdependent set of descriptors, similar and complementary to the rights of the child. Together, they help inform and enrich the community's description of child well-being, through participatory dialogue with community members, stakeholders and partners. In Figure 7.6 below four key outcome areas require that children 'Enjoy good health', 'Are educated for life', 'Experience love of God and their neighbours' and 'Are cared for, protected and participating'.

Goal	Sustained well-being of children within families and communitites, especially the most vulnerable			
Aspirations	Girls & Boys:			
	Enjoy good health	**Are educated for life**	**Experience love of God and their neighbours**	**Are cared for, protected and participating**
Outcomes	Children are well nourished	Children read, write, and use numeracy skills	Children grow in their awareness and experience of God's love in an environment that recognises their freedom	Children cared for in a loving, safe, family and community environment with safe places to play
	Children protected from infection, disease, and injury	Children make good judgments, can protect themselves, manage emotions, and communicate ideas	Children enjoy positive relationships with peers, family, and community members	Parents or caregivers provide well for their children
	Children & caregivers access essential health services	Adolescents ready for economic opportunity	Children value and care for others and their environment	Children celebrated and registered at birth
		Children access and complete basic education	Children have hope and vision for the future	Children are respected participants in decisions that affect their lives
Foundational Principles	Children are citizens and their rights and dignity are upheld (including girls and boys of all religions and ethnicities, any HIV status, and those with disabilities)			

Figure 7.6   World Vision outcomes for the sustained well-being of children (World Vision International, 2011)

A strong focus on outcomes enables a more integrated approach and creates an evidence base for World Vision's work across strategy, programming and advocacy (World Vision International, 2011, p.9). Foundational to the theory of change, and to DPA, is an ecological understanding of child well-being. It requires consideration of 'the different relationships, institutions, systems and structures that create a positive environment where children can develop to their fullest potential. Analysis of the ecology of the child shows the different levels and types of influence on a child's development, from the closest (for example, families and peers) to the farthest (for example, political and cultural systems and structures)' (World Vision International, 2012). In Figure 7.7, analysis at the micro level recognizes the impact on children of parents, siblings and peers, however acknowledges the importance of influence at the meso, exo and macro levels. Ideally, effective project planning should demonstrate awareness of each of these. DPA involves working with local partners to consider the complete picture or the full ecology of the child: the child, family, community, civil society, national and global institutions, and systems. All these levels interact with and influence each other to the point that 'Effective approaches to address root causes affecting child well-being require mature and sustained cooperation and collaboration between all levels of partners and stakeholders' (World Vision International, 2012).

Through a life-cycle approach, interventions at various life stages link health, nutrition, education and protection outcomes with economic development and advocacy issues. This significantly improves

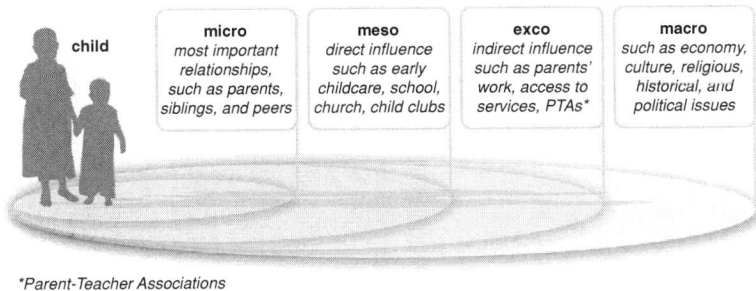

| child | **micro**
most important relationships, such as parents, siblings, and peers | **meso**
direct influence such as early childcare, school, church, child clubs | **exco**
indirect influence such as parents' work, access to services, PTAs* | **macro**
such as economy, culture, religious, historical, and political issues |

*Parent-Teacher Associations

Figure 7.7   The ecology of the child
(World Vision International, 2012)

the spiritual, cognitive, social, emotional and physical development of children. It also recognizes the special needs of girls and boys at each stage of development (World Vision International, 2012). Although the needs of children differ, World Vision International conceptualizes three life cycle stages of children that may be used to prioritize interventions, notable, health, nutrition and early stimulation in children prenatal to five years, basic education and life skills to children aged six to 11 and life skills and vocational education for children ages 12 to 18 years. Essential at all stages are caring, protective relationships and economic development in families and communities.

For World Vision, part of our mission is to include the most vulnerable children. This requires the building of social protection: 'a set of policies and programmes that help poor and vulnerable children and their families to counter deprivation and reduce their vulnerability to risk' (World Vision International, 2012). This also requires equitable access to social protection services, in order to strengthen the care and protection of children within different contexts. And in turn, advocacy at community and national levels is essential to assure equitable access to these services (World Vision International, 2012). Children's participation is another cornerstone of child-focused development.

So within DPA, the child becomes the point of integration for World Vision's development programming and advocacy. CS has shaped World Vision's understanding of development by requiring individual accountability for our macro-level programmes. The individual, any vulnerable child, cannot be allowed to slip by hidden within statistics that might otherwise sound like success. This individual accountability of CS has brought into sharp focus the most vulnerable children and

prenatal to 5 years	6 to 11 years	12 to 18 years
Health and nutrition	Basic education	Lifeskills
Early stimulation	Lifeskills	Vocational

Caring, protective relationships and economic development in families/communities

Just systems that ensure equity for all children, especially the most vulnerable

Figure 7.8   The life cycle stages of children
(World Vision International, 2012)

the human dimension of development. Sponsorship has contributed to World Vision's emphasis on promoting child rights through programming and a strong advocacy base.

At the same time, key CS practices have been significantly reshaped by a growing understanding of development theory and practice. The rest of this chapter describes the transition of sponsorship-specific practices to be more equitable and inclusive, and to making a direct and sustainable contribution to community capacity to care for and protect children.

Sponsorship-specific principles and practices

Strong integration of sponsorship processes within the development programme has proven to be a critical success factor (World Vision International, 2008). There are specific requirements related to CS, such as correspondence with sponsors or selection and monitoring of registered children. These can be labour-intensive and costly by taking time and effort away from direct development work. The activities planned with children for sponsor communication can easily become extractive. For instance, there is the risk that children might be pulled aside to write letters without any clear strategy to ensure their participation in these activities contributes to their own well-being and development. Or thousands of hours of volunteer time might be spent simply to assure children are participating in the sponsorship projects. For World Vision it has been important to ask in what ways these practices can be modified to assure that they contribute to local efforts for sustainable change.

All of these types of activities can be rethought and intelligently integrated into community processes and children's participation. This can result in stronger affinity between development outcomes (increased child well-being, working with communities and local partners) and the organizational needs (to attract and foster relationships with sponsors). In the past, these sponsorship requirements for monitoring and communications were managed separately from the development work and were primarily designed as accountability to sponsors. Now the monitoring is undertaken by the community wherever possible to promote community-based child protection. Correspondence activities are integrated with children's participation, thoughtfully designed to integrate within the programme. This is called 'sponsorship in programming', a discipline that began to develop in World Vision from 2006 and has grown out of the research and development for DPA.

Sponsorship in programming also includes thoughtful and systematic mitigation of each of the challenges traditionally associated with sponsorship and outlined in the learnings above. This has allowed World Vision to take CS intelligently (with clear contextual analysis and response) into contexts traditionally considered too difficult, such as urban, scattered rural or culturally complex environments. Sponsorship risk mitigation includes: cost efficiency; addressing jealousy/stigma, suspicion or welfare expectations (often associated with CS); formal measurement and mitigation of risk factors, such as migration; difficult contexts; economy-of-scale calculations; ability to maintain regular contact with children; local cultural factors; and many others.

Key principles of sponsorship in programming

CS is most effective when it is part of an integrated, child-focused programme, working with local partners to promote the well-being of children within the community. A child focus brings the community together to focus on all children, especially the most vulnerable. In World Vision programmes all children are valued and have a role in the process, even though not all have sponsors. CS practice focuses on community capacity to promote care and protection. In contributing to scaffolding that strengthens local child protection systems, World Vision provides opportunities for local advocacy, and contextualized projects that contribute to and sustain other well-being outcomes, including health and nutrition, education, life skills and resilience.

In World Vision's programming, CS practice focuses on children's agency and voices. Children are agents of change in their community and also towards their sponsors. Donor communications are a by-product of this process. Shared direct benefits are practiced to enable an equitable approach with meaningful outcomes for children. In this way, all children in the targeted population, whether sponsored or not, can participate and benefit from the approach. Contextual challenges and messaging are managed for optimal results. Without credible analysis large CS programmes can result in high dropout of children, poor economies of scale, poor communication, cancellation of sponsors and even the closure of programmes. For some of these reasons all World Visions ADP activities closed in Papua New Guinea in 2000.

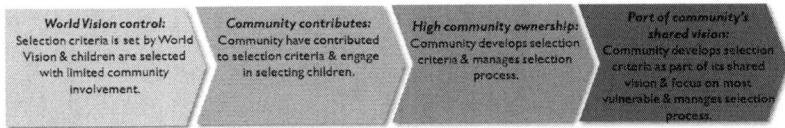

Figure 7.9   The changing nature of child selection
(Jeyakumar et al, 2012)

The importance of child selection and effective monitoring

Some real opportunities emerge from repositioning sponsorship-specific practices. One is the way that the practice of selection and monitoring of children can serve as a catalyst to strengthen the community's own focus on children, building community-based care and protection. When community groups are empowered to identify need, select children and liaise with INGO staff, the result can be renewed interest in the community in children, their rights and potential to participate in development processes. Arguably, this was not the case in historic CS programmes when NGO staff selected beneficiaries themselves. Currently, children are selected for monitoring by local partners and actors to explore issues of children's vulnerability and progress through ongoing, one-to-one monitoring. A process of reflection by stakeholders for thoughtful inclusion of the most vulnerable has become necessary as World Vision has moved away from organizational control of the process to a model involving high community ownership with a shared vision for child participation (see Figure 7.9 below).

World Vision seeks to ensure that every single registered child benefits through programme activities, without special interventions for only registered children. This means managing two critical issues, which at first glance appear paradoxical. Firstly, every sponsored child must benefit: if each sponsored child does not benefit, the child, family and donor expectations will be compromised. Secondly, activity must follow 'Do No Harm' principles: Singling out individuals for exclusive assistance over their siblings and peers raises ethical questions. In the past some considered that special treatment was required to provide incentives for participation of families in CS. It is now clear that such special treatment is unnecessary. Currently, the most vulnerable children are selected where possible because sponsorship monitoring provides a sample of vulnerable children and ensures that their issues are brought to the attention of a community-based monitoring group.

'Shared direct benefits' reflects World Vision's commitment to ensure each sponsored child benefits through the programme efforts, whilst avoiding exclusive focus on or handouts to sponsored children. Children are selected from amongst target groups for intervention, as informed by the programme design. The benefits sponsored children receive through participation in the programme are shared with their siblings and neighbours, thus addressing exclusivity and welfare expectations often associated with CS in the past. This approach can be effective with strong family participation in most contexts if the foundations of a programme are managed with strong communication (McKenzie, 2008, p.14).

> There is a high degree of alignment between specific project interventions and selection of Registered Children, in terms of their age range and communities in which they live. As a result, Registered Children do not have to be exclusively targeted in order for them to benefit from the program, but are naturally included through normal targeting mechanisms of the project...program objectives and indicators are articulated around the well-being of children and based on the life-cycle approach to children's growth and development (World Vision Peru staff).

The range of issues facing vulnerable children is complex and varied, and often beyond the scope of World Vision's multi-sectoral development programmes. So a critical role is to build the community's child protection mechanisms: the broader paradigm of systemic response to abuse and neglect. In more sophisticated communities this may include formal government child protection, but in most contexts this is largely community-based. As such, the monitoring of children can bring together and strengthen local mechanisms to identify and respond to specific issues facing vulnerable children. It can also help to bring together other existing community-led monitoring, such as health or education.

Typically a coalition of duty bearers and local actors work together as a network as part of shared efforts to promote children's well-being, to track the progress of children. CS brings an additional opportunity for the network to select and monitor individual children, and this can supplement existing community monitoring data. The advantage of this mechanism is that the narrative around the complexity of children's lives becomes apparent in the individual stories. Where thematic issues emerge, the monitoring or reflection processes are designed to ensure children who are not monitored are included in interventions. For this reason, the sponsored children are selected from among of the broader population in the community, with special emphasis on the most vulnerable.

Initial learnings show that this is very effective and tends to catalyse the local network focused on children. In Senegal for example:

> ...children who were previously socially marginalized can now enjoy a better social life. This has emerged through dialogue around use of the child selection tool, and people have begun to attach importance to all children. A girl who used to be shut in her room before the sponsorship program... now she is all smiles during visits (De Soysa, 2009).

Since not every child is selected by the network for monitoring, there are deliberate processes to ensure other children are considered when planning interventions. For example, the deceptively simple Four Questions Tool helps a frontline volunteer or monitoring committee to address root causes, and to identify the spread of the issue within the community, and the relevant duty bearers or actors best placed to respond. The tool requires identification of an issue, consensus on root causes, analysis of impact of the problem on stakeholders and agreement on response.

The continuum below (see Figure 7.10) communicates the paradigm shift from previously organization-centred CS practice, towards practices that strengthen community capacity to care for and protect children.

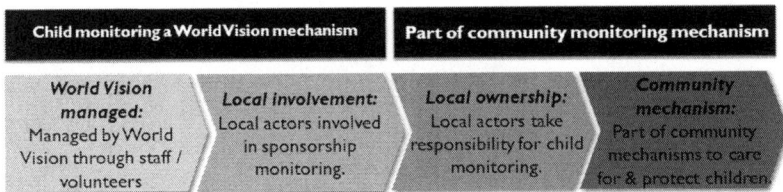

Child monitoring a World Vision mechanism		Part of community monitoring mechanism	
World Vision managed: Managed by World Vision through staff / volunteers	*Local involvement:* Local actors involved in sponsorship monitoring.	*Local ownership:* Local actors take responsibility for child monitoring.	*Community mechanism:* Part of community mechanisms to care for & protect children.

Figure 7.10 Levels of monitoring responsibility
(Jeyakumar et al, 2012)

This continuum reflects the shift in sponsorship monitoring towards a community-led monitoring approach where child monitoring is integrated with local child protection and advocacy efforts. The data and learnings from selection and monitoring of the more vulnerable children contribute strongly to community capacity to care for and protect children. In practice, the makeup of any coalition involved in community-led monitoring may vary considerably. Where present, it naturally involves stakeholders such as representatives working (both formally and informally) in child protection, schools, health and local organizations. In contexts with low civil society representation, it may commence with perhaps one or two interested partners.

The importance of promoting children's participation, life skills and voices

World Vision's CS enables children to share their hope and influence with their communities. The communications to sponsors, wherever possible, emerge from children's participation and voice within their own community. It is the overflow from the vibrant experience of children that is shared with child sponsors. Importantly, the activities are inclusive of non-sponsored children. Having said this, for World Vision every sponsorship-related activity, even the sending of a letter, needs to demonstrate how the activity itself contributes to the children's lives. This is essential for effective development education and provides for donors clear evidence that though they sponsor an individual, they do so in a way that impacts all children in the community. The continuum below (Figure 7.11) shows how sponsorship communication activities can contribute to children's lives when they move away from extracting stories and letters from children, to a meaningful process of engaging with children, promoting their voice and reporting their crucial role as actors in development.

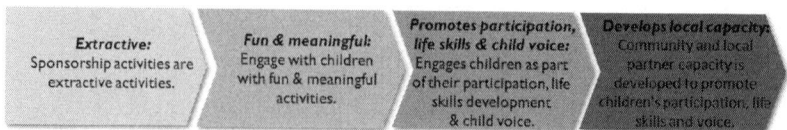

| Extractive: Sponsorship activities are extractive activities. | Fun & meaningful: Engage with children with fun & meaningful activities. | Promotes participation, life skills & child voice: Engages children as part of their participation, life skills development & child voice. | Develops local capacity: Community and local partner capacity is developed to promote children's participation, life skills and voice. |

Figure 7.11   Child participation and life skills through sponsorship activities (Jeyakumar et al, 2012)

It is true that reports, communications or photos for sponsors are still gathered as the basis of sponsorship communication however this best takes place during activities that promote children's participation, life skills, or Development Assets (Search Institute, n.d.), or at other times that involve child participation, such as advocacy activities. For World Vision staff in Vietnam:

> Children and families seem to appreciate this time that teachers spend with the children because letters were found to help children express their thoughts and feelings, which is not common in local culture. Additionally, the children establish closer relationship with the teachers and this helps both teachers and children as their interaction during classes improves (Vietnam staff).

The integration of child communication with sponsors through innovative activities is an important component of World Vision strategy. In the example below, sponsored individuals might, through a variety of means, report their involvement in activities that affirm their voice as partners in development rather than recipients of aid:

> Sponsorship empowers children as right holders by forming a collective to voice their views through children's forums – children's clubs and child parliament/council. Children (sponsored and non-sponsored) from the target communities were trained in a Child Rights Assembly, and provided space to articulate and advocate for their rights by assessing the service providers, particularly government, on issues affecting their lives related to health, education, protection and low budget allocation for children. Children collectively handed over a 'manifesto' to the leaders and policy makers. Children were invited by the press and by the eminent leaders of the nation – state level and national level – to share their concerns and to advocate for their rights (Clara Raphael, Manager, Child Rights and Protection, World Vision India).

Annual reports for sponsors in programmes in Malawi are completed during the Most Significant Change (MSC) monitoring activities. All children participate and their reflections help to shape the future programme and community priorities. The reports for sponsors are a by-product of children's voices within their own development – yet marketing research confirmed the positive impact on donors in hearing the MSC story of the specific child they sponsor:

> The Most Significant Change approach has helped the community and children to see how they can realize their own potential and opportunities, both by including the children in the process and by encouraging them to reflect on and communicate the significant events and what is important to them (World Vision Malawi staff).

Children's participation can readily translate into donor communications, enriching it in the process. In 2010 children in World Vision India projects planted 211,567 trees in open community land, homes, schools, as well as agricultural lands around the country. The day included different awareness-building activities in various ADPs, like poster competitions, essay competitions, invited talks, skits/street plays et cetera, apart from plantation. The theme selected for the activity was 'Green Age'. As a result of this:

> In each village, every child planted a sapling and each child created a leaf rubbing from their tree to show the sponsor the tree planted in their name. The sponsors too were requested to plant a sapling if possible and send a photo back to the child (Bertha David, Director Sponsorship Operations, World Vision India).

Managing the challenges and contextualizing

A critical aspect of sponsorship in programming is the need to mitigate the challenges to good sponsorship performance. Prior to entering a community, the context is analysed for potential challenges, such as poor communications infrastructure, population movement, cultural issues, economy-of-scale or the presence of other agencies (Pierce, 2009). CS can bring its own set of challenges, particularly if misunderstood (World Vision International, 2008). Careful communication is required to avoid overtones of welfare expectations, exclusivity and jealousy, undermining of parental dignity or other issues (Pierce, 2011).

Sponsorship risks are mapped during assessment and strategies are employed in the design to mitigate each challenge. This process systematically addresses all risks that have been identified in World Vision's experience globally. For instance, one of the vital processes for mitigating risk is to manage the understanding of CS within diverse

Low understanding of sponsorship: Community has poor understanding of sponsorship resulting in problems.	Basic understanding & engagement: Community has a basic understanding & engagement with sponsorship.	Strong understanding: Community understand sponsorship & participate, & actively own key sponsorship processes.	High ownership: Community use sponsorship to strengthen their own monitoring & care for the well-being of children in the community

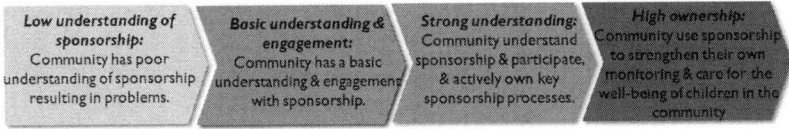

Figure 7.12   Sponsorship understanding and ownership
(Jeyakumar et al, 2012)

community groups. World Vision works carefully to avoid programming in communities with low understanding of its sponsorship practices and seeks strong understanding associated with high ownership (see Figure 7.12 below). Experience and research has highlighted the importance of community preparation around World Vision's approach and the role of CS (World Vision International, 2008).

Initial learnings from the sponsorship in programming approach

The set of continuums presented above help to define a paradigm of sponsorship programming quality (Jeyakumar et al, 2012). Initial analysis has found that newer World Vision programmes are achieving higher levels across all the continuums. This suggests that the new approach represents a fundamentally different conversation and practice with the community, altering community capacity to care for children, and children's participation in the process. Meeting sponsor needs and other organizational requirements in this paradigm can be done in harmony with community processes.

One of the immediate outcomes has been stronger community ownership and the strengthening of genuine community-owned volunteerism. In the past, local volunteerism was often viewed as challenging, with a strong tendency towards a requirement for remuneration. But since this is now a shift towards a community-based protection, initial promising findings are that the volunteers recognize it as clearly beneficial to their own community. The engagement and passion of volunteers is evident in the following statement:

> I always had very low self esteem. I used to often say to myself, 'stupid Maria.' As I became involved in monitoring children I discovered a new Maria inside of me... I see the value of monitoring

because I can see exactly how the children are going. I felt a real change in myself, because before I didn't really participate in anything. Then once I became involved in monitoring I realized I had something valuable to contribute because I can see when any child is in trouble. I spend a lot of time with the children! (Maria, local volunteer, Pierce, 2012)

The new emphasis on child protection coupled with empowering children is spawning networks of children, and leading towards children's movements. In Latin America, for instance, this has led to the creation of diverse 'Networks of children, adolescents, and youth empowered and connected through relationships of solidarity, to contribute to the social movement for the defence and enforcement of the rights of children and adolescents in their respective countries and throughout the Latin American region' (Horna, 2012). As at April 2013, in Latin

Figure 7.13   Indian youth use film to exercise their right to freedom of expression
Article 12 and 13 of the UN Convention on the Rights of the Child gives every child 'the right to freedom of expression' and 'the right for their views to be respected.' The youth in the picture above were part of the initiative 'My life is a story. My story is my country.' Approximately 100 children from Goa, Malda, Delhi, Jaipur, Chennai, Kolkata and Bangalore were part of a series of workshops that World Vision India conducted over six months, leading to their production of films.

America alone, more than 160,000 children are actively participating in 4,287 self-organized local, regional and national networks and organizations supported by World Vision in the 14 countries. CS is at the heart of this movement that is inclusive of all children defining their needs and influencing local and national political agendas, from concerns about discipline practice in schools in a rural village in Nicaragua right through to proposals adopted into the constitution of the Dominican Republic (Horna, 2012).

Conclusion: Building on past strengths

World Vision has always sought to bring people together to improve the lives of children. In the beginning, this meant recruiting sponsors from overseas to help children in orphanages. A Development Planning Approach integrating CS brings many actors together: parents, schools, local organizations, government representatives, policy makers and – importantly – children themselves. It has become a powerful catalyst within communities to deepen awareness and promote action to build stronger communities where children can thrive.

Children are a vital part of this collaborative process. Children's voices are heard when they raise concerns at their school, with their parents, community leaders or even at government through children's parliaments or other advocacy. It might be as simple as changing discipline practice in a school in Nicaragua. Or it may involve child advocacy for far-reaching policy change at the national level, or the coordination of children's voices from many districts. By connecting the children's voices from isolated communities even greater influence is possible; in 1998 a group of World Vision sponsored children were nominated for the Nobel Peace Prize for taking a stand against violence in Colombia by forming a national children's movement (Carillo and Homer, n.d.). While such outcomes are exciting, they are a reminder that a balanced approach is needed. World Vision is aware that National-level advocacy without grassroots change and community development will struggle to see a difference in the lives of children. Grassroots efforts without policy change may be hamstrung.

This is where a real strength of CS keeps coming to the fore – the balance of individual accountability within macro-level programmes and advocacy. Every policy change or initiative to improve the lives of children at a national level needs to be matched by the individual attention of parents, schools or local people who can contribute to children's lives. And individual children – sponsored or otherwise – with their own personal world of struggles, hopes and opportunities, can experience and contribute to real change. In World Vision's experience 'The developmental approach recognizes that the family and community in which the child lives has the primary responsibility for the child's well-being. Our task is to help empower the community to bring about changes in the conditions that perpetuate poverty' (Irvine, 1996, p.217).

Bibliography

Carillo, J. and Homer, K. (n.d.) *World Vision Today, Peacebuilding in Colombia: A Noble Cause*, http://www.worldvision.org/worldvision/imagelib.nsf/main/ WVTODAYaut98mayerly.pdf/$file/WVTODAYaut98mayerly.pdf, date accessed 15 October 2013.

Christian, J. (ed.) (2001) *Experiments with Development – Area Development Programmes* (Monrovia, USA: World Vision International).

De Soysa, N. (2009) *Assessment of the Use of the Sponsorship Tools in IPM Pilots*, World Vision or [unpublished internal document].

Horna, P. (2012) *MARCO DE REFERENCIA REGIONAL PARA La participación de niños, niñas y adolescents*, internal strategy document for World Vision Oficina Regional para América Latina y el Caribe. San Jose, Costa Rica.

Irvine, G. (1996) *Best Things in the Worst Times* (Monrovia, California: World Vision International).

Jeyakumar, S., Pierce, B.C. and Thompson, B. (2012) *Sponsorship in Programming Reflection Tool*, World Vision or [unpublished internal document].

McKenzie, K.A. (2008) *Synthesis: IPM Sponsorship Programming Case Studies*, unpublished, World Vision International.

Pierce, B.C. (2009) *Sponsorship Feasibility and Risk Management Tool*, http://wvi.org/guidancefordevelopmentprogrammes, date accessed 21 June 2013.

Pierce, B.C. (2011) *Community Engagement Tool*, http://wvi.org/guidancefor developmentprogrammes, date accessed 21 June 2013.

Pierce, B.C. (2012) *Child Sponsorship and Child Protection San Carlos ADP*, unpublished case study (Monrovia: World Vision) or [unpublished internal document].

Search Institute (n.d.) 'Developmental assets: Preparing young people for success in college, career, and citizenship', http://www.search-institute.org/ assets, date accessed 21 June 2001.

World Vision International (2008) *Sponsorship Research Study – A Summary Document* (Seattle: World Vision) or [unpublished internal document].

World Vision International (2011) *The Handbook for Development Programmes*, http://www.childhealthnow.org/bs/node/1312, date accessed 8 October 2013.

World Vision International (2012) *Child Well-Being Reference Guide*, http:// www.wvi.org/child-rights/publication/child-well-being-reference-guide, date accessed 8 October 2013.

World Vision International (2013) *Registered Children: Facts & Figures FY13 2nd Quarter*, unpublished internal document (Manila: World Vision) or [unpublished internal document].

8
Compassion International: Holistic Child Development through Sponsorship and Church Partnership

Alistair T.R. Sim and Mark Peters

Introduction

Compassion International is a Christian, non-denominational, evidence-based, non-government child development organization active in 26 countries. At the heart of Compassion's unique sponsorship approach is individual child development in partnership with local churches and international sponsors. Children are the most vulnerable and marginalized people group as a result of poverty, yet they represent the hope and the future for their families, communities and countries. The inherent plasticity and enormous potential of children offers remarkable opportunities for lasting societal change, but, conversely, failure to directly address both the effects and root causes of poverty in childhood, where cognitive, emotional and physiological effects can become irreversible, limits many poverty alleviation strategies. A key element of Compassion's individual child development is the sponsor who is considered to be much more than a financial benefactor. Rather, he/she is an integral part of the development strategy and, in turn he/she is themselves developed through engagement with the work and the child.

Compassion's work is built upon four foundations that underlie its interventions (Christian or Christ-centred, Church-based, Child-focused and Commitment to integrity). Whilst churches and faith-based organizations are now well recognized as effective and arguably critical components of international aid and development strategies, Compassion's commitment to the local church goes beyond its role as implementer. As a Christian organization, Compassion's commitment to partnership with the local church is viewed as a fundamental responsibility and strategy arising from the lasting message of hope that is the true and often misrepresented message of Christianity. Compassion is therefore committed to building the capacity of the local church to fulfill its mission as a change agent for good; to seek justice and to intervene on behalf of the poor. To ignore this aspect of Compassion's approach is to ignore a key element of Compassion's programmatic philosophy. Moreover, spiritual aspects of international development continue to gain practitioner and academic recognition as essential elements of effective development. Compassion is also committed to integrity, not only in financial management, but also in the application of rigorous and conservative measurement of programme effectiveness, both internally and through academic collaboration of the highest possible standards. In the following chapter we will develop further an understanding of the rationale for child development and present evidence-based arguments for the effectiveness of Compassion's distinctive model of child sponsorship.

History of Compassion International

Compassion's early work began in 1952 when founder and evangelist Everett Swanson visited war-torn Korea and was moved by the plight of orphaned children he met on the streets of Seoul. Through Swanson's personal contacts, funds were raised by donors in the USA to meet the immediate needs of 35 children. A small, individual child sponsorship programme for additional South Korean orphans was established in 1954, providing funds for shelter, medical care, food, clothing and Bible lessons. In 1963 the name Compassion International was adopted to replace what was then called the Everett Swanson Evangelistic Association. Compassion's work expanded to Indonesia, India, Haiti and Singapore in 1968 when the programmatic strategy was formalized through the establishment of a Family Helper Program, similar to the successful conditional cash transfer systems (Behrman, 2005; Bobonis and Finan, 2009; World Bank, 2009) where funding is provided to beneficiaries specifically for school tuition, meals, medical care and other benefits. In addition to provision of material resources, even in these early days, some Compassion staff were on hand to provide emotional support to impoverished families. Increased recognition of the fundamental need for high-quality educational support led to the establishment in the mid-1970s of Compassion-assisted educational

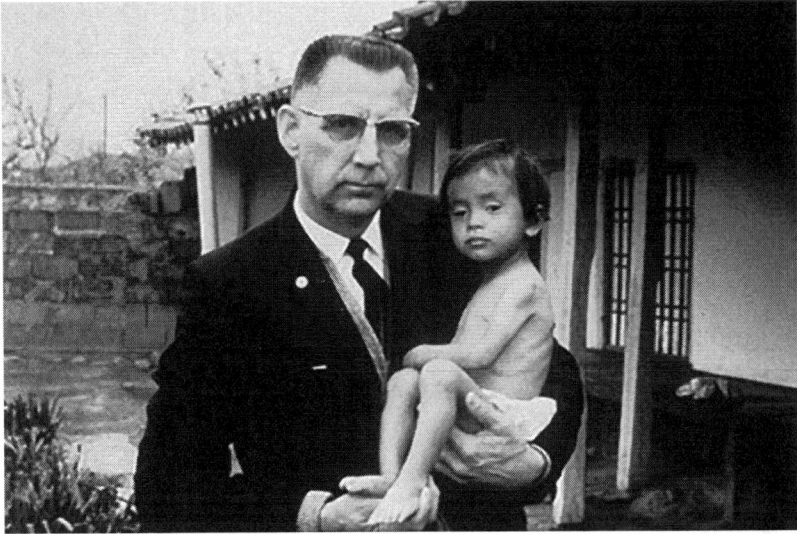

Figure 8.1   Everett Swanson with a Korean child in the 1950s
Everett Swanson founded Compassion in 1952 after he witnessed the ravaged lives of orphans resulting from the Korean War. His initial care for 35 orphans rescued from the streets resulted in the formation of Compassion International which provides holistic child development through local churches to children living in poverty.

centres for children who were unable to attend normal school through lack of resources or restrictive availability of schools.

Several years later, Compassion diversified child support work to working directly in partnership with local churches in developing communities. The establishment of these Compassion-assisted, church-owned and church-operated child development centres allowed for greater attention to the comprehensive and contextualized needs of each child. This represents the true beginnings of Compassion's holistic child development model. Beyond addressing physical and educational needs, so called Non-Formal Education (NFE) gave attention to socio-emotional, cognitive and spiritual development objectives, where children deepened their own understanding of their intrinsic value and their potential to manage their circumstances and work towards an improved future for themselves and their community. At the heart of this approach is the consistent Compassion message that every individual child matters, all children can have a better future and can influence their world for good. Such positive messaging of hope, self-efficacy and aspiration is counter to the often fatalistic perspectives of those living in poverty, but is increasingly recognized as a critical but often neglected component of international development (Banerjee and Duflo, 2011; Dalton et al, 2011).

In Compassion's experience, partnership with the local church ensures local ownership of the work and reliable delivery of support within local contexts, needs and perspectives. It also allows Compassion to practice the true and unambiguous motivation behind our work; namely representing the Judeo-Christian belief in the compassionate heart of God for the marginalized and disadvantaged and the enormous God-given potential of each and every child. At the time of writing, Compassion supports over 6,000 church-based child development centres and over 1.4 million sponsored children in 26 countries throughout Africa, Asia and Latin America. Through funds raised globally, many children have escaped the ravages of poverty and are now serving others as leaders in their communities in a diverse array of roles including doctors, nurses, teachers and members of parliament (see later section on programme effectiveness). Whilst the details of programmatic strategies have evolved over the years, Compassion's fundamental model has remained essentially the same – individual child development through sponsorship and partnership with the local church. The current model, with its comprehensive attention to the physical, cognitive, socio-emotional and spiritual needs of children in a non-school setting, sets Compassion apart from most other contemporary child sponsorship organizations, making it difficult to benchmark or make comparisons. One consequence of this for Compassion has been the need to develop strong mechanisms to monitor and assess programme effectiveness, a feature that is addressed in the coming sections.

The holistic child development model

The importance and strategic role of children in international development is understood by most child sponsorship organizations, yet it is important to fully understand Compassion's own perspective and unique approach to holistic child development. The term holistic is a much used and perhaps overused term, yet it remains a major descriptor of Compassion's programme. In short, Compassion takes the view that a holistic approach to child development seeks to simultaneously and contextually address the physical, emotional, relational, intellectual and spiritual aspects of a child's life in order for him or her to reach their full potential. This aligns with the view that poverty is a complex multi-dimensional condition, the alleviation of which requires attention to both its causes and effects, both external influences and internal constraints such as mindsets and beliefs. Compassion defines poverty as 'a condition characterized by the deprivation of basic human needs, the denial of opportunities and the deficiency of internal assets that prevent a person from realizing his/her basic, God-given potential' (Compassion International, 2010). Compassion's distinctive focus on individual child development is based upon the premise of transformational thresholds; simply, that effective poverty alleviation requires sufficient, comprehensive and sustained investment throughout childhood for lasting change to be realized. Equally important to physical well-being is a child's need to be nurtured emotionally, socially and spiritually and it is in these areas that Compassion makes a unique contribution, a mandate which is reinforced by recent neurobiological research.

Neurobiology research clearly indicates that children's brains are inherently plastic (or flexible) until the age of 24 and can be positively or negatively influenced throughout this period (Cauffman and Steinberg, 2000; Giedd et al, 1999). The emerging multi-disciplinary field of eco-biodevelopment is revealing that early life experiences and environmental conditions can have long-term effects on the very genetic core of an individual, thereby influencing physical and mental well-being, potentially for life (Shonkoff et al, 2011; Murgatroyd and Spengler, 2011). Convincing evidence shows a strong correlation between poverty and sustained activation of physiological stress pathways (Fernald and Gunnar, 2009). Such chronic activation of stress pathways, or 'toxic stress' as it is now called, impairs adult well-being and rational decision-making (Hare et al, 2009; Van den Bos et al, 2009), hence perpetuating the often paralysing self-destructive effects of poverty (Banerjee and Duflo, 2011).

Importantly, toxic stress can, through epigenetic changes, shape a child's development, not only in physical and cognitive dimensions, but also in perpetuating a state of fear, anxiety and hopelessness (Fernald and Gunnar, 2009; Hare et al, 2009). Children, then, need focused, multi-dimensional (holistic) nurturing for the long term, not only for their own future but for the sustained alleviation of poverty. Attention to the more tangible and visible aspects of poverty has indeed been shown to effectively reduce the physiological symptoms of toxic stress (Hare et al, 2009). However, studies have also determined that differences in quality of care and emotional support influence adult cognition and psychopathy for generations to come (Murgatroyd and Spengler, 2011). This nexus between biological and social sciences represents a relatively new paradigm in the understanding and management of poverty (Fernald and Gunnar, 2009). Although representing a complex interplay of sciences, this paradigm was recently, perhaps over simplistically, defined in the popular media as 'a (new) poverty solution that starts with a hug' (Kristoff, 2012), yet is one which has been intuitively known and practiced in Compassion's model of child development for decades.

Critically, we believe that, through such individual and positive investment, children, individually and collectively, can become effective and indeed vital agents for change in their communities and beyond. Ultimately, changed children change families and changed families change communities. This approach and philosophy also aligns well with the growing discipline of positive youth development, in which children, particularly adolescents, are viewed as resources with unique strength and capacity to be developed, not problems to be managed (Lerner et al, 2005). Children and youth are now being recognized as effective agents of change in a number of international development programmes (Fien et al, 2008; Ginwright and James, 2002; Mitchell et al, 2009) where they learn and practice skills within a context of effective contribution to society (Becker et al, 2005) and are motivated by a true sense of contributing to success (Makhoul et al, 2012).

Case study

Ntale David knows when an animal isn't well. He can look into the creature's eyes and see that although it is alive, it isn't thriving. Perhaps that look is familiar to him because of his childhood. 'Life was not good at all,' says David, now 33. 'We used to sleep on the ground with no mattresses.' David's parents, who couldn't read or write, were what he calls 'peasant farmers' in rural Uganda. The maize, cassava and beans they grew provided just enough to feed the family — on a good day. 'Sometimes we used to eat once a day, sometimes twice and, when lucky, thrice a day,' David recalls. He, his parents and his siblings lived in a home with no electricity, and they walked more than a mile to reach the nearest well for drinking water. In a family so dependent on farming, David began looking after animals even before he entered Compassion's Child Sponsorship Programme at age nine. But it was at the Compassion-assisted child development centre that the boy learned even more about herding goats, sheep, pigs and cows. He also learned about gardening, carpentry, personal hygiene, nutrition and the gospel. A financial gift at Christmas time from his Compassion sponsors was used to buy the family a pig. Subsequent gifts became a Christmas tradition of sorts, helping to grow the family herd. Breeding and selling the animals provided a meager income for the family. As David grew, so did his passion for farming. With the education and resources cultivated during 13 years in the Child Sponsorship Programme, 21 year old David enrolled at Farm School where he studied general farming and, after graduation, he got a job at a veterinary clinic. Word about David's knack for treating animals quickly spread and soon farmers from nearby villages sought out David's services. 'I became very popular and people gave me a lot of business,' David says. 'This encouraged me to become self-employed.'

So David started a nursery growing coffee plants, pine trees and fruit trees. 'I would sell the plants and get money,' he says. 'I also continued to treat animals, and both of these ventures brought in money for me.' By 2011, David had saved up enough money to open a shop selling animal medicine, crop fertilizers, seeds, herbicides, pesticides and fungicides. He also owns 1.5 acres of banana trees, four acres of coffee plants, and four acres of nursery trees. To give back to his community, David donates coffee seedlings to churches every season. He has also started a Christian ministry to teach others how to rise above poverty. Through his ministry, he emphasizes the importance of both prayer and hard work; he wants people to know that both are crucial to success. 'I would be a failure if it was not for Compassion,' David says. 'I would have no food for my family, no plan and no visibility.'

Clearly long-term investment of this kind, also requires practitioners themselves to have realistic hope, confident patience and delayed gratification which are perhaps inconsistent with a modern western world view that includes pessimism and consumerism. Yet, it is these same positive characteristics that we and others believe to be essential for effective development (Ali, 2011; Karlan and Appel, 2012) and we have chosen to not only emphasize them in our programme, but also to model these same characteristics in our own behavior and attitudes.

Compassion, then, in partnership with implementing local churches, engages with each child, viewing him or her as a complete person with unique potential and protecting and nurturing them in all aspects of their growth.

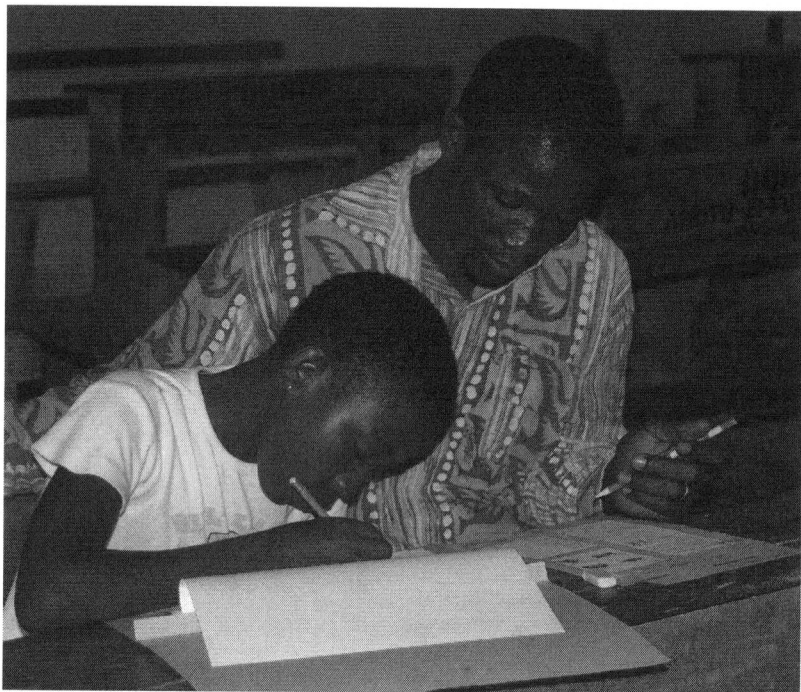

Figure 8.2   Child being assisted with letter writing
Each child development centre at a neighbourhood church is staffed with adults who invest individually into the lives of the children for whom they care holistically.

Features of Compassion child sponsorship

Selection of children for sponsorship is based on the principle of non-discrimination, including religion. Currently children may be enrolled for sponsorship between the ages of three to nine in order to address the developmental constraints as early as possible (a separate Child Survival Programme provides home-based care for pregnant mothers and children aged zero to three). The neediest and most vulnerable children are prioritized for sponsorship by the local church partners according to international and local poverty indices. Each Field Office updates a country strategic map every three years to ensure that they continue to target the poorest children within their reach. In order to benefit as many households as possible, a maximum of three children per family may be sponsored. Whilst Compassion's intensive focus on individual children contrasts strongly with other broad-based community development child sponsorship strategies, it should be recognized that all aid and development is selective, whether through limited resources or strategic targeting (Dollar and Levin, 2006). Selecting recipients of aid and development always requires difficult choices and there are limitations to all models. Compassion has chosen to consistently focus on helping the neediest children in families and communities reach their own personal transformational thresholds, whatever that may take for each child and we acknowledge that this leaves other potentially needy children in the community unsupported. Our own experience is that families and communities generally understand these selection restrictions and by involving families and communities in child selection and ongoing development of the child such perceptions of 'unfair selectivity' are rarely expressed, except in terms of 'can you not take more?' Moreover, other programmatic attention to the 'wider context' (see later section) addresses some of these perceived limitations.

Once registered in the programme, the child, along with 150–600 (an average of 250) of the neediest children from the same community, attends a child development centre, operated and staffed by a local church for at least four hours per week. The number of days a child attends the centre varies by country according to local contexts. Here the children receive both formal and informal opportunities to develop in an environment where they are individually known, loved and protected by caring staff, volunteers and church members. Indeed every child is assigned a case worker who knows and cares for them and regularly documents their progress in the cognitive, socio-emotional, physical and spiritual domains. A significant component of the programme is the training children receive through Compassion's holistic curriculum. This contextualized curriculum is designed to help children reach age-appropriate developmental milestones in each outcome area. Lessons address age-appropriate topics such as personal hygiene, social interaction, critical thinking and problem solving, effective listening, and spiritual disciplines, such as prayer and Bible reading. Highly disadvantaged children may also receive assistance needed to attend or remain in school and participate in extra-curricular activities. In some cases, adolescents may receive skill training for future income generation. To assist with their physical growth and development, sponsored children receive regular health screenings provided by appropriate local healthcare providers and are given nutritional and medical assistance as required. Each child development centre is responsible for ensuring that standard routine vaccinations are administered by local or visiting health professionals. Adolescents are provided with a culturally appropriate life and career planning tool as part of a life-skills mentoring approach and all programme participants are given an age-appropriate Bible or scripture portion. Children are strongly encouraged and are provided with support to write to their sponsor at least twice per year. The letter writing activity is a necessary link to donors; however, it can also be developmental as it provides children with the opportunity to organize their thoughts and express themselves creatively.

The role of religion and the local church

According to Deneulin and Rakodi (2011, p.52) 'It is important that development studies acknowledge the religious dimension of people's lives.' And whilst there is an often publicized and indeed popularized western concern over religious persuasion by faith-based organizations, Compassion is unashamedly a self-described Christian ministry, motivated by a biblical mandate to serve, not control, the poor. Most reliable data indicates that fear of religious persuasion is largely a minority neo-atheistic view that, although gaining popularity in some quarters, has little reality amongst the majority of the world's population, particularly those living in poverty. World Bank survey data shows that religious belief and practice are considered an important part of most poor peoples' actual well-being and development (Narayan et al, 2000).

Whilst religious conflict can be an issue in some communities, a recent multi-country survey in sub-Saharan Africa found that the vast majority of people felt very free to practice their religion and there was a high degree of tolerance and respect between Muslims and Christians (The Pew Forum, 2010). Two thirds of people worldwide 'give God high importance' and the total number of people who profess adherence to one of the world's major religions is still growing, particularly in developing countries (The Pew Forum, 2010). Indeed, another study finds that 88 per cent of the world's population is religious and predicted to reach 90 per cent by 2020 (Center for the Study of Global Christianity, 2013). However, international development has been historically slow to capitalize on and address these facts. A summary of key practitioner views in 1980 (Wilber and Jameson, 1980) stated, 'a view which sees religion as a major factor in the moral base of the society and consequently as a social limit on development is likely to provide a more fruitful view of how religion and development inter-

Figure 8.3 Compassion children receiving encouragement and support from a religious leader
In Compassion International's experience, individual attention, role modeling and mentoring from local partners are key experiences necessary for children's development.

twine'. Changes in minority world social and political policies and attitudes meant that this concept failed to gain traction in development practice for over a decade. However, Deneulin and Rakodi (2011) in their 2010 review of religion and development conclude that 'changes in development thinking have made the subject of religion no longer avoidable in development studies'.

Whilst most informed development practitioners would now accept the church as a reliable and strategic aid and development implementer, Compassion fundamentally believes in the importance of Christian faith and the church to an individual's well-being and destiny. Failure to address an individual's spiritual needs is therefore to limit their development. Note that Compassion does not, however, purposefully use development programmes as tools for spiritual conversion. Rather, Christian principles and teachings are naturally integrated into the holistic programme in both content, and as the source of moral and ethical frameworks and foundational hope for a better future. Children and their families clearly accept and understand that programmes are delivered in partnership with the local church and that they will therefore be exposed to Christian teaching. In many cases the local church is highly active and respected in the (often multi-religious) communities, such that concerns about forced conversion are not necessarily a generalized local reality. Compassion's local church partners do not force conversion, yet honestly seek to present the Christian message of hope and the opportunities that it presents. Ultimately Christianity and indeed secular humanity are both about freedom of choice. Failure to provide opportunity to understand and choose something (Christianity), which Compassion fundamentally believes in, in our view, only serves to disempower further those living in poverty, for whom choice is already severely limited or denied.

The role of the sponsor

Letter writing between sponsored children and sponsors has long been criticized as time consuming, expensive, divisive and primarily a donor-orientated marketing tool, although it must be acknowledged that no research to support these criticisms has been published. However, Compassion's experience is different and the sponsor-child relationship is at the heart of Compassion's child development strategy. More than an effective fundraising strategy, the one-to-one relationship between sponsor and child is held primarily as a critical element of our child development strategy, as well as sponsor transformation. To that end, sponsors are encouraged to write, pray for, send gifts to and indeed, if possible, visit their sponsored child to reinforce the message of hope that is fundamental to our mission.

Currently the majority of sponsored children receive at least one letter from their sponsor each year and the majority of these receive more than one, with evidence of clear socio-emotional outcome (see later). There is indeed substantial literature to support the notion that regular communication with a 'significant other' is a critical component of child thriving (King et al, 2005), particularly where difficult family backgrounds and community circumstances limit positive interactions with others. Letter writing has a significant history in human communication and has found significance in clinical psychology and family therapy (Moules, 2009). So called 'therapeutic letters' have been clearly shown to have significant impact as an adjunct to clinical therapeutic interventions (Pyle, 2006; Kindsvatter et al, 2013).

In response to receiving letters 'the experience of being seen by a thoughtful other with sustained attention is believed to be uniquely powerful' (Hamill et al, 2008), with recipients feeling known and valued (Freed et al, 2010). Appropriately worded letters were shown to promote connectivity to the writer and the intervention, as well as demonstrate commitment of the writer to the recipient beyond the writer's primary responsibility as a therapist (Pyle, 2009). Letters were also shown to consolidate and reinforce intervention messaging and facilitated greater engagement of the recipient with the therapy. Importantly, therapeutic letters provided validation, encouragement, increased self-esteem, meaning and greater self-confidence in the re-cipient (Pyle, 2009). Lastly the long-term benefits of therapeutic letters were noted, providing recipients with the opportunity for ongoing reinforcement, direction and lasting internalization (Hamill et al, 2008). Whilst the content and style of therapeutic letters are critically important to the clinical impact (Moules, 2009), the extrapolation of this concept to sponsor/child communication is an attractive hypo-thesis. Sponsors are able to regularly communicate and reinforce the message that the child is indeed loved, valued and has a positive future.

Using the framework from therapeutic letters, we have demonstrated a causal link between the frequency of receiving sponsor letters and child self-esteem (Sim, 2011). Using a fixed and random effects regres-sion model to account for other contributing factors, it was shown that child self-esteem, measured on both a standardized Search Institute self-esteem scale (Benson et al, 1998) and a contextualized self-esteem scale, increased significantly ($P<0.004$, N=3397) with increasing frequency of letters (Figure 8.4).

In-depth qualitative analysis of a random subset of these children uncovered a depth of feeling towards both the receipt and non-receipt of letters. Whilst receiving letters was broadly reported to promote a sense of personal worth and well-being, the most frequently raised issue was that letters facilitated a greater sense of connection to the sponsor. Letters were widely referred to as the most valued evidence of sponsor love for the child: 'It's easy to send money. Gifts don't show their love in the way a letter does' (13+ year old sponsored child). Thus whilst sponsored children benefit from many 'significant others' through interaction with caring church members, project staff and vol-unteers, the active role of the sponsor was clearly viewed by children and their parents as an important contributor to the child's develop-ment. Indeed there appears to be a special role for the distant person

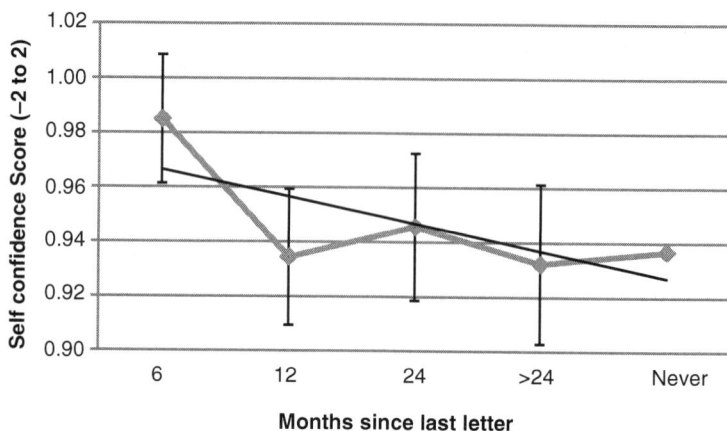

Figure 8.4   Effect of sponsor letters on child self esteem
(Adapted from Sim, 2011)

who, through their support and communication, conveys an additional sense of value on the child; 'even though we haven't met, the letter shows that they care for me and are part of our lives' (9–12 year old). Importantly children consistently refer to the fact that they regularly revisit their letters, particularly in their difficult times, where they are reminded of their value and their hope is reinforced. The value of sponsor connection is also appreciated through understanding the feelings of children who do not receive letters. Although the vast majority of Compassion sponsored children receive letters from their sponsor, many of those who do not receive letters from their sponsor feel the disappointment deeply. When a group of 16 year old boys were asked to draw a picture representing how they felt about their sponsor they drew a tree with no leaves and the caption 'this is a tree with no leaves, resulting from it not being looked after. The same happens to a person, when they are not appreciated they become sad. Each branch represents one of us, without love'. Further probing indicated that this was because none of them had ever received communication from their sponsors. The predominant response to not receiving letters was one of disengagement and demotivation. Despite these strong feelings of disappointment, many projects mitigate these negative consequences through sensitive management of letter distribution. Moreover, through improved sponsor engagement strategies, such as helping sponsors develop the habit of writing early on in the sponsorship and providing web-based communication capabilities, Compassion is seeking to further increase sponsor-child communication, with the goal of each child receiving some form of encouraging communication on a regular basis. In addition, sponsors are educated on appropriate and meaningful letter content to improve the quality of communication.

Sponsors themselves are also impacted by their relationship with their sponsored child. The communication they receive from their sponsored child expands the sponsor's understanding of the child's reality and how the sponsor can best encourage the child. Thousands of sponsors have become advocates for children in poverty, speaking out within their spheres of influence and actively drawing new sponsors to Compassion. Countless blogs and personal anecdotes document life-changing experiences of sponsors who have visited their sponsored child and become familiar with Compassion's work in poor areas.

The wider context of the child

Compassion believes that 'If we can improve the surroundings we can improve the wellbeing of the child' (Compassion International Board Policy A-1.1). For this reason, Compassion strives to ensure that each registered child is known, loved and protected. Whilst Compassion child sponsorship provides comprehensive support to individual children, we do recognize the importance of providing children with a safe and supportive environment in which to grow, one which can not only be provided whilst attending the project, but which must also involve their home, family and community. To address this, firstly, our partnership with the local church encourages and supports the church to engage in and seek means of support for other programmes in their community. For example many churches engage in community health programmes, community clean-up programmes and adult education classes, in all of which the sponsored children are themselves often involved, learning from the outset to serve and give back to their communities. Secondly, child case workers (the majority of whom are highly motivated and committed local volunteers) and project staff (themselves often on the boundaries of poverty and living in the community) regularly visit the homes of children's families with whom they form relationships to encourage each other and, where necessary, assist with specific needs. Compassion fundamentally believes that such individualized attention, care and follow-up by case workers is a highly effective preventative or at least early intervention strategy to tackle most challenges a child may face, particularly abuse, prostitution and exploitation (Clay et al, 2012; Landgren, 2005). Indeed case workers and staff receive regular training in the recognition and management of key child issues, including child abuse, and often go to extraordinary lengths to restore an abused or neglected child. Compassion is staunchly committed to child protection and subjects all staff, sponsors and volunteers to training, checks and accountability.

In addition to these partnership-based measures to improve the wider context of the child, a Complementary Interventions programme exists to supplement and enhance the Child Sponsorship Programme by removing significant obstacles to holistic child development for children registered in the programme. For example, funds raised specifically for Complementary Interventions are used to respond to large-scale disasters, enhance church or community facilities (for example toilets, clean water, classrooms and so on), provide HIV/AIDS education and other health programmes, distribute water filters and malaria nets, and fund income-generating activities. Complementary Intervention projects are funded on a needs and proposal-based system, which includes specific monitoring and evaluation components. This programme amounts to approximately 7 per cent of overall Compassion revenue. In all of these broader scale ventures, the focus remains on the child development outcomes, hence the term Complementary Interventions.

Strategy and challenges for measuring programme effectiveness

Compassion is an outcome-driven organization and is committed to empirical measurement of overall programmatic effectiveness of the highest possible standards. Indeed Compassion's model affords some particular advantages in this arena. Firstly, Compassion's commitment to individual child development means that detailed records and regular reports (Child Development Progress Reports) for each and every child are kept at the project and used specifically to measure the child's development against clearly defined outcomes in the four areas of holistic development (physical, cognitive, socio-emotional and spiritual). Comprehensive programme management and field manuals provide a level of consistency across all projects, but they also allow considerable and necessary freedom for local contextualization and application.

In addition, a global Program Effectiveness Research Team exists within The International Program Division as a resource for programme management. This team's primary role is to carry out novel research studies on a range of topics to both independently assess routine child development data and investigate programmatic effectiveness in depth, with increasing responsibility for identifying causative elements of the child's development. This team has intentionally avoided the use of the term 'evaluation' in order to distinguish their role in the organization from policing performance or assessing value, towards one which partners with practitioners to manage and improve programme. Clearly such integration of programme effectiveness research within programme management also has the potential for bias and less objective reporting. Yet a commitment to excellence and programmatic improvement ensures such bias is limited. Indeed excellence and integrity are not only two of Compassion's stated core values, but also a fundamental characteristic of good research. Therefore, the framework under which the team operates includes a commitment to rigor, integration with programme decision-making, effective communication and appropriate follow up of results.

Commitment to rigorous research, however, presents significant challenges within a donor-funded corporate environment where resources are limited and where deadlines for results can be restrictive to empirical methodologies. Moreover, the discipline of international development research has seen considerable change in recent years with strong methodologies from public health and econometrics gaining considerable ground. Ultimately these changes are positive and continue to be embraced by Compassion. The programme effectiveness team carries out multiple major research studies each year, based on primary questions raised by programme directors. Both qualitative and quantitative methodologies are applied where appropriate, with a strong commitment to the counterfactual (see evidence of programme effectiveness) to allow assignment of causation to outcome measurements wherever appropriate. The team also has an increasing role in the design and effectiveness measurement of pilot programmes. Often the domain of limited summative external studies, involvement in the design phase of pilot programmes has afforded the team opportunity to design and embed novel effectiveness measurement strategies into the programmes themselves. This reinforces a culture of ongoing effectiveness reflection amongst practitioners, rather than measurement of effectiveness being viewed as primarily an external, secondary activity. Note that such integration does not exclude the need for secondary validity research; rather it provides an initial source of evidence to guide practitioners that in turn becomes one source of data that can contribute to an overall measuring effectiveness strategy.

Enthusiasm, and indeed requirement, for frequent reporting of programme impact also has the potential to force an organization down a path that leads to the generation of poor quality and even meaningless data, particularly at a time when data is somewhat easy to generate and visualize. However, only good data can inform good decisions and a recent business review suggested that the cost to an organization of using poor quality data can be up to 30 times more than the cost of making business decisions based on correct data. Indeed the use of poor data has been estimated to typically cost 10 to 20 per cent of company revenue (Redman, 2004) or 6 per cent of GDP in the USA (Eckerson, 2002). Organizations cannot afford to assume that their data collection methods and systems are accurate or reliable and must invest in data quality and methodological rigor in an environment that is rapidly changing. For example, the randomized, controlled trial (RCT), once the exclusive domain of drug trials and ignored by social science evaluators is now gaining significant traction in development evaluation methodologies (Banerjee and Duflo, 2011). The randomized controlled trial is often referred to as the gold standard quantitative methodology, a position that is hotly debated in evaluation circles. Like all methodologies, it has its limitations (Ravallion, 2012), but its rising prominence illustrates the changing landscape and the need to stay current, rigorous and apply the most appropriate methodology that resources and time allow. Good development evaluators should avoid the often heated polarization between particular methodological camps and be prepared to embrace and apply any appropriate approach to measuring effectiveness, particularly when outside their own comfort zone or experience.

Evidence of programme effectiveness

Case study – Ateku

When his son was born in 2012, Evans Ateku surprised some of his relatives by naming the baby Albert rather than a family name. But the Kenyan father could think of no better way to honor the California woman who sponsored him when he was a child in Compassion's programme. Now Evans is hoping to have a daughter. 'I know what my girl's name will be. It will be my sponsor's first name.' Before he knew the name of his sponsor a young Evans would watch his mother leave early each morning in search of food for their family of seven. Her desperate attempts, which often didn't end until late at night, weren't uncommon in his village. 'I remember that food was scarce,' Evans says. 'People fought for food.' Then in 1987, Compassion staff learned of Evans' situation and registered him as one of the first students at a Child Development Centre. Evans says he fondly remembers days when he would go to the centre and see his friends and eat a meal. 'My favorite dish was githeri [maize and beans]. I still remember how good it tasted.' When Evans received a financial gift from his sponsor his family used it to buy a goat. Soon the goat gave birth. Selling the baby goats allowed the family to purchase a cow that eventually proved more valuable than they could have imagined. After the high-achieving student graduated from Compassion's Child Sponsorship Programme in 1997, Evans was eager to go to college but doubted he could afford tuition. Then he remembered his sponsor's gift. He sold the family cow and some of her calves to pay his tuition. Evans went on to study math and chemistry, graduating with a Bachelor of Education degree. Experiencing the power of education firsthand motivated him to help all four of his siblings complete college. Their jobs now include government officer, forwarding agent, lab technician and accountant. 'I am grateful to God, first for allowing me to be alive, to have the strength to work hard,' says Evans, who now serves the Anglican Church of Kenya by overseeing its spiritual and financial development. 'And now, [for] the beautiful wife and child He has given me.'

All organizations, including Compassion, can find and report 'success stories' such as this one. More often than not, these stories are true for these individuals, yet the causative factors remain unclear and the extent to which these stories are representative of all beneficiaries is generally unknown. Even the definition of the word impact lacks clarity. As an organization, most practitioners are concerned with the tangible effects of programmatic activities on beneficiaries. Evidence of true impact, particularly in poverty alleviation and individual trans-formation strategies, must wait until beneficiaries have left the pro-gramme and can demonstrate sustained change and independence. Compassion, therefore, defines impact as long-term sustained change and accepts that considerable time must pass before evidence of impact can be seen. Therefore, programmatic changes amongst existing beneficiaries represent short-term impact and are referred by us as pro-gramme outcomes to distinguish them from true impact.

The key to effective outcome and impact measurement strategies on a global scale is the counterfactual; the comparison group which repre-sents the outcomes or impact had the programme not existed. Without careful attention to the counterfactual, any measurement of outcome or impact cannot be reliably attributed to programmatic activities, as distinct from other life and environmental influences. Identifying an appropriate counterfactual represents a considerable challenge, particularly for broad-based community development programmes. However, the individual focus of Compassion's programmatic model has afforded the, perhaps unique, capacity for quantitative research using strong counterfactuals to assess the impact of Compassion's child sponsorship programme (Wydick et al, 2013). In 2009 Wydick's team began an independent six country study of adult life outcomes amongst adults who were formerly sponsored as children by Compassion. Data was collected on 10,144 individuals, including formerly sponsored children, their siblings and former eligible, but not sponsored, children and their siblings. The study took advantage of three eligibility rules which limited the number of children per household, required children to be within a defined distance of the project and established a maximum age beyond which a child cannot be sponsored. These eligibility criteria allowed the establishment of strong counterfactuals, which, together with a number of robust estimation techniques, that included household fixed effects, an instrument variable and regression discontinuity, allowed true impact of our programme to be measured. Results showed that the Compassion sponsorship programme significantly, substantially and specifically increased educational, employment and leadership outcomes compared to those who had not benefited directly from the programme (Figure 8.5). Across all six countries, formerly sponsored children, now adults, benefited from an average of almost 1.5 extra years school education. The biggest impacts in education were seen in the secondary school completion rates. Whilst the baseline rates for completion of tertiary education were understandably low in the communities studied, Compassion sponsorship resulted in almost doubling the likelihood of a person graduating. These impacts are of similar or greater magnitude than other significant educational programmes such as PROGRESA/Oportunidades programme, which is often cited as a gold standard programme and where a size effect of an additional 0.66 school years was found and is considered highly successful (Schulz, 2004). The Wydick study also showed large and significant increases in the likelihood of employment, particularly in white collar jobs, and major increases in likelihood of holding leadership roles in their communities and or church.

Whilst the Wydick study represents the most rigorous peer reviewed study of any child sponsorship programme to date, because its focus

Parameter	Effect Size
All school years (additional years)	1–1.5 Years
Primary Completion (greater likelihood)	5–13%
Secondary Completion (greater likelihood)	27–40%
Tertiary Completion (greater likelihood)	50–80%
Employed (greater likelihood)	14–18%
White Collar Employment (greater likelihood)	35%
Community Leader (greater likelihood)	30–75%
Church Leader (greater likelihood)	40–70%

Figure 8.5 Summary of former sponsored children's adult life outcomes (Adapted from Wydick et al, 2013)

was limited to Compassion Child Sponsorship, results cannot be extrapolated to other sponsorship programmes. Moreover, this study, whilst specific to the impact of Compassion child sponsorship did not directly address the key elements of the programme that are responsible for these impacts. However, Wydick also refers to three follow-up studies in which he examines how these adult life outcomes might have been shaped by elements of Compassion's programme. These studies focused on the theory that Compassion's focus on internal constraints played a significant role in these adult outcomes. Results, still to be published, but introduced in Wydick's peer reviewed paper, suggest that Compassion sponsored children, when compared with a similarly constructed counterfactual, have significantly improved education and employment expectations, happiness, self-efficacy and hope; similar outcomes that we have seen can also be boosted by sponsor letters (Sim, 2011). Indeed Wydick suggests that 'The most salient characteristic that distinguishes Compassion's program from comparable interventions is its emphasis on raising children's self-esteem, reference points and aspirations' (Wydick et al, 2013). These unpublished findings, however still do not establish a direct causal link to adult impacts but are consistent with Compassions' programmatic philosophy, other qualitative research data and current development thinking (Dalton et al, 2011).

Whilst such independent studies, with strong methodological rigor, provide the strongest validation of our programmes to date, they also represent the pinnacle of a commitment by Compassion to rigorous methodological approaches to measuring programme effectiveness. Current internal studies, which increasingly rely upon mixed-method approaches, apply similar levels of rigor within the constraints of limited resources and time to demonstrate ongoing programme effectiveness. For example, an independent meta-analysis of a five-year multi-informant qualitative study of 13 countries identified several key global drivers and barriers (Birmingham, 2011) that formed the framework for a new qualitative and quantitative programme outcome effectiveness measurement (POEM) strategy. Key drivers of global programme effectiveness were qualitatively found to be staff mentoring and child follow-up, family and community inclusion, biblical principles, extra-mural activities (for example camps, sports, community service), peer support groups and My Plan for Tomorrow, a programmatic exercise which was reported to provide a strong message of hope and empower-ment for the future. These findings confirm the importance of attention to internal constraints for effective poverty alleviation programmes.

Quantitatively the POEM utilizes a strong counterfactual which relies upon the existence of waiting lists of eligible children and their siblings who subsequently were unable to enter the programme. With this counterfactual framework, an ever changing array of tools to measure specific child development outcomes can be applied, allowing continued evolution of the effectiveness measurement programme. The POEM is proving to be an effective approach to informing Compassion's outcome-driven programme. For example in the Dominican Republic current sponsored children have been shown to have 1.4 times higher odds of having an income-generating skill than unsponsored children. In Haiti and Ghana sponsored children have 40 per cent and 120 higher odds respectively of completing primary school than unsponsored children (Heryford, 2013b). Moreover, these same children also showed significant improvements in socio-emotional outcomes such as altruism (Haiti) and self-esteem (Ghana).

Similar counterfactuals were recently used to measure the effectiveness of Compassion's Complementary Intervention programme in Africa. Here, households who had a child on the waiting list for spon-sorship at the time the Complementary Intervention was implemented (up to four years ago) represented the counterfactual. These households subsequently had a child sponsored, but did not receive the Complementary Intervention. In other words they had received the benefits of child sponsorship for many years and experienced the same community challenges but not the Complementary Intervention over the same time period. Using this approach, Complementary Intervention was shown to have caused a 52 per cent reduction in child sick days in Uganda, 26 per cent decrease in incidence of Malaria in Burkina Faso and, in Tanzania, households receiving food security interventions were significantly more likely to produce more food and save for the future than families that had not received these interventions (Heryford, 2013a). While UNWater estimates that only 2 per cent of worldwide projects are followed up on and maintained sufficiently, 89 per cent of Compassion's WASH intervention projects were found to be in good working order after two years with almost 80 per cent of communities trained in all areas of repair to provide for their own sustainable maintenance (WHO, 2012).

Future state and issues

Compassion's commitment to a holistic child development model, together with local church empowerment, has served the communities within which we have operated well and the evidence indicates that children are influenced well into adulthood, many of whom are taking positions of leadership in their communities (Wydick et al, 2013). Nevertheless, increasing environmental and political complexities, changing funding landscapes as well as vast improvements in economic development require ongoing flexibility and contextual application and development of our core model.

For example, whilst the exchange of letters between sponsor and child has been shown to contribute significantly to child development (Sim, 2011), the concept of physical letter writing is outdated to many sponsors. This means that our communication model will need to change. Whilst transitioning to an electronic format is being pursued we also need to recognize that children like to keep the physical letters, often referring to them when they need encouragement (Sim, 2011) and also many of our church partners still have significant challenges with digital technology. New innovations are needed to facilitate meaningful and timely communication between sponsors and children that serve the needs and capacities of both.

Moreover, our commitment to local ownership and management of the programme is being more strongly pursued with the introduction of Qavah (Compassion International, 2013), a participatory tool that promotes self-discovery, local ownership and collaboration between church and community to address local issues. Qavah is built upon a rich history of participatory development and evaluation tools (Cousins and Earl, 1992; Chambers, 1983), the most recent of which is called Umoja (Njoroge, 2010). However, greater empowerment of local actors has the potential to conflict with a growing western need for programmatic influence and evidence of effectiveness. For example, sponsorship pressure to know if we are truly serving the poor raised questions surrounding child selection and poverty measurement, yet Compassion, whilst providing broad guidelines, leaves selection of children to local church and community representatives. This is where an integrated research strategy using trusted but objective researchers can contribute in a way which doesn't appear to challenge local ownership and trust. For example, a recent comprehensive study of poverty, using economic indicators and the multi-dependent poverty index (Alkire and Santos, 2010) showed that, using local indicators and processes to select eligible children, over 82 per cent of recently registered families were indeed below their national poverty lines and in Africa and Asia, over 80 per cent of recently registered families were found to be poor (<$2PPP per day or >0.2 MPI). Given that Compassion is committed to the local church long term, this is comforting data which validate the efforts of our partners. Nevertheless, the challenge remains to ensure healthy partnerships while reaching the neediest in the countries in which we work. Indeed, in the same study in the Latin American Region (LAR) approximately 70 per cent of recently registered families were found to be poor, consistent with the considerable recent economic development in that region. These and other findings then served to inform a revised strategy to reach the neediest, including the establishment of daughter churches by these partners and parallel initiation of Compassion's child sponsorship programme.

As strategies within our core model of child sponsorship continue to evolve, identifying key elements that drive outcomes will become increasingly important. Moreover, as governments in developing nations and international bodies continue to remove the external constraints to poverty reduction, attention to identifying and relieving the internal constraints will increase. Ultimately we believe that this is where Compassion's individualized holistic model of child development thrives. Our combined attention to both external and internal constraints is producing unquestionable results (for example Wydick et al, 2013) in which we believe hope (a belief in a better future and a belief that those living in poverty have the capacity to influence that future) is the greatest driver of success. Whilst the evidence is beginning to support this hypothesis it will require new, integrated research approaches and methodologies that cross discipline boundaries to prove it empirically. After 60 years of holistic child sponsorship, the future is still exciting.

Acknowledgements

This chapter represents the words of two men who represent an army of past and present staff, church members, project staff, volunteers, children and families across Compassion's more than 3,000 employees, 6,500 church partners and 1.4 million sponsored children. All have contributed in some way, shape or form to this work and it is not possible to identify each and every contribution except collectively. We would, however, specifically like to thank Paul Moede, Dinah Myer, Wolf Riedner, Brenda Kerls, Kurt Birky, Kate Heryford, Maria (Weng) Campos, Judy Webb, Dustin Bell and Shona Sim for suggestions, material and reviewing of this chapter. Whilst representing the work of Compassion International, any errors therein, however, are solely the responsibility of the authors.

Bibliography

Ali, S. (2011) 'Learning self control', *The Quarterly Journal of Economics*, 126, 2, 857–893.

Alkire, S. and Santos, M. (2010) *Acute Multidimensional Poverty: A New Index for Developing Countries* (NY: UNDP).

Banerjee, A. and Duflo, E. (2011) *Poor Economics. A Radical Rethink of the Way to Fight Global Poverty* (NY: Public Affairs Publishing).

Becker, A.R., Randels, J. and Theodore, D. (2005) 'Project BRAVE: Engaging youth as agents of change in a youth violence prevention project', *Community Youth Development*, Fall (Special Peer Reviewed Issue), 39–52.

Behrman, J.R. (2005) 'Progressing through PROGRESA: An impact assessment of a school subsidy experiment in rural Mexico', *Economic Development and Cultural Change*, 54, 1, 237–253.

Benson, P., Leffert, N., Scales, P. and Blyth, D. (1998) 'Beyond the village rhetoric: Creating healthy communities for children and adolescents', *Applied Developmental Science*, 2, 3, 138–159.

Birmingham, B. (2011) *Meta Evaluation of Compassion International Child Sponsorship Program Evaluations* (Colorado Springs, CO: Compassion International).

Bobonis, G. and Finan, F. (2009) 'Neighborhood peer effects in secondary school enrollment decisions', *Review of Economics and Statistics*, 91, 4, 695–716.

Cauffman, E. and Steinberg, L. (2000) 'Immaturity of judgement in adolescence: Why adolescents may be less culpable than adults', *Behavioural Science Law*, 18, 741–760.

Center for the Study of Global Christianity (2013) *Christianity in its Global Context, 1970–2020: Society, Religion and Mission*, Gordon-Conwell Theological Seminary.

Chambers, R. (1983) *Rural Development: Putting the Last First* (Harlow, UK: Longmans).

Clay, R., CdeBaca, L., De Cock, M., Goosby, E., Guttmacher, A., Jacobs, S., Pablos-Mendez, A., Polaski, S., Sheldon, G. and Steinberg, D. (2012) 'A call for coordinated and evidence-based action to protect children outside of family care', *The Lancet*, 379, 9811, e6–e8.

Compassion International (2010) *Poverty: Compassion's Ministry Philosophy Series* (Colorado Springs, CO: Compassion International).

Compassion International (2013) *Qavah Learning Community*, http://qavah.compassion.com, date accessed 13 June 2013.

Cousins, J. and Earl, L. (1992) 'The case for participatory evaluation', *Educational Evaluation and Policy Analysis*, 14, 4, 397–418.

Dalton, P.S., Ghosal, S. and Mani, A. (2011) *Poverty and Aspirations Failure: A Theoretical Framework. CentER Discussion Paper Series*, Social Science Research Network No. 2011–124, http://arno.uvt.nl/show.cgi?fid=121266, date accessed 1 November 2013.

Deneulin, S. and Rakodi, C. (2011) 'Revisiting religion: Development studies thirty years on', *World Development*, 39, 1, 45–54.

Dollar, D. and Levin, V. (2006) 'The increasing selectivity of foreign aid, 1984–2003', *World Development*, 34, 12, 2034–2046.

Eckerson, W.W. (2002) *Achieving Business Success through a Commitment to High Quality Data*, The Data Warehousing Institute, http://download.101com.com/pub/tdi/Files/DQReport.pdf, date accessed 10 October 2013.

Fernald, L. and Gunnar, M. (2009) 'Effects of a poverty-alleviation intervention on salivary cortisol in very low-income children', *Social. Sci. Med*, 68, 12, 2180–2189, date accessed 10 October 2013.

Fien, J., Neil, C. and Bentley, M. (2008) 'Youth can lead the way to sustainable consumption', *Journal of Education for Sustainable Development*, 2, 1, 51–60.

Freed, P., McLaughlin, D., SmithBattle, L., Leanders, S. and Westhus, N. (2010) 'It's the little things that count: The value in receiving therapeutic letters', *Issues in Mental Health Nursing*, 31, 4, 265–272.

Giedd, J., Blumenthal, J., Jeffries, N., Castellanos, F., Liu, H., Zijdenbos, A., Paus, T., Evans, A. and Rapoport, J. (1999) 'Brain development during childhood and adolescence: A longitudinal MRI study', *Nature Neuroscience*, 2, 10, 861–863.

Ginwright, S. and James, T. (2002) 'From assets to agents of change: Social justice, organizing, and youth development', *New Directions for Youth Development*, 96, winter, 27–46.

Hamill, M., Reid, M. and Reynolds, S. (2008) 'Letters in cognitive analytic therapy: The patient's experience', *Psychotherapy Research*, 18, 5, 573–583.

Hare, T.C., Camerer, C. and Rangel, A. (2009) 'Self control in decision-making involves modulation of the vmPFC valuation system', *Science*, 324, 649–658.

Heryford, K. (2013a) *CIV Effectiveness Study: The Effect of WASH, Malaria, Health and Food Security in Uganda, Tanzania, Rwanda and Burkina Faso* (Colorado Springs, CO: Compassion International).

Heryford, K. (2013b) *Program Outcome Effectiveness Measurement in Dominican Republic, Ghana and Haiti* (Colorado Springs, CO: Compassion International).

Karlan, D. and Appel, J. (2012) *More than Good Intentions* (NY: Plume).

Kindsvatter, A., Desmond, K.J., Yanikoski, A. and Stahl, S. (2013)' The use of therapeutic letters in addressing parent-child attachment problems', *The Family Journal*, 21, 1, 74–79.

King, P., Schultz, W., Mueller, R., Dowling, E., Osborn, P., Dickerson, E. and Lerner, R. (2005) 'Positive youth development: Is there a nomological network of concepts used in the adolescent developmental literature', *Applied Developmental Science*, 9, 4, 216–228.

Kristoff, N. (2012) 'A poverty solution that starts with a hug', *The New York Times*, 7 January.

Landgren, K. (2005) 'The protective environment: Development support for child protection', *Human Rights Quarterly*, 27, 1, 214–248.

Lerner, R., Lerner, J., Almerigi, J., Theokas, C., Gestsdottir, S., Naudeau, S., Alberts, A., Ma, L., Smith, L., Bobek, D., Richman-Raphael, D. and Simpson, I. (2005) 'Positive youth development, participation in community youth development programs and community contributions of fifth grade adolescents', *Journal of Early Adolescence*, 25, 1, 17–71.

Makhoul, J., Alammeddine, M. and Afifi, R. (2012) '"I felt I was benefiting someone": Youth as agents of change in a refugee community project', *Health Education Research*, 27, 5, 914–926.

Mitchell, T., Tanner, T. and Haynes, K. (2009) 'Children as agents of change for disaster risk reduction', *Children in a Changing Climate Research*, Working Paper No. 1 (Brighton, UK: Institute of Development Studies).

Moules, N. (2009) 'The past and future of therapeutic letters: Family suffering and healing words', *Journal of Family Nursing*, 15, 1, 102–111.

Murgatroyd, C. and Spengler, D. (2011) 'Epigenetics of early child development', *Frontiers in Psychiatry*, 16, 2, 1–15, https://www.ncbi.nlm.nih.gov/pmc/articles/PMC3102328, date accessed 10 October 2013.

Narayan, D., Chambers, R., Shah, M. and Petesch, P. (2000) *Voices of the Poor: Crying Out for Change* (New York: Oxford University Press).

Njoroge, F.R. (2010) *Umoja, Transforming Communities Facilitator Guide, TearFund* (Teddington, UK: TearFund).

Pyle, N. (2006) 'Therapeutic letters in counselling practice', *Canadian Journal of Counselling*, 40, 1, 17–31.

Pyle, N. (2009) 'Therapeutic letters as relationally responsive practice', *Journal of Family Nursing*, 15, 1, 65–82.

Ravallion, M. (2012) 'Fighting poverty one experiment at a time: A review essay on Abhijit Banerjee and Esther Duflo, poor economics. World Bank', *Journal of Economic Literature*, 50, 1, 103–114.

Redman, T. (2004) *Data: An Unfolding Quality Disaster*, http://www.estgv.ipv.pt/PaginasPessoais/jloureiro/ESI_AID2007_2008/fichas/TP06_anexo2.pdf, date accessed 29 October 2013.

Schulz, T.P. (2004) 'School subsidies for the poor, evaluating the Mexican Progesa Povery Program', *Journal of Development Economics*, 74, 1, 199–250.

Shonkoff, J., Garner, A. and The Committee on Psychological Aspects of Child and Family Health, Committee on Early Childhood, Adoption, & Dependent Care and Section on Developmental and Behavioral Pediatrics (2011) 'The lifelong effects of early childhood adversity and toxic stress', *Pediatrics*, 129: e232–e246, https://pediatrics.aappublications.org/content/early/2011/12/21/peds.2011-2663, date accessed 10 October 2013.

Sim, A. (2011) *Impact of Sponsor Communication* (Colorado Springs, CO: Compassion International).

The Pew Forum (2010) *Tolerance and Tension: Islam and Christianity in Sub-Saharan Africa*, Pew Research Center. Available online at https://www.pewforum.org/2010/04/15/executive-summary-islam-and-christianity-in-sub-saharan-africa/, date accessed 10 October 2013.

Van den Bos, R., Harteveld, M. and Stoop, H. (2009) 'Stress and decision-making in humans', *Psychoneuroendocrinology*, 34, 10, 1449–1458.

WHO (2012) *UN-Water Global Annual Assessment of Sanitation and Drinking-Water (GLAAS) 2012 Report: The Challenge of Extending and Sustaining Services*, WHO, http://www.who.int/water_sanitation_health/publications/glass_report_2012/en/index.html, date accessed 10 October 2013.

Wilber, C. and Jameson, K. (1980) 'Religious values and social limits to development', *World Development*, 8, 7–8, 467–479.

World Bank (2009) *Conditional Cash Transfers: Reducing Present and Future Poverty* (Washington, DC: The World Bank).

Wydick, B., Glewwe, P. and Rutledge, L. (2013) 'Does international child sponsorship work? A six-country study of impacts on adult life outcomes', *Journal of Political Economy*, 121, 2, 393–436.

9
Children at the Centre: Children International, Child Sponsorship and Community Empowerment in Underserved Areas

Jim Cook and Damon Guinn

> In Children International, we discover, practice and enhance our talents and skills...from elementary to college, from every pencil to uniform, from toothpaste to kitchenware, from toothache to hospital bills – they gave me a chance to have a better future.
>
> *May Ann, Philippines,*
> *Former sponsored youth and preschool teacher*

From its beginning as a small food relief charity to its current role as a worldwide humanitarian organization focused on early childhood, youth and community development, Children International (CI) has become a reliable presence in numerous underserved communities. What sets CI apart from other child sponsorship (CS) organizations is its unique community centres. The newest facilities are highly functional and modern and are designed to provide impoverished children, youth and families with essential benefits and services that are often inaccessible in their communities. These include free medical and dental care, educational resources, nutritional aid, material assistance, skills training, recreational opportunities, comprehensive youth programmes and disaster relief.

CI provides comprehensive programmes through more than 80 community centres that serve more than 335,000 impoverished young children, youth, and their families, in urban slums and other marginalized areas of Chile, Colombia, the Dominican Republic, Ecuador, Guatemala, Honduras, India, Mexico, the Philippines, the United States and Zambia. Staffed by local residents who understand the

191

specific needs and challenges of each community, the centres offer a safe reprieve from the social and environmental hazards that threaten children and their families in deeply impoverished areas, while also providing a diverse variety of programmes and activities that foster personal growth, citizen security, self-sufficiency and improved community cohesion.

This chapter explains how CI has evolved to meet a wide array of needs within disadvantaged communities and why its community centres are ideally suited to create lasting change in some of the world's most underserved areas.

A foundation built on food and faith

CI's approach to alleviating poverty has radically changed since the organization was founded in 1936 by Ralph Baney, a Baptist minister. Baney initially raised funds through speaking engagements in communities and churches across the Midwestern and South-Central USA. In keeping with its roots as a religious-based charity, the organization was known as the Holy Land Christian Mission until the name was officially changed to Children International in 1987. Despite its origins as a Christian charity, there were no explicit religious or denominational requirements for beneficiaries. In the early years, both Jewish and Muslim families were assisted in the West Bank without regard to religious affiliation.

From its headquarters in Kansas City, Missouri, CI's early efforts focused on helping impoverished women, children and families in Bethlehem and Jerusalem. The very first benefits the charity provided were food baskets with basic staples, which were distributed on a monthly basis to families the organization's local church affiliates identified as most vulnerable. A small, one-room medical clinic was opened as well to treat minor infections and illnesses among its beneficiaries. As the charity's efforts expanded during the 1940s, CI added an orphanage to its facilities and began providing clothing to boys, girls and other beneficiaries in its social welfare programme.

When a polio outbreak spread through the West Bank in 1952, the charity launched a successful direct mail campaign in the United States to fund the expansion of its medical clinic to provide higher quality treatment than was available to disadvantaged children and their families through under-resourced public clinics. The additional revenue raised through direct mail appeals in the USA made it possible for CI's clinic to perform orthopedic surgeries and provide therapeutic services

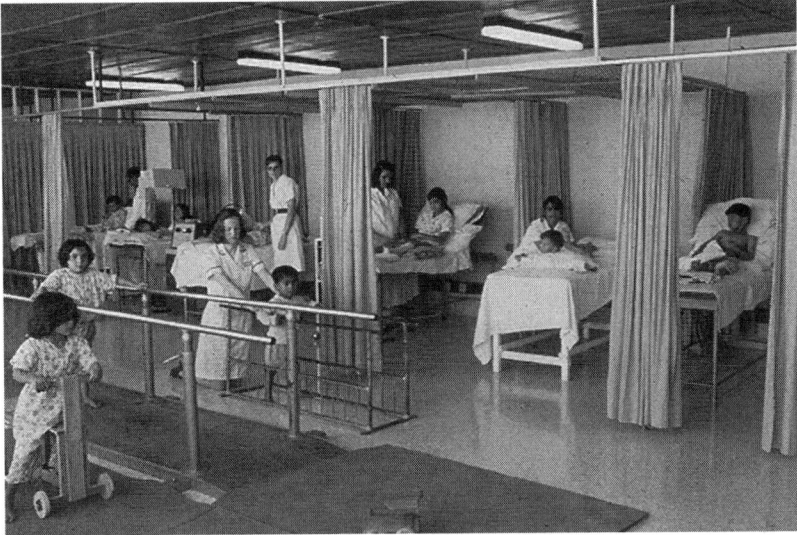

Figure 9.1   The Mount of David Crippled Children's Hospital
The hospital operated in Bethlehem until the 1990s, providing the initial impetus for the organization's child sponsorship programme.

for children disabled by polio, club foot and other debilitating bone disorders, a degree of care that most impoverished families in the region could not afford to cover without international assistance.

As demand for specialized medical services continued to grow, CI converted its clinic to a full-service hospital in the early 1970s before building the Mount of David Crippled Children's Hospital in the early 1980s using support from USAID grants with funds raised through an ongoing capital campaign. The larger, state-of-the-art hospital had the capacity to treat approximately 20,000 patients a year, and continued to operate and perform sophisticated orthopedic surgeries until the mid-1990s, when it was sold to a private Jordanian business group due to political volatility in the area and the organization's strategic shift to sponsorship of children.

CI made its first foray into CS in the mid-1970s. Donors were mailed information about individual boys and girls who needed specialized medical care and asked to 'sponsor' those children by making ten dollar monthly contributions to cover their health needs at the Mount of David Hospital. The charity budgeted for the hospital's expenses and the degree of care each child required by pooling sponsors' donations. Doing so made it possible for CI staff to schedule treatment in advance and request additional funds as needed. In exchange for their support, sponsors in the USA received annual photos and progress reports about the children. Sponsorship provided a mutually beneficial relationship: children received the medical care they needed while their sponsors gained a sense of satisfaction from helping those boys and girls overcome very real, often debilitating conditions.

The pilot CS programme in the West Bank yielded such a strong response that by 1980 CI started soliciting support through sponsorship to provide groceries, clothes and kerosene stoves to widows through a programme it called Widows Aid. More importantly though, it set out to launch a worldwide, non-religious CS programme. The decision coincided with UNICEF's 'Child Survival and Development Revolution,' which urged governments and INGOs to fight child mortality and curb preventable diseases (UNICEF USA, 2013). CI joined those efforts by launching one-to-one sponsorship programmes in Honduras, Guatemala, Chile, Colombia, Thailand, the Dominican Republic, followed by India and the Philippines. To get the programme off the ground, the organization partnered with non-profit agencies that were based in developing areas. Together with the help of volunteer mothers and community leaders, local staff began enrolling children they considered to be in dire need of help because of insufficient monthly income and sub-standard living conditions.

CI's early CS programme initially focused on providing food relief. Groceries were distributed to children and their families as a result of sponsors' monthly donations. As was the case with the previous programme in the West Bank, each sponsor received an annual photo and two letters from their sponsored child, with news updates about benefits and the child's circumstances. More than 2,390 children and their families were benefiting from monthly food assistance through the sponsorship programme by the end of the first year, with potential for growth in nearly every area. Eager to extend sponsorship to more needy children and families, the staff at CI set an ambitious goal of building community relations, enhancing operations, enrolling additional children and recruiting new sponsors. Those efforts led to the enrollment of thousands of children in deeply impoverished communities around the world, including the Tondo district of Manila, Philippines, one of the most densely populated and disadvantaged in the region. Renowned for its extreme poverty and hazardous conditions, Tondo became emblematic of the communities CI sought to support through sponsorship – areas without safe housing, adequate sanitation or reliable access to health, education and social services;

neighbourhoods with high unemployment and even higher underemployment, where government services were overwhelmed by the scale of need and where the safety and well-being of children was constantly in jeopardy.

A new era of child sponsorship

As CI extended one-to-one sponsorship to tens of thousands of children throughout the 1980s, the organization underwent a second major transformation under the leadership of a newly appointed president, Joseph Gripkey. Following a brief name change to Mission International, the charity adopted its current name (Children International) and launched an advertising campaign on cable TV to recruit sponsors at twelve dollars a month instead of ten. CI rapidly gained popularity as one of the most affordable CS organizations available in the USA, and a surge in new sponsors, along with the corresponding increase in revenue, made it possible to provide additional benefits to children and their families. In areas where food relief was less critical, sponsorship began covering the costs of healthcare, medicine and essential clothing items. By the end of the decade, CI had opened two more sponsorship programmes in Ecuador, in Guayaquil and Quito, effectively reaching 134,000 children in eight countries. Between 1980 and 1990, cash income increased from US$5.6 million to US$22.8 million, allowing CI to both expand and professionalize.

Beginning in the 1990s, CI set out to redefine its processes and strategy for helping children in need. The organization created a field manual that formalized financial controls – including budgeting policies, procurement procedures for benefits, and auditing practices – while also instituting a core set of benefits for every sponsored child along with guidelines and procedures for administration and distribution of benefits at the field level. Core benefits to individual children included an annual health examination, follow-up care and free medicine, nutritional aid, educational assistance in the form of school uniforms and supplies, plus material aid such as clothing and shoes. Providing a standard set of benefits to every child, regardless of location, made it possible for CI to improve monitoring and reporting, thus improving the efficiency of operations and accountability. Under the new system, budgeting for benefits was more effective, since clothing, shoes and other material items could be purchased in bulk at a cheaper price. CI also began securing and distributing product donations to bolster the benefits it provided to children and families, beginning with 23,000 pairs of shoes provided by Nike Corporation in 1991. From that point forward, donations ranging from school text-books to hygiene supplies and vaccines offered invaluable budget relief and, in some cases, higher quality goods than the organization might have been able to purchase through its suppliers.

Standardized benefits and stronger budgetary and procurement prac-tices further ensured that CI could provide uninterrupted care to boys and girls whose sponsors had discontinued their support, a number that hovered around 5 per cent of total enrollment each year. Rather than suspend benefits and possibly thwart children's progress while they waited to be sponsored again, the organization began allocating a portion of its annual budget to cover the costs of ongoing support for children whose sponsorships had lapsed. CI then placed those children on a priority waiting list and used direct mail acquisitions and appeals to secure new sponsorships as quickly as possible.

Improvements in budgeting and field operations created efficiencies that gave CI the capital to start a domestic sponsorship programme in the United States. In 1994, it partnered with the University of Arkansas at Little Rock (UALR) to form what would become its only USA-based programme. At that time Arkansas had one of the nation's highest rates of children living in poverty, and UALR possessed the staff and facilities to deliver direct assistance to low-income children in the city's elementary schools. Sponsored children received standard benefits such as material aid and school supplies, similar to the international sponsorship programme, but the programme office in Arkansas placed a greater emphasis on educational development through afterschool activities such as art classes, a chess club, dance, and music (in 2013 CI was funding and operating afterschool programmes at four schools). Over the years, enrollment grew from 300 to 3,000 participants, and CI and UALR established partnerships to open the state's only elementary-based dental clinic.

Addressing the needs of a broader cross section of children

The addition of the USA programme meant that more than 200,000 children in nine countries were benefiting from CI's sponsorship pro-gramme by the end of the 1990s. With CI's growth and commitment to maintaining an ongoing presence in communities over long periods of time came the realization that the population of sponsored children was not only growing larger, it was becoming older too. As the new millennium approached, there were more than 60,000 sponsored youth between the ages of 14 and 19 whose emotional and physiological needs were far different from younger children. Those needs were not being addressed by basic sponsorship programming that guaranteed provision of medical services and necessities.

Prior to 1999, CI's policy was to stop providing benefits to youth 14 and older when their sponsors discontinued. It was often easier to find replacement sponsors for younger children who were perceived to be more vulnerable. Unfortunately, the previous directive had left many youth cut-off from the community of support that had nurtured them since early childhood. Furthermore, CI staff found that youth who were forced to leave the CS programme were less likely to stay in school. CI addressed the problem by adjusting its budget so youth could remain enrolled until the age of 19, regardless of whether or not they had a sponsor and urged sponsors to continue their support until the youth officially graduated from the programme.

To better understand the needs and priorities of youth in the communities it supported, CI conducted surveys through its international field offices to determine which programmes and services youth believed were most beneficial. The general consensus indicated that they wanted opportunities to learn social skills in a safe setting and the means to complete their formal education through secondary or vocational school. They also expressed a strong interest in developing life skills, a better understanding of reproductive health, and a desire for career counselling. CI responded by launching an official youth programme, the costs of which were covered by unrestricted donations and discretionary income that stemmed from an increase in monthly sponsorship from US$12–US$14.

With more young children being added to the rosters and more youth remaining in the CS programme through to late adolescence, CI's programme needs began to outgrow the organization's original project facilities, pushing the limits of many buildings beyond their capacity. As a result, the scheduling of services and delivery of benefit distributions became logistically challenging and time-consuming for staff and families alike. Beginning in 1990, CI began to allocate funding for purchasing and building larger multi-use facilities in centralized locations to absorb current and projected growth. The new facilities, which were officially called Service Area Centres but were more commonly known as community centres, had to be large enough to house waiting and examination rooms for health checkups, libraries, meeting spaces, benefit storage rooms, and at certain locations, dental clinics and pharmacies. They also had to be situated in areas that were easier to access by programme staff, volunteers, and the majority of sponsored children and families than the older, more remote facilities, which were often situated farther away from modern infrastructure.

CI's new community centres became the impetus behind a strategic growth plan to more effectively deliver sponsorship benefits and services in geographically concentrated urban slums, and by extension, provide a source of stability that would increase community member security within those areas. The first centre based on the new model was built in the deeply impoverished colony of Asentamientos Humanos, or 'Human Settlements,' outside San Pedro Sula, Honduras, in 1991. The community was a squatter settlement inhabited by a rapidly growing population of migrants from other parts of the country. As such, it was located in an undeveloped area with few paved roads, limited drainage, no waste disposal and very few public services. For most of the residents enrolled in CI's sponsorship programme, the centre offered the only access they had to medical care, nutritional aid and other forms of support. It became a central meeting place for sponsored children and their families to learn about health and hygiene and participate in other instructional workshops. CI used the blueprint for Honduras to add new centres in Ecuador and the Philippines, thanks in part to Debt for Development exchanges, in which the government of the USA forgave countries' debts with the condition that the governments matched expenditures by USA charities operating there. The exchanges allowed CI to build community centres on land with perpetual leases deeded 'free and clear' by their host countries.

Since 2000, CI has used the new community centre model to open sponsorship programmes in Mexico and Zambia and to build or rehabilitate community centres in all of the countries it serves. As of 2013, it was operating more than 80 community centres in 11 countries for the benefit of more than 335,000 children, youth and their families.

Community centres: A world of difference, by design

Open year-round, some up to seven days a week, CI community centres serve as the focal hubs for the delivery of benefits, services and community-wide support. Many are modern, highly functional buildings unlike anything else in their local settings, and their physical presence symbolizes CI's commitment to promoting real and lasting change. They are centrally located in poor, underdeveloped areas to provide convenient access to essential services such as schools, hospitals, main roads and public transit, while also providing impoverished children and youth with services that are limited or unavailable in their communities.

Worldwide, CI staffs all its centres exclusively with local professionals (approximately 1,200) and community volunteers (more than 8,000) who understand the unique needs and demands of the catchment areas. Each newly constructed centre is designed with sufficient space to provide benefits and services to as many as 5,000 children. The surrounding communities where children and families live are divided into sectors, each consisting of up to 1,000 sponsored children and youth assigned to a field officer. The field officers, working together with volunteers, notify children and their families about scheduled medical and dental exams and benefit distributions, letter-writing and photo requirements, and other community centre activities, while also keeping a watchful eye on environmental and social conditions in the communities.

Delivery of services and benefits within limited and geographically strategic catchment areas is desirable for several reasons: it reduces cost of delivery, increases transparency and improves monitoring. Referring to the direct benefits provided by CS organization Islamic Relief, Van Eekelen (2013, p.475) states that the large efficiency gains in one-on-one sponsorship programmes can be made 'simply by adhering rigidly

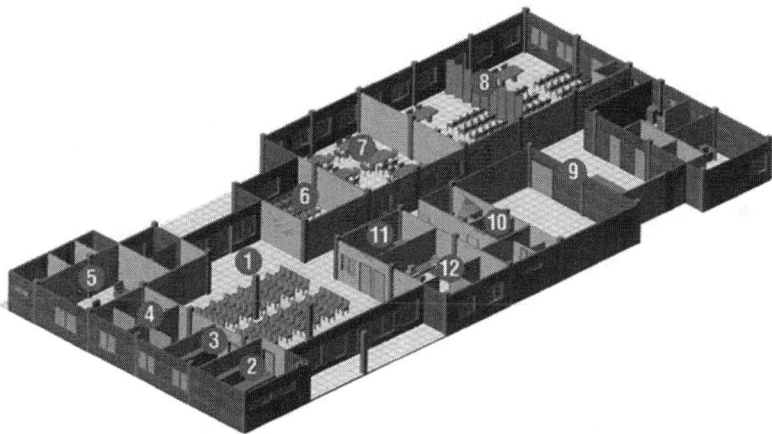

Figure 9.2 A typical modern CI community centre floor plan:
1. Waiting area, 2. Pharmacy, 3–4. Medical Clinic and Exam Rooms, 5. Dental Clinic, 6. Youth Activity Centre, 7. Library, 8. Community Enrichment Hall, 9. Benefit Distribution Centre, 10. Restrooms, 11. Computer Room, 12. Staff Office

to catchment areas beyond which nobody is eligible for sponsorship, and by situating the sponsorship offices in the middle of these catchment areas' (2013, p.475). CI's community centre model and staffing paradigm are on target in terms of keeping operating costs down while maintaining highly efficient delivery practices.

The centres are far more than physical structures, however; they are points of hope and refuge for children, youth and families who rarely have safe places to gather and engage in constructive activities. Enrolled at an early age, sponsored children visit the centres regularly, attending health and dental exams, picking up clothing benefits, writing letters to their sponsors, using the library or playground, and interacting with each other and the staff. They grow up receiving care from individuals who have their well-being and best interests in mind. The added sense of security, both psychological and physical, that children and youth derive from those routine interactions was noted in a 2003 survey carried out by the Aguirre Group, an independent auditing firm, which evaluated sponsorship services funded by CI in Ecuador, Guatemala and the Philippines:

> ...There seems to be a 'community of sponsorship' – a community that may be lacking for many young people at home or school or in their neighborhood. The staff and directors of the [community centres] are well-known to the children and youths as being there for them in difficult times. [...] In the Philippines, Multi-Purpose Centres provide a 'safe haven' from the streets. It is a place where sponsored children and youth can hang out without fear of being hassled by drug dealers. It is a place where friends can meet and talk after school (Aguirre Group, 2003, p.95).

The personalized care and positive reinforcement staff and volunteers provide at the community centres instills confidence in children and youth, imbuing them with a sense of hope and purpose. 'I see the community centre as something good for both me and the society – for families,' says Yusiva, a sponsored youth in Barranquilla, Colombia, 'because it is always helping somehow...it is always teaching us to be better people.' Surrounded by supportive role models, young people who grow up visiting the community centres are able to envision a better future for themselves and their communities. It is a transformative process for many children that can begin the moment a child sets foot in a CI community centre to receive his or her very first benefit or access a service.

Figure 9.3 A before-and-after look at Children International's community centre in Los Tanquecitos, Dominican Republic

A healthy start

The communities assisted by CI centres are characterized by pervasive environmental and social hazards that threaten children's health, potential and well-being. From the densely packed urban slums of India and the Philippines to the sprawling squatter settlements of Colombia and Ecuador, a lack of sanitation services and access to potable water, along with overcrowding and substandard housing conditions, leave children exposed to parasitic and respiratory infections and illnesses like dengue, malaria, and tuberculosis. Many sponsored children come from communities situated in areas prone to flooding, fires, erosion, and other natural disasters, which can lead to severe injuries, disability or death.

The combination of CS with innovative programmes and services provided at community centres (see Figure 9.3 for pictures of community centre buildings), ensures that a health checkup and malnutrition screening are the first benefits every child under 12 receives. The majority of centres are equipped with medical and dental clinics staffed by local professionals. Most have fully stocked pharmacies that provide free antibiotics, pain relievers and other medicine to children and their families. CI's medical staff also monitor and chart each child's medical history from the first checkup, using an electronic medical records system that adheres to clinical guidelines developed by the World Health Organization.

Because families of sponsored children and youth have regular access to CI's medical and dental clinics, they are able to seek treatment more often than they would at public clinics, which are usually overcrowded, poorly equipped and require patients to pay for medicine and supplies. In 2012, for example, the community centre clinics performed 390,050 medical checkups and 251,061 dental exams and screenings for children and youth. Those numbers are significant considering how difficult it can be for families in impoverished communities to see a doctor. 'You ask for an appointment at the civil hospital, and the doctor tells you to get an appointment when you can,' explained Patricia, the mother of Marisol, a sponsored child in Jalisco, Mexico. 'But it might be six, eight months down the road.' Prior to sponsorship, Marisol had been prescribed medicine at a public hospital to help control seizures, but her mother was unable to arrange a follow-up visit to check the dosage. Marisol's dosage was finally checked more than a year later, but only after she was enrolled in sponsorship and had a medical exam at CI's community centre clinic. The staff doctor ordered blood tests and discovered that Marisol's dosage was too high. She was gradually being poisoned by her own medicine. 'I tell my husband how grateful I am for the care she gets,' Patricia remarked. 'Even the kids can tell the standard of care they receive is better.'

When the Aguirre Group surveyed CI sponsorship beneficiaries in Ecuador, Guatemala and the Philippines, they found that sponsored children had 'significant increases in access to medical consultation, as well as overall dental health...' (Aguirre Group, 2003, p.5). According to the parents surveyed, sponsored children saw a doctor during their last illness at a rate one and a half times greater (73 per cent) than their non-sponsored children (54 per cent), while sponsored youth were twice as likely as their non-sponsored peers to get an annual checkup. The study also found that 'almost one-quarter more sponsored youth receive medications when ill (97 per cent) compared to non-sponsored youth (73 per cent)' (Aguirre Group, 2003, p.5).

The health services that sponsored children and youth receive do not end at the community centre. CI medical staff make referrals to specialists for follow-up treatment and therapy through a network of public and private health providers and make arrangements for emergency medical care for cardiac and orthopedic surgeries and other critical operations. They may be called upon to provide emergency triage when natural disasters affect sponsorship communities or participate in health campaigns such as anti-parasite treatments and tuberculosis prevention for sponsored and non-sponsored participants alike. Likewise, nutrition seminars and lunch programmes are held at centres and at homes within communities, where volunteers take turns preparing nutritious meals to rehabilitate children with moderate to severe malnutrition. School-based feeding programmes at community schools outside Lusaka, Zambia, simultaneously address the problem of hunger and increase school enrollment.

Sponsored youth are encouraged to play a part in improving community health. As volunteers in CI's Youth Health Corps (YHC), they receive training to raise awareness of reproductive health, drug abuse and hygiene. Julieth, a Colombian youth, became a peer educator and began educating other youth about the dangers of drug use after her own recovery from drug addiction. 'The youth look to me for advice, and I visit them at their houses,' she shared. 'Now I want to rescue all the young women who are addicts today.' Likewise, Dr. Delhy Delgadillo – a CI staff doctor in the Dominican Republic who was once a sponsored child herself – has devoted her life to improving the health of her communities. '...We work to help and protect children and youth, who are among the neediest people because they cannot defend themselves...,' she stated when interviewed. 'In my role as doctor for the program, I can work, advise, serve and help all at the same time.'

Children international sponsorship opens doors to education

Like CI's medical and dental clinics, the libraries at community centres also fill a void in severely impoverished areas – they are an indispensable resource for children and youth who rarely have access to books in their neighbourhoods and who frequently lack sufficient electricity or space to study at home. According to Krashen (2011), libraries play a fundamental role in helping impoverished children overcome socio-economic barriers. His research found that libraries had a similar impact on reading scores as wealth, thereby closing the 'achievement gap' between children from high- and low-income families.

More than 98,000 children, youth and community members visited CI libraries in 2012 to do their homework, attend tutoring sessions, participate in reading programmes and educational activities, or simply hang out and play games. Tutoring services have been especially helpful. In India, CI internal research found 95 per cent of fifth-grade students who attended a year of tutoring at CI libraries in Kolkata demonstrated a 50 per cent improvement in their test scores at the end of the year. There are also 30 community centres with computer labs, where children, youth and adults can learn basic operating skills, work on school assignments, do research or create resumes. Each lab has up to 15 computer stations and a full-time lab assistant to help users develop their skills. Several CI field locations have expanded their library services by forming partnerships with local library associations, government programmes and publishing companies to provide a wider selection of titles and resources.

Natividad, a ten-year-old sponsored girl in Guatemala, is typical of the children who have benefited from CI's library services. Without books at home or school, she struggled with reading and comprehension, eventually failing second grade. After she was enrolled in the CS programme she spent the following summer practicing reading and writing at her local community centre library, stating that she learned to read better than the other children and had received congratulations from the teacher for her improved grades. Commenting on the level of disadvantage experienced by children in her area she said:

> There is nothing like this place. Neither here in Ciudad Vieja, nor in the school. The most similar thing is a place that is almost always closed and has few books. They also do not give books to small children, only to older young people doing research. But here is different. Here are books to read, encyclopedias and games to play in a safe place with other children or young people. With all this and the music, the colors...this is more than a place to read. Here is the place where we all want to be!

In the absence of effective government services, the existence of a well-resourced, accessible library in a disadvantaged area can have significant impact, providing economic and academic benefits. When a CI library in Quezon City, Philippines, was opened to the general public from three different communities (more than 400,000 residents total), there was a flurry of activity. In assessing the impact of the library, CI's local education coordinator remarked:

> Our visitors, especially the students, are able to save time and even money... They can do Internet research for free. Instead of buying reference materials for school, they can come and look for what they need. They can instead divert their savings to food.

Combined with the core educational assistance sponsorship provides – school supplies, uniforms, tuition and transportation assistance – educational services at community centres help boost school attendance and performance in areas where children may be forced to drop out of school due to lack of resources.

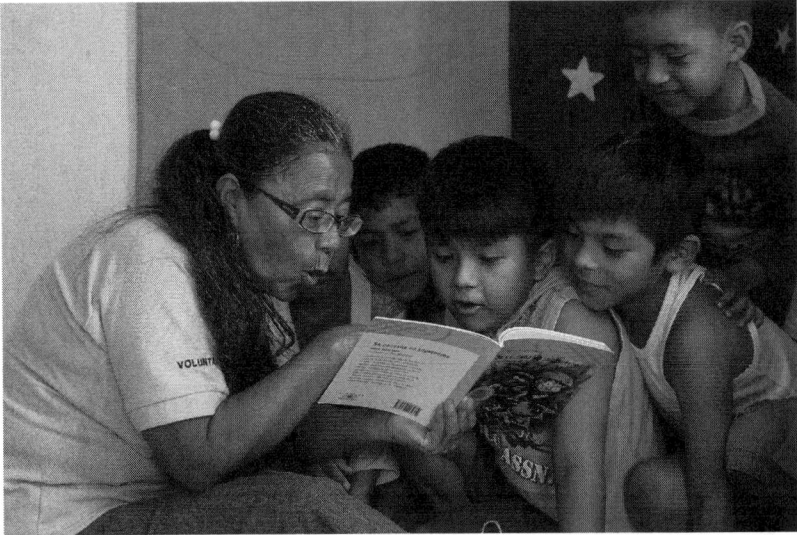

Figure 9.4 Local volunteers and tutors play an active role in promoting literacy and learning at Children International's community centre libraries around the world

The positive benefit Children International's educational assistance provides was first noted when the organization conducted a programme evaluation at its field locations in 1994. Using the Child Welfare League's Child Well-Being Scales, 12 scales were selected to measure programme-related care, such as healthcare, education, clothing and environmental sanitation among a random sample of 4,764 sponsored children at 16 different CI locations against a control group of 627 children waiting to be sponsored. The results indicated a statistically significant positive change for sponsored children in terms of adequacy of education, academic performance and school attendance (McDonnell and McDonnell, 1994, p.203). The study was relatively small, and took place much earlier, but the results appear to be complemented by the groundbreaking work of Wydick et al (2013, pp.396–397) who found several positive impacts of Compassion sponsorship, including that children tended to stay in school a year to a year and a half longer than their non-sponsored peers, were 27–40 per cent more likely to finish secondary school, and 50–80 per cent more likely to complete a university education. Although the authors state that they could not make claims about the positive impact of all sponsorship programmes, they did note 'some of the other major child sponsorship organizations, such as ChildFund and Children International, retain a focus on the nurturing and development of individual children, similar to Compassion's approach' (2013, p.29). In this sense, Compassion and CI share a common emphasis, one that merits further study.

Volunteers: The heart and soul of every Children International community

CI's sponsorship programme and community centres would not have undergone such rapid growth without the contribution of volunteers. They have been an integral part of community efforts since the organization launched its international sponsorship programme in 1980.

The majority of the more than 8,000 volunteers who assist CI are mothers of sponsored children and youth who help the staff identify and enroll children in need of assistance and inform families about upcoming activities, appointments and changes. Each volunteer works with approximately 42 sponsored children, but they also effectively serve as role models to the community at large, helping build trust and establish strong community relations. Because volunteers interact with sponsored children and families nearly every day, they are usually the first to learn about illnesses and health concerns in their communities. Most attend educational workshops on topics such as leadership that CI field locations host to help volunteers recognize and report health needs. Some also receive specialized training to become community health promoters. They use that training to help raise awareness about common health risks in their neighbourhoods and help administer anti-parasite medications and other forms of treatment during health and hygiene campaigns.

Although CI recruits volunteers to efficiently communicate with sponsored beneficiaries and help with the administration of benefits, many say they have benefited as much as the children they serve. In addition to the knowledge and leadership skills they have gained, volunteers say they feel empowered to improve their own lives, their families and their communities. Many have witnessed the growth and progress their own children and families have undergone through sponsorship and want others to reap the same rewards. And since the majority of volunteers are female, the added influence they gain is imbuing them with the right to make decisions and play a more prominent part in traditionally patriarchal societies that have had high rates of alcoholism, domestic violence and absentee fatherhood. The Aguirre Group noted that 'all volunteer mothers interviewed expressed strong feelings of satisfaction with their contribution. They describe this satisfaction as deriving from feeling '"useful," from increasing their knowledge through new information and skills, and from contributing to the benefit of needy families in their communities' (Aguirre Group, 2003, p.21).

The sense of empowerment reported by CI volunteers is linked to the development of social capital – the productive and beneficial social relations crucial to all communities. According to sociologist Brian Christens, psychosocial benefits 'accrue' to individuals fortunate enough to avoid trauma and other risk factors as well as those who become actively engaged in community organizations '...that permit many people to play meaningful roles, those that provide social support, those that provide access to social networks in different organizations, and those that implement community action' (Christens, 2012, p.539).

The sense of empowerment volunteers derive through participation is highlighted by the case of Guadencia, a volunteer mother in Manila, Philippines, whose two sons graduated from the sponsorship programme. Guadencia has served as a nutrition volunteer, a health educator and, most recently, a TB treatment partner, who assisted the CI staff doctor during medical checkups and administration of TB medication:

> Way back in 1995, when I was not yet volunteering for Children International, I was a loner, an introvert, and I had a feeling I was inferior compared to others. In the process of volunteering, I changed. I overcame my shyness and other weaknesses. I learned many things. I met many people. I became known to most residents in our community. Now I receive the respect and appreciation from them.

Replicated many times over, such stories illustrate that the sponsorship of children through CI programmes has a direct though less tangible benefit for the many volunteers who assist in its centres. These accounts are anecdotal, but their prevalence warrants further study.

Community support during times of crisis

The direct, personal relationships that are nurtured through sponsorship and reinforced by volunteers and staff have enabled CI to establish an extensive network of support that can respond rapidly to community-wide needs. Community outreach starts at centres, where families are invited to attend workshops on topics such as hygiene and nutrition, but fans out across surrounding neighbourhoods during annual anti-parasite campaigns, disease-prevention efforts, and community lunch programmes for malnourished children.

CI's community outreach is most noticeable, however, when the organization responds to natural disasters and builds community infrastructure. In 1998, when Honduras was devastated by Hurricane Mitch, CI quickly secured grants from the Cooperative Housing Foundation through USAID and launched a massive housing reconstruction programme in three different areas. Safe, stable land was acquired and nearly 700 hurricane-resistant homes with running water, electricity, bathrooms and kitchens were built along paved roads for sponsored families, most of whom had lived without those amenities prior to the storm. One of the housing sites, Colonia de los Apadrinados, or 'The Neighborhood of the Sponsored,' showed immediate signs of progress because many of the beneficiaries themselves took part in the area's development and reconstruction process.

The same can be said of Mabuhay Village in the Bicol region of the Philippines. Mabuhay, which means 'welcome' in Tagalog, is a thriving community that embodies the resilience of its people. CI funded rebuilding of the relocated community in the aftermath of 2006's Typhoon Durian, a violent storm that displaced as many as 100,000 people in Legazpi and Tabaco, including many of the 36,000 sponsored children and families who lived in the area. Local staff and volunteers quickly responded to the disaster by providing emergency food relief, medical support, and assistance with temporary housing. Families who had lost most of their possessions during the storm were ushered to community centres to pick up new clothes and shoes that had been donated by CI's corporate partners. In the months that followed, a relocation site was selected on land classified as a 'hazard-free zone' by the Philippines Mining and Geosciences Bureau, and construction began on 100 homes with fortified foundations and anchored roofs. 'During the recovery process, I witnessed how people become so supportive of one another in times of need,' observed the mother of a sponsored child and a recipient of one of the homes. 'We are happy in our new environment, and we are starting a new life here, leaving behind the pains that we've experienced during the typhoon.'

Following this successful intervention, CI partnered with UNICEF to form Disaster Preparedness Committees in 14 communities in the

Philippines, designed to help families overcome psychological trauma following disasters. The long-term presence of community centres provides an ideal base for such activities and volunteer and youth participants are trained in first aid and basic life support and pledge to be among the first on the scene when disasters strike. CI has also joined efforts to set up 'child-friendly spaces' at evacuation centres to help keep vulnerable boys and girls safe in their temporary and often insecure settings. Beyond that, CI volunteers carry out therapeutic psychosocial sessions that include group interaction, counseling and storytelling to help children confront frightening memories associated with disasters. In recognition of these combined efforts, CI received the 'Best Civil Society Organization on Humanitarian Assistance' award from the Philippines National Disaster Risk Reduction and Management Council from 2010 to 2012.

Elsewhere in the world, CI has helped families recover from numerous other disasters – from earthquakes and mudslides to floods and fires. The organization has partnered with donors, local governments and private businesses to build and renovate schools, construct community wells, and install latrines to improve living conditions and create safer environments.

Youth: The power of participation

If young people are to have any hope of breaking the intergenerational cycle of poverty, they need more than basic healthcare and education – they especially need opportunities to develop useful skills and behaviors that will keep them safe and lead to gainful employment. According to USAID (2012, p.4), youth programmes and services can ameliorate conditions such as high rates of school dropout, youth unemployment, teen pregnancy, HIV/AIDS infection and poor nutrition. Increasing investment in youth, USAID adds, 'will amplify and sustain important health and social gains from childhood interventions'.

CI's specialized youth programmes provide young men and women opportunities to build upon the benefits they receive through basic sponsorship. Unlike many of their non-sponsored peers, sponsored youth grow up receiving regular encouragement from their sponsors as well as guidance from culturally attuned role models at community centres. They learn to emulate the altruistic actions of sponsors, staff, volunteers, and their sponsored peers and then replicate that behavior at home and in their neighbourhoods. 'They see and later begin to be participants and agents of change in the broader community. We often forget how much learning takes place simply by observing, and CI's children are observing a community of caring,' noted Dick Roberts, a lifelong educator who coordinated afterschool programmes for the Los Angeles Unified School District and who now serves on CI's Advisory Council.

USAID (2012, p.8) stresses the importance of 'engaging young people in creating safe environments – safe schools, safe neighborhoods, safe jobs, safe cities.' Consequently, CI encourages all sponsored beneficiaries 12 and older to actively participate in youth programmes and begin to develop their individual aptitudes, life skills, social awareness and confidence. Besides helping youth manage the challenges of adolescence, the programmes are designed to address specific needs which go largely ignored in impoverished communities: leadership and life-skills training, community-service projects and participation, financial education and resource management, health awareness, scholarships for continuing and higher education, and job training and apprenticeships for gainful employment.

In addition to teaching youth crucial skills for their own personal progress, the youth programmes support several of the United Nations Millennium Development Goals, such as the promotion of gender equality, ensuring environmental sustainability, improving maternal health, and combating HIV/AIDS and other diseases. In the Youth Health Corps (YHC), for instance, sponsored youth raise awareness about preventing early pregnancies, drug and alcohol abuse, HIV and other sexually transmitted diseases during formal classroom and community presentations and one-to-one peer interaction. YHC efforts are helping to reduce the spread of dengue in sponsorship areas, curb adolescent pregnancy among sponsored youth, and increase young people's understanding of HIV infection. In 2012, 2,383 sponsored youth were trained as peer educators, who in turn discussed health

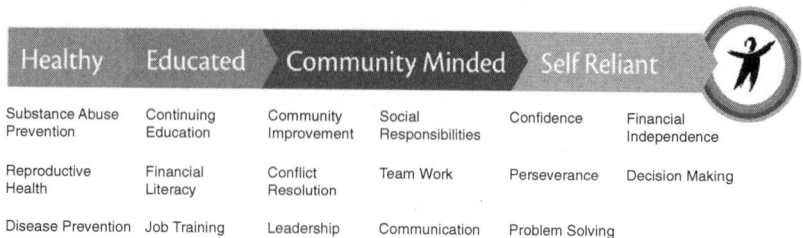

Healthy	Educated	Community Minded	Self Reliant		
Substance Abuse Prevention	Continuing Education	Community Improvement	Social Responsibilities	Confidence	Financial Independence
Reproductive Health	Financial Literacy	Conflict Resolution	Team Work	Perseverance	Decision Making
Disease Prevention	Job Training	Leadership	Communication	Problem Solving	

Figure 9.5   Focal points of CI's youth programmes

issues with more than 183,000 individuals in their communities. CI's 2012 Youth Health Corps Survey found that 93 per cent of the 2,383 peer educators could identify two ways of preventing the sexual transmission of HIV after a year of training, from a baseline of 47 per cent at start. Among that same group, 90 per cent indicated that they would use condoms during sexual intercourse, compared to a 62 per cent baseline at the beginning of the year.

'The importance of YHC is well-known in the community,' explained Jocelyn, a sponsored youth participant in Guatemala. 'We see adolescents who know their rights, respect their bodies and eradicate drug use and violence.' Through their participation in youth programme activities, sponsored youth are building self-esteem and core competencies they can use to become self-reliant, contributing members of society. Based on the 2012 exit survey CI gave to 11,853 graduating sponsored youth at its field locations, 84 per cent of those who participated in six or more youth activities during the year indicated that the programme motivated them to reach their goals, while 82 per cent believe they are now better able to solve problems in their communities due to programme participation. It is the observation of CI staff and others that the longer a student is sponsored, the more likely he or she is to exhibit more self-esteem, greater leadership skills, and a higher commitment to volunteerism.

Sponsored youth are also empowered to use their abilities for the greater good of their communities. This is evidenced in widespread participation in community-service projects using the Youth Empowerment Fund, an annual grant averaging US$20,000 that is awarded to Youth Councils at each of its programme offices. Sponsored youth have used the Fund to build classrooms in Guatemala so young children do not have to walk to school along dangerous roads. Among other projects, they have installed a well in Honduras to provide clean water to rural residents with no other safe option, and launched a community-garden project for impoverished families in Mexico who were struggling with hunger as a result of rising food costs.

In the derelict Kanyama compound outside Lusaka, Zambia, sponsored youth built a latrine at a public health clinic that serves hundreds of thousands of residents. Over 100 youth helped to build six modern, flushing toilets following a cholera outbreak. 'This is the first time the community has come together to build a structure at the clinic to assist patients,' the clinic's director remarked. 'And what makes it so special is that this structure has been built by youth who are fondly said to be future leaders. If this is the type of thinking the youth will bring when they become leaders, then we are assured a bright future.'

Conclusion: Future challenges

Children International places children at the centre of community and at the heart of collective action. Child sponsorship is an essential part of this process, and allows CI to invest in the long-term well-being and empowerment of impoverished people through community centres and dedicated staff that have become conduits for change in extremely disadvantaged communities. Direct, continuous support and provision of fundamental services can and does help children thrive from early childhood through late adolescence, while fostering hope and progress among families, community members and volunteers.

A key challenge going forward is to validate CI's internal evaluations and indicators of success through external study and peer review of CI's community-centre-based programme, measurable impacts on its population of children and youth, and ultimately on the communities served. Efforts to do so are already underway, and the results will dictate the continued evolution of CI's delivery systems and pro-grammes for beneficiaries. By extension, CI will be challenged to gain funding for programme improvements and programme expansion for areas of greatest impact. Further, boosting CI's 32 per cent youth-participation rate is essential if it hopes to truly assist in the transforma-tion of troubled communities.

Despite these ongoing challenges, it is evident for Children International that CS will remain key to funding, operation and expan-sion of community centres. Research will play an important role in linking the presence of community centres to broader community development. A 2013 assessment of CI's community centre services by Jim Copple – the founder of Strategic Applications International – noted that 'the synergies, the opportunities, and the outcomes are much more easily identified and have a larger community impact than most people realize. I fully suspect this is an untapped research area in the new collective impact themes in community development' (Copple, 2013).

Bibliography

Aguirre Group (2003) *Children International: An Assessment Report on Core Benefits to Sponsored Children* (Washington DC: Aguirre Group).

Christens, D. (2012) 'Targeting empowerment in community development: A community psychology approach to enhancing local power and well-being', *Community Development Journal*, 47, 4, 538–554.

Copple, J. (2013) Personal communication.

Krashen, S. (2011) 'Protecting students against the effects of poverty: Libraries', *New England Reading Association Journal*, 46, 2, 17–21.

McDonnell, W.A. and McDonnell (1994) 'Quality evaluation in the management of child sponsorship programmes', *Journal of Tropical Medicine and Hygiene*, 94, 4, 199–204.

UNICEF USA (2013) The child survival revolution 2.0, www.unicefusa.org/news/news-from-the-field/a-child-survival-revolution-fifth-birthday.html, date accessed 4 October 2013.

USAID (2012) 'Realizing the demographic opportunity', *Youth in Development*, USAID Policy – Youth (Washington, DC: USAID).

Van Eekelen, W. (2013) 'Revisiting child sponsorship programmes', *Development in Practice*, 23, 4, 468–480.

Wydick, B., Glewwe, P. and Rutledge, L. (2013) 'Does international child sponsorship work? A six-country study of impacts on adult life outcomes', *Journal of Political Economy*, 121, 2, 393–436.

10
Baptist World Aid: Transition to a Child Centred Community Development Approach

Anthony Sell and Felicity Wever

Introduction

Baptist World Aid Australia is a not-for-profit, non-governmental organization (NGO) tasked with linking Australian Baptist churches and their members to international community development, emergency relief and advocacy programmes. Founded in 1959 as the Australia Baptist World Aid and Relief Committee, the organization has undergone several name changes however is referred to in this chapter as Baptist World Aid Australia (BWAA). BWAA originally specialized in supporting refugees through the provision of disaster relief, financial assistance, food, shelter and clothing. In 1974, the child sponsorship (CS) programme 'Support an Orphan' (SAO) was founded by a group of volunteer women who sought to involve Baptists in the care of destitute children in developing countries. Consistent with the activities of many other CS organizations in the 1970s, the SAO programme included direct cash transfers to families and payment of children's educational and medical costs by individual sponsors.

Between 1974 and 2000, many children sponsored by BWAA were supported in hostels located close to education providers. In India for example, sponsored children from remote areas often lived in hostels or boarding facilities in the vicinity of government schools, thereby enabling them to continue their education. Here, the children were taught basic life skills including childcare, raising chickens, cooking and cleaning. During these early stages, the programme partnered with local churches including Baptist Unions in India, Sri Lanka, the Philippines, Bangladesh, Kenya, Uganda and Zambia. Sponsorship of orphans and destitute children was enthusiastically embraced by Baptist supporters and was central to the church's identity in Australia.

Figure 10.1 Historic BWAA school-based child sponsorship featured the support of children in hostels so they could attend schools

CS provided a predictable, increasing flow of income and anecdotal evidence suggested to staff that many children had benefited from long-term support. One historical document records that 'Although they had little, the children were safe and very happy with their secure shelter, care and food. Their eyes expressed their joy' (Semmens, 2006, p.7). In common with staff sentiment expressed in other CS INGOs that emphasized schooling, BWAA staff valued education as critical in empowering children to escape a life of poverty.

Despite the popularity of the SAO programme with sponsors, and decades of support by Baptist Churches in Australia, changing circumstances resulted in a robust debate about the future of the SAO programme in the 1990s. Opposition to traditional *CS* had begun to increase in the Australian aid sector, with critics suggesting that it resulted in manipulation by religious groups, children becoming vulnerable to exploitation, dependency being bred and many other issues inimical to the development of children and communities. In 2000, BWAA shifted away from a traditional welfare model of international aid to an integrated, community development approach. An increasing emphasis was placed on supporting sustainable, community-based organizations focused on agriculture, education, health and savings-based credit activities. Following strategic reflection on the organization's mandate, a decision was formally made to transform the Support an Orphan programme into the Share an Opportunity (SAO) programme. By 2005, the numbers of sponsored children peaked, with 12,041 children in seven countries being sponsored by approximately 8,500 donors. However, despite growing commitment to integrated, community development in various projects, many children were still receiving individual support in the SAO sponsorship programme. The reality of changing a decades-old system proved challenging.

By 2009, the SAO programme entered the first phase of its shift to a Child Centred Community Development (CCCD) approach. This transition phase was designed to continue to move the organization's CS activities from a partially reformed programme to a child rights-based approach, which pools funds to benefit all children in the community. For BWAA, the transition has been fraught with difficulty. At times it has been divisive, burdened with complexity and costly. However, the evolution of the programme has also been necessary, rewarding and ultimately beneficial to the children and their families impacted by CS. We hope that in sharing our journey, other small CS organizations contemplating a similar journey can learn from our mistakes and triumphs.

The rationale for a shift away from individual support

When the SAO programme began, the prevailing thinking within BWAA regarding child poverty was that education was the key to breaking the poverty cycle. Like many other sponsorship programmes, BWAA's most important goal was to ensure that children were educated to at least high school graduation level. This was achieved by paying school fees and associated costs for selected sponsored children and where necessary, funding hostel accommodation to enable their access to secondary schooling. Individual children were identified, documented, photographed, enlisted in the programme, matched to a sponsor and provided with tangible benefits. Over the course of each year, sponsors received pictures of their child, letters and progress reports.

The concept of formal education as an effective means of reducing poverty was first questioned when a child, who had been sponsored in Bangladesh, died directly after completing school at the age of 18. His mother was a widow who had seen the sponsorship programme as a way out of poverty. In her mind, her child's education would ultimately result in employment, care for her in old age and a more secure future for her son. After his death, the bereaved woman was left with little hope and no means to help herself. Without a son, her safety net and her solution to poverty were gone. Clearly, years of sponsorship had done nothing to improve this woman's capacity to help herself, or other members of the family. Although this represents just one anecdotal account, and other anecdotal accounts have been much more positive, it was helpful for programme staff in triggering discussion about impact and sustainability.

It became clear to programme staff that the SAO programme outcomes – such as improved and extended education through the provision of fees, uniforms and resources – were often not sustainable and that ensuring access to education for one member of a poor family was not consistently lifting families from poverty in the short or longer term. Questions arose among the programme's implementing partners about the policy of only allowing sponsorship of one child per family. According to these partners, this approach created jealousy and division in families and was not based on which child had the highest capacity to succeed in school. From a child welfare perspective, it made sense to subsidize the most vulnerable child's costs at a hostel, orphanage or school. However, from a perspective of sustained, longer-term impact on families, subsidizing the most talented individual with the highest chance of acquiring a good job seemed a preferable approach. In both cases helping only one individual allowed for exclusion of others. Further, as BWAA became more interested in evaluating the impact of interventions on families and communities, it became evident that individual child welfare and access to schooling had limited capacity to reduce poverty for entire families and communities. Anecdotal evidence left no doubt that some children benefited greatly from sponsorship, especially academically gifted ones, however it was equally apparent that many families remained poor, despite long years of educational assistance and cash transfers. Although individual support of children in a school setting did contribute to individual child welfare, and was popular with individual children and their families, it often did not contribute to poverty reduction in a wider sense.

During the mid-2000s, several of BWAA's partners successfully introduced community development activities into their sponsorship-funded programmes, combined with reduced educational handouts such as school fees, uniforms and basic school supplies. Community development activities were mostly contingent on income generation, health, and social mobilization activities, implemented through the formation and strengthening of self-help groups. As BWAA's implementing partners began to see success in the community development activities, a momentum towards expansion of these programme components grew. In some instances, community development activities were extended into communities where no children were being sponsored. These activities arose through contiguous expansion of specific programmes. Self-help groups were established in areas around the target communities, and began to grow as awareness of the benefits spread. These benefits included accumulated savings, small loans, reduced social isolation and increased social support. Implementing partners began to support grassroots groups, which were also exploring opportunities for alternative funding sources.

By 2007 rigorous BWAA monitoring and evaluation had led programme staff to the conclusion that pooled funding for community development was highly valued by communities and had significant impact on participating families. Consequently, some partners of BWAA expressed interest in only receiving community development funding and not expanding sponsorship which benefited individual children. This was extenuated by the fact that the provision of school fees and other welfare for sponsored children was perceived by project

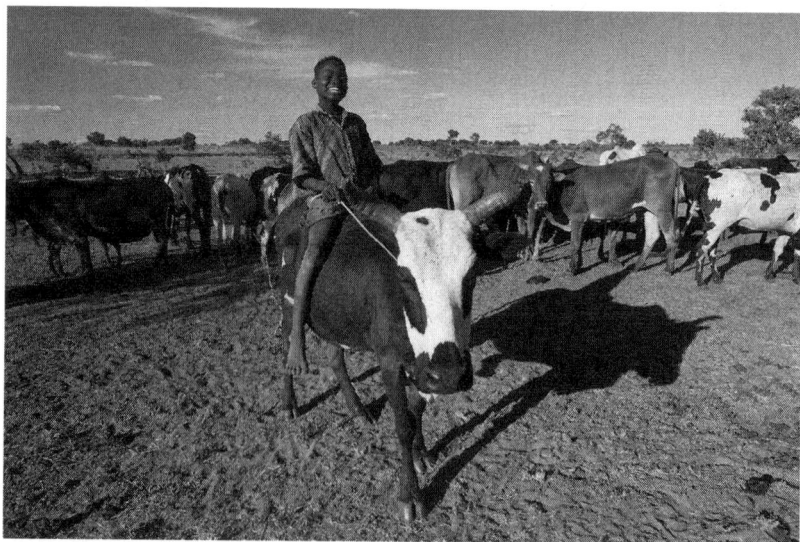

Figure 10.2 Child sponsorship for community development symbolized by a boy on a cow engaged in productive livelihood activities

staff to be yielding less motivation for beneficiaries than funding for community development activities with higher levels of participation. Thus child-focused spending in the form of educational reimbursement declined in the sponsorship programme and handouts to children and their families became largely tokenistic.

Despite the lack of a strategic framework integrating sponsorship with community development, BWAA and its partners continued to monitor and evaluate the shift towards community development and poverty reduction within its child sponsorship programme. However it had become evident some partners were achieving more effectiveness than others and direct handouts to beneficiaries or individual support continued in various forms. Recognizing that further progress was needed, BWAA staff began to assess current partner activities, past evaluations and best practice in the field of development. Assistance was sought from other development agencies and a consultant from World Vision International was appointed to support the reflection and planning process. The result was an adaptation of a Child-Centred Community Development programme grounded in child rights.

Child-centred community development

The principles of CCCD had been developed and implemented widely by Plan International and its partners well before BWAA considered it as a platform to shape its own CS programme. In 2003 Plan International adopted the Child-Centered Community Development Approach as a framework for its poverty reduction programming. This represented '...a significant departure from Plan's previous approach to development work, which was characterised by individual support to sponsored children, direct provision of goods and services, and a welfare-based model of NGO interventions' (Vijfeijken et al, 2011, p.5). Plan International (2010, p.17) describes CCCD as a rights-based approach that relies on the collective action of civil society to empower children, necessitating '...changes in policy, political will, public attitude and systemic change in service delivery...' CCCD has also been interpreted as involving 'child-centredness', 'child participation' and 'empowerment' evidenced in communities strong enough to claim their rights (Brouwer et al, 2009, p.4). Although BWAA is not large enough to influence government policy, political will or systemic change in service delivery, as Plan seeks to do, BWAA has adapted the CCCD approach to improve the well-being, rights and life opportunities of children in poor communities.

Currently, BWAA and its designated CCCD programme partners jointly develop project designs based on a situational assessment, thorough child rights mapping and detailed project framework. Programmes developed in this way seek to achieve change in four outcome areas, aligned with the UN Convention on the Rights of the Child (UNCRC) – survival, development, protection and participation. BWAA has adopted four key programming principles in the CCCD approach: equity and non-discrimination, sustainability, child participation and accountability (see Figure 10.3).

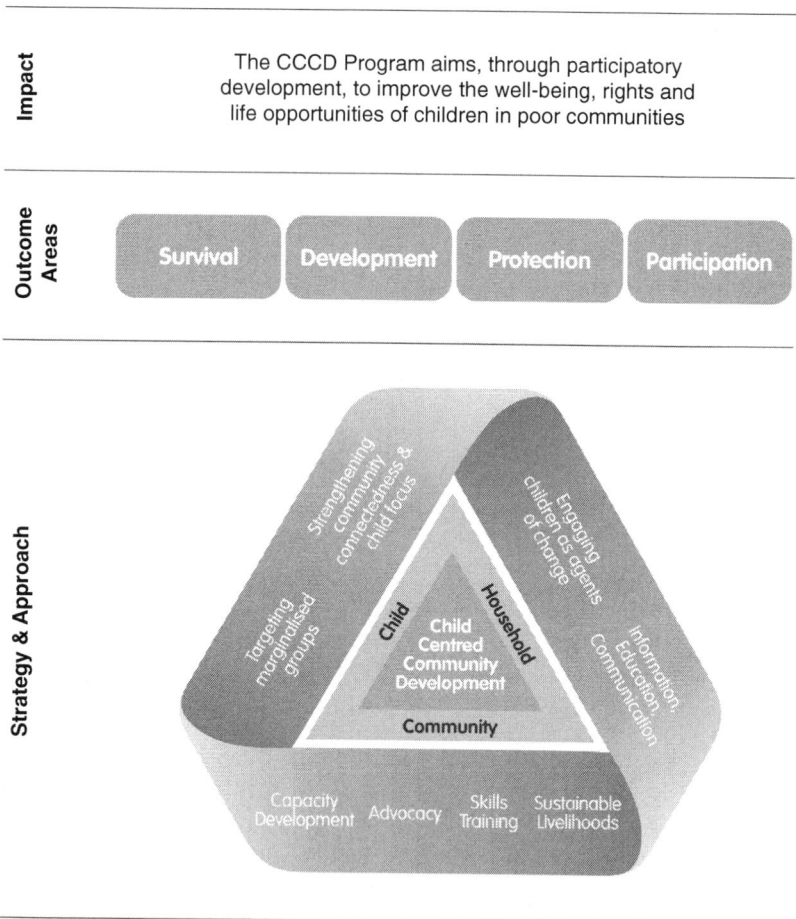

Figure 10.3   Baptist World Aid Australia's CCCD strategy and approach (BWAA, 2012, p.13)

The role of sponsored children and selection committees in CCCD

BWAA staff agreed that if sustainable long-term funding of CCCD projects was to be effectively linked to the CCCD Programme, Australian supporters would still need the motivation of being connected with a specific child who represented the positive impacts of the development project they supported. Sponsored children became known as Child Partners and act as community representatives for Australian supporters, communicating positive changes. Secondly, Child Partners actively participate in monitoring and evaluation. They may be asked to participate in reviews involving a random sample of children in the target area, with regular data collection providing a picture over time of changes in the lives of children in relation to baseline data. Unlike the earlier sponsorship programme, Child Partners do not receive any individual assistance or benefits. They do not attend additional project activities that are not open to other children. All children in the target area, regardless of their sponsorship status, theoretically have equal opportunity to be involved during project design, project activities, and monitoring and evaluation of the project.

Prior to the integration of CCCD principles in the sponsorship programme, sponsored children were selected by staff members of partner organizations, based on their own assessment of the child's needs. There was tendency to view children as passive beneficiaries while NGO staff were 'all powerful'. Now, Child Partners are selected by the community through a Community Child Partner Selection Committee, comprised of members representing community groups, parents, children and other stakeholders. Child Selection Criteria are negotiated between the implementing agency, BWAA and the local committee. Ideally, when a final list of children has been created and there is clarity about the roles and responsibilities of Child Partners, the collection of Child Partner details, including photographs and introductory letters, follows.

In many cases, the implementation of this process has been warmly welcomed and BWAA partners have developed ability to assist formation of effective committees that are not dominated by community members with vested interests. Evaluations of the Community Child Partner Selection Committees have found a diverse range of willing participants, including school teachers with strong community strengthening philosophies, parents who had come to understand the potential of the programme, community leaders who had chosen to volunteer their time, members of civil society groups that liked the consultation process, and children who often expressed their excitement at being involved in the project and with project staff.

A key role of the Community Child partner Selection Committee is to identify potential Child Partners who will be tangibly, though not exclusively, impacted by the project activities and who are able to articulate the benefits of the project to sponsors via letters, cards and creative forms of communication. Child Partners are selected from areas where activities will occur during the early stages of project implementation, and from groups that will have early involvement in the programme. Interviews conducted with Child Partners to understand their motivation for becoming involved in the programme, have revealed a common response. Children have seen participation as an opportunity to increase their knowledge and help them achieve ambitions to enter professions like school teaching, social or community work and community leadership – vocations associated with project activities. Through knowledge of other micro finance groups, the children were also often aware that savings or self-help groups could support people to become leaders and to achieve their ambitions for work and community involvement. Typically, children from lower castes or minority groups reported that their involvement as Child Partners offered an opportunity to acquire some status in the community. Children with natural leadership skills also saw the possibility to become part of something that was going to bring about change in their lives.

The formation of the Community Child Partner Selection Committee is important for several reasons. It empowers the community, assists the relationship-building process between the implementing organization and the community, improves community ownership of the project, reduces feelings of unfairness or jealously and respects the community's knowledge of the children and families.

In transitioning to its model of CCCD, BWAA recognized that sustained impact would require implementation of programmes in a much tighter geographic area, involving up to 800 children per project (clustered target areas) with corresponding resource and activity focus. Additionally, BWAA sought to deepen project impact through longer-term commitment evidenced in a nine-year commitment following the initial preparation phase, which would include community engagement, programme communication strategies and group formation.

Child rights

Like other organizations engaged in rights-based activity, BWAA recognizes that effective, responsive and accountable government systems are crucial for long-term, sustainable development in any country. Aligning project activity with relevant government policies and objectives is more likely to benefit children than well-intentioned assistance to individual children. Further, a rights-based approach to poverty reduction attempts to not only ensure that the duty bearer (such as local government) is held accountable, but that the duty bearer is also appropriately networked and assisted. This ensures that an effective delivery mechanism is established without creating a dependency on the project or NGO to provide these services.

Though education had historically been identified by BWAA as critical for children, and remained an important goal in the new CCCD approach, it was clear that the outcomes of the CCCD programme needed to be broadened to include a range of changes at child, household and community or institutional levels. Additionally, BWAA sought to include four key rights of children identified by the UNCRC: survival,

Figure 10.4 BWAA sponsorship emphasizes the importance of child rights and community capacity to protect and nurture children

development, protection and participation. Child survival was understood to mean that a child would have good quality healthcare, safe
drinking water, nutritious food, information and a safe environment.

Case study 1: Child survival

BWAA's CCCD partner in Zambia helped the community form a
Mother's Nutrition Group after community health workers trained by
the project found that 26 children in the village aged under five were
underweight. The mothers meet once a fortnight to participate in
cooking demonstrations. They contribute ingredients and are shown
how to use local foods to provide adequate nutrition for their children.
The mothers are also taught to recognize the warning signs of malnutrition. After the first month of meetings and training children were
returning to normal weight, and soon, mothers were expressing
confidence in their ability to prepare food for their young children,
and judge how often they needed to eat.

Child development would focus on supporting children to develop
to their full potential, facilitating opportunities for formal and non-
formal education that would help them develop their personality,
talents and abilities. This would include quality primary education, the
right to relax and play and a wide range of cultural and artistic recreational activities. However, emphasis shifted from directly assisting

	Child	Household	Community/Institutional
Child survival	Knowledge and attitudes towards health issues and prevention. Nutrition and weight. Prevalence of disease (diarrhoea, malaria, skin infection, respiratory infection). Immunisation.	Knowledge and attitudes towards health issues and prevention. Health seeking behaviour and prioritisation. Availability of nutrition, medicine, clothing, shelter. Household income. Food security and agricultural yield.	Availability of education on health issues and prevention. Access to health services. Healthy environment. Maternal and newborn mortality and health. Clean water and sanitation facilities. Health infrastructure (clinics and health workers). Access to immunisation. HIV/AIDS awareness and education (or reproductive health).

Figure 10.5 Child survival areas and changes at different levels

individual children to identifying reasons for non-enrolment and high drop-out rates, identifying duty bearers, and building capacity within the family and community to address the root causes of low formal educational attainment. Non-formal education opportunities have also been emphasized.

Case study 2: Child development

In Bangladesh, child clubs are formed. Child members are given the opportunity to take on club leadership. Children vote for leaders who then hold the position for a set period of time. This allows all children in the club to learn the responsibilities of different leadership positions; strengthen social cohesion; address power dynamics in the group; and gives the children greater ownership of leadership responsibilities. Children, adolescents and adults work together to identify the issues they care about, plan activities that will address the root causes, implement strategies and timelines.

For BWAA and its partners, protection would involve boys and girls being shielded from sexual abuse, trafficking and exploitation, the worst forms of labour, violence, living without a family, involvement in armed conflict, forced migration (refugee/IDP), negligence, discrimination and drug use. Child protection requires a whole of community commitment.

	Child	Household	Community/Institutional
Child development	Attendance at school. Literacy and numeracy. Test scores/achievement. Involvement in training. Involvement in recreation and cultural activities. Involvement in environmental sustainability activities. Household awareness of healthy homes.	Knowledge and attitudes towards education for boys and girls. Ability to send children to school and resource education. Literacy and numeracy.	Enrolment (primary, secondary). Gender parity. Completion and drop-out rates (primary, secondary). Class size and teacher to student ratios. Teacher absenteeism. Teacher qualification. Education infrastructure (early childhood, primary, secondary). Use of accessible language in school.

Figure 10.6 Child development areas and changes at different levels

Case study 3: Protection

In Malawi, our partner has worked with communities to establish Child Protection Committees consisting of up of ten members for each community, including a teacher, two children, a church leader, two out-of-school youth, one local police representative, one village leader and two community representatives (male and female). The role of the committee is to advocate for children's rights within the community, to encourage children to participate in project activities, and to report any issues shared by children to the committee including child labour and human rights abuses. Weekly meetings address children's welfare regarding food, family violence, child rights, and school attendance, creating a mechanism for open discussion and intervention.

For BWAA participation, commonly seen as an approach or methodology, would also be regarded as an outcome in and of itself as one of the key rights of children enshrined in the UNCRC. Programmes seek to ensure active, meaningful and productive participation by children in family and community life. This would be expressed in a range of ways, including forming associations to serve boys, girls and society and facilitating ways for children to express their opinions and have them valued.

	Child	Household	Community/Institutional
Child protection	Knowledge and awareness of child rights. Instance of claiming rights. Instance of reporting violations and use of policy and legal provisions. Suffering from abuse, neglect, exploitation and violence. Support at home, knowledge and access to safe places. Contact with supports and networks.	Knowledge and awareness of child rights, and/or how to get help and who is responsible. Instance of reporting violations and use of policy and legal provisions. Involvement in (and toleration of) forms of abuse, neglect, exploitation and violence. Contact with supports and networks, safe places for women and children.	Availability of social supports and networks. Development of partnerships around problems (such as child protection networks). Existence and use of policy and legal provisions, safeguards, monitoring mechanisms that can identify victims of violations. Involvement in (and toleration of) forms of abuse, neglect, exploitation and violence.

Figure 10.7   Child protection areas and changes at different levels

Case study 4: Participation

In Nepal, school students participated in child clubs to implement a 'Learning Without Fear' programme. The programme involved advocacy to teachers about the negative results of beating students with sticks. As a result, child-adult relationships in the schools improved, and children developed greater confidence to talk about issues that were important to them. In Cambodia, young people in a Savings Group established small enterprises and supported family members. They reported stronger relationships with each other and developed skills to work together, save, purchase study materials and assist family members.

The overall programme goal of BWAA has become one of improving the well-being, rights and life opportunities for boys and girls in poor communities. Although the translated testimony below is just one example, it serves to show how programming has moved beyond individual benefits to projects emphasizing empowerment and rights.

	Child	Household	Community/Institutional
Child participation	Active participation in school and community life. Active participation in family life and household. Involvement in activities and associations that serve their own interests. Sense of influence in decision-making that affects their lives. Access to information. Expression of opinions and feelings.	Opportunities for the involvement and influence of children in activities and decision-making that affects them. Attitudes and support towards children's participation in school and community life. Involvement of activities that serve the interests of children. Availability and provision of information.	Opportunities for the involvement and influence of children in school and community activities and decision-making. School and community plans and activities that serve the interests of children. Availability and provision of information.

Figure 10.8   Child participation areas and changes at different levels

Nepali project participant testimony

Namaste... Before the project began in my community I was extremely shy, and I used to hide whenever people came to visit my house. I was married at the age of 13, and was still very young and really scared to talk with others. My mother-in-law and my husband have not been kind to me and I was abused often. At first this made me scared to join the other mothers in the Self-Reliant Group (SRG), but after the staff member visited my house and invited me to join the Group, I began to change. Before the project I didn't know how to write names or how to greet others. In the past women were not allowed to speak with others and we used to speak very roughly.

Before I became a member of the SRG I didn't care whether my child went to school and had an education. Because I was illiterate, married young and missed out on an education, I did not see the importance for my child. Through the literacy campaign launched by the mothers' group, I came to understand the value of education, not only for my child, but for everyone. Now I can write my name and I know how to greet others.

I realize education is the most important tool for community development and it's necessary for every child, not just my child. In the past I didn't used to care about others' children, but now even though my children are grown up, when I see other children on the way to school, I take them with me to make sure they are safe and they attend.

Through my participation in the mother's group and SRG I have helped look after the kitchen garden in the school, built fences for safety of the children, learned how to cook and look after the children better and always make sure children have an education and are valued.

My only wish is that I knew about a project like this before I got married, and my life would be different. I don't want any girl to have the problems I had. The change in our community means a girl can have education first and then get married.

Impact of the transition on partners

In 2009 when the decision was made to transition the SAO sponsorship programme to the CCCD approach the transition strategy sought to phase out direct handouts and educational assistance within a three to five year period, and commence a number of new programmes with new and existing implementing partner agencies. The new programmes would have a strong assessment and design phase, ensuring active participation by the community, including children and youth, to identify the key challenges for children and contextually appropriate responses. It was understood by BWAA that this would mean a gradual reduction in child partner numbers, as children graduating from the old sponsorship programme would not be replaced. A directive was given to existing partners by BWAA to not select any new children for sponsorship from old project areas that were operating under the pre-existing model.

Some BWAA partners strongly disagreed with the new approach, arguing that without the incentive of handouts, children and families would not stay in any programme. This belief came from direct experience with communities that had a definite welfare dependency and were expressing great resistance to the removal of the handouts. Furthermore, these communities and families were angry that the programme was to be phased out over the next three to five years. Clearly, there was an expectation that the programme would be provided indefinitely, a view that was at times reinforced by poor communication of time frames during the initial engagement of those communities and the fact that BWAA projects had historically remained in communities for extensive periods of time.

BWAA was aware that, for existing partners, transitioning the sponsorship strategy away from individual support to CCCD underpinned by rights-based approaches would be difficult. All previous 'SAO' partners were expected to transition to the new model over three-to-five years, drop welfare components of project activity as soon as possible and cease provision of handouts or designated gifts and opportunities. The shift represented enormous changes for partners who were required, in some cases, to radically change field operations, levels of community engagement, commitment to new project activity and its associated planning and design, donor relations, governance, effectiveness and efficiency and general viability.

BWAA developed a rigorous partner selection and orientation process. Over the course of transition, eight new partners were selected from six countries. Rather than select partners that were aligned in values and area of geographic interest, emphasis was placed on ability to design and deliver projects according to the CCCD Project Framework which provided a much clearer set of expectations and guidelines for partners and also provided a Monitoring, Evaluation and Learning Framework (MELF) to improve the way in which results were measured across the programme, and incorporate a strong focus on learning to improve effectiveness. Furthermore BWAA sought to build a community of practice through bi-annual partner forums and exposure visits that bought implementers from around the world together and expose them to each other's work.

BWAA also prioritized organizations with demonstrated ability for community participation, including proven community entry and mobilization skills using participatory approaches, skilled staff, strong levels of prior community engagement and a track record of experience in rights-based approaches. This was a consistent point of negotiation as such expectations had never before been stipulated. The notion of 'implementing' partner and 'funding' partner was changing and a new form of joint partnership was being forged, at times painfully. These expectations had been made clear to all CCCD partners prior to signing up, but for some, the initial experience was that BWAA was 'forcing' their own processes and systems upon partners, creating tensions that were often associated with paternalism.

For one development agency in Nepal, the heavy requirements for active participation by the community and children in particular, had an extremely rewarding outcome. In responding to a debriefing question about the highly participatory design process integral to CCCD, one staff member said: 'I was not sure about this type of participation, asking so much before the project even begun...now I realize we have never really done development like this—it is a big improvement from simply coming and saying "this is what we are going to do."' However, another agency in South East Asia withdrew, realizing that the programme components required to address gaps in children's rights were beyond their mandate, expertise and level of staffing.

Impact of the transition on BWAA

Like many organizations that have tried to transition their model of sponsorship, BWAA found it difficult to shift CS as individual support, to CS for community development and later to pooled sponsorship for CCCD. Many sponsors still expected the majority of their funds to benefit an individual and, from a marketing perspective, the sponsorship product was deeply entrenched into the Australian psyche. Understandably, marketing staff were concerned that the loss of a tangible 'hook' that a child profile created would result in the failure of a very important and successful fundraising mechanism. Meanwhile, programme staff wanted to increase sustainable outcomes in the field, leading to poverty reduction. Wanting to enhance the dignity and rights of children, they questioned whether sponsorship and sponsorship language, in whatever form, was a new form of colonialism, which positioned Australian sponsors as the saviour of people living in poverty. This questioning included whether sponsorship was exploitative in its use of children for fundraising purposes.

These very real concerns of programme staff contrasted sharply with those of marketing staff, who worried that rapid change in CS interventions and rapid change in CS fundraising would lead to a further decline in a beleaguered revenue stream. Aware of their concerns, BWAA was determined to press forward, hoping that clear communication with BWAA donors, including many long-term, faithful supporters, would be enough to avoid a backlash. In an attempt to re-educate donors and reinforce the change in programming, the term 'sponsorship' was dropped from the fundraising product, which became the 'SAO Program'. Children linked to sponsors were termed 'Child Partners' rather than 'sponsor children'. Unfortunately, after a 12-month period, it was deemed that BWAA was losing traction in the sponsorship market and was struggling to engage new sponsors. Not being a market leader, BWAA was also vulnerable to competition from other agencies that were using CS language and messaging more strongly, and thereby connecting with people's paradigms about helping children in poverty. The result was a difficult reappraisal of BWAA's idealistic stance.

Despite its idealism, BWAA had to accept that the notion of CS was deeply entrenched in the Australian psyche. For potential supporters, a donor proposition involving CS immediately triggered an understanding of what was required of them without further explanation (a monthly gift that was used to assist a child). It appeared that trying to explain the way that CCCD worked confused donors. Nevertheless, BWAA surveyed its supporters and found that a large proportion of the donor base was aware that CS programmes no longer gave money directly to children but rather allocated funds for community-based projects that assisted the child, their family and the wider community. A new communication strategy was needed that would reinforce this awareness while educating donors about the full realities and merits of a rights-based CCCD approach over time.

The lack of traction of new sponsorship language came at a difficult time. For a number of years prior to the transition of the sponsorship programme, there was unwillingness within BWAA to continue expanding programmes by increasing the numbers of sponsored children. The research, development and adoption phase for CCCD across the agency took several years and during this period sponsored child numbers stagnated for a variety of reasons. By 2009 and 2010 BWAA had communicated to partners that direct benefits to newly sponsored children would not be funded, essentially meaning that new children could not be selected until the CCCD programmes were up and running. Many of the long-running programmes experienced natural attrition as children dropped out, reached 18 years of age or graduated from school. These children were not replaced in the existing programmes that were preparing for closure during the long process of adopting a CCCD approach to programming.

As well as natural attrition and delays in replacement, the closure of two major, long-term partners had accelerated the reduction in sponsored child numbers. Further, a programme in Bangladesh, which was due to phase out, reached its natural conclusion. The overall result of all the closures and phase outs was the loss of approximately 4,500 children from the 12,041 sponsored children recorded at the start of the transition. The financial stability of the agency, reliant on CS and other sponsor contributions for the bulk of its income, was threatened as the number of children's profiles dwindled and replacement sponsor children could not be provided to donors to secure their continued support. Loss of income from the closure of the two partners equated to over 10 per cent of annual sponsorship income, but the overall loss of the 4,500 sponsored children was equivalent to over a third of sponsorship income.

Overall, BWAA leadership and programming staff are supportive of the CCCD approach and confident that the transition has strengthened outcomes for children and reinvigorated the sponsorship programme. However there is an acknowledgement that the transition has at times bought the agency to points of great difficulty.

Impact of the transition on sponsors

At face value, little had changed for donors by the late 2010. Children were still sponsored, documented, photographed and encouraged to write to their sponsors. Despite a brief exploration of moving away from traditional sponsorship language, marketing staff at BWAA in Australia still used the language of individual sponsorship and provided an individual child focus. However, even though there was increasing communication explaining the shift to poverty reduction through community development, some donors found it confusing that the funds they had given to help their sponsored child were being used for community development activities, particularly in situations where the benefits to individuals were less tangible. Some sponsors were very committed to their individual child. They valued being able to make a difference in the life of one individual. For them the value proposition seemed diluted by having the funds benefit the whole community. Many had to make a decision to either migrate to another sponsorship organization that maintained a traditional one-to-one approach or remain with BWAA.

Impact on beneficiaries and communities of the transition

Between 2000 and 2009 BWAA was forced to choose new partners and transition out of some programmes. This required an end to sponsorship in some areas. For those families and children who gradually lost ongoing support this must have been very difficult indeed. For some parents and children who continued to benefit from sponsorship, but were now receiving fewer handouts or cash transfers, the slow change prior to the introduction of CCCD in 2009 led sometimes to accusations that project staff were 'eating their money'. Beneficiaries pushed back against the decision to reduce handouts. At times children were removed from programmes, families threatened to not cooperate with ongoing activities and false scandals about the implementing partners were created. Rumours in some communities began to spread, claiming that the programme was a scam and the organization would steal money accumulated by savings groups. The implementing partners – already overwhelmed with the responsibilities of change management – felt such negative reaction very strongly. Where this occurred field staff had to work hard to calm communities and explain the logic of the changes while still coming to terms with the philosophical reasoning of the shift themselves. Some expressed resentment about the change, even though they could see the long-term impact of dependencies created by traditional welfare activities.

Unfortunately, the pre-CCCD programme strategy was not clearly designed around the impact on children, and the approach and its benefits to children were not clearly articulated to sponsored families. As a result, the linkages between community development activities and sponsorship were perceived as weak and problematic. To complicate matters, sponsorship was far from uniform across programme locations. Some partners still emphasized individual support while others had moved to pooling funds for development activities. In hindsight, the uneven push towards CS for community development initiatives between 2000 and 2009 would have been better served with a coherent approach, initiated over several years, with high levels of communication between BWAA, partners and beneficiaries in CS programmes.

Conclusion

After three years, the transition at BWAA to a child-centred development agency continues. By the end of 2012, the CCCD Programme was operating through 11 partner agencies (including one in preparation stage) across Africa, South and South East Asia. Transitioning from CS for individual child and family support, to CS for CCCD has been a challenging process for all and complicated by a lack of readily accessible guidance for small CS NGOs seeking radical change to sponsorship programming. Nonetheless, it was necessary. Aware that much of this chapter has emphasized the journey of BWAA, rather than the journey of child partners, it is fitting to conclude with an anecdote and a short testimony. As BWAA continues to gather evidence about the impact of the CCCD approach, such stories have reinforced the sense that the pain in the transition has been justified. Referring to the emphasis on child rights in CCCD, a young person wrote recently in Malawi,

> Before the CCCD project, I used to be abused and be given a heavy workload above my age. I did not realize that I had the right to speak out against that. I didn't realize it was wrong, and so I didn't say anything. After joining the project, I learned a lot about child rights and now I am able to object when someone gives me a heavy workload or abuses me physically. It wasn't easy to speak out, and since I was young I never said anything because it was my mother giving me a heavy workload. After joining the project, I explained things to her and she finally understood that I was young and needed a smaller workload.

It was always anticipated that changing the public perception of 'sponsorship' would be a significant challenge. BWAA staff thought that the CCCD approach included sufficient checks and balances, in the form of programming imperatives, to ensure that children and communities would understand what the programme would and would not provide (that is opportunities, not things), and to ensure that the notion of Child Partners as representatives of the community, which would ultimately benefit from the programme, rather than direct recipients. However, this issue has not been so simple to address and the challenge to shift the paradigms of donors, implementing partners and communities is an ongoing one.

Many of BWAA's partners avoid using the terminology of child sponsorship in the field because of the impact it will have on their communication strategies. The mere fact that children still have to provide written correspondence, a photo and profile information often means that families become suspicious that the new CCCD project in their community is really a traditional sponsorship project with individual benefits, and that the field workers are stealing the handout money. One of the most significant factors affecting the transition to a new model is the pace of paradigm shifts between Australian supporters and the realities in the field. CS is a deeply entrenched concept in many developing and donor countries.

The good news for BWAA is that surveys of supporters are showing a continuing trend of recognition that their sponsorship does not entail direct welfare inputs to the Child Partners. Although donor understanding of the CCCD approach lags behind the reality of programmes, communication strategies continue to reinforce the importance of whole of community benefit and child rights outcomes. Though the journey from individual child benefits to community development and child rights informed CCCD has been difficult, the result will ultimately be better educated supporters, effective implementing partners, and much greater potential for poverty reduction that sustainably impacts children.

Bibliography

Brouwer, H., de Boer, F., van Uffelen, G. and Wigboldus, S. (2009) 'Strategic evaluation study on child-centred community development: Synthesis report', http://edepot.wur.nl/247880, date accessed 29 September 2013.

BWAA (2012) *Sharing Skills and Knowledge: Effective Child Centred Community Development Implementation through Learning* (Sydney: BWAA).

Plan International (2010) *Promoting Child Rights to End Child Poverty: Achieving Lasting Change through Child-Centred Community Development* (Woking, Surrey, UK: Plan Limited).

Semmens, T. (2006) *Continuing the Call: History of Baptist World Aid Australia 1984–2004*, Internal BWAA publication (Sydney: BWAA).

Vijfeijken, T.B., Gneiting, U. and Schmitz, H.P. (2011) *How Does CCCD Affect Program Effectiveness and Sustainability? A Meta Review of Plan's Evaluations*, Transnational NGO Initiative, Moynihan Institute of Global Affairs, http://www.maxwell.syr.edu/moynihan/tngo/Publications/, date accessed 29 February 2012.

11
Through the Eyes of the Sponsored

Brad Watson and Anthony Ware

Child sponsorship (CS) international non-governmental organizations (INGOs) have a long history of using individual change stories in their marketing materials. However, a feature of the ongoing debate over the merits of CS-funded programmes is the reality that those parts of the discussion accessible in published literature have often been dominated by Northern journalists, aid industry insiders and academics. Often, the perspectives and lived experiences of those who are, or who have been sponsored in the South, have been marginalized and pushed to the periphery of discussion by experts in their haste to pass judgment on the legitimacy of CS-funded interventions. Yet, of all the perspectives on CS one might explore, perhaps one we should consider to be equally significant, is that of sponsored children and previously sponsored adults. The lived experience of those who grew up within a CS scheme, their own analysis of that experience, and the impact the experience has had on their lives, is an important set of perspectives to capture in a volume of this nature.

Unfortunately, any attempt to provide a cohesive, representative sample of sponsored child experience and perspective presents an insurmountable task. It is impossible to accurately reflect the incredible diversity of experiences that millions of children have had, across hundreds of countries, through numerous CS INGOs. Conceding this reality, the following chapter presents seven short contributions from individuals who participated as beneficiaries in an assortment of CS schemes. Collectively, they represent a small range of positive change stories. They are not in any way representative of every child's experience, or even of the average sponsored child. Rather, because they come from individuals of differing ages, socio-economic background and education levels, they are best seen as anecdotal, diverse, and illustrative of the positive impact CS can have in at least some, if not a vast majority of cases. Notably, the voices of children who have been superficially impacted or perhaps even negatively impacted by sponsorship are conspicuously absent below.

The Third Girl Child

by Sadhna (sponsored in a World Vision Area Development Program)

Hello friends, my name is Sadhna. I am 15 years old and I am in tenth grade. I live with my family in South Delhi in a resettlement colony. I have two elder sisters and two younger brothers.

I am the third girl child. My mother told me that when I was born it was one of the saddest days for my grandparents and for our relatives. They cursed my mother for giving birth to a daughter for the third time and they did not allow my vaccination. It hurts growing up where your presence is neglected and ignored. It is painful when your family members taunt you for being a girl. There was a time when I went into a shell of loneliness.

When I was eight years old, I was enrolled in World Vision's sponsorship programme. Today, I am 15 years old. This journey of seven years has been very beautiful and I have understood the definition of sponsorship, which means to share love and to accept someone else as your own. As time passed I made new friends within the sponsorship programme, but the turning point in my life was when I was called for a 'child journalism' workshop.

Twenty children were selected out of 40 to 50 for further training and I was one of them. I participated whole-heartedly in the workshop and learnt a lot, not only about journalism but also about enhancing our personalities. Now I have a dream for a new life. My ambition is to be a journalist or a TV reporter. I am just waiting to complete my school, so I can pursue my dream. Today, I have left all my sorrows somewhere behind and it is a time when I am happy about being a girl.

I am very active in my school academic and cultural activities. Now I am able to understand my lessons very well. My teachers appreciate my understanding and my ability to ask the right questions. My friends in school come to me for my advice and trust me. If they are undergoing any issue, especially gender discrimination,

I counsel them and their parents or guardians. Today I am a member of the youth club.

My parents support me and love me. They played the most important role in my success by allowing me to participate in World Vision's programmes. The biggest day of my life was when my father said, 'I am proud of you – I am proud of you being my girl, my daughter. If I knew girls could be like you I would have never desired for a boy.' He also said, 'Today people and children know me by your name. I am happy and proud to be your father.'

I thank God and World Vision for making me what I am today; for being my guide, my supporter and my teacher. I want to tell everybody: stop discriminating, start loving, start accepting and believing, only then will we have a beautiful world where we can live. Have faith in God and in yourself and never miss any opportunity. You never know when an opportunity can work magic in your life.

I feel very good about coming into sponsorship because, whoever my sponsor is, I have not met them but I know that they love me very much. Just like how I have never seen God but God helps me – so also my sponsors help me a lot. I have not received letters from them but every year I have sent them an APR (Annual Progress Report) and photos. I also do drawings for them with my own hands and write messages for them. I feel very happy with this.

I am confused about this matter: they don't know me and have not met me, but for seven years they have been with me and have helped me and my community. I feel very good when sponsors send the children letters and photos. But I also feel a little sad that I have not met my sponsor. I really wish to meet them.

World Vision has helped many people in my community: they helped with educational support, provided notebooks and books, helped widows, provided water filters for clean and pure water, and gave mosquito nets to protect us during summer.

World Vision helps everybody, not just sponsored children. They give everyone equal opportunities. They conduct life school for transformational development (LSTD) through which the children receive a good education. They have also started youth clubs and children's clubs, through which much change has happened.

The best thing is that through children's clubs and youth clubs we discuss the issues in our society and we awaken people – raise awareness – through plays. We conduct big programmes on these issues. We ourselves, the children, call police officers and people from different organizations and government officers to make them listen to our voice.

There are many changes I have seen in the lives of the children in my community. Arjun would not go to school and would take tobacco and sniff drugs. He used to steal and gamble. Today, he and his three friends run the Little Champ Children's Club. In his club, there are 21 children, who were once caught in such habits but today they have changed and are going towards a better life.

Maya was a girl with no identity. She came from a very traditional family and used to be sick, frequently experiencing fits. So, she was very weak, physically and mentally. Through the letters from her sponsors, and with the counselling, direction and love from World Vision, Maya is very happy today. She is also very good in her studies.

Poor children, orphaned children and children who have fallen into bad habits and are not in school were provided education as a result of help through World Vision's youth clubs. Today, four out of the 20 children have obtained admission in regular schools. The remaining children will also get admission in July.

Change has come in the lives of these children. Today, they dream of a beautiful tomorrow. Today, they know what they want to become. For me:

Tomorrow was dark under the shadows of sadness,
suddenly a silver light shone through the darkness.
Someone held my hand; I held it tight and just followed the light

I entered a new world, a world which is my today;
full of joy and happiness, sorrow and darkness all washed away,
A new life has come, where there is no sorrow or sadness; just hope and dreams to live and win.

With thanks to Amrita Upali Singh, Community Development Coordinator, South Delhi Area Development Program for facilitating this story, and to Joan Nirupa, World Vision India, for translating Sadhna's work into English.

Figure 11.1   Sadhna
Sadhna dreams of becoming a journalist or TV presenter, and has participated in World Vision child journalism workshops.

Grateful I Am

by Lina Marcela Trujillo (formerly sponsored in a SOS Children's Village)

My name is Lina and I would like to tell you a bit about my life: about growing up in SOS Children's Village, and how my sponsors have made me extremely happy.

I lived in the Municipal district of Valle de San Juan, in the Tolima district in Colombia. I lived there very happily with my parents and my five brothers and sisters. My Mama loved us a lot. I remember that we were always playing and the big children looked after the smaller ones.

Mother died when I was six. Father could not cope and did not have the financial means, so he abandoned us. I was really scared because I did not know what would happen. After the funeral, one of our aunts took my sisters and me to SOS Children's Village Ibagué, near where we lived. She did not have enough money to take care of us all.

I clearly remember the day when I arrived. It was a lovely place with 16 houses all near each other, and nine children living in every house. They were looked after by a woman, many children called her 'Mother'. When I saw so many boys and girls, I felt calm. I understood that I was not the only one who had lost her parents.

They organized a welcome party with balloons and lots of delicious food. I then met the other children who would become my brothers and sisters: Liliana, Diego, Mauricio, José, Ovidio and Paula.

I felt really calm when Nohelia hugged me. She looked after us lovingly, waiting for us when we came home from school. I will never forget those moments. Although we had no blood ties, we formed a loving bond that still unites us. Nohelia became our guardian angel, a blessing and the greatest inspiration to start new adventures. She taught us respect and a passion for life, and reminded us to value every little thing that God gives us daily.

I remember the first time Nohelia told us about the sponsors. To be honest, because we were so small, we did not really understand. However, I found it amazing that people who lived far away thought about me, and wanted to help me.

It was a great joy to get wonderful presents such as Christmas and birthday cards with my name written in them. It made me feel valued and important! Even though they were written in another language, I understood that when things are heart-felt, the universal language of love touches us all. Sponsors from far away gave me not only affection but also the chance to go to school, to have a family, to play and to do many things that I would not have been able to do. When I was about 11 years old I joined a children's choir, took dance lessons, art classes and I learned how to play the guitar. The money gifts the sponsors sent were kept in a bank account until I was bigger.

Suddenly, one day I started getting photographs and letters addressed to me! I enjoyed seeing their beautiful traditional dresses. I learnt that there were seasons in other countries and the weather was not always like it was here in Colombia. I found their way of dressing and their dances strange! I wanted to write to them about my own experiences, tell them about my daily life, thank them for all the good things they were doing for me. I knew that I was only able to go to school, eat and have a happy life thanks to their generosity and love.

When I was around 15 years old I had a phase where I found it hard to follow the rules and keep the agreements I had made. My SOS mother, Nohelia, talked to me and we agreed that it might be better if I spent some time with my aunt. I was not too sure, but agreed to go and I spent one year and three months with my aunt.

I began to miss the place where I had grown up: my brothers and sisters, my family, my mother and my home were all there. It was a difficult time for me. I also thought about all my plans, those that I had told my sponsors, and I felt I was going to let them down.

I decided to return, to change, to improve, and to understand that what they asked me to do was for my own good because they wanted me to be happy. I realized that I had a great path ahead of me, and the chance to write a different story for me and my brothers and sisters.

When I was 18, I started on my path to independence. This is when most of us begin to live outside the Children's Village. It was hard at first. I was not sure what I wanted to do. Life can be quite hard, especially alone and living outside the SOS Children's Village. I then met a great friend called Adriana; she and her family helped me all the time. But I can also tell you that the thought of Nohelia fed my soul daily. I knew she would never abandon me, she has always been there for me and I can rely on her.

When I was 19, I was interested in starting a vocational training course at SENA (National Learning Services of Colombia). I studied to be a beautician because it is a good way to earn a living and I can improve people's mental and physical health. I got a lot of pleasure from studying this, but I was always worried because I knew it was very difficult to find a good job in Ibagué. This is why I thought about setting up my own business.

When I told the youth worker in the SOS village about my plans, she said I could open my business with money that had been saved for me from my sponsors. I was so excited when I realized my sponsors had been so generous and that my dream could come true!

I wrote a project proposal and worked out the costs. Now I am my own boss and I am independent. I sell Colombian artifacts to tourists, made from recycled materials, so it is good for the environment. For example, I sell 'Manillas', bracelets designed with different textures and colors; and 'Mochilas' – hand-woven bags that are popular not only in Colombia but also abroad. I also make small bamboo souvenirs.

I have not been lucky enough to personally meet my sponsors, but I do not lose hope that I will one day. I want to see them, and to say thank you with a smile, a hug and thousands of words. I want to let them know how grateful I am for all the good they have done. May God bless them!

With thanks to Ms. Julia Braunegg, Assistant to Head of International Donor Services, SOS Kinderdörfer, for facilitating this story.

Figure 11.2   Lina
Lina sells Colombian artefacts and woven products to earn a living. She is pictured displaying some of the items sold in her store.

My SAO Life

by Nerissa P. Soledad (formerly sponsored by Baptist World Aid)

'God is good all the time and all the time God is good'. This will always be my declaration of thanksgiving to the Lord for his goodness even though life in the Philippines was not easy for us in 1981. There were six children in the family and I was the second child and only girl. We lived in an urban area in the western part of the Visayas. My mother was a Catholic however my father had no religion.

Our home was made up of light materials, coco lumber as wall, palm thatch roof, and sand as floor. If it rained, it was also raining inside because our roof was dilapidated. When my father had no job or contract for carpentry works, my mother and I accepted laundry from other people in exchange for just enough money to buy our food, rice, vegetables and fish. I would often assist my mother rinse and dry the clothes. She suffered from asthma and I was happy to help.

I was only six years old when I entered the Baptist Australia Share An Opportunity Sponsorship programme, as a first grader in my elementary school. Because of the various activities, I was able to overcome my shyness and actively become involved. I received monthly financial assistance and this was used for my school uniform, school supplies and other needs. There were also instances that we were given items like blankets, mosquito nets and some basic grocery items through the sponsorship. We also had annual medical and dental checkups. At first we were required to go to church but later on it was my own free will to attend. It has reaped its reward because through it I became a faithful Christian and have joyfully served the Lord until this time. I developed a relationship with the Lord in which I truly enjoy.

When I was yet a child, I would always witness the hardships in our daily lives and this compelled me to strive to finish my studies and to have a regular job. I believed that only education could uplift our economic situation, through hard work and the financial assistance I received monthly from my sponsor, Kylie Brown. She supported me for 11 years of school and four years accounting course. I successfully graduated from College in April 1995, with a degree in Accountancy. My first dream was to become a Teacher but because of financial incapacity I wasn't able to pursue this course.

By the grace of God, I got a job as a bookkeeper in a local newspaper two months after I graduated from College. My sponsorship had a ripple effect on myself and my family, because I was able to support my siblings' schooling needs as well as needs in my family. I was so happy when our house was repaired through my salary. I was also able to support the medicine my asthmatic mother needed. I could sense the changes in the way they treated me. They would often wait for my decision in some situations, and because I am the only one who earns regularly, they would always depend on me for their daily need.

In September 1999 I got the opportunity to visit Australia to promote the sponsorship programme, during the 25th anniversary. More than 300 Australian friends committed to sponsor a child.

And the most wonderful thing that happened was, my sponsor Kylie decided to support again another child after seeing the result of her help to me.

In 2000 I was assigned as a Holistic Development Facilitator, working directly with children and parents in the community. I was also placed in charge of sponsorship in our area. This was truly very meaningful to me, being a former sponsored child. One of my assigned tasks has been to distribute financial support to the children, and to facilitate letter writing. The first time I did this I got so emotional, because I could relate to the joy of the children when they receive their support and wrote letters to their sponsor. Seeing them transformed and living a fulfilled life is a great accomplishment for me. My dream and utmost desire for them is to see them finish their education and have a regular job to sustain their daily needs.

The present programme focuses mainly in empowering children. We run various activities focusing on things like values formation, character building, advocacy on environmental protection, personal hygiene and value of savings. In my own assessment, this is truly beneficial to them. The participation of the children is sincere and they signify that they are thankful to be a part of the programme and they know from the very start they do not get monetary assistance. With the old programme, which was more welfare, their involvement sometimes was anchored on what they can get in terms of monetary handout. But right now, I can actually discern that their participation is purely because they want to become developed individuals and not because they can get something.

I am now a mother of five children, and the wife of a Pastor. Furthermore, I am a Holistic Development Facilitator working directly with the children. I am a living testimony that indeed sponsorship can make a great difference in the life of a child. Just like the Lord Jesus who placed much value in children, it is always my prayer that the Lord will use me as His instrument in touching the lives of the children under my care and continue on making a difference in their lives which will eventually impact their family and the whole community as well. To God be the Glory!

With thanks to Anthony Sell, Director of International Program, Baptist World Aid Australia, for facilitating this story.

My Story

by V. Masilamani (formerly sponsored by Compassion International)

I, V. Masilamani, was born on 5th January, 1975 in a village near Madurai city in Tamil Nadu, India. My parents were proud to have a son and the meaning of my name is 'faultless gem'. My sister's name is Nallathai, meaning 'good mother'. My father only studied to fourth grade, and my mother did not go to school at all. They were farmers and worked together on a small 1.5 acre plot. For them farming was like gambling. Success was largely dependent on rainfall, which is a random process. My parents also owned some buffalos whose milk was our other source of income. Of eight children born to my parents, only my sister and I survived, by God's grace.

There was a Church of South India primary school in our village, started by American missionaries in 1887. Due to our poor economic situation and the lesser importance placed on girls' education at that time, my parents did not send my sister. Instead, Nallathai looked after the buffalos from the time she was just seven years old. By God's grace, I studied. After my fifth grade, I was asked to look after our buffalos and my sister was sent to help my mother as an agriculture laborer.

When school reopened in June 1980, after summer holidays, all my friends headed to a high school about three kilometers from our village, but I continued to go behind the buffalos. One fine day, a month after school reopened, my primary school teacher came to our house and fought with my father. He said that if my father refused to send me to school, my teacher will consider me as his own child and give me an education. By God's grace, my father enrolled me in high school after that intervention by my teacher.

Every day I walked to school. A month after I was admitted, my primary teacher told my father about a Compassion project in a small town called Batlagundu, about 50 kilometers away. Being the only son, my mother refused to send me. She was afraid. However, my teachers convinced my parents. I registered for sponsorship along with many others in 1986. There were two hostels in the same campus; one was a World Vision project, the other a paying hostel. Students in the fee-paying hostel needed to pay Rs.100 per month (approximately USD6.5 at that time). Those of us who registered for sponsorship still needed to pay half of this, until we received sponsorship. By God's grace, I was sponsored the next year by Mr. MacClanakhan from the USA, who helped me for two years. From my village alone, five students received sponsorship, and a Compassion home, the Martin Memorial Children's Home, was started in Batlagundu.

Our first warden was Mr. Rathnakumar, a science teacher. Every day we had morning and evening prayers and he delivered the word of God powerfully through songs and stories. We all really enjoyed this, and this prayer time experience has been so useful till today. I was thrilled to have good food in the hostel. In my village, our regular food was made from cooked ragi seeds. Only occasionally did we eat rice at home, and we could only afford meat during festivals. But in the Compassion home, we ate rice every day, and non-vegetarian at least once a week.

Because we were sponsored, we were given two sets of school uniform, one set of color dress, textbooks and notebooks, as well as soap, oil, et cetera every year. My parents were so happy. On the education side, since our hostel was on the school campus, we found it very easy to go to school. After classes, we were given tuition. I started reading newspapers and periodicals very enthusiastically. We were also given music lessons and sports equipment. I greatly enjoyed cricket and kabadi. Above all, we were given very good spiritual food. Some of us were trained by missionaries from Campus Crusade for Christ, and did village ministry with them during holidays.

Unlike most of the others, I stayed in the home until I completed my 12th grade. The facilities, as well as spiritual and academic guidance, in the hostel really shaped my future. One of our tutors encouraged me to do post-secondary study.

Through God's grace my sponsorship continued. Between 1992 and 1998 I received a Bachelor of Science in Mathematics and a Master in Science from The American College, Tamilnadu. Then I enrolled in a Master of Philosophy in Mathematics at Madras Christian College so I could become a Lecturer. I graduated in 1998 and immediately got a Mathematics Lecturer job in an engineering college in Chennai. I worked for three years, and then I quit the job to study a Master of Technology degree in Computer Science from the best engineering institute in our country, the Indian Institute of Technology, Kharagpur. It was a dream come true for me!

After I graduated, I got a job as in-charge of computer science and engineering department in an engineering college. During this period I married Josephine Lilly Chithra, a qualified mathematics teacher. We have two sons: Joel is ten years old, doing fifth grade, and Josh is three years old. In 2004, I commenced a doctorate in computer science and engineering at the prestigious Indian Institute of Technology, Madras. I graduated in 2009 and joined the Indian Institute of Information Technology, Design and Manufacturing, as an Assistant Professor in computer engineering. I am enjoying my work, and planning to do a course on theology to do effective church ministry.

My Lord and saviour Jesus Christ has blessed me abundantly through various people including my sponsors, Compassion home officers, wardens, teachers et cetera I always remember my sponsors and the primary teachers who brought me back to education, and also to the Compassion home. After I informed Compassion India I had dedicated my thesis to them, I was thrilled to receive an email from my former sponsors, the Todds. I came to know that they are also professors living in New Jersey.

To radiate the love and kindness shown onto me by my sponsors, God has given me an opportunity to support my sister's son's education from his 7th grade to his Diploma in Mechanical Engineering. Now he is running his own business and he is supporting my sister's family. My parents are still living in our village, and we often visit them or have them come and stay with us for a few months. May God help us to reflect his image in all our lives.

My Life Growing Up in Poverty

by Cindy Petro (formerly sponsored by Children International)

My name is Cindy Petro. I was born in the Boston neighbourhood of Cartagena, Colombia, in 1992. My community has had many problems with safety, violence and sanitation. It is located on the edge of a trash-filled swamp that would flood our neighbourhood during heavy rains and make us sick. There were no paved streets. Everything turned to mud – even the dirt floor of the wooden shack where my family and I lived.

My childhood was made more difficult because my parents separated when I was just two. My father went to Barranquilla, leaving my three siblings and I living with our very sick mother. Our economic situation wasn't good. Every morning my mother would take me with her to her friends' house, where she would help them do the chores. As payment, they would give us food. Later, she worked as a maid with the condition that they would let her be with me. That's how she took care of my needs. My maternal grandmother also supported us. What I remember with great admiration was the care and love that my mother always expressed to me and my three siblings, no matter what she was going through. Still, I always yearned for the love of my father.

When I was five, Children International came to my community. They enrolled me in the sponsorship programme, and soon an angel appeared and sponsored me. Such happiness! When I received my first gift, I was excited. I liked the clothing very much. And the first time I received the education kit was very exciting for me. I liked it a lot because I felt very special when I went to school with all my school supplies.

Up until then, I didn't know how important Children International would be in my life. I happily received all of the gifts during my 12 years of sponsorship. Medical and dental care, including medicines, were always available. People in the community medical centre kept me in good health. They were very kind to me when I arrived, and they always took care of me. For me, the community centre was a place where I was appreciated and assisted to have better health. All of that made me feel better and more secure.

Because I was sponsored I was also included in the Youth Programme. I participated in the workshops, which really strengthened me. I learned that we can overcome problems if we really want to (that poverty can be overcome), to value ourselves as people, to have a life project and to set goals for ourselves. I had a lot of fun playing, sharing in group, being tolerant and responsible.

This programme helped me clarify my goals and strive to achieve them, no matter the difficulties that get in the way. I always wanted to be a nurse, and Children International helped me to make that dream a reality. When I finished high school, I applied for a HOPE scholarship through Children International. I was very happy when I heard that it was approved. I was supported during all my semesters.

They paid for everything; I didn't pay for anything, not even the graduation fee. Without this help I could never have succeeded.

Thanks to God and Children International, now I'm a nursing assistant. I stood out as the best student because I really wanted it and I wanted to improve more and more each day.

I feel really happy to have had Children International's help, because they contributed to the realization of my dreams. Having studied nursing, and now practicing it, means changing my life story – a story full of love, but also with many economic challenges. My dream today is to become a head nurse, or a teacher of young children. I want to serve people and work with boys and girls.

Now my life is different. Although I have a daughter and I'm a single mother, I can take care of her needs and also help my own mother. My goal is to continue on with becoming a professional in my career, to offer my daughter a good future, never forgetting to give her love, and to help my family, my mother, my stepfather (who gave me a father's love) and my siblings, from whom I have always received unconditional love and who give me the strength to move forward.

Figure 11.3 Cindy
Cindy works as a nurse's aide for the Infant Development Center of the Juan Felipe Gómez Escobar Foundation in Cartagena, Colombia. She provides daily nutritional, educational and emotional care to underprivileged children of teenage mothers. Pictured is Cindy with her daughter.

A True Testimony

by Edwin Sithole (formerly sponsored by Plan International)

Reminiscing the era before Plan's direct involvement in my life is like a torturous experience to me. After my father died, my mother could go to some cities to work as a domestic worker to raise money to meet some necessities. I grew up in the hands of my grandmother. Our home was the tiny, dust-impregnated village of Zamchiya, in Zimbabwe.

I vividly remember each time the school headmaster would enquire about outstanding school fees, my name was always featured on top of the list. Each time we were sent home to collect the fees, others would indeed return with the money but for me there wasn't anyone to give me help. Well-wishers in the village, after granting me some manual jobs and house chores, would donate some paltry payments which I saved 'till I had the required amount. By the time I could get enough money for fees almost half of the term would have lapsed!

I was always lagging behind in terms of my performance, simply because of this arduous task of looking for school fees. When Plan International came to our area offering fee support, at first we were suspicious. Like many who grew up in the remotest parts, I was very skeptical. Conspiracies were extremely rife. One of the most dubious was that the organization's sponsorship scheme was a guise, whose real intention was to kidnap children and traffic them for forced labor and slavery in Europe!

Somehow my name was taken and I was sponsored in 1993 at Zamchiya Primary school. Suddenly I did not have to worry about school fees. My tenacious life totally changed and the rough life I had experienced came to an abrupt end. Every year, I would look forward to Christmas cards, and photos of my Japan-based foster parent. Gifts of reading books, pencils, pens and writing pads made me a hero in the village. My esteem as an individual was lifted. I liked being photographed together with Plan's staffers in our school compound. At times I would call my friends and my grandparents simply for a snap photo.

I was able to finish school in 2002 when I was in my Ordinary-level studies. I was replaced by my sibling and was accepted for

Plan's support for higher education. With Plan's help I am now walking tall, having attained a National Diploma in Mass Communication only offered at Harare Polytechnic. Today I can humbly walk with pride because my full potential has been cultivated and sprouted out. I have convinced myself that no one will ever act as a barrier to anything that I want or dream in life. I have become more of a juggernaut.

Through the educational scholarship of Plan I am proudly leading our own local development community-based Non-Government Organization, Alight Zimbabwe Trust (Plan Alumni) as its founding national coordinator. My role with the Alight Zimbabwe Trust has given me a good platform to help others, something I had longed for since I was including within the scheme of Plan. My mentor, mother and friend from Japan, Yoko Sakurai Nakamura, imparted in me the humanitarian imperative that has permanently left me with a burning desire to always look forward to helping others in the best way possible.

After Plan helped me, I feel no one can make a meaningful living on this earth without being helped in one way or the other. My life is a full testimony joyfully shouted to my society and the entire world that a hopeless future can be positively changed into an inspiring, meaningful and promising life, made possible through compassionate and tender intervention. Who knew that one day I would be able to fend for my siblings, who are all doing well in their education and industry? That I would become an inspiration to my younger brothers and sisters? That in my lovely village, they all look forward for great things from me? They now realize that it is possible for a little boy whose skin never knew jelly, whose torn clothes a needle could no longer mend, whose lips where always cracked due to under-nutrition, could have a life worth reckoning! Hope of attaining a national qualification was a fantasy, the hallucinating of an orphaned boy whose major childhood preoccupation was herding cattle and goats, chopping firewood, picking wild fruits and gathering insects for a living. There has never been a journalist in my family or compound's genealogy. I broke the ranks, but such a jump start was only made possible by this organization used by God.

Today's sponsorship programme in Zimbabwe is different from the one our generation went through, because in our time it was needs-based. We could eat and forget, even though the importance of education was not in some of us. Today is now a rights-based approach. If someone is empowered through this rights-based approach, obviously there is a sustainable development. The most crucial thing one can do for an orphaned child like myself is, simply, affording him or her equal opportunity to education. Non-Governmental Organizations' activities have been popular largely because they offer food handouts and food hampers, but somehow this has crippled people's initiative. Affording someone opportunity to attend school is the greatest empowerment a society can be granted. One cannot give a colleague fish, but should give the fishing rod itself. That is the starting point of the lifeline. Education is the vital cog that breaks the vicious cycle of poverty.

From Rescued to Rescuer

by Rajendra Gautam (formerly sponsored by Asian Aid Organisation)

My name is Rajendra Gautam. My life in the mountains of Nepal started with high expectations, as the first born son of the Hindu priest in a village called Nayagaon 6 in the state of Kavhre, approximately 80 kilometers south east of Kathmandu. I was destined to be heir of the holy rituals and our family wealth. Even when I was just small, my father had begun grooming me to be a priest, and his successor when I was older. However, his life was suddenly cut short when he died of Tuberculosis in 1983. I was only four years old.

My whole family's world changed in that instant; my mother was cursed for 'eating her husband' and deceitful villagers took our house and family land away from us. We had to live hand-to-mouth to survive, with just a few chickens, a cow and a goat. My mother, along with my younger sister, eked out our existence for a couple of years but then my mother also took seriously ill with Tuberculosis. Before she died she asked kind village people to carry her to Scheer Memorial Hospital in Banepa for treatment.

Despite this being a Christian hospital, my mother believed she would be cared for and, more importantly, she knew that they would also care for her children. It was arranged that I would go to boarding school in Roorke, India while my sister stayed in the care of Nepalese hospital staff Pr. Naseeb and Mrs. Rama Basnet. Because I was now orphaned, I stayed with them in Banepa during my summer vacations and my sister lived with them for some long years until she got married.

My years at boarding school were a mixture of tumultuous problems that included; racial discrimination from teachers and fellow students, language difficulties and adapting to a new culture and religion. This contrasted with my ongoing academic success. I did not have very much and survived on what little I was given or could work for, yet I had one thing many of the other boys did not have: a photo. The photo was a picture of my sponsor and his wife, and I clung to this as if my life depended on it. This photo gave me hope. It gave me courage to carry on when times became unbearable. This photo represented people that loved and cared for me even though I had never met them. My solace was this love and the letters that arrived at irregular intervals, saying that I was important and encouraging me to keep doing my best in my studies.

I did not know it then, but my sponsors started with a monthly commitment of $30 to Asian Aid. By the end of my schooling they were paying $50 a month. The money was given to the school to cover tuition, books and boarding. Extra contributions around Christmas time helped buy gifts that keep us clothed. Yet, my whole schooling experience was shadowed by pain and loneliness of having no parents for support, love, protection or guidance. It was this blend of emotion that spurred me to become a school prefect and advocate for my fellow Nepali students, who were treated poorly.

Asian Aid gave me hope in providing an education, uniforms and boarding through the sponsorship programme in Australia. As the Australian director of Asian Aid, 'Mummy Eager' regularly visited my school to ensure that sponsored children were cared for appropriately and to smother us with some motherly love, which we all so desperately craved. She was a constant in my life which motivated me to strive to please her and my sponsors with hard work and dedication. Mummy Eager continues to mentor and support me as I run a charity organization that I am director of.

My sponsorship continued throughout my years at school, 12 years in all, and provided me with the motivation to progress to further study and ultimately begin a career as a pastor and missionary. In reality, the sponsorship has continued my whole life. Being sponsored does not always mean financial assistance, but can be having people who pray for and look out for me and my family. Around the time I moved to Pokhara with the aim of starting a church in 2004, Dad and Mum (my sponsors, Peter and Fiona) initiated further sponsorship to help with my ministry. This continued to build the bond that I had shared with my sponsor parents when I was a child into a family connection that still continues to grow and strengthen as each year passes.

In 2011, my family and I were overjoyed to be visited by Dad, Mum, Josh and Nicole. It was a time of celebration in finally meeting face-to-face and bonding as only families can. Being a Seventh-day Adventist pastor allowed me the unique opportunity to baptize my sponsor 'sister' Nicole in a ceremony which will be remembered by us all as a defining moment in our families' history.

Sponsorship has given me the opportunity to be educated, to build a life of my own and to be able to give back to my community of fellow Nepali's by offering the same opportunity to children in similar or worse circumstances than what I was. God has guided me in building a school to provide education, starting a safe house for rescued girls who had been sold to sex traffickers, and to be part of a vibrant community here in Pokhara that is committed to continuing the mission of being the hands and feet of Jesus.

I can truly say that I was fortunate enough to be rescued from a life of poverty and am now honored to have been called to be a rescuer of my fellow Nepali men and women, boys and girls.

With thanks to Rajendra's sponsor for facilitating this article.

Discussion

The seven stories presented above are delightful and heart-warming. They are drawn from children and adults sponsored by seven different organizations, across five different countries. Read together, they provide a tribute to the potential for CS to profoundly impact the lives of sponsored children. They highlight the strengths and potential of several CS-funded interventions, and as first-person narratives, they provide us with a glimpse of what successful child sponsorship looks like from the perspective of the sponsored. The stories are from the perspectives of those who are still being sponsored, from those only recently out of such a programme, and from those who are well-and-truly adults looking back on their formative years. Yet despite this diversity, there are a number of significant commonalities and themes that run through most or all of these stories.

Poverty is often described in terms of material deficits. However, implicit in the narratives above is an understanding of poverty as being lack of opportunity and capability, driven largely by marginalization and resulting in a debilitating sense of hopelessness. What these stories illustrate is the power of CS to provide hope, evidenced through powerfully affirming relationships. At one level, relationships are formed with individual sponsors. On another, they are formed with CS INGO staff and other children enrolled in sponsorship programmes. To some extent this accounts for effusive thanks offered to CS INGOs. Perhaps the most lovely evidence for this claim occurs in the narrative of Sadhna, a 15 year old student sponsored through World Vision for whom sponsorship provided a timely escape from restrictive gender roles, a restoration of fatherly pride, and the possibility of a career in journalism. For Sadhna:

Tomorrow was dark under the shadows of sadness,
suddenly a silver light shone through the darkness.
Someone held my hand; I held it tight and just followed the light.

Another recurring theme is the value placed on new or greater educational opportunity. Each of the stories functions as an account of unlikely success, with children rescued from a life of manual labor or economic disadvantage by the opportunity to attend school and participate in various related programmes. In these narratives education is positioned as key to success, with the CS INGO functioning as a catalyst, removing barriers and enabling school attendance, encouraging academic progress and facilitating the achievement of individual potential. Edwin Sitholes' remarkable transition to respected journalist provides an evocative account of success insofar as, 'Hope of attaining a national qualification was a fantasy, the hallucinating of an orphaned boy whose major childhood preoccupation was herding cattle and goats, chopping firewood, picking wild fruits and gathering insects for a living'. From an individual's perspective, such commentary offers a stern rebuke to those who have mocked the idea that a small monthly donation could change the life of a child.

For the authors of these stories, there is what Nerissa P. Soledad refers to as a 'ripple effect'. Education has resulted in improved self-esteem, formation of life-purpose, affirmation of self-efficacy and, ultimately, employment and attainment of income and the means to choose life outcomes. For each narrator the opportunity to attend and complete school has been transformational, leading to the conclusion that, 'Education is the vital cog that breaks the vicious cycle of poverty.' In the case of Cindy Petro, 'Although I have a daughter and I'm a single mother, I can take care of her needs and also help my own mother. My goal is to continue on with becoming a professional in my career, to offer my daughter a good future, never forgetting to give her love...' The dignity inherent to the possibility of personal choice amid difficult circumstances shines in each of the narratives.

Common to the narratives above is the explicit reasoning that the personal nature of sponsorship was an important factor in individual success. While critics have linked sponsorship to paternalism and dependency, the narratives above suggest that for some children sponsorship, confusing as it may be, communicates a level of compassion and care by a distant stranger which creates a sense of encouragement, and is motivational in a way that whole community assistance, arguably, is not. Put simply, being singled out for special treatment was instrumental in high achievement and high self-esteem for these individuals. Thus, through CS, children and youth may feel valued, loved, cared for and personally connected to powerful, perhaps even God-like actors in their lives providing hope in counterpoint to the harsh realities of poverty and disadvantage. For Rajendra Gautam, 'I had one thing many of the other boys did not have: a photo. The photo was a picture of my sponsor and his wife, and I clung to this as if my life depended on it.' Having said this, it is also clear that the role of the sponsor in this is just one of many. Personal attention and relationships with local school teachers, mothers of orphan homes, tutors, INGO staff and various other concerned adults, each played a crucial role in leveraging sponsorship as a vehicle for personal improvement.

Beyond merely knowing they had a sponsor, communication and quality of relationship with sponsors is a recurring issue in the success stories of sponsored children. All the individuals expressed gratitude for sponsorship, the majority felt affirmed by being selected for support, and most seemed to value sending letters and receiving gifts. The sense of personal connection was sometimes accompanied by a strong desire to meet sponsors (or a least learn more about them). For some, this promoted learning about places and people beyond their otherwise narrow experience. For others, this sense of personal connection with sponsors led to a desire to fulfill the expectations they felt were inherent in the sponsorship relationship, perhaps expressed in the dreams they shared in correspondence with sponsors. In the case of Lina Trujillo, the decision to return to her orphanage and to make something of her life was partially because, 'I also thought about all my plans, those that I had told my sponsors, and I felt I was going to let them down.' We note a sense of confusion or disappointment in some cases that the sponsor is not known, as well as a degree of dignity and pride associated with knowing names and meeting sponsors in person.

Throughout most of the narratives there is a recurring belief expressed that a higher power is responsible for the sponsorship and resultant transformation. In part, this may be because a number of the CS INGOs featured are Christian. However, this is also due to the religious worldview of many sponsorship beneficiaries. Rather than sponsorship being viewed as a charitable transaction, sponsored beneficiaries may make sense of their sponsorship by framing it within the context of a spiritual journey. For secular readers this may seem strange, especially given the recurring historic tendency to criticize CS INGOs for evangelizing and forcing their religion on vulnerable others. In these narratives, at least, religion has been perceived in terms of a personal journey in which they retained agency, rather than an experience of coercion. For Rajendra Gautam the opportunity to meet his sponsors and baptize his sponsor's daughter is accompanied by a deep sense of pride, intimacy and blessing. V. Masilamani accounts for his ongoing sponsorship as due to God's grace, while Nerissa Soledad is emphatic that her life is testimony to God's goodness. With respect to secular critics, it is evident that for some sponsored children at least, the attainment of sponsorship and the success derived from ongoing support, may be richly significant in terms of one's faith.

In a number of the stories, receiving personalized help rather than institutionalized assistance has fuelled a personal commitment to help others. This desire to give back, or pay it forward, might be referred to as development of a virtuous circle in which sponsored beneficiaries determine to give back to their own families and communities. Beyond being inspired to dream for a better future for themselves, the accounts of sponsorship above reveal potential for sponsorship to inspire service and compassion in young people who have been recipients' of others' compassion, and allowed to participate in society as equals rather than being poor and singled out. Nerissa Soledad's account typifies accounts in which sponsored children grow up and 'pay it forward'. Writing enthusiastically from a Christian world view she asserts, '...it is always my prayer that the Lord will use me as His instrument in touching the lives of the children under my care and continue on making a difference in their lives which will eventually impact their family and the whole community as well.' Without reference to religious belief, Sadhna enthuses that, 'My friends in school come to me for my advice and trust me. If they are undergoing any issue, especially gender discrimination, I counsel them and their parents or guardians.'

Many a story is untold in the narratives of this chapter. What, we may ask, has been the experience of young people who were individually sponsored yet did not thrive academically? To what extent did they benefit and what might they write about their experience of sponsorship? Did they also frame their support through a religious world view? Having experienced compassion, do they find less evident ways of paying it forward? Nonetheless, what is significant about the themes explored above is that the impacts described here appear across the boundaries of institution, country, and even the model of child sponsorship. It would appear that at its best, the personalized support of child sponsorship at the time children are at their most vulnerable, can have a deeply personal and transformational impact in a way other institutional support and programmes most likely could not.

At time of writing, sponsorship spans orphan care, education, family support, pooled funding for community development, rights-based interventions and use of representative children who may receive no direct, tangible benefits. An ongoing challenge for CS INGOs is to collect and disseminate positive and negative change stories that give voice to children in CS programmes in ways that respect the integrity of their narratives, diversity of experience, and potential as change agents in CS processes. While this chapter honors those who have benefited from CS, it flags the need to honor other, less effusive voices marginalized in the ongoing quest to improve the lives of children through child sponsorship.

12
World Vision, Organizational Identity and the Evolution of Child Sponsorship

David King

Introduction

World Vision is the world's largest religious humanitarian organization, a multi-faceted global partnership operating in nearly 100 countries with around 45,000 employees and an annual budget over USD2.7 billion. While World Vision now operates as an elite international non-governmental organization (INGO), the initial success of child sponsorship (CS) served as the key that led World Vision to distinguish itself from peer evangelical agencies in terms of budget, popularity and global reach. Yet, CS itself only partially accounts for World Vision's meteoric growth. The evolution and interplay of World Vision's practices, theology, rhetoric, and organizational structure over its 60 year history illustrates sweeping change. In particular, debate over its evangelical role as well as its approach to child sponsorship have been instrumental in shaping its identity and programming, positioning World Vision as an important case study for scholars interested in the development of religious INGOs.

The origins of World Vision's child sponsorship programme

With America's new global cachet and heightened international curiosity in the wake of World War Two, a new generation of American evangelicals sought to export a style of American revivalism designed to win the world to Christ. Billy Graham was the most well-known however other short-term evangelists also reported conversions in the thousands and returned to interpret the world to American audiences. In 1948, Baptist preacher Bob Pierce travelled to China for a summer of crusades. His rallies met with intoxicating success, recording more than

17,000 decisions for Christ (Graham and Lockerbie, 1983, p.66). Yet he claimed it was his encounter with a single child that served to alter the course of his life and the genesis of World Vision.

There are variations of Pierce's initial encounter. Most begin with Dutch Reformed missionary Tena Hoelkeboer's invitation to preach at her school of 400 girls. In one version Pierce invited the students to 'Go home and tell your folks you're going to be a Christian' (Graham and Lockerbie, 1983, p.73). When one of Hoelkeboer's students – White Jade – did as she was asked, she was described as beaten by her father and thrown out of the house. Hoelkeboer demanded of Pierce, 'What are you going to do about her?' (Graham and Lockerbie, 1983, p.74) Pierce gave Hoelkeboer all the money he claimed to have left and promised to send more. Once home, he asked his audiences how anyone could ignore 'the half of Asia that goes to bed hungry and without knowing Christ' (Gehmen, 1960, p.184). Yuen (2008, p.42) points out that subsequent narrative variation subtly influences reader perception of intent and vision, and Pierce's account changed slightly over time. Yet the heart of the story remained the same, confronting American audiences with an individual need and the question, 'What are you going to do about it?' (Anderson and Pierce, 1949, p.104)

Under Pierce's guidance, World Vision emerged from an American evangelical subculture that had long prioritized evangelism over social action. Debates among American Protestants in the early twentieth century had led to clear divisions. The Fundamentalist-Modernist debates of the 1920s had split several denominations into conservative and liberal factions, both of which forfeited the name evangelical for other labels. Fundamentalists argued that essential doctrines were being sacrificed for cultural relevance. Pointing to theologians such as Walter Rauschenbusch and his social gospel, those same fundamentalists accused the modernists (the forbearers of later mainline Protestants) of preaching a gospel of social salvation that trumped the primacy of the need for individual conversion.

The same struggle ripped apart the Protestant missionary enterprise. Conservatives withdrew from denominations to form their own mission agencies. Both at home and abroad, defining the priority of revival and reform divided American Protestants throughout much of the twentieth century. Whether the distinctions were real or imagined, many identified one party (liberal, mainline or ecumenical Protestants) with social reform while associating the other (including fundamentalists and evangelicals) with a primary emphasis on individual conversions. A few organizations like World Vision attempted to maintain a tenuous middle ground.

Bob Pierce typified a new generation of post-war US evangelicals who emerged from the fundamentalist subculture in the mid-1940s eager to reach the world for Christ and reclaim an evangelical identity. Pierce claimed, 'I had gone there to preach the gospel, true enough, but I had also gone there to capture the need of the people and to bring that need back to America' (Anderson, 1948, p.16). Ultimately, he returned with a message that challenged evangelicals to prioritize the care of orphans. When Communist control closed China to Western missionaries in 1949, Pierce followed American troops into Korea. He founded World Vision in 1950 to carry the gospel as well as American food and clothing to those in need.

Pierce spent the rest of the Korean war alternating between meeting humanitarian needs on the frontlines in Korea and returning with fresh images of Korean Christians, missionaries, American soldiers and communist aggressors to raise support in churches in America. He helped fund hospitals and leprosariums, bought jeeps for missionaries and funded biblical training for South Korean military chaplains. Pierce regaled American evangelicals with images and first-hand accounts of daily life, the bright colors of the market, the smell of kimchi, or the human-drawn rickshaws. Yet he also showed them poverty, physical deformities and squalor. He told stories about the torture and death of Korean pastors, filmed leper colonies and shocked audiences with images of malnourished children.[1]

Pierce became convinced of the importance of orphan care. 'I never intended to be in the orphanage business,' Pierce said, but 'taking care of orphans' was 'the little job God has given me to do' (Pierce, n.d.). While many missionaries operated orphanages throughout Korea, by the end of the war, the number of orphans had become a major problem. In 1954 orphanages could only house 5,000 of an estimated 170,000 orphans (Correll, 1954, p.3). For this reason Pierce funneled resources through existing orphanages established by western missionaries as well as building new ones which he subsequently turned over to missionaries or Korean Christians to administer.

In 1953, Pierce recruited Ervin and Florence Raetz who had served with the China Children's Fund (CCF), tasking them with replication of a similar programme on World Vision's behalf (Dunker, 2005, p.101). In 1954, World Vision unveiled its own CS programme. For ten dollars a month, an American could sponsor a Korean orphan through Christian institutions with fixed percentages used for food, clothing, education and religious teaching. Sponsors exchanged photos and letters with their 'foster' child with provision for extra gifts such as clothes, candy, and Bibles. From 1954 to 1956, the annual funds devoted to orphanages mushroomed from $57,000 to $452,538. By the end of the decade World Vision donors sponsored more than 13,000 orphaned children throughout four countries (World Vision, 1982).

In the late 1950s, World Vision continued to fund individual missionaries while also training indigenous pastors and organizing evangelistic crusades. Yet, its work with orphans soon encompassed the vast majority of the organization's time and money and CS quickly became the fundraising engine for the organization. CS was so successful that the organization was sometimes forced to 'borrow' funds designated for orphans to cover other budgeted expenses. When several of the orphanages became embroiled with government over accusations of misappropriation of funds, Pierce began to worry. He lamented entry into the 'orphanage business,' and prepared to jettison his marquee ministry. Pierce despised the headaches of institutional bureaucracy preferring to travel the world to evangelize and support the needs of individual missionaries (Pierce, 1958). Yet, the majority of staff within the organization already realized that World Vision's success or failure was tied to CS.

The initial success of child sponsorship

World Vision's leaders believed CS would succeed by rousing a complacent Western Christianity to respond to a world in need and Pierce filmed what he encountered. The efforts coincided with a cultural moment when Americans turned their attention eastward and during the 1950s, World Vision averaged more than one film a year. It screened them at churches, mission conferences, and civic auditoriums, sometimes attracting audiences of 5,000 to 6,000[2] (Bernard, 1957, p.4).

Pierce's films put World Vision on the map, but he soon invested in other media, including a weekly coast-to-coast radio broadcast in 1956. On 'Bob Pierce Reports,' Pierce recounted his international travels, interviewed missionaries and indigenous pastors, and asked for help to support World Vision's work around the world.[3] In 1957, World Vision began publishing the monthly magazine, *World Vision*, which not only won national awards for its reporting but was credited with doubling annual income (Graham, 1997, p.294).

By the end of the first decade, the child had become the centrepiece for most World Vision marketing activities. Pierce's films, radio sermons and print publications featured personal stories and images of children he encountered and offered direct connection through sponsorship. Pierce shocked with graphic pictures of destitute orphans overseas juxtaposed with well-fed, middle-class American children, however he also encouraged donors to think of their sponsored child as part of their extended family. From the programme's inception, donors could select the gender and age of their sponsored child and communicate as much as possible.

Pierce promoted CS a tangible, life-changing form of humanitarian action motivated by evangelical zeal and love. Pierce often repeated the refrain that motivated his ministry, 'Let my heart be broken with the things that break the heart of God' (Gehman, 1960, p. 171). He chastised audiences, urging that 'they should not let their inability to do everything keep them from doing something' (Pierce, 1952). The unemployed or addicted rarely made it into World Vision's promotional materials. Instead, Pierce offered images of widows, martyred pastors, and most often individual children and victims who suffered through no fault of their own: 'If you believe God is interested in your aches and pains,' Pierce offered, 'don't you think He hears the cry of starving children?' (Pierce, 1949, p.17) With that framing, few among his evangelical audiences would disagree.

World Vision balanced its abundant images of need with testimonies of success. It contrasted pictures of orphans before and after sponsorship: the malnourished Korean orphan in one photo appeared in a later one as a healthy and happy child (VanderPol, 2010, p.77). It also told stories of long-term success: young boys who became pastors as a result of their Christian education or girls who earned jobs through the vocational training they received in World Vision orphanages. CS exposed donors to immense global need, providing an opportunity to save children in the temporal world and for eternity.

Pierce was conscious that World Vision often crossed the traditional boundaries dividing American Protestants. He was clear that conversion came first, yet because he prioritized conversion, conservative evangelicals listened to his call for social amelioration. He shrewdly tied evangelism and social concern together with insider evangelical language that avoided the social gospel that conservatives despised. Yet, Pierce called for Christian charity, not for structural justice. Initially, World Vision had little understanding of the systemic character of poverty, and it compelled donors by illustrating need one individual child at a time.

Expansion and growth in the 1960s

World Vision's innovative marketing continued to propel the organization's rapid growth in its second decade. Alongside its magazine, the organization also sent donors glossy pictorials, modelled after similar gifts from *LIFE* and *National Geographic*, as a thank-you to sponsors. It also sent appeal letters several times a year written in Pierce's voice and brimming with emotive language and snapshots of children in need. The CS-funded orphan care programme itself changed very little even as the numbers continued to balloon from 13,000 to 32,600 over the decade (World Vision Annual Reports 1950–1959). However, by 1967, a geographic shift was evident. Vietnam had become the centre of World Vision's public appeals to sponsor children, build hospitals, administer relief aid to refugees, and train local communities in agricultural and vocational skills.

Registration with the USA's Agency for International Development (USAID), enabled World Vision to receive commodities and grants for humanitarian relief. Pierce remained cautious about dependence on government, but he pursued limited connections to capitalize on available resources (Rohrer, 1987, pp.138–139). The size and growing complexity of World Vision's humanitarian commitments, its first foray into federal funding, as well as the limited size of Vietnam's local Christian population forced World Vision to develop its own delivery structures that began to sideline the direct engagement of churches and missionaries.

In Vietnam, WV staff began rubbing shoulders with mainline, Catholic, and secular NGOs. While leading humanitarian agencies like Catholic Relief Services, CARE, and Church World Service often continued to look askance at World Vision as an unsophisticated and naïve evangelical upstart, World Vision began to re-examine its own identity as a missionary organization. Even so, it still romanticized its origins as existential and unpremeditated, driven by '...a summons from Christ to act and to act now' (World Vision, 1978). By the close of the 1960s, new challenges forced the organization to reassess. World Vision President Graeme Irvine reflected:

> Anyone looking at World Vision would see an organization that was action oriented, centered around Bob Pierce himself, strongly evangelical, innovative, and progressive. As with most things, there was another side to the coin. These apparent strengths had corresponding weaknesses: instability, dependent on the ideas and personality

of one person, narrow relationships and limited international per-spective (Irvine, 1996, p.22).

By 1967, Pierce had resigned from the organization. World Vision kept one foot firmly planted within evangelical missions, but ventured slowly outside an exclusively evangelical orbit. It was still more mis-sionary agency than humanitarian INGO or development organiza-tion, but new interactions offered exposure to new conversations and vocabularies that slowly began to chip away at its insular evangelical-ism and reshape its practice.

World Vision's evolution and growth in the midst of change – 1970s

The 1970s marked the beginning of World Vision's explosive growth. In little more than a decade, World Vision's annual income grew from USD4.5 million in 1969 to USD94 million by 1982 (Waters, 1998, p.69). The growth came as a result of a number of factors. For one, by the 1970s, Western evangelicals themselves began to reconsider the direction of the missionary enterprise. Reflecting this trend and rein-forcing it, Billy Graham's 1974 International Congress on World Evangelization in Lausanne, Switzerland resulted in an unprecedented international evangelical statement on the need for Christians to resist poverty, hunger and injustice.

World Vision was well positioned to benefit as the global evangelical movement began to broaden its definition of mission. At the same time World Vision expanded into large-scale relief work prompted by high-profile disasters in the early 1970s. In 1970 it responded with emergency aid to a massive cyclone, tidal wave, and civil war in East Pakistan (now Bangladesh) that left 500,000 dead and displaced 10 million people. In 1972 it received its first large government grant to coordinate relief after a devastating earthquake in Nicaragua. In Africa, it launched programmes to feed people during famines in Biafra (Nigeria) and Ethiopia (World Vision, 1982, pp.145–149).

These and similar interventions brought increased media attention and more donations from evangelicals.[4] That support led to new kinds of evangelical agencies: Christian relief and development organizations that operated outside the sphere of evangelical missions. While tradi-tional mission agencies may still have received the majority of evangel-ical support, the new relief agencies expanded at an astonishing rate with an average annual growth of 17 per cent throughout the 1970s, twice the rate of traditional evangelical mission organizations. Some of these agencies adopted CS; others avoided it (Smith, 1986, pp.104–108).[5]

Critics from within the humanitarian aid community often ignored World Vision efforts to embrace local partnerships and extend its growing expertise in humanitarian emergencies. Critics instead still saw World Vision as too American, too narrowly evangelical, and perhaps too wedded to CS. Those identities may have sometimes hurt its reputation overseas, but it aided fundraising at home. During the 1970s, World Vision grabbed the greatest share of headlines and support among U.S. evangelicals on its way to rapid institutional and popular growth. Government funds still made up only a fraction of World Vision's budget. It continued to expand primarily through emergency appeals and monthly pledges of its child sponsors.

The fall of Vietnam and Cambodia to communism in 1975 resulted in the loss of one third of World Vision programmes consisting of 23,000 sponsored children and USD3 million of sponsorship revenue. Staff hastily established operations in Latin America and Africa, seeking new children to sponsor (Watkins, 1998). It continued to broker relationships with local missionaries and evangelical churches, however, World Vision management knew it must learn to work with other Christian factions; mainline Protestants, Catholics, and Pentecostals vied for influence with the organization. As it moved into large-scale relief, it also became more operational, establishing its own programmes, hiring staff and often interacting with other relief agencies in the field.

World Visions' expansion into the medium of television served as the catalyst for the organization's further growth. Hoping to increase support beyond church-going Americans, in 1972 it introduced hour-long television documentaries that did not preach at the audience but used images and stories of hungry children to compel viewers to sponsor children. It soon specialized in multi-hour hunger telethons. Images of poverty and starvation alternated with upbeat musical numbers by celebrities like the Muppets and Julie Andrews. In the words of one producer, 'World Vision productions couched the organization's Christian motivation in language the average person could understand. We did not want to hide the Christian purpose, but to express it in general terms more appropriate for a television audience' (Waters, 1998, p.70).

The success of television fundraising brought expanded budgets and programmes at the same time that the organization began to reconsider its own theoretical approaches and institutional structure. CS dollars still made up the bulk of World Vision's fundraising while sponsorship programmes made up the majority of the expenditures and took up the majority of time among programme staff in the field. By the end of 1977, World Vision had over 130,000 sponsored children in 40 nations with over 70 per cent of its field budget spent on sponsorship programmes. Staff began to worry that the organization's policies and procedures fell short. Often the quality and design of its programmes differed quite drastically from place to place as each country decided independently what sponsored children should receive. Under a new structure labelled Childcare Ministries, World Vision leadership instituted policy and procedures to monitor the status of sponsored children alongside minimum benefits packages for all children and mandatory training of childcare workers. Simultaneously, it began to move slowly away from an orphanage to a family-focused model. Acknowledging critiques of institutionalization, and heeding internal advice from programmes staff, World Vision directors realized that shifting the benefits of sponsorship from individual orphans to children within extended families would help with the long-term goal of community change[6] (Watkins, 1998; Rohrer, 1987, p.121).

Inevitably, voices within World Vision began to challenge the organization's structure. Pierce had referred to his organization as World Vision International since 1966, yet it largely remained an American agency funding programmes run by local missionaries and churches overseas. By the late 1960s, it had opened support offices in Canada, Australia and New Zealand to serve as fundraising branches of the American-based World Vision International. By the 1970s, these new offices wanted to help make decisions and plan programmes[7] (Rees and Kamaleson, 1976). They also argued that to become a peer among international humanitarian NGOs, it must abandon a provincial Americanism for a more global geopolitics.

Leadership from support offices argued that true internationalization would open the way for greater representation and participation; it would also require more democratic structures and the delegating of accountability (Whaites, 1999, p.414). Others within World Vision argued that internationalization was more than a question of organization; it was a matter of theology in which sending missionaries to act on behalf of native peoples had become an 'anachronism'. Evangelical missiology now viewed Western missionaries as partners or servants of indigenous churches. While World Vision articulated a supranational and supracultural church, its organization was clearly still American (Rees and Kamaleson, 1976).

Attempts to 'express spiritual internationalism in organizational terms' led to real structural change. By 1973, World Vision's second president, Stan Mooneyham, promised to replace most American expatriate personnel with an indigenous workforce while helping field countries establish autonomous boards[8] (Mooneyham, 1978). That same year World Vision began its official internationalization. By 1978, the United States office handed over control to create World Vision International (WVI), a new legal entity governed by a board comprising all five support offices. The U.S. office remained the most influential, but now sat at the table as one among several voices making decisions about strategic planning, field operations, and budget[9] (McCleary, 2009, p.117). While the new organization was not as international as many hoped, the goal was a centralization of programmes as well as space for new voices to be heard in a spirit of partnership (Irvine, 1996, p.83).

As it internationalized and professionalized, World Vision also began to experiment with community development as a part of its ministry programmes. Other humanitarian agencies had for some time derided World Vision as an ambulance chaser that sped in with emergency relief and rarely stayed to help with lasting change. Many of World Vision's field staff agreed that emergency relief alone was inadequate. By 1974, World Vision decided to make development a key part of its ministry, and it soon became the organization's new buzzword[10] (Irvine, 1978). At the beginning, long-time staffer Bryant Myers admitted that World Vision knew little about community development, yet predicted that over the next ten years it would make up 75 per cent of the organization's work (Myers in Rohrer, 1987, p.153). Explicit missionary language waned as World Vision increasingly began to refer to its staff as aid workers and it no longer shied away from describing programmes as enterprises in healthcare, family planning, land regeneration, income generation and vocational training.

World Vision believed its newfound development approach went hand in hand with its theological outlook. If evangelical missionaries had once considered development as a form of 'secularized missions,' many now began to see it as an appropriate form of Christian mission, striving for a holistic gospel over what they had come to see as an unbiblical division of efforts. Development discourses also gave World Vision's growing non-western staff a language to advocate the need to privilege the dignity and agency of local individuals over the imposition of western answers and technologies. Still other staff adopted development strategies because it gave them a language to address issues of structural injustice (Sider, 1982, p.99).

In the early 1970s, World Vision organized its work into separate departments for childcare, evangelism, and relief/development that allowed for greater efficiency and expertise. Yet, some began to argue that separate departments undermined the organization's commitment to a more holistic theology. How could it talk of doing away with dichotomies between evangelism and social concern when it divided the two into separate departments? By 1978, a movement for 'ministry integration' led to the integration of evangelism, childcare, and relief/development into each local programme (Irvine, 1978).

In the early 1970s, childcare expanded from institutions to families, but sponsorship still provided fixed assistance packages to individuals. By 1979, World Vision pledged to move half of its childcare projects to embrace community development methodologies by 1984. It was considering changing from an organization that asked donors to support individual children into an agency that would pool sponsorship dollars for community development. World Vision leaders felt the adjustment helped bring the structure and fundraising practices of its child sponsorship programmes in line with its theology and development practice, but they worried about risking too much adjustment to the programme that brought in the bulk of its annual income (Watkins, 1998; Myers, 1987).

Reconsideration of child sponsorship in the 1980s

By the 1980s, some within World Vision were ready to renounce CS. Externally, child sponsorship agencies had begun to face increased scrutiny and negative publicity. Investigative journalists uncovered isolated cases of negligence or fraud in various organizations (see Stalker, 1982). Other mainstream media sources, including a few evangelical publications, questioned whether CS was the best way to raise money for humanitarian causes (Hayes, 1983). Internally, World Vision admitted that CS was difficult to administer and required enormous overhead costs associated with letter writing, gift-giving and child tracking. In some cases, it had been forced to subsidize sponsorship with non-sponsorship funds to meet its own minimum standards. Some field staff argued that individual CS ran counter to the organization's new commitment to development while many others turned their attention to the influx of funds and government grants designated for the large-scale emergency relief in the well-publicized Ethiopian and Somalia famines. Yet, World Vision's marketing managers knew that sponsorship remained the most reliable and largest source of annual income (Watkins, 1998).

By 1983, despite having over 300,000 sponsored children, an internal Sponsorship Task Force recommended a move away from the sponsorship programme (World Vision, 1983). The fundraising offices in the USA, Canada, and Australia experimented: instead of assigning donors a specific child, World Vision sent information about a 'representative child' and spoke of helping children in community. Overwhelmed with funds designated for the Ethiopian famine in 1984, World Vision decided to stop acquiring new sponsors altogether. After two years, however, World Vision saw a substantial decline in its sponsor fulfillment rates. The organization's marketing specialists realized that people were not connecting to a 'representative child' (Watkins, 1998).

By 1985, budget shortfalls after the height of the Ethiopian famine, led World Vision to return to and expand CS. It no longer used a sponsor's monthly pledge to support only a single child or a family, but integrated the funds into community development programmes. It realized, however, that donors needed a one-to-one connection with the ability to correspond and receive updates on 'their' sponsored child[11] (Watkins, 1998; Myers, 1989). By the end of the decade, World Vision had enrolled more than 1,000,000 children in sponsorship. Not everyone was happy with the decision. Some field offices refused to sign up kids for sponsorship just for the money that sponsors would bring to their programmes (McNee, 1989, pp.8–10).

A debate over development education illustrated the divisions. Most western fundraising offices had little knowledge of development and compartmentalized the work they did 'at home' and the development work done 'in the field.' The development staff resented the pictures of malnourished children that World Vision US and others used to raise funds, arguing that such images implied a call for charity that undermined the dignity of the people they served as well as the organization's commitment to development.[12] They claimed that World Vision had a responsibility to educate staff and donors on development. WVI leadership defined the conflict as one between idealism and pragmatism (Houston, n.d.). While they agreed donor education was important, marketing studies told fundraisers that images of hungry children brought in more financial resources than explanations of crop rotation or reforestation. As World Vision marketers debated the ethics of their approach, they knew pragmatically that World Vision management evaluated them on money raised over the message portrayed[13] (Gruman, 1985).

1990s–2000s: World Vision – More than a child sponsorship agency?

Despite internal conflict over the ongoing evolution of the CS programme in the 1970s and early 1980s, World Vision had developed considerable expertise in emergency management and community development. It continued to expand dramatically as its annual budget more than doubled through the 1980s to over USD200 million. By the end of the decade, it had gained consultative status with the United Nations High Commissioner for Refugees (UNHCR) and United Nations Children's Fund (UNICEF) as well as the World Food Program (WFP) and the World Health Organization (WHO). It entered the 1990s among the top ten largest INGOs in the world. Its size and hard-earned reputation as one of the leading relief and development organizations afforded it a seat at the table alongside industry leaders (McCleary, 2009, pp.25–29).

As relief and development became more central to World Vision's operations, its leaders became more confident in the organization's approach. As development discourse evolved, World Vision adapted its language. Bryant Myers, who had initially admitted both his excitement and naïveté in navigating World Vision's embrace of development principles in the 1970s, now felt confident in the organization's experience and expertise as World Vision's Vice President of International Program Strategy. He argued that secular development was just now beginning to discover what religious agencies like World Vision had been arguing for decades: the importance of the role of religion and culture as part of the development process. *Walking with the Poor*, Myers' account of transformational development, was first published in 1999 and remains the standard work used by evangelical seminaries and development agencies.

Having moved beyond the dichotomies between evangelism and social action that earlier dogged evangelical organizations, Myers defined World Vision's approach to transformational development as 'restoring relationships, just and right relationships with God, with self, with community, with the "other," and with the environment' (Myers, 1999, p.36). He couched World Vision's approach in Christian terms, relying on the best development experts, but resisting the claim that he was merely spiritualizing secular theory. Arguing that poverty was relational, he claimed that the powerlessness of the poor resulted from sin, broken relationships with God manifested in 'relationships that do not work' on personal and psychological, social and structural levels (Myers, 1999, p.36; Christian, 1999, pp.67–71).

Programming evolved alongside the changes in World Vision's theory of development. By the early 1990s, World Vision moved beyond scattered local community projects toward expansive Area Development Programs (ADPs). These ADPs identified pockets of poverty in a geographic area that encompassed multiple communities and populations of 20,000 to 40,000 people. Programmatically, ADPs offered World Vision a model that combined funding from multilateral organizations such as the World Health Organization with the support of individual child sponsors to offer the stability of long-term planning. ADP programming recognized that social structures perpetuating poverty often extended beyond a single community and that larger projects would allow it to implement its holistic principles. World Vision pledged to support each ADP for ten to 15 years until it could turn over complete control to the local communities (McDonic, 2004, p.66; Grellert, 2007). Since 2011, World Vision has adopted a new Development Programming Approach that further focuses on eliminating dependency by concentrating on the agency of local communities in light of its own child-focused development approach. In the field, World Vision has continued to adapt CS into its overall development strategy, continually revisiting programmes and measurements to gauge their success in meeting child well-being outcomes.

By 2003, World Vision International's annual budget was well over a billion US dollars, and it had risen to become the world's second largest INGO in real revenue (McCleary, 2009, p.28). It was also the largest INGO distributor of food aid and trailed only the Red Cross in responding to disasters and complex humanitarian emergencies[14] (Myers, 2005). Increased capacity meant the ability to apply for multi-million dollar governmental grants and receive generous gifts-in-kind (GIK), donated commodities that it could distribute to those in need or monetize for supporting other programmes.[15] Yet as it expanded and diversified, CS still made up the greatest percentage of World Vision's funding. World Vision had spent decades reconsidering CS. Despite its high operating costs, the criticism of CS from development theorists, and journalistic exposes, the steady stream of monthly support was too lucrative to abandon (Tackett and Jackson, 1998; Bornstein, 2001). While other INGOs depended on government grant cycles and the latest development fads, World Vision's devoted base of individual donors afforded it a measure of financial stability (Bergstrom, 2010).

Child sponsorship: Marketing, education, advocacy

World Vision also began to reconsider CS not only as a fundraising mechanism but also as an educational tool. When Pierce founded the organization, his vision was not only to raise funds for foreign missionaries but also to educate evangelical congregations on global issues. As it expanded into mass marketing via television in the late 1970s, dollars raised trumped education. Marketers understood the medium succeeded more through shocking images of malnourished children over lessons in historical, political contexts[16] (Gruman, 1985). By the 1990s, World Vision followed other organizations to present positive images of children as well as more intentionally educate donors on the processes of development. Not only did marketing studies point to the fact that positive images could raise more funds than negative ones, they also felt the obligation and pressure to merge marketing and education (Dyck and Coldevin, 1992, pp.572–579).

In educating its donor base, World Vision US often pointed to its AIDS work as it greatest success. While its donor constituency differs among various World Vision national offices, in the USA, World Vision's donor base remains solidly evangelical with 91 per cent of English speaking sponsors identifying as born-again Christians (World Vision, 2006). Having penetrated the evangelical market more than the general public and having honed its marketing strategies to reach it most effectively, World Vision could continue to focus on an American evangelical subculture and still maintain steady annual growth, but WVUS also felt an obligation to push American evangelicals beyond their comfort zone.

Its AIDS initiative served as a case in point. World Vision arrived later than most other humanitarian agencies to the AIDS crisis, and WVUS worried that the issue had little traction among its evangelical constituency. In the 1990s, the disease was not well understood, and most evangelicals still associated it with homosexuality and sexual promiscuity. World Vision's marketing staff worried that talking about AIDS would hurt the organization's image. A 2001 Barna poll proved World Vision's assumptions correct. It found that 'evangelical Christians were significantly less likely than non-Christians to give money for AIDS education and prevention programs worldwide'. Only 3 per cent of evangelical Christians would consider supporting World Vision's AIDS efforts (Barna, 2001).

World Vision still pressed ahead and established its Hope Initiative in 2000 as its global response to the HIV/AIDS crisis. Marketing costs would be higher and returns on investment much lower, but World Vision decided that education would be as important as the fundraising. In 2003, WVUS launched its first Hope Tour to educate American Christians and their churches about AIDS. Taking its message to major cities across the country, it parked its 2,500 square foot interactive, World Vision Experience, in church gyms, civic centres and even New York's Grand Central Station. As people made their way through the exhibit, they followed the story of a child affected by AIDS. At the conclusion, participants had the opportunity to sponsor a Hope Child, a designation given to children awaiting sponsorship in communities devastated by AIDS[17] (Tu, 2008). In a single year, World Vision saw the percentage of evangelicals willing to support HIV/AIDS work jump from 3 to 14 per cent (Barna, 2004; Shapiro, 2006).

WVUS President Richard Stearns points to success stories like the Hope Initiative in his best-selling book, *The Hole in our Gospel*. If World Vision worked throughout its more than 60 year history to overcome the divisions between evangelism and social reform, Stearns and others within the organization began to see the need to preach their holistic message more explicitly to its donor constituencies as well. Stearns claimed that 'being a Christian requires much more than just having a personal and transforming relationship with God. It also entails a public and transforming relationship with the world' (Stearns, 2009, p.2). Sensing that a number of Christians had shifted their views alongside World Vision's own evolution, he claimed both 'evangelism and social action as indivisible parts of the whole gospel' (Stearns, 2009, pp.199–200).

Conclusion

Despite its work as a leading relief and development organization, World Vision is still most often labelled as a CS INGO. Yet despite its continual heavy marketing of sponsorship, it is no longer the same organization that introduced CS to large numbers of American evangelicals in the 1950s and 1960s. World Vision has debated its relationship and approach to CS over the past 60 years as its leaders revisited the organization's theology, methodology and institutional structure. Tensions within the organization over CS no doubt continue, but such a case study illustrates the diversity among child sponsorship agencies, their intentional reflection upon their own practice, and the centrality of their role in the larger field of global humanitarianism. World Vision also demonstrates that while the analysis of humanitarian work often lumps organizations into simplistic categories of either religious or secular camps, the categories and divisions are rarely so simple. Analysing World Vision's grappling and retention of its faith commitments demonstrates how the religious identity of a faith-based organization is not isolated but often intertwined with the structural shifts the organization undergoes over time, the tensions it encounters from both internal and external pressures, and the practices and production of its humanitarian work.

Notes

1 Pierce had served as a journalist and had filed stories for numerous American evangelical publications such as *United Evangelical Action* and *Eternity* as well including images in his own sermons and fundraising efforts.

2 Over a typical ten month period in 1956–1957, World Vision recorded 58,914 people attending one of its travelling films. For a study of World Vision's film ministry, see John Robert Hamilton, 'An Historical Study of Bob Pierce and World Vision's Development of the Evangelical Social Action Film' (Hamilton, 1980).

3 At its peak, World Vision broadcasted 'Bob Pierce Reports' on 140 stations. In addition to offering stories of missionaries, they challenged listeners to sponsor orphans or otherwise support World Vision's work. They gave away gifts (records, tracts, books) for those who supported their ministry, and they even tracked which giveaways produced the highest return of supporters.

4 Seven new evangelical agencies were founded in the 1970s.

5 Smith notes that nine new evangelical organizations were founded in the 1970s.

6 World Vision realized that sponsored children were getting opportunities that un-sponsored children in the same community did not receive. Sometimes parents would give non-orphaned children to World Vision for care because they saw the added benefits of sponsorship.

7 The World Vision Canada office opened in 1957 and was incorporated in 1959. World Vision opened offices in Australia and New Zealand in 1966. Australia incorporated in 1969, and New Zealand in 1974. An office opened in South Africa in 1975. Along with the U.S., these became known as World Vision support countries in contrast to field or national countries that received funds to operate programmes.

8 A later discussion became not only moving to an indigenous workforce but also diversity in senior leadership. By 1978, Mooneyham claimed that two of three vice-presidents were non North Americans. One was Australian. The other was Indian. Sam Kamaleson of India became the first WVI Vice President from a former Third World country. He had first participated in evangelistic crusades with Pierce in Asia. Mooneyham recruited him to head World Vision's work with pastors' conferences.

9 Because World Vision US contributed the greatest proportion of funds to the partnership (75 per cent), it held a higher proportion of board seats:

4 US, 2 Canada, 2 Australia, 1 New Zealand and 6–8 at large. In early 1975, World Vision reported an income of $15 million. $11 million came from the US, $2 million from Australia/New Zealand, $1.5 million from Canada and $250,000 from South Africa (Mooneyham, 1975, p.10).

10 World Vision added 'developing self-reliance' to its core objectives in 1974. This was the first objective that World Vision had added since it the organization's founding. The six objectives were: 1) ministering to children and families; 2) providing emergency aid; 3) developing self-reliance; 4) reaching the un-reached; 5) strengthening leadership; 6) challenging to mission.

11 World Vision created a new Childcare Policy approved by the International Board in 1987.

12 Under pressure from the field offices, World Vision's marketers undertook a major study in the early 1980s to develop a fundraising philosophy that respected the dignity of people (World Vision, 1981).

13 In World Vision's research into its donor base, it knew that appeals for immediate relief and impoverished children proved most successful. World Vision later drafted guidelines on what it could and could not film (for example, unclothed women and children, or children with flies in their eyes) (Mussa, 2010).

14 World Vision measured its global position in various 'product lines' within the humanitarian industry including sponsorship, humanitarian response, food aid, advocacy, and development. Specifically, in regard to food aid, it was the largest recipient of World Food Programme commodities.

15 Organizations like World Vision often have come to monetize much of their GIK (sell the product on the open market) and use the income generated for other programme expenses.

16 By the late 1970s, 86 per cent of donors came through television.

17 Today, over 50 per cent of the children that World Vision donors sponsor are Hope children.

Bibliography

Anderson, K. (1948) 'Ambassador on fire', *Youth for Christ*, June, p.16.

Anderson, K. and Pierce, B. (1949) *This Way to the Harvest* (Grand Rapids: Zondervan).

Barna Research Group (2001) *World Vision: Orphan and Vulnerable Children (OVC) and HIV/AIDS Research*, January (WVUS Archives).

Barna Research Group (2004) *World Vision: Orphan and Vulnerable Children (OVC) and HIV/AIDS Update Research*, November (WVUS Archives).

Bergstrom, A. (2010) Interview with author, November, 16, Federal Way, WA.

Bernard, L. (1957) Editorial, *World Vision Magazine*, June, p.4.

Bornstein, E. (2001) 'Child sponsorship, evangelism, and belonging in the work of World Vision Zimbabwe', *American Ethnologist*, 28, 3, 595–622.

Christian, J. (1999) *God of the Empty-handed: Poverty, Power, and the Kingdom of God* (Monrovia, CA: MARC).

Correll, S. (1954) 'Korea: Shining star for Christianity', *United Evangelical Action*, 1 February, p.3.

Dunker, M. (2005) *Man of Vision: The Candid, Compelling Story of Bob and Lorraine Pierce, Founders of World Vision and Samaritan's Purse* (Waynesboro, GA: Authentic Media).

Dyck, E.J. and Coldevin, G. (1992) 'Using positive vs. negative photographs for third-world fund raising', *Journalism & Mass Communication Quarterly*, 69, 3, 572–579.

Gehman, R. (1960) *Let My Heart Be Broken with the Things That Break the Heart of God* (Grand Rapids, MI: Zondervan).

Graham, B. (1997) *Just as I Am: The Autobiography of Billy Graham*, 1st ed. (San Francisco, CA: HarperSanFrancisco).

Graham, F. and Lockerbie, J. (1983) *Bob Pierce: This One Thing I Do* (Waco, TX: World Books).

Grellert, M. (2007) Interview with author, 22 June, Monrovia, CA.

Gruman, E. (1985) *1984–5 Donor Research Study* (WVI Central Records).

Hamilton, R. (1980) *An Historical Study of Bob Pierce and World Vision's Development of the Evangelical Social Action Film*, PhD thesis, University of Southern California.

Hayes, K. (1983) 'Child sponsorship: Mything the mark', *The Other Side*, March, pp.36–37.

Houston, T. (n.d.) *Idealism vs. Pragmatism* (Houston Papers, WVI Central Records).

Irvine, G. (1978) *Ministry Integration: What Is Meant By It and Why We Need It*, 7 October 1978 (Irvine Papers, WVI Central Records).

Irvine, G. (1996) *Best Things in the Worst Times: An Insider's View of World Vision* (Wilsonville, OR: BookPartners).

McCleary, R.M. (2009) *Global Compassion: Private Voluntary Organizations and U.S. Foreign Policy Since 1939* (Oxford: Oxford University Press).

McDonic, S. (2004) *Witnessing, Work and Worship: World Vision and the Negotiation of Faith, Development and Culture*, PhD dissertation, Duke University.

McNee, P. (1989) 'Sponsorship: Can it be a two-way street', *Together* (April–June), pp.8–10.

Mooneyham, S. (1975) *What Do You Say to a Hungry World* (Waco: Word Books).

Mooneyham, S. (1978) *Remarks on Aspects of Internationalization*, prepared especially for presentation to Australia/New Zealand Boards, 1 February 1978 (WVI Central Records).

Mussa, J. (2010) WVUS, Senior Vice President, Donor Engagement, Advocacy and Communications, Interview with author, 19 November, Federal Way, WA.

Myers, B. (1987) *Childcare Position Paper* (WVI Central Records).

Myers, B. (1989) *World Vision's Sponsorship Ministry: The Ministry and the Money*, Report to World Vision International Council's Ministry Review and Evaluation Committee, 11 March (WVI Central Records).

Myers, B. (1999) *Walking With the Poor: Principles and Practices of Transformational Development* (Maryknoll, NY: Orbis).

Myers, B. (2005) *Our Future Orientation*, March (WVI Central Records).

Pierce, B. (n.d.) Untitled sermon, approximately 1956–1957 (WVI Central Records).

Pierce, B. (1949) *Youth for Christ Magazine*, September 1949, p.17.

Pierce, B. (1952) Message given at Missionary Conference of American Soul Clinic, 12 October 1952 (WVI Central Records).

Pierce, B. (1958) President's Report, WV Board of Directors' Meeting, 7 October 1958 (WVI Central Records).

Rees, P. and Kamaleson, S. (1976) *Theology of Internationalization*, Report of World Vision Internationalization Study Committee (WVI Central Records).

Rohrer, N. (1987) *Open Arms* (Wheaton, IL: Tyndale House).

Shapiro, N. (2006) 'The AIDS evangelists', *Seattle Weekly*, 15 November, http://www.seattleweekly.com/2006-11-15/news/the-aids-evangelists/, date accessed 15 June 2011.

Sider, R.J. (ed.) (1982) *Evangelicals and Development: Toward a Theology of Social Change* (Philadelphia, PA: Westminster Press).

Smith, L.D. (1986) *An Awakening of Conscience: The Changing Response of American Evangelicals toward World Poverty*, PhD dissertation, American University.

Stalker, P. (1982) 'Please do not sponsor this child', *New Internationalist*, 111, http://www.newint.org/features/1982/05/01/keynote/, date accessed 15 June 2011.

Stearns, R. (2009) *The Hole in Our Gospel* (Nashville, TN: Thomas Nelson).

Tackett, M. and Jackson, D. (1998) 'Myths of child sponsorship: The miracle merchants', *Chicago Tribune*, 22 March.

Tu, J. (2008) 'Bringing message on AIDS home — via Africa – Changing attitudes exhibit gaining notice among evangelical churches', *The Seattle Times*, 9 May, http://seattletimes.com/html/localnews/2004402500_aidsexhibit09m.html, date accessed 25 October 2013.

VanderPol, G.F. (2010) *The Least of These: American Evangelical Parachurch Missions to the Poor, 1947–2005*, PhD dissertation, Boston University School of Theology.

Waters, K. (1998) 'How World Vision rose from obscurity to prominence: Television fundraising, 1972–1982', *American Journalism*, 15, 4, 69–94.

Watkins, S. (1998) *Understanding Child Sponsorship: A Historical Perspective*, 20 March 1998 (WVUS Archives).

Whaites, A. (1999) 'Pursuing partnership: World Vision and the ideology of development – A case Study', *Development in Practice*, 9, 4, 410–423.

World Vision (1950–59) *Annual Reports – Missionary Disbursements, 1950–1959* (WVI Central Records).

World Vision (1978) *Declaration of Internationalization*, 31 May 1978 (WVI Central Records).

World Vision (1981) *World Vision Promotion and the Dignity of People*, 2 December (WVI Central Records).

World Vision (1982) *World Vision Factbook, 1982* (WVI Central Records).

World Vision (1983) *Report on Sponsorship Task Force*, WVI International Affairs Committee, February, pp.14–17 (WVI Central Records).

World Vision (2006) *Comprehensive Donor Survey*, 5 July 2006 (WVUS Archives).

Yuen, P. (2008) 'Things that break the heart of God': Child sponsorship programs and World Vision International', *Totem: The University of Western Ontario Journal of Anthropology*, 16, 1, 41–42.

13
Give and Take? Child Sponsors and the Ethics of Giving

Frances Rabbitts

Introduction

It is self-evident that child sponsorship (CS) should be set up to benefit the lives of its recipients in some way. Plan UK assures potential sponsors that 'Your donations help a whole community through funding projects such as building schools, digging wells and providing vaccinations' (Plan UK, 2013). Compassion UK argues that in its direct benefit programme 'the faithful financial support of the individual sponsor equips the child for the future by providing for their core needs' (Compassion UK, 2013). SOS Children, which provides homes for orphaned and abandoned children, explains its vision as 'a loving home for every child', where sponsorship provides children with 'new families for life' (SOS Children, 2013). Despite its varying setups, then, CS is unfailingly sold as a charitable act that can make a tangible difference to beneficiaries. Its success is measured and marketed accordingly, often (for instance) through 'success stories' of sponsored children who have become high achievers, or through statistics about community welfare. Understandably, then, debates about sponsorship focus mostly on its material and social impacts on recipients, with attention rarely paid to its other dimensions. And yet, sponsorship constructs meaning in more ways than one, shaping and impacting international non-governmental organizations (INGOs) themselves, and drawing together beneficiaries and INGOs with sponsors in sponsorship 'relationships'.

For some CS INGOs it is also self-evident that sponsorship can be transformational for sponsors. Save the Children's website, for instance, claims that 'Through child sponsorship, two lives are changed forever: yours and the life of your sponsored child' (Save the Children, 2013). Despite such promotional claims, questions about how CS impacts donors remain largely unconsidered, as are their motivations for giving: it is not self-evident at all how sponsorship might also be beneficial to sponsors themselves. The only accounts available are simplistic, positivist testimonials used in INGO marketing, such as the following: 'Being a child sponsor has helped me as much as it's helped the children. In giving I've received so much more than I could have imagined' (Anne Peel, Toybox, 2013). Chris Evans, ActionAid sponsor, explains that 'when I get a letter from [my sponsored child], it's really important to me...the feedback that you get from them gives you an insight into their world' (ActionAid UK, 2013). Such reports are occasionally supplemented or challenged by opinion pieces in newspapers, or by references in popular culture, such as the 2002 film 'About Schmidt', which portrays CS as a positive, self-affirming experience for sponsors. Despite these periodic mentions, no sustained work exists more thoroughly examining why people sponsor, what meaning it has to them, and how it becomes part of their daily lives. Unfortunately a common presumption is that 'Although it is possible for meaningful relationships between sponsors and sponsored children to exist, these seem to be a rarity and are not essential to the process' (Ove, 2013, p.6).

A perennial philosophical question about ethical action more generally is whether a concern with giving dynamics really matters. Some judge giving motivations as of little concern, as long as the end result is right and good (for example utilitarian theorists such as Peter Singer). In contrast, philosophical work on 'virtue ethics' (associated with the writings of Aristotle) judges the moral worth of giving according to motivations, rather than giving consequences. The jury is still out, therefore, on these centuries-old debates. However, questions about what happens in people when they give, how sponsorship gets performed and made meaningful, nonetheless provide a fascinating alternative to questions about sponsorship's impacts 'in the field'. Furthermore, these topics have multiple practical significances: they concern people's decisions to sponsor and to keep sponsoring, hence underpinning INGOs and sponsorship programmes themselves; they impact the way that sponsor-child relationships are understood and practised; and they shape the communities and cultures to which INGOs must direct their marketing efforts. In terms of CS more broadly, therefore, the real mechanics of donation 'matter' very much.

In addition to this, if the sponsoring process is not unpacked, some common but problematic understandings of charity donation risk becoming further embedded. One positions charitable activity as primarily egoistic, allowing givers to invest in a self-gratifying sense of their own personal goodness, in what Rebecca Allahyari (2000) has termed 'moral selving'. In a critical self-analysis, World Vision sponsor Samantha Selinger-Morris (2012) explains:

> If pressed, I would say I initially clicked on Jordan's photo on the charity's website...out of a creeping sense of middle-class guilt. That I was buying bespoke muesli week after week while children were literally starving elsewhere in the world was an incongruity that stuck uncomfortably to me like a burr, mocking my perception of myself as a Good Person.

Although Selinger-Morris infers a deeper sense of altruism here, the point remains that sponsorship's personable feel-good factor often works because it flatters sponsor egos. However, this reading is not only cynical, but also woefully partial.

A related narrative, visible in the wealth of social scientific work critiquing manifestations of 'neo-liberalism', reads contemporary Western charity as increasingly focused around notions of global citizenship (with personal charity being encouraged as a vital counter-response to the pro-social failures of neo-liberal capitalism), rhetoric of individual, consumer choice, and service-delivery goals. Most CS INGOs allow donors some choice in who they sponsor (be it the child's location, gender or age), and market sponsorship as allowing donors to monitor the impacts of their donations: 'Our staff in the child's community will send you two newsletters a year, so that you can really understand how your donations are working to change lives. It will include detailed figures on where your money is going, and stories of individuals whose lives you have helped to change' (ActionAid UK, 2013). CS therefore seems to fit this reading as well, emphasizing consumer choice and boasting measurable results.

A third reading positions internationally-focused charity within a much broader trajectory of Western philanthropic involvements in 'Other' countries, rooted in colonialism. For Ove (2013, p.13) '...the construction of good (white) people(s) is predicated upon an histor-ically oppressive association with helping poor (black) Others. In this way, the work of international development in general, and CS in par-ticular, can never truly be separated from the perspective of 'the white man's burden.' In such readings CS comes to embody long-standing power relations of Western patronage, most clearly visible in tradi-tional representations of white adults nurturing black children (see also

Burman, 1994; Manzo, 2008). Such arguments have been directed at sponsorship for a long time, as this 1989 critique from the *New Internationalist* shows: '[Through letter-writing] the sponsored child is constantly reminded that they are the "poor relation". They must always be prepared to show gratitude to the "rich cousins" on whose charity they depend'. Thus, sponsorship becomes unavoidably associated with problematic relational patterns, whether or not its practical content fosters neo-colonial attitudes. One view of CS posits that 'Because of the apparently miraculous capacity of their donations to forever alter some poor child's life, sponsors are able to attain the status of extraordinary person that is so desirable in Western culture' (Ove, 2013, p.12).

The problem with these narratives is that they employ particularly partial readings of donation, fostering simplistic, cynical assumptions about what charity is. What follows argues for a richer reading, drawing on interviews with sponsors from two very different CS INGOs, Compassion and the Kindu Trust, carried out in 2011–2012. I seek to show how (firstly) the ethics and (secondly) the practice of CS are caught up in everyday spaces, relations and senses of identity, and (thirdly) how these interweave with broader configurations of identity, community and INGO strategy. The complexity of CS donation is not a distraction from the 'real issues' which plague sponsorship more broadly: it could, I argue, provide an alternative way to open these up, underpinning more radical approaches to development.

Charitable ethics

The basic recognition of philosophical and sociological work on gift-giving is that no gift is ever purely altruistic, always involving the self somehow (for example Mauss, 1924; Derrida, 1992). Sponsor-child dialogue, for instance, is a particularly obvious example of reciprocity being built into charity; through it sponsors can track their giving investment and very often obtain some sense of personal satisfaction, whether in terms of knowledge that their money is being used wisely, or emotional feedback from feelings of 'making a difference'. Whilst such self-gain might render sponsorship vulnerable to arguments of 'moral selving' or hedonistic charity, it need not always be viewed negatively (Barnett and Land, 2007). This is important: the question is not whether givers are or are not wrapped up in their giving, but the merits of how they are involved.

CS often provides a vehicle through which sponsors, egoistically or not, invest in and 'work up' (Barnett et al, 2005) certain moralized senses of personal identity (see also Rabbitts, 2012). One influential set of ethical frameworks around which this can be organized is Christianity, historically – and still – a significant source of charitable prompts and resources, and long influential in landscapes of international development. Today, over half the INGOs offering CS schemes in the UK publicly affiliate themselves with Christianity.

The Christian faith is very often understood and practised in ways which emphasize the intertwining of generous action with self-investment: Biblical endorsements of love for others, particularly the poor, are connected strongly to narratives of personal righteousness and holiness, out of obedience to God and through His power:

> [Sponsorship] was something I felt God poked me about, and I really didn't want to go into it lightly...it was kind of learning that what I have is His anyway, so if everything I own is God's...it should be a real blessing to be able to [sponsor]...you know as part of walking with God, we're told to serve other people, we're told to see other people as better than ourselves. So I'm actually changing my attitude towards that (Tony, Compassion sponsor).

This notion of one's ongoing spiritual self-development clearly interweaves not only with threads of theology, but also with ideas of personal relationship with God. Thus, charitable giving can often be connected with senses of spiritual experience:

> One day we had somebody [from Compassion] speaking at church...and I sat there and listened and I suddenly knew, 'today's the day, [I'm] going to get another child!' After he'd finished speaking, I just went up to the table for Compassion and [a Compassion volunteer] was standing there...she saw me there and she gave me this [profile] – 'that's your child, [Lucy]' – I didn't choose, but this was the one, I just looked at [this child] and thought 'you are gorgeous!' ...I thought yeah, this is God putting the two of us together (Lucy, Compassion sponsor).

Some note that faith-based giving, Christian or otherwise, can tend towards uncritical self-involvement and the reproduction of neocolonial attitudes, especially if concerns for proselytism are approached insensitively (for example Cloke et al, 2005). Evangelistic motivations can form a central part of Christian giving, for instance; Compassion mobilizes this as a key selling point for its programme, where sponsored children are 'given opportunities to hear and respond to the gospel' (Compassion UK, 2013). This, according to Cloke et al (2005), can prompt questions about what sort of changes or conversions are required of sponsored children in order to be counted as 'successful' recipients. As previous examples show, nevertheless, faith can also frame responses which spill beyond narrow conceptions of self-interest, expanding to include responsibilities to both God and others (see also Korf, 2006), in ways which highlight the importance and potential of Christian caritas or charity as a motivation and ethical framework.

Similar ethics of generosity, empathy and social justice are also apparent in the responses of sponsors with no expressed religious affiliation, though they can be packaged differently, and often involve very different attitudes to the self. Cloke et al (2005), after Coles (1997), identify secular forms of humanitarianism as another key driver of charity; whereby God-centred or God-founded views of charity are substituted by human-oriented views, with ethical prompts to help others being founded on assumed universal, 'objective' moral norms, such as discourses of human rights. Jim Al-Khalili, President of the British Humanist Association at the time of writing, argues thus: 'Reason, decency, tolerance, empathy and hope are human traits that we should aspire to, not because we seek reward of eternal life or because we fear the punishment of a supernatural being, but because they define our humanity' (BHA, 2013).

Self-involvement, in this context, is judged according to reigning frameworks of ethical subjectivity which, I have found in my work, involve a mixture of modern and postmodern ideas (see also Cloke et al, 2005). Within modernist frameworks, purely 'altruistic' giving is perceived to be quite achievable, with the self being able to be kept objectively separate from the giving process, lest it might compromise the purity of the gift. Adam, a sponsor with no religious affiliation, responded:

> It's been good to know that I am helping someone less fortunate than me...[but sponsorship should] be approached from the point of view of doing it for the child and not for yourself, i.e. don't do it if it's only going to inflate your own ego (Adam, Kindu Trust sponsor).

The idea that charity is less charitable if there is a benefit to the giver, and that sponsorship is depreciated if there is an emotional reward for sponsors, is further implied by Kindu Trust sponsor Mathew, who commented: 'I mean it's really simply a sort of charitable act rather than anything personal.'

Where postmodern conceptions of selfhood are influential, sponsors frequently identify a tension between their desire to help people in need, and a fear of imposing their own world-view on others. This internal tension often produces unease, such that sponsors distance themselves (often quite paradoxically) from sponsorship as much as possible. Milly, for instance, explained her decision to not communicate with her sponsored child thus:

> I don't feel like I have any claim on him just because I'm able to give him money...I don't have any control over his life, and I don't want to, I feel like what I'm doing is acknowledging some sort of great injustice, but I don't want to make him feel obliged to be in touch with me, or thank me (Milly, Kindu Trust sponsor).

Of course, in practice 'Christian' and 'secular' frameworks of charitable ethics, themselves diverse, overlap and interact in ways which are very difficult to tease apart. A useful way of comprehending this is to note a distinction in attitudes between those who draw charity around rigidly defended boundaries of belief (whether religious or secular), and those who are more willing to lay these boundaries aside in favour of more broadly accessible grounds for action (see also Cloke and Beaumont, 2012). Overall, what is important to note from the responses above is that, depending on their ethical logics and understandings, many sponsors clearly recognize and negotiate their inevitable self-involvements in giving (particularly in CS where felt senses of reciprocity are heightened) quite differently.

Giving inspirations

Giving involves not only the self and senses of self-identity, but also many other relations and ethical concerns. Initial prompts to sponsor, for instance, can be far more complex than usually assumed – rarely do people become sponsors purely because they see an advertisement. One's own family and friends, for example, can significantly shape decisions to give. For Kindu Trust sponsors, the majority of who are recruited through personal contact with its Ethiopian projects, prompts to sponsor children through the Trust's scheme often issue from admiration for these projects, seen first-hand, as well as for its staff – particularly its founder, Kate Eshete, who was the driving force behind the charity until 2009 (Director of Operations, personal communication, 15 February 2012). Many Kindu sponsors narrate their giving not as primarily concerned with the novelty of sponsorship, nor as about responding to broader moralities or imaginaries of poverty, but as inspired by far more proximal relations and the charisma of particular people. In this case, the charisma belongs to an INGO founder and staff member, though of course similar inspiration could be derived from the work of volunteers, or from the use of celebrities in CS campaigns – an increasingly popular fundraising method amongst INGOs.

Similarly, Compassion puts a strong emphasis on face-to-face recruitment methods, meaning that whilst few Compassion sponsors have physically visited a Compassion project, most can identify a staff member, volunteer or evangelistic friend or family member who has helped to prompt their decision to give. Thus, charitable action is not simply prompted by the figure of the needy child or some pre-existing altruistic urge, but also by other relations and inspiring performances.

Furthermore, in many ways CS becomes intertwined with the everyday social contexts of donors, such that the distance and difference between sponsor and child are made more accessible by being understood through familiar lenses of personal experience and identity:

> My role now is a family support worker so I'm visiting families who haven't got very much, but by comparison with Kindu they've got loads, you know, more than one room to live in! And also, when I was young and first a mum, not everything was as rosy as it was painted, so...I think it's an appreciation of how tough it is (Pat, Kindu Trust sponsor).

Similarly, the monetary commitment of sponsorship is often rationalized through comparison to everyday purchases and activities: 'It's a round of drinks in the pub' (Peter, Kindu Trust sponsor), 'it's a takeaway every week, and think how much healthier we would all be' (Annie, Compassion sponsor).

These proximal lenses not only affect the way that sponsorship is understood and done; they themselves can be re-invested through sponsorship, as seen in the two extracts below:

> When I used to work in a college I used to take [photos and information about my sponsored child] in to the students, because I

was [teaching] Early Years, and you know, 'this is the other side of life, girls' (Pat, Kindu Trust sponsor).

My family chose to sponsor a child who is approximately the same age as my granddaughter, because we wanted her to understand how blessed she is and that she has a responsibility to fight the corner of the less fortunate...our granddaughter is in a single parent family and has no contact with her father. Her life is tougher than many of her friends but we encourage the thought that her life is still easier than that of our sponsored child (Charlotte, Compassion sponsor).

This 'ethical embeddedness' (Hall, 2011) of CS suggests that its ethical dynamics spill far beyond the relation between sponsor and sponsored child, intertwining cross-distance giving practices with more proximal caring relations.

Thus far, it becomes extremely difficult to encapsulate the ethical dynamics of CS donation by narratives of moral selving, consumerism or colonial patronage. Though these undoubtedly still have purchase, charity donation should be understood as folding together multiple relations and ethical demands, in ways which are shaped uniquely by the contexts of each sponsor. These suggestions are now further explored through a discussion of how CS is practised and performed.

Charitable practice

CS stands out within international humanitarian charity because it seemingly offers sponsors an opportunity to engage regularly and actively with the aid process, following it and feeling able to contribute to it, whether via letter-writing, gift-sending, visits, or less obvious engagements such as prayer, for sponsors of faith. Not all sponsors take up these opportunities or attach meaning to them in the same ways, and INGO allowance of such opportunities varies widely; nevertheless, they remain vital elements of sponsorship's appeal and experience.

Importantly for this discussion, frequently overlooked are the ways in which these active engagements become embedded in sponsors' everyday lives and relations. These can be offered up as part of the gift, and shared with sponsored children:

[I write] 'I like to play with horses' and that's because I think that the people in these 3rd world countries horses for them are work animals, they don't see them as loved or cared for, so I can say that you know, I've learned to help other people understand their horses better which is what I like to do...I keep it simple and I just tell them I have two daughters and what age they are, and you know, one's married and I've got a cute little granddaughter... (Lucy, Compassion sponsor)

Gabby, a Compassion volunteer who sponsors several children, spends much of her spare time encouraging sponsors in her local area to creatively engage with letter-writing. She regularly produces colorful activity sheets themed around local landmarks and life in rural England, designed to be interesting and informative for young children, and a talking point for sponsors. This highlights the rich creativity with which sponsors can approach the traditional element of dialogue (see also Bornstein, 2001).

Correspondingly, sponsorship becomes embedded in spaces and rhythms of sponsor lives; photographs of children take pride of place on window sills and notice-boards, suitable gifts are sought as part of everyday shopping routines, household budgets are readjusted, and daily tactics are adopted to further integrate activities like letter-writing and prayer. The following extracts indicate that for some sponsors, the act of sponsorship becomes wrapped up in their daily lives and material surroundings in ways which are imbued with meaning and purpose:

When I was at uni, I had a big board on which I could pin things, and I would pin [the drawings done by my sponsored child] up...when my friends came into my room I could tell them how she was, and I put the pictures I had of her up as well so I could see her and it reminded me to pray as well. (Kat, Compassion sponsor)

We have our sponsored children's photos displayed in the house, and there is not a day where I don't think about them, pray for them, wonder how they are doing... Sponsorship has had an impact on our budget – we have reallocated money towards it that would have been spent on non-essentials – our sponsored children need it more than we do! (Natalie, Compassion sponsor)

Not dissimilarly to fundraising ventures like alternative gifts or Tearfund's 'Toilet Twinning' scheme, the material and practical elements of sponsorship are here displayed within daily life in ways which regularly prompt sponsors to remember to care, and allow for others to notice and engage. In their analysis of Fairtrade supporters,

Barnett (et al, 2005, pp.31 & 38) argue that such performances work to govern the self, 'making one's own life a project of self-cultivation' through routine activities; and govern others, seeking to display ethical credentials to friends and family and inspire them to follow suit.

Importantly, from these daily environments sponsors derive knowledge, skills and resources which shape their practical engagements with giving. Many sponsors, for instance, inform their giving by their own experiences of parenthood, or their own career trajectory, whether in terms of some kind of caring or child-related expertise (for example teaching, healthcare), or prior work with charitable organizations. Kindu sponsor Julia provides one such example:

> I used to be a charity fund-raiser...so I knew the drill, essentially how it works, and I know the wastage in charities as well, which I was sort of worried about...[Kindu] is a very small charity, so I felt like the wastage wouldn't be too much. And because it was registered in UK, that gave me a bit more confidence as well...because of corruption, which is the sad truth.

Others utilize opportunities and resources already available within their own lives; for instance, Compassion sponsor Lucy writes out Bible verses and song lyrics in Portuguese to her sponsored child in Brazil, using a Portuguese Bible and Portuguese songs she has because of her Brazilian son-in-law.

This notion that sponsors creatively put their own stamp on their giving challenges neo-liberal conceptions of donors which locate 'expertise' with the INGO and position sponsors as consumers, rather than active shapers of (and potential contributors to) the sponsorship process. Indeed, recognizing the situated knowledge and expertise which sponsors bring into their giving could found a much more productive set of engagements between INGOs, development issues and Western publics. Whilst managing sponsor involvements can be a point of continuous difficulty for INGOs, demanding tender balances to be struck between involving sponsors and pandering to them, and involving contradictory claims to expertise; nevertheless, some of the most inspiring and interesting schemes currently in existence remain those where INGOs take seriously the unique contributions and skills of sponsors, treating them as people rather than as sources of money.

At the Kindu Trust, for instance, where most sponsors are personally known by staff members and sponsors often visit children, a particularly organic organizational culture lets sponsors contribute even more directly to development projects. If sponsors see a need they feel should be addressed, on top of the remit of traditional CS, they can freely collaborate with the Trust to take action, often bringing to bear their own expertise on the situation as they go. Thus, many Kindu sponsors occupy quite untraditional roles, involving elements of donation, volunteering and collaborative, staff-like encounters.

In many ways strains of colonial philanthropy are visible here, where patrons and benefactors demand a more central role in deciding how their giving is disseminated. How Kindu manages sponsor engagements alongside its own professional expertise, and what imaginaries of Western development efforts are deployed in the process, are therefore clearly important questions to ask if such heightened involvements are to not conform to such critiques. However, more positively, Kindu's open, collaborative culture flies in the face of professionalized, service-delivery charity, where CS is a product that sponsors can take or leave, where INGOs are responsible for implementing projects and demonstrating a return on sponsors' investments, and where outside-the-box engagements cannot easily be synthesized with increasingly managerial organizational cultures. This again gestures to the potential of CS to exceed the giving parameters endorsed by neo-liberal frameworks and, if approached appropriately, also those critiqued by post-colonial thought. Undoubtedly, Kindu's small size helps to make its 'case-by-case', organic organizational culture possible; if it grows, it will be interesting to see to what extent this is sacrificed in the face of pressures to become more corporate and bureaucratic.

Charitable networks

CS, it is now apparent, can emerge from and invest in both the self and relationships with more proximal others. It should not, therefore, be surprising that this also involves certain senses of community to which sponsors belong. It has already been shown, for instance, that sponsorship can invest in one's own family, particularly in one's children, which builds into it another set of 'parent-child' dynamics often passed by, particularly by post-colonial critiques.

Additionally, sponsorship is often taken up by schools, being a longer-term project focusing on a face with which school-age children can identify, and which can be productively factored into several different curricula; here, sponsorship becomes about investing in the education of other children (see also Smith, 2004), and in their senses of 'global citizenship', as much as (or more than) about the gift itself.

Similarly, sponsorship can play a role in cultivating senses of church community, easily interweaving with Christian moral discourses of helping the poor and establishing God's kingdom, and providing a practical way for whole congregations, youth clubs, Sunday Schools and Bible study groups to practise what gets preached. This not only re-invests in localized senses of belonging and collective action, but, as Bornstein (2001) has argued, also helps establish senses of 'global Christian family' that centralize notions of brotherhood rather than ethnic or cultural difference (I would add that evangelism is very often a key intersecting motivation, though one which is often wrongly tarred with a very simplistic brush). Thus, what is done through CS is done inseparably from these broader, multiple, overlapping senses of community (including global-scale formulations of collective citizenship, earthly or heavenly), meaning that sponsorship is rarely as individualistic as it appears at first glance.

Out of these various collective efforts, new networks can spin into existence. Many churches and community groups across the UK, for instance, hold letter-writing groups for sponsors; this not only re-invests in the practice of CS, but also cultivates new friendships and senses of collective action. Similarly, INGOs themselves can be responsible for bringing such networks into being. Compassion, for instance, has created an online social networking platform for its sponsors, 'OurCompassion', through which sponsors can write letters electronically, create their own profiles, interact with other sponsors, browse project locations and access updates provided by the managers of each project. This latter example gestures towards the broader importance of understanding how sponsor networks become interwoven with the marketing efforts of INGOs. These are not only visible in purpose-built online platforms, but also in the strategic targeting of other collective spaces with tailored resources and discourses (for example school curricula, church services).

In the UK Compassion employs a wealth of different tactics in order to integrate their brand of CS with senses of collective Christian life. From the top-down, they sponsor key national Christian events, garner the support of Christian celebrities and forge partnerships with well-known Christian media organizations, in order to establish a strong brand presence in those larger-scale movements, discourses and spaces from which many local churches and church-goers derive inspiration. From the bottom-up, Compassion has a network of volunteers and staff advocates who embody its discourses at a face-to-face level. Packs of promotional resources are produced targeting different segments of church community, and entire congregations; and local volunteers are encouraged to put up church displays and do presentations during services.

These efforts demonstrate that INGO presences in the networks surrounding CS are complex and rarely easily separable from the various strands and senses of community to which sponsors belong. In other words, neither INGOs nor sponsors act from some sort of social vacuum, but from within broader communal existences. This does not always unfold in the same way; churches might provide certain opportunities for INGOs like Compassion to weave CS with senses of community and belonging that are not provided by marketing venues such as shopping centres; festivals undoubtedly provide different opportunities to community groups, and so on. Nevertheless, charity donation cannot be thoroughly understood without an appreciation of how it interweaves with such dynamic contexts. These will necessarily have their own political and ethical dynamics which spill out beyond INGO control. They are not consistent, homogeneous or devoid of political struggle. Of interest then, is firstly how INGOs dialogically shape and get shaped by these networks and spaces, and secondly how these interactions might be politically productive: not in ways which romanticize supporter communities, but in ways which open up real dialogue.

Discussion

Whether discussing the ethics of giving, its practice, or the networks surrounding these, it is clear that child sponsors (and charity donation more broadly) deserve a richer, more dynamic reading. This is not to resoundingly reject the narratives described at the start, for these undoubtedly have purchase, but instead to argue for integrating these with a recognition of the intricate social and spatial fabrics which imbue and undergird charity: the other ethical flows, the other people, the other elements of sponsor lives and identities which get caught up in CS, and how these change the character of giving. It is also to recognize that charitable giving becomes embroiled in the performance of these relations, spaces, senses of self and community, in ways which are thoroughly ethical.

These sorts of recognition are not merely matters of conceptual tweaking. They demand a thorough re-theorization of the donation process, and a deeper appreciation for how charity can have many layers of meaning. The undeniable presence here of ethical positives, of flows of generosity, which far exceed narratives of 'moral selving', neo-liberal individualism and neo-colonial patronage, should alert us to the blinkered accounts of charity which such readings prescribe. The ethics and practice of giving involve more complex ways of relating and more dynamic flows of power; furthermore, these complexities may be mobilized and enhanced by INGOs in inspiring ways.

This, then, attests rather more hopefully to the broader question of whether or not CS might be put to work in opening out more radical engagements between Global North and Global South. Sponsorship would seem uniquely placed for such projects because of its built-in opportunities for dialogue; moreover, there certainly seems to be much opportunity for INGOs to creatively engage with the complexities of donation. There is no singular pathway forward here; simply the notion that if INGOs are seeking ways to deepen their approaches to development, the potential roles sponsors might play in this process should neither be underestimated nor circumscribed by organizational pressures or broader [neo-liberal] sector discourses. The figure of the 'donor' (even this term is unnecessarily prescriptive) must be rethought with more hope, even – especially – in the face of so many pressures to package sponsors up in easy boxes and, often, leave them there.

Now for some caveats. The ways in which such opportunities might be opened up will clearly depend upon a variety of factors, not least the setup of each scheme and the specificities of each INGO. Furthermore, they should necessarily be held in productive tension with a critical awareness of the many pitfalls and problems which cling determinedly to CS, in practice and in public and professional imaginations; these should not be forgone in exchange for a totally positive reading, but continually wrestled with. Finally, I am not saying here that INGOs (in all their wondrous variety) do not appreciate their sponsors, nor that attempts to engender such engagements are not already in existence; rather, that public engagements with development via CS are complex and dynamic, unable to be encapsulated easily with demographic markers or ethical allegations, and as such, they can always be approached in more creative ways.

In other words, it is high time for a critical yet hopeful discussion of exactly what it means to be charitable, and what kinds of exciting, inspiring movements might be engendered by taking sponsors more seriously, as able to contribute in more ways than just finance, as more than ignorant targets for 'development education' and neo-liberal projects of 'global citizenship'. Better understanding of their richly messy engagements may, it is true, primarily serve to stimulate ever-more creative recruitment methods from INGOs. But this is not the point: the point is that the complexity of charity can and should be a platform from which to build better approaches to aid and development, and more inspiring attitudes to our being in the world. For this project, particularly given its in-built potential for dialogue and for encouraging high levels of interest from donors, child sponsorship (despite its baggage) may provide a particularly good place to start.

Bibliography

ActionAid US (2013) *What You'll Receive*, http://www.actionaid.org.uk/sponsor-a-child/what-youll-receive, date accessed 3 June 2013.

Allahyari, R. (2000) *Visions of Charity: Volunteer Workers and Moral Community* (Berkeley: University of California Press).

Barnett, C. and Land, D. (2007) 'Geographies of generosity: Beyond the "moral turn"', *Geoforum*, 38, 6, 1065–1075.

Barnett, C., Cloke, P., Clarke, N. and Malpass, A. (2005) 'Consuming ethics: Articulating the subjects and spaces of ethical consumption', *Antipode*, 37, 1, 23–45.

BHA [British Humanist Association], (2013) *BHA website*, http://www.humanism.org.uk, date accessed 3 June 2013.

Bornstein, E. (2001) 'Child sponsorship, evangelism, and belonging in the work of World Vision Zimbabwe', *American Ethnologist*, 28, 3, 595–622.

Burman, E. (1994) 'Poor children: Charity appeals and ideologies of childhood', *International Journal of Psychology and Psychotherapy*, 12, 1, 29–36.

Cloke, P. and Beaumont, J. (2012) 'Geographies of postsecular rapprochement in the city 1', *Progress in Human Geography*, 37, 1, 27–51.

Cloke, P., Johnsen, S. and May, J. (2005) 'Exploring ethos? Discourses of "charity" in the provision of emergency services for homeless people', *Environment and Planning A*, 37, 3, 385–402.

Coles, R. (1997) *Rethinking Generosity: Critical Theory and the Politics of Caritas* (New York: Cornell University Press).

Compassion UK (2013) *About Sponsorship*, http://www.compassionuk.org/about-sponsorship, date accessed 3 June 2013.

Derrida, J. (1992) *Given Time: Counterfeit Money* (Chicago: University of Chicago Press).

Hall, S. M. (2011) 'Exploring the "ethical everyday": An ethnography of the ethics of family consumption', *Geoforum*, 42, 6, 627–637.

Korf, B. (2006) 'Geography and Benedict XVI', *Area*, 38, 3, 326–329.

Manzo, K. (2008) 'Imaging humanitarianism: NGO identity and the iconography of childhood', *Antipode*, 40, 4, 632–657.

Mauss, M. (1924) *The Gift: The Form and Reason for Exchange in Archaic Societies.* Trans. W.D. Halls (London: Routledge).

New Internationalist (1989) *Simply...Why You Should Not Sponsor A Child*, Issue 194, April 1989, http://newint.org/features/1989/04/05/simply/, date accessed 3 June 2013.

Ove, P. (2013) '"Change a life. Change your own": Child sponsorship, the discourse of development, and the production of ethical subjects'. Doctoral thesis, Faculty of Graduate Studies, University of British Columbia.

Plan UK (2013) *Sponsor a Child*, http://www.plan-uk.org/sponsor-a-child/, date accessed 3 June 2013.

Rabbitts, F. (2012) 'Child sponsorship, ordinary ethics and the geographies of charity', *Geoforum*, 43, 5, 926–936.

Save the Children (2013) *Sponsor a Child*, http://www.savethechildren.org/site/c.8rKLIXMGIpI4E/b.6146367/, date accessed 1 October 2013.

Selinger-Morris, S. (2012) *I Was Dumped by My Sponsor Child*, http://www.stuff.co.nz/life-style/6639200/I-was-dumped-by-my-sponsor-child, date accessed 3 June 2013.

Smith, M. (2004) 'Contradiction and change? NGOs, schools and the public faces of development', *Journal of International Development*, 16, 5, 741–749.

SOS Children (2013) *SOS UK homepage*, http://www.soschildrensvillages.org.uk/, date accessed 3 June 2013.

Toybox (2013) *What Our Sponsors Say*, http://www.toybox.org/uk/give/child-sponsorship/what-our-sponsors-say.aspx, date accessed 3 June 2013.

14
Child Sponsorship as Development Education in the Northern Classroom

Rachel Tallon and Brad Watson

Introduction

Child sponsorship (CS) marketing has been described as the pre-eminent lens through which many people in the Global North see the South (Smillie, 2000, p.121). Since the 1980s the repetitive use of images of malnourished, unclothed, sad and de-contextualized children by some international non-governmental organizations (INGOs) has been questioned and it remains apparent that '...no matter how effective the image, the message can be very destructive' (Coulter, 1989 p.2). A growing body of literature has emerged, concerned with the portrayal of the 'Other', particularly with the narrow format of a close-up picture of a passive child that CS has so often used (Manzo, 2008). Ongoing speculation suggests that some messages and images continue to 'ignore Northern complicity in creating inequality' while they 'portray people as helpless victims, dependent, and unable to take action...' (Plewes and Stuart in Bell and Coicaud, 2007, p.24). Further, the positioning of children at the centre of advocacy, advertising and interventions has led to claims that the dominant image of the child in many CS campaigns may have become a symbol for many places and people in the Global South (Paech, 2004; Strüver, 2007). As such, a more recent concern about CS marketing is that people in entire regions of the Global South may come to be seen by Northern donors as needy, passive and childlike through the dominance of CS representations (Dogra, 2012). This may be especially true for impressionable students in Northern schools where CS is advertised by international non-governmental organizations (INGOs) and facilitated by teachers in the absence of a pedagogically sound development education curriculum. A key issue is how students make meaning of their interaction with CS INGOs and how they construct the 'Other' in response to marketing strategies that continue to utilize evocative images.

To their credit, ethical CS INGOs are increasingly concerned about their portrayal of people in the South and have paid particular attention in recent years to issues of respect and ethics regarding images of the vulnerable (see Mittelman and Neilson, 2011; CCIC, 2008 for discussion on the ethical use of images). INGOs have also carried out extensive research concerning how the public interprets their messages (VSO, 2002; Darnton and Kirk, 2011). Many large CS INGOs are not dissimilar in this regard. For example, in Australia, in keeping with standards promoted by the Australian Council for International Development for all INGOs in Australia, World Vision Australia's communication guidelines require that images 'ensure the respect and dignity of the subject is maintained' and 'represent situations truthfully' (World Vision Australia, 2009, p.4). Though such guidelines do not address the concern that a predominance of child images may render the South as childlike in the minds of donors, they do reflect improved standards and awareness embraced by leading CS INGOs in North America, Europe and other donor nations. Signatories to the Irish Association of Non-Governmental Development Organizations, including CS INGOs such as Plan, agree not just to 'Avoid images and messages that potentially stereotype, sensationalize or discriminate...' but to 'Truthfully represent any image or depicted situation both in its immediate and in its wider context so as to improve public understanding of the realities and complexities of development' (DOCHAS, 2006, p.2).

To date much of the scholarly commentary has been on adult perceptions of the Global South and how their knowledge levels and perceptions may be shaped by CS INGOs (see Plewes and Stuart, 2007; Manzo, 2006) with little research conducted into how CS advertising impacts young people in the North (Smith and Yanacopulos, 2004). Research conducted with youth in New Zealand demonstrates that well-intentioned teacher use of CS to complement development education is potentially complex and can reinforce binary divisions regarding the world. This may undermine effective development education for young people whose depth of understanding and motivation for informed engagement will impact North-South interactions in the future.

Moving beyond recognition of the potential to create problematic misunderstandings, this chapter argues that the promotion of CS in schools and mobilization of Northern children to sponsor Southern children is best used as a possible quiver in an effective teacher's bow, with others aimed at advancing student understanding of poverty, exclusion, geographic disadvantage, unfair trade, colonial legacies and a range of related issues. It should not be assumed by CS INGOs that young people in the Global North receive the idea of CS homogenously, positively, or in a manner likely to advance a global citizenship education (GCE) agenda.

Development education: From radical roots to consumerism?

The promotion of CS in schools and to youth is not a recent phenomenon. In 1929 the Save the Children Federation Journal reported that an enquiry made in some schools in Geneva (probably private schools) which sponsored children 'revealed genuine enthusiasm for it among teachers. The teachers were unanimous in declaring that their pupils took a greatly increased interest in the country of their adopted children, "but", they added, "the exchange of letters is absolutely necessary if the zeal of children is to be maintained"' (Schatzmann, 1929, p.9). Schatzmann argued that the benefits of adoption included the formation of real friendships, 'the weaving of a web of friendship throughout the whole world', and asserted that children who had adopted a little foreigner:

> naturally begin to take an interest in his environment, his town, his country. They are keen to learn all the customs of the country, its history, its national festivals, its buildings, its costumes. Visits are often planned, and more than once the adopted child has been asked to spend his holidays with his foster-parents (Schatzmann, 1929, p.10).

From the 1980s, a number of increasingly powerful INGOs spent significant funds on media and resources to raise the level of awareness of the Northern public about global inequalities and the need for conceited action to address them (Lidchi, 1999, gives an overview of the conflict within INGOs between education and fundraising). These broad efforts were designed to develop 'global awareness', and alert audiences to '...events and conditions in distant parts of the globe...' moving them beyond the 'motivational threshold of the average unconcerned citizen' (Lissner, 1977, pp.140–141). Loosely-termed development education, such efforts were not dissimilar to the early awareness raising agenda of S.C.F. in Great Britain however it encompassed questions including 'do we pay proper attention to the explicit and implicit values which we convey to the public...?' (Lissner, 1977, p.145) For the most part, attempts to inform compassionate response with greater awareness was commendable although Duke (2003) has raised concerns that the very discourse of development education may conceal unconscious attitudes of superiority evident in calls for compassion. While some early development education efforts had radical underpinnings, challenging the 'pity them' framework and calling for a political response to global inequality (Bourn, 2011) many CS INGOs have allocated the large majority of their public communication funds to marketing CS as a product rather than a vehicle for informed giving and advocacy for sustainable change. For much of the twentieth century INGOs had ignored or paid lip service to Eglantyne Jebb's 1920s argument that 'Help should not be a gift from above but rather help aimed at self-help between equals where, everyone contributes according to their ability...' (in Save the Children, 2008, p.5).

McCloskey (2012, p.113) has differentiated between UK INGOs who consider their role to be that of donor and aid provider, and those who consider that they have a more transformational role in society to move beyond aid provision to draw attention to and address the structural causes of poverty. Although some INGOs have blended both, in theory the latter are arguably more likely to call for justice than compassion, and political or economic change rather than more aid. They are more likely to embrace development education encompassing the concept of Global Citizenship and a relatively new emphasis on GCE. According to Davies (2008) GCE is substantially different to the Global Education or World Studies agenda utilized by schools and colleges around the world since the 1970s insofar as 'Citizenship clearly has implications in terms of rights and responsibilities, duties and entitlements, concepts that are not necessarily explicit in global education.' Oxfam UK (1997, p.1) embraces this distinction, defining a 'global citizen' as someone who is not just aware of the wider world and their role in it but '...is outraged by social injustice, is willing to act to make the world a more equitable and sustainable place, participates in and contributes to the community at a range of levels from the local to the global. Simply put, effective GCE in a school setting might aim to equip students to embrace an informed personal commitment to social justice and poverty reduction on local and global scales.

Child sponsorship within Northern schools

There are many positives identified by teachers in having CS in a school environment and it is not uncommon for classes or whole schools to sponsor a child. In some instances a picture of a sponsored child is framed and displayed on a wall as a prominent display of altruistic action which advertises and supports religious or humanitarian goals of school communities and outcomes relating to global education or GCE. For teachers CS can be embraced as a practical way for engaging students in humanitarian action that builds a sense of community amongst sponsors, advances their geographic knowledge and forges links with a sponsored child and their country. Additional, although rarer benefits include the opportunity for visiting the child by some of the school children – and contribution to a sponsored child's community – CS is an act of compassion that most Northern children can contribute something to, even a few dollars, ensuring an element of inclusiveness. The difficulty of ensuring that altruism and compassion are encouraged without development of negative attitudes and paternalism is the tricky part for both elementary and secondary school teachers. In the absence of a broader, age-appropriate GCE curriculum, CS can become an act of enthusiastic, unquestioned consumerism rather than an educative process rooted in informed giving and development of young people as advocates for justice. Offered without sufficient thought, it may patronize young people in the North as well as young people and their communities in the South.

Development education and GCE that seeks to unsettle normative or traditional conceptualizations of poverty and development in Northern youth often finds CS initiatives uncritically adopted in schools. The reality of CS in a school setting is that in the absence of effective development education or a broader curriculum designed to promote GCE, the main signifier is often the single child and the act of giving to a single child signifies a benevolent transfer to a relatively passive 'South'. Whether part of a school or class-based activity, the enthusiastic support of a sponsored child and resulting correspondence has been criticized for being a form of 'soft' development education (Andreotti, 2006). This is largely because it often prioritizes a Western-intervention development narrative which portrays the Global South as passive, in need of help and stresses charity. The relationship often proposed is largely one-way. The student in the North potentially makes a small financial contribution and feels good; very little other sacrifice is called for and the sponsored child makes no unreasonable demands on the student in the North. A relationship with any people 'over there' can become confined to a one-way, minimalistic financial transaction, inspired by superficial communication and benevolent feelings exercised as an expression of charity.

Evidence from research

This section draws upon findings in a doctoral research project conducted in the New Zealand school context (Tallon, 2013). The aim of the research was to explore the meanings young people make from INGO messages about the Global South. 118 young people aged 13 to 15 years were surveyed in 2011 and 2012 with a qualitative methodology to canvass what impressions they gained from INGO images and media. Field research involved seven teachers and their year ten social studies students in five secondary schools chosen to represent a diverse selection of socio-economic communities. In the focus group activities that were part of the data collection, CS was not specifically mentioned in any question but in the students' responses, CS television advertisements and CS posters in their community were what they recalled the most when asked to think about the INGO sector. This is an important finding in itself as the CS poster was a prominent (and in some cases the only) signifier of the Global South identified by many of the participants. For a least a quarter of the students in the study, the child image of CS was the Global South. Disaster relief aid or other types of positive images were a distant second.

The study confirmed research by Bryan and Bracken (2011) and Seu (2010) concerning the mixed reception of audiences to INGO messages. In one of the six classrooms in the research described above, CS had been utilized as a teacher initiative to highlight water issues in the sub-Saharan region. Through focus groups it became evident that the students enjoyed the topic and expressed a sense of achievement associated with the child sponsorship that was an optional activity chosen by the class after the unit of learning. One student genuinely wanted to sponsor a child herself. It was apparent that the students strongly linked their knowledge of the region with the child sponsorship activity and when the topic was concluded, a picture of their sponsored child remained on the classroom wall. The extract below from a focus group discussion illustrates how this region came to be remembered by the students.

B2: People had to struggle to get water.

B3: Where we live in the city where it's...

B1: And we were fundraising money for...

B3: And we don't have to walk 200m or 200km or 200miles.

B1: Yeah, we learned about Niger and pretty much you have to walk like three ks just to get a bucket of water.

B3: Five meters or something.

B1: That wouldn't be everyone. That was just that specific person.

B2: And we sponsored a child.

B3: And then we had to do a test to see how long it would take us to get water from a certain spot, didn't we? We went out with a bucket carried on our heads...that was fun.

B1: Yeah.

B2: Cool topic anyway.

[School 1, group C]

Given the realities of a crowded curriculum and time limitations, many junior high school teaching staff would be pleased that the students know that Niger exists, understand the difficulty faced by some people, recognize global differences and inequalities in access to safe drinking water and enjoyed learning. At first glance, the above extract seems benign, if not positive. The students have learnt about someone else's need, engaged in a practical, memorable activity, and in this case they fundraised. However, a critical analysis should ask whether these outcomes are appropriate for the age-group involved. Is it enough for students to learn about them, then fundraise for them? (Bryan, 2011). In effect this may signal to the Northern student that the South is in deficit and we learn about them, never from them. Given Kothari's (1988) argument that where colonialism left off, development took over, INGOs in general and CS INGOs in particular are advised to consider if they are reinforcing or challenging the old divides inherent to a colonial mindset. Had the interview been with senior high school students there would be room for concern that students did not refer to complex reasons for water shortages, INGO partnerships, postcolonial issues confronting Niger and accuracy of representation. However, are these first impressions the most important and is this how the people in the South might wish to be remembered?

The attractive pull of being able to engage students in an activity to improve the lives of the 'Other' as part of learning about them, should be balanced with awareness of pitfalls. Taylor (2011) argues that rather than shifting the ontological basis of the student, a pedagogy which promises absolution largely through a colonialist 'we can help you' framework, is a pedagogy of consolation (p.180). The sufferer is the student feeling guilty that they are wealthy/privileged and this space is uncomfortable and quickly resolved through fundraising efforts. There is a certain seductiveness for teachers because they can maintain a social conscience through encouraging action. What is offered is 'consolation rather than the critical and ethical tools to respond to this crisis' (p.181). This was in evidence in the classroom described above. For the majority of students, a geographical region became remembered by its need and the students felt empowered through their benevolence. The political, historical and environmental reasons for the global inequalities were certainly taught, and with some of the students they recalled these, but the lasting impression was the Global South's need.

Sponsoring a child was mentioned by at least 20 of the students in the study as something they approved of, that their family did or that they had reservations about. For the majority of students their empathy towards the plight of those in need was evident in their talk concerning the child sponsorship advertisements they saw on television as this extract demonstrates:

> B2: Kids don't get an education when I see the [child sponsorship] ads, and when I see them I feel like I want to sponsor someone from the poor countries and help them to get a better future than yeah, get a better education and follow their dreams.
> [School 5, group E]

This response is both positive and complicated. On the one hand, this boy shows a caring response and yet on the other hand, context appears to have been forgotten, the Global South is remembered as homogenous, passive and awaiting his help. It is a powerful subjectivity that he can embody and emotion is a driving force. This is one of the key concerns: that CS, through a benevolent action creates patrons rather than partners. There may be nothing inherently wrong about patronage, but when a young person in the Global North comes to see themselves as a powerful giver to people in the South, disparity is not erased, it is reinforced. This development of a superior/inferior relationship is unlikely to be one that INGOs desire and yet, commentators such as Jefferess (2002, 2008) are concerned with the unintended effects of benevolence. The question is how partnership can be the frame by which the relationship is presented, so it become less about 'us fixing/helping them' and more about 'being in this together' or 'learning from each other'. Unfortunately, the much greater material wealth, higher levels of English literacy, sophisticated information technologies and different world views of Northern students exposed to INGO messages of Southern need are unlikely to develop genuine, mutual respect or a sense of solidarity unless there is a definite strategy in place to unsettle the historical ways of relating.

Returning to evidence from the study, diverse attitudes and receptions towards CS were recorded. At least half the students expressed positive feelings towards CS marketing, saying that they were informative about the needs of others. Approximately a quarter of the students in the study were both critical and questioning of CS marketing in particular. This next extract illustrates some of the tensions that were present.

> G1: I think that I think the words on the poster 'Donate Now, you can make a difference' [referring to a clip art in the questionnaire that is of a stylized CS poster] are all bullshit really. I think that we can't make a difference as one person to one person. They say that if you provide $40 a month you're going to make a change to the whole community and yet they only have one person showing on the poster...
>
> B1: I also agree with that opinion, but then, there's another way of looking at it...if you are helping one child, one community, one town or city that's one less that you'll need to help in the future, or hope that you won't need to help. But also, that there may not be as much money as we think going into it.
>
> G1: Yeah you can help one person, but you have to keep helping them.
>
> G2: How would you feel if you were in the community and you weren't the person on the poster?
>
> B1: That like if you're the one that wasn't being helped, like would the $40 get shared between the 1000 people in the community?
>
> G1: Yeah so that's not going to go a long way is it?
>
> B1: No well, I mean do your math sort of thing, y'know.
>
> B2: And with all the kids and how they show all the children on the posters and stuff, why can't they just stop having kids?
>
> [School 2, Group D]

In G1's second comment 'you have to keep helping them' concern about dependency and the endlessness of aid seems to be entrenched.

At the end of this extract B2 remarks that in his opinion, the advertisements are evidence of overpopulation, leading him to accuse the 'Other' of irresponsibility. In both cases initial empathy has dissipated. Doubts, voiced scepticisms and even anger at INGO's marketing are notable and the students appear to be building up defenses (Seu, 2010) for why they do not wish to donate or take part. They critique the effectiveness of the CS initiative on offer as well as the marketing techniques. Similar friction in relationships between Northern publics and with the INGO sector has researchers worried as it may be the culmination of several factors. Seu's (2010) work in this area is useful, as is the work by Smith (2004), Smith and Donnelly (2004) and Dalton et al (2008).

Researchers are moving beyond singular causes, such as 'compassion fatigue' and considering how people negotiate the INGO demand and position themselves in response. These complex negotiations were in evidence with these young people in their talk concerning CS. Ideally, this would occur in a context where students consider what development is and how CS is a part of this sector. Then the students should consider the benefits and disadvantages of different forms of CS funded intervention, such as community development initiatives emphasizing self-help and community mobilization rather than ongoing individual assistance. They would also be encouraged to consider CS rationally as opposed to emotionally. Often emotion is engaged first (Manzo, 2006) and this lack of deeper critical engagement can create only a surface understanding and appreciation of development, a concern that has emerged from other research (Edge et al, 2009; Marshall, 2005).

The research found that the young people were empathetic towards the distant and vulnerable 'Other' but that the cumulative marketing of need by CS INGOs and a shallow engagement with ideas about development created a barrier for over two-thirds of the students canvassed. Often the students could only see a financial transaction (donate now or sponsor) as the main way to engage with the 'Other' and address global poverty. These responses mirror work by Smith and Donnelly (2004) that showed that young people were not engaged in debates around development; they saw themselves (often negatively) as targets of INGO campaigns. Other messages about aid and development were present (such as governments trading fairly) but they were a shadow of the main emphasis to donate. In a school setting, effective GCE is likely to require considered intervention by teachers utilizing good development education pedagogy and effective curriculum materials, a reality with implications for teacher training. Dalton et al

(2008) found that even among the university students who participated in their study, CS marketing was losing its emotional pull. The students in this study with the younger students did not have compassion fatigue, but many were starting to exhibit a form of demand fatigue. Limited options had been presented to them and they had begun to both tire and be wary of the INGO's call to help.

In a study on how generation Y (born between 1979 and 1991) perceive of international aid and charity (Urbain et al, 2012), traditional concepts of duty and guilt were not seen in a positive light by young people. Other emphases such as sharing and volunteering were identified as more influential. Examining the visual face of CS marketing and the practice of sponsoring a child for its political, ethical, relational, and educational impacts on youth is significant for understanding how attitudes and ideas about other people may be formed. In the research of year ten students reported in this chapter, one teacher remarked that You Tube clips allowed young people overseas to directly talk to her students and this created a more even relationship. She commented that her students could identify with their distant peers when they were more than a static image. Emotions other than pity or compassion were generated and the interest in the issues was much higher than for other media and programmes. The teacher concluded that having the active voice of the people speaking produced in her students 'the best personal reflective writing' for the topic. Baillie Smith (2008, p.15) reports that in research with young people, 'they particularly valued being engaged in debate and being introduced to and having various choices explained to them, without the pressure to act in a particular way'.

Considerations for child sponsorship INGOs

Writing in 1977, Lissner (1977, p.145) traced the emergence of a 'rather lively (and at times tense) debate within voluntary agencies about their educational responsibilities' to the 1960s. At the core of the concerns regarding the marketing of INGO initiatives, is that they may silence radical voices from the South, reify the role of the Northern donor, emphasize charity over structural change, misrepresent the 'other' and run contrary to principles of effective development education unfamiliar to marketing staff and senior administrators in many INGOs. Marketers and managers in INGOs who are not grounded in development theory may not realize that the call to compassion may limit other ways of thinking about people who may be suffering from global injustice. Teachers may be similarly prone to this. Baillie Smith (2008, 2012) has observed that even when INGOs do not seek to explicitly promote fundraising, schools and teachers often default to raising money, as it offers action and closure. To move forward beyond a charitable framework, to a more equitable representation that reflects the actual relationships INGOs have with the Global South, Andreotti (2007, 2011, 2012) argues that critical self-reflexivity on Northern political and economic practices is crucial to INGO initiatives in education in the Global North. This is consistent with Dogra's claim that 'It is time for INGOs to decide if they would like to project deeper contexts of global poverty (and prosperity) and instill new attitudes or carry on with small, individual stories without the context of global relations' (Dogra, 2012, p.193).

Studies in the UK have found that short-term campaigns and messages that focus on individual solutions to poverty can cause development fatigue (Darnton and Kirk, 2011) and a sense of cynicism may set in, causing two researchers to term current UK knowledge of international development 'A mile wide and an inch deep' (Hudson and van Heerde-Hudson, 2012). Arguably, effective development education in schools is less about the right materials, or how much money is going to be raised, or who to support, but more a considered approach to influencing hearts and heads for sustainable change through effective development education and sometimes by linking INGO development education to GCE. In the table below the HEADS UP acronym developed by Andreotti (2012) can be used by both marketing and education staff in INGOs to consider their messages critically, mindful that 'Fundraising campaigns and any other attempts to communicate to the public carry with them explicit and/or implicit 'message' about the development problem' (Lissner, 1977, p.147) This being the case, CS fundraising brochures, posters and images produced by marketing staff should be assessed for their cumulative impact to ensure they do not undermine development education. Beyond asking for money, marketing staff of CS need to consider what else and what other messages are being transmitted through the marketing. If used effectively, Andreotti's acronym challenges thinking around historically embedded patterns and ways of knowing.

For CS INGOs in particular, the alignment of implicit and explicit messages in their marketing and development education strategies requires resourcing, cooperation across departments, high levels of self-reflection and strategic development of age-appropriate development education materials. Although GCE is contested, and may not translate

Concepts that may inform INGO activities and education material	Questions for INGO staff to consider
Hegemony (justifying superiority and supporting domination)	How can an initiative like CS support or counter the idea that the Global North is superior? What is the underlying message of a CS initiative?
Ethnocentrism (projecting one view, one 'forward', as universal)	How can CS address ethnocentrism and seek to portray a more complex notion of 'going forward' and alternative futures that include a range of voices?
Ahistoricism (forgetting historical legacies and complicities)	How can CS avoid the single simplistic history of places and people and provide wider contexts to current issues?
Depoliticization (disregarding power inequalities and ideological roots of development initiatives)	CS has been criticized in the past for being apolitical. How can this be addressed, without confusing and alienating people, or dominating the debate with simplistic or idealistic solutions?
Salvationism (framing help as the burden of the fittest)	Are young people who engage in CS able to see themselves more as learners than saviors? How might CS in development education reduce the 'illusion of superiority and the disenchantment of inferiority'? Can this be done without crushing generosity and altruism?
Un-complicated solutions (offering easy solutions that do not require systemic change)	This has been a strong critique of CS: that the monthly donation requires little commitment. How may CS initiatives address this beyond writing letters to a child? People may want simple solutions; how can INGOs help move people beyond just a 'donate now' option to a deeper engagement with complex issues?
Paternalism (seeking affirmation of superiority through the provision of help)	How can initiatives like CS draw upon what is good about altruism without belittling or infantilizing those who have asked for assistance?

Figure 14.1 'HEADS UP'
(Adapted with permission from Andreotti, 2012)

easily to curriculum in various Northern countries, OXFAM's Education for Global Citizenship (2006, p.5) has made some progress in stimulating thinking regarding age-appropriate outcomes spanning knowledge and understanding, skills and values and attitudes. For example knowledge and understanding outcomes in OXFAM's guideline include: Social justice and equity; Diversity; Globalization and interdependence; Sustainable development; Peace and conflict. Usefully, in the realm of social justice and equity, OXFAM's guidelines encourage beginning with concepts of fair and unfair or rights and wrongs for children under five, extending to awareness of rich and poor for ages 5–7, widening to causes and effects of inequality for ages 7–11, and delving into rights and responsibilities by age 14 and deepening student awareness by age 16 to causes of poverty and different views on its eradication and students' roles as a global citizen. No doubt this pedagogical progression would be much debated by educators however few would contest the need for nuanced, age-appropriate resources or presume that marketing materials would suffice. All marketing materials need to be evaluated for their educational influence and CS initiatives are no exception to this.

In some cases, opportunity exists for strategic networking between leading CS INGOs and non-CS INGOs to partner with elementary and secondary education providers in the development of age-appropriate curriculum and development education resources. For example, in Australia, World Vision, OXFAM, Caritas, Save the Children and Plan (and others) have formed a Global Education Working Group with terms of reference to seek best practice in Global Education and also to advocate for 'global perspectives' and non-paternalistic attitudes in the development of the new nationwide Australian curriculum. Large INGOs are increasingly interested in influencing what is taught in schools. In the Australian context for example, the publication 'Global Perspectives: A framework for global education in Australian schools' (Curriculum Corporation, 2008) has been funded by the Global Education Project, which is supported by the Australian Government's Overseas Aid Program. The reference group included academics from leading Australian universities and representation from prominent INGOs such as World Vision Australia, a geography teachers association, plus various foundations and entities. Collaboration at this level may not be feasible for small CS INGOs however even for them there is a need to consider that the development of empathy for people overseas is desirable though far from being a simple process.

As well as familiarizing themselves with advances in development education and the broader debate over the role of GCE in schools, the following guidelines are suggested for CS INGOs to consider when developing and presenting their initiatives, particularly CS, to young people in the North. They may be read as a synthesis of the concerns raised by Andreotti's HEADS UP, Baillie Smith's (2008, 2012) concerns over INGOs role in development education, Graves' (2007) view and the concerns of Pardiñaz-Solis (2006).

Development education should feature Southern voices

Inclusion of a diversity of Southern voice in development education for school children is necessary. The presence of Southern voice is of paramount importance. According to Graves:

> People of the South are seldom presented as agents of their own change. Materials produced by charities and churches focus on information from their projects. Their 'partners' present the Southern dimension. This means 'witness', case studies and inspiring stories. These voices are necessary, as is Southern analysis and research but agency material and development education material seldom draw on this. Overview and analysis rests with the North. Editorial control rests with the North. Presentation belongs to Northern people. These controlling processes usually exclude Southern people (Graves, 2007, p.89).

Questions for INGO staff and teachers interested in effective development education include: Whose voice is privileged; who is the hero in the story? Are the diverse voices of Southern people and children present? Who is representing whom? Are people aware of different views about development and the diversity within the South? Are Southern people shown as actively working towards their own development? These questions challenge what some commentators are calling a form of narcissistic humanitarianism, whereby the Northern donor is given super powers by INGOs (Chouliaraki, 2010; Jefferess, 2008, 2012). Graves' call is to 'Support people in the Global South as agents of their own change by challenging the notion that Southern people are disempowered and incapable of their own agency' (Graves, 2007, p.89).

It is important to acknowledge historical and political complexity

Questions to consider include: Is the marketing campaign balanced with educational resources that recognize complexity? What will the 'poor' be remembered for? Considering what is being left out, is complexity being sacrificed for a quick donation? While marketing imperatives demand simple messaging, complexity tells a fuller story, and gives dignity to people (Adichie, 2009). Effective global education or development education avoids overwhelming emphasis on isolated, de-contextualized representations and stereotypes. Campaign managers and resource writers for schools should assume that their resource may be the only information that is being presented to young people concerning a people or region. They need to remember that all campaigns are educating people about people.

It is important to encourage older students to contest representations of poverty and development

INGOs face an internal tension regarding education and fundraising. While there are constraints, there are also opportunities. Offering young people a choice, opening up the debate around development within an age-appropriate pedagogy and eventually presenting CS (and the sector) in a frame that challenges hegemonic ideas of development is a more effective and ethical way of engaging young people, especially older high-school students. This may be a leap too far for many INGOs which lack the ability, funds, time or resources to interface with schools, but connecting with those INGOs that do is important. Seeking quick closure to an issue, provision of one-off fundraising events and considering schools just as sources of potential donors does wider development education a disservice. Moving students from compassionate acts of charity to informed engagement is key.

Promote holistic development grounded in partnership

Bryan (2011) has argued that the 'fun, fasting and fundraising' model is limited in its ability to engage youth in the long term. A deeper and more diverse engagement may bring in less money, but may herald a change in long-term attitudes. Questions to consider for marketing staff include: What is the short-term aim of a CS campaign? What are the long-term aims? What type of relationship is suggested and promoted – is it one of partnership? Finally, are Northern students invited or pressured to respond out of a sense of guilt or paternalism?

Conclusion

INGOs continue to have an important role in mediating relationships across geographic, cultural and economic divides. INGOs, and CS INGOs in particular need to consider if they are barriers to effective development education, or facilitators committed to respectful advertising, appropriate images, design and dissemination of age-appropriate, pedagogically sound education materials designed to disrupt the inequality that exists, expand global awareness and encourage practice of effective citizenship. What is at stake is future global South-North relations. As young people interact with their peers across the divides, they will seek diverse ways of relating and promoting social justice that may include individual child sponsorship, but hopefully, will be so much more.

Despite Bryan's (2011) view that development education has lost its radical edge, the extent to which CS INGOs were ever radical in school settings is questionable. The recommendations offered in this chapter allow CS INGOs to consider not just their immediate aims, such as more donors, but the frames in which they are presenting people, including themselves, their constituents and their partners in the South. If INGOs are to move beyond just marketing their interventions in schools, to active agency in development education and commitment to giving voice to the South, they will need to influence curriculum in context with the broader discussion over the future of Global Education and GCE. This requires not just self-awareness, and isolated self-reflection, but active partnership and collaboration across the sector.

Acknowledgements

The authors of this chapter would like to thank Dr. Steve Tallon, Dr. Fiona Beals, Dr. David Jefferess and Dr. Matt Baillie Smith for their feedback on earlier drafts of this chapter. The authors would also like to thank Prof. Vanessa Andreotti for permission to use the HEADS UP framework and Rod Yule, World Vision's Manager Global Education, for his input.

Bibliography

Adichie, C. (2009) 'The danger of the single story', http://www.ted.com/talks/chimamanda_adichie_the_danger_of_a_single_story.html, date accessed 2 May 2012.

Andreotti, V. (2006) 'Soft versus critical global citizenship education', *Policy and Practice – A Development Education Review*, 3, 40–51.

Andreotti, V. (2007) 'An ethical engagement with the Other: Spivak's ideas on education', *Critical Literacy: Theories and Practices*, 1, 1, 69–80.

Andreotti, V. (2011) *Actionable Postcolonial Theory in Education* (New York: Palgrave Macmillan).

Andreotti, V. (2012) 'Editor's preface: "HEADS UP"', *Critical Literacy: Theories and Practices*, 6, 1, 1–3.

Baillie Smith, M. (2008) 'International non-governmental development organisations and their northern constituencies: Development education, dialogue and democracy', *Journal of Global Ethics*, 4, 1, 5–18.

Baillie Smith, M. (2012) 'Reimagining development education for a changing geopolitical landscape [Editorial]', *Policy and Practice – A Development Education Review*, 15, 1–7.

Bourn, D. (2011) 'Discourses and practices around development education: From learning about development to critical global pedagogy', *Policy and Practice – A Development Education Review*, 13, 11–29.

Bryan, A. (2011) 'Another cog in the anti-politics machine? The "de-clawing" of development education', *Policy and Practice – A Development Education Review*, 12, 1–14.

Bryan, A. and Bracken, M. (2011) *Learning to Read the World? Teaching and Learning about Global Citizenship and International Development in Post-Primary Schools* (Dublin: Irish Aid).

CCIC (2008) *Focus on Ethics: Addressing Tensions in Choosing Fundraising Images* (Ottawa: Canadian Council for International Co-operation).

Chouliaraki, L. (2010) 'Post-humanitarianism: Humanitarian communication beyond a politics of pity', *International Journal of Cultural Studies*, 13, 2, 107–126.

Coulter, P. (1989) 'Pretty as a picture', *New Internationalist Magazine*, 194, 10–12.

Curriculum Corporation (2008) (2nd edition) *Global Perspectives: A Framework for Global Education in Australian Schools* (Australia: Education Services).

Dalton, S., Madden, H., Chamberlain, K., Carr, S. and Lyons, A.C. (2008) '"It's gotten a bit old, charity": Young adults in New Zealand talk about poverty, charitable giving and aid appeals', *Journal of Community and Applied Social Psychology*, 18, 492–504.

Darnton, A. and Kirk, M. (2011) *Finding Frames: New Ways to Engage the UK Public in Global Poverty* (London: Bond for International Development, UKAID, Oxfam).

Davies, L. (2008) 'Global citizenship education', *Encyclopedia of Peace Education*, Teachers College, Columbia University, www.tc.columbia.edu/centers/epe/.../Davis_ch13_22feb08.doc, date accessed 19 September 2013.

DOCHAS (2006) *Code of Conduct on Images and Messages* (Dublin: The Irish Association of Non-Governmental Development Organizations).

Dogra, N. (2012) *Representations of Global Poverty: Aid, Development and International NGOs* (London: I.B. Tauris).

Duke, R. (2003) 'The discourse of development education', in R. Tormey (ed.) *Teaching Social Justice: Intercultural and Development Education Perspectives on Education's Context, Content And Methods*, pp. 201–212 (Dublin and Limerick: Ireland Aid and Centre for Educational Disadvantage Research).

Edge, K., Khamsi, K. and Bourn, D. (2009) *Exploring the Global Dimension in Secondary Schools – Final Research Report* (London: Institute of Education).

Graves, J. (2007) 'The changing landscape of development education', *Policy and Practice – A Development Education Review*, 5, 86–91.

Hudson, D. and van Heerde-Hudson, J. (2012) '"A mile wide and an inch deep": Surveys of public attitudes towards development aid', *International Journal of Development Education and Global Learning*, 4, 1, 5–23.

Jefferess, D. (2002) 'For sale – peace of mind: (Neo-) colonial discourse and the commodification of third world poverty in World Vision's "telethons"', *Critical Arts: A South-North Journal of Cultural & Media Studies*, 16, 1, 1–21.

Jefferess, D. (2008) 'Global citizenship and the cultural politics of benevolence', *Critical Literacy: Theories and Practices*, 2, 1, 27–36.

Jefferess, D. (2012) '"Africa for Norway", aid, and the problem of representation', *Culture and Decolonization*, http://blogs.ubc.ca/davidjefferess/2012/11/26/africa-for-norway-aid-and-the-problem-of-representation/, date accessed 14 March 2013.

Kothari, R. (1988) *Rethinking Development* (Delhi: Ajanta).

Lidchi, H. (1999) 'Finding the right image: British development NGOs and the regulation of imagery', in T. Skelton and T. Allen (eds) *Culture and Global Change*, pp. 87–101 (London: Routledge).

Lissner, J. (1977) *The Politics of Altruism: A Study of the Political Behaviour of Voluntary Development Agencies* (Geneva: Lutheran World Federation).

Manzo, K. (2006) 'An extension of colonialism? Development education, images and the media', *The Development Education Journal*, 12, 2, 9–13.

Manzo, K. (2008) 'Imaging humanitarianism: NGO identity and the iconography of childhood', *Antipode*, 40, 4, 633–659.

Marshall, H. (2005) 'Developing the global gaze in citizenship education: Exploring the perspectives of global education NGO workers in England', *International Journal of Citizenship and Teacher Education*, 1, 2, 76–92.

McCloskey, S. (2012) 'Aid, NGOs and the development sector: Is it time for a new direction?' *Policy and Practice – A Development Education Review*, 15, 113–121.

Mittelman, R. and Neilson, L. (2011) 'Development porn? Child sponsorship advertisements in the 1970s', *Journal of Historical Research in Marketing*, 3, 3, 370–401.

OXFAM (1997) *A Curriculum for Global Citizenship* (Oxford, UK: Oxfam).

OXFAM (2006) 'Education for global citizenship: A guide for schools', http://www.oxfam.org.uk/~/media/Files/Education/Global%20Citizenship/education_for_global_citizenship_a_guide_for_schools.ashx, date accessed 19 September 2013.

Paech, M. (2004) *A Photograph is Worth More Than a Thousand Words: The Impact of Photojournalism on Charitable Giving*, Master's thesis, Master of Science in Development Studies, University of London.

Pardiñaz-Solis, R. (2006) 'A single voice from the South in the turbulent waters of the North', *The Development Education Journal*, 12, 3, 4–7.

Plewes, B. and Stuart, R. (2007) 'The pornography of poverty: A cautionary fundraising tale', in D.A. Bell and J.-M. Coicaud (eds) *Ethics in Action. The Ethical Challenges of International Human Rights Nongovernmental Organisations*, pp. 23–37 (Cambridge: Cambridge University Press).

Save the Children (2008) 2008 Annual Report, http://www.savethechildren.org.au/__data/assets/pdf_file/0017/5480/2008_Annual_Report.pdf, date accessed 10 February 2014.

Schatzmann, E. (1929) 'Education for world peace: The "adoption" system of the Save the Children movement', *The World's* Children, Vol. X, October 1929–1930, pp.9–11, SCF Box A670.

Seu, B. (2010) '"Doing denial": Audience reaction to human rights appeals', *Discourse and Society*, 21, 4, 438–457.

Smillie, I. (2000) 'NGOs: Crisis and opportunity in the new world order', in J. Freedman (ed.) *Transforming Development: Foreign Aid for a Changing World*, pp. 114–133 (Toronto: University of Toronto Press).

Smith, M. (2004) 'Contradiction and change? NGOs, schools and the public faces of development', *Journal of International Development*, 16, 5, 741–749.

Smith, M. and Donnelly, J. (2004) 'Power, inequality, change and uncertainty: Viewing the world through the development prism', in C. Pole (ed.) *Seeing is Believing? Approaches to Visual Research*, 7, 123–145 (Bingley, UK: Emerald Group).

Smith, M. and Yanacopulos, H. (2004) 'The public faces of development: An introduction', *Journal of International Development*, 16, 5, 657–664.

Strüver, A. (2007) 'The production of geopolitical and gendered images through global aid organisations', *Geopolitics*, 12, 680–703.

Tallon, R. (2013) 'What do young people think of development? An exploration into the meanings young people make from NGO media', Doctoral thesis in Development Studies, Victoria University of Wellington.

Taylor, L. (2011) 'Beyond paternalism: Global education with preservice teachers as a practice of implication', in V. Andreotti and L.M. De Souza (eds) *Postcolonial Perspectives on Global Citizenship Education*, pp. 177–199 (Abingdon: Routledge).

Urbain, C., Gonzalez, C. and Le Gall-Ely, M. (2012) 'What does the future hold for giving? An approach using the social representations of Generation Y', *International Journal of Nonprofit and Voluntary Sector Marketing*, 18, 159–171.

VSO (2002) *The Live Aid Legacy: The Developing World Through British Eyes – A Research Report* (London: Volunteer Service Overseas).

World Vision Australia (2009) *Representing Global Poverty: Image Guidelines for World Vision Australia Communications* (Melbourne: World Vision Australia).

15
Child Sponsorship: A Path to its Future

Matthew Clarke and Brad Watson

Introduction

Concluding a book of 15, diverse chapters on child sponsorship (CS) is a challenging task, made more difficult by the fact that there is no precedent to such a text. This is remarkable considering the many millions of children who have been assisted through sponsorship programmes since the inception of individual CS in the 1920s. As the first of its kind to deal explicitly with CS, this volume is a significant contribution to the broad foreign aid literature, blending perspectives of academics, practitioners, journalists and sponsored youth. Limited by its emphasis on a relatively small number of CS INGOs, this volume provides a series of stepping stones or direction markers, allowing for navigation through a veritable swamp of dated criticism, and a starting point for further discussion and analysis of key issues.

As a text, this volume is timely if somewhat overdue. Each year, developed nations provide around USD150 billion in official development assistance (or foreign aid) to address humanitarian needs globally, considering their own needs and vested interests in the process. Bilateral Foreign Aid is rarely given for purely altruistic reasons. Feeny and McGillivray (2008, p.522) have noted that DAC bilateral aid donors consider *both* recipient need *and* donor interests in determining aid allocations while Maizels and Nissanke (1984, p.891), have previously argued that 'bilateral aid allocations are made...solely...in support of donors' perceived foreign economic, political and security interests'. Further funds are channelled through private foundations and NGOs, among whom CS INGOs form an important sub-set. Wydick et al (2013) estimates that there are more than 9 million children currently being sponsored and CS agencies raise more than

USD3.3 billion annually from the sponsors of these children. According to Kharas (2008), World Vision International, the world's largest CS organization, delivers more than US$2 billion annually to address the needs of the world's poor, using children as the focal point of fundraising. As symbols of common humanity, the children offered to sponsors by INGOs are often still presented to Northern publics as the bearers of suffering with little or no responsibility for its causes (Holland in Burman, 1994, p.31).

Through their actions CS INGOs are engaged in a much broader process of constructing and deconstructing ideals of childhood, sacralizing them '...in a definitive shift from economic to emotional value', resulting sometimes in a disjunct between cultures in which members of Northern countries conceptualize children as priceless, non-labouring, non-productive, play oriented, innocent yet morally valued members of society (Bornstein, 2001, p.601). Consequently, CS has unprecedented appeal and legitimacy for the general public in the North. Beyond this, CS can not only boast longevity as one of the oldest sources of foreign aid, its popularity has surged and CS INGOs continue to proliferate. As a source of substantial aid flows from North to South, CS programmes in their various forms impact millions of children, families and communities in the South in ways that are rarely studied.

Additionally, CS advertising and advocacy impacts donors in the North, sometimes in keeping with tenets of good development education. Despite this, the origins and evolution of CS have been poorly documented, critique has often been perpetuated without reference to a typology, discussion is hindered by a stunning absence of effective, longitudinal research and CS INGO response to critique is rarely acknowledged. From an academic perspective, it is perplexing that such an important phenomenon should be so poorly documented and so little researched! In providing a number of case studies by a range of INGOs this volume has provided insights into the tensions CS institutions grapple with and manage. The volume is not uncritical of CS though, with a number of chapters challenging perceived wisdom around CS and the impact it has on both the lives of the children sponsored but also on perceptions of global poverty within developed nations.

Unlike perhaps any other foreign aid activity, CS has become entrenched in both developed and developing worlds, with the transfer of funds from the wealthy to the poor transacted on a very personal and private level. Increasingly however, CS is a fundraising model with inherent internal tension. On one side of the model is the focus of improving the lives of children, evident for over 90 years and justifying continuation of enormously successful one-to-one linkages which form the backbone of CS advertising and public relations. On the other is emergent knowledge that the best way to help children in the long-term is to fund development interventions or empower communities to demand their rights, in a way that can improve the lives of poor children through the communities, people and supportive structures surrounding them. Reconciling the two provides an ongoing challenge for CS INGOs restrained by the weight of public expectation associated with the individual sponsorship paradigm. International NGOs that do not use CS also experience tension between international programming and the fundraising required to support these interventions. As will be discussed with regards to CS there is also little work on the fundraising activities of development agencies – see Clarke (2008) and Feeny and Clarke (2007) for exceptions.

The balance of this final chapter seeks four outcomes: to review why sponsorship continues to be attractive to CS INGOs; to acknowledge the progress leading CS INGOs have made in responding to internal and external critique which peaked in the 1990s; to outline 13 key principles for all CS INGOs, regardless of the model of intervention followed; finally, to suggest direction for additional research.

Positive features of historic child sponsorship

The longevity of CS indicates a number of benefits to CS INGOs, donors and beneficiaries. These are shown below in Figure 15.1.

Humanized aid through relational giving

For sponsors and the INGOs that broker donations from them, the appeal of direct links to an individual has endured since its early use. In 1925 Save the Children UK staff wrote 'One of the most human aspects of the Save the Children Fund work is the photo-card adoption scheme, whereby necessitous children of many lands are being saved from misery' (SCF, 1925, p.36). Referring to the use of numbered photo-cards of ill and undernourished children showing name, address and age of the child, the author explained the importance of personal bonds formed through direct correspondence. The result was, according to Save UK staff, '...many a pathetic story of the friendships which are established between adoptive "parents" and their children' (SCF, Vol. 5, p.36). Similarly, staff of what is now Plan International

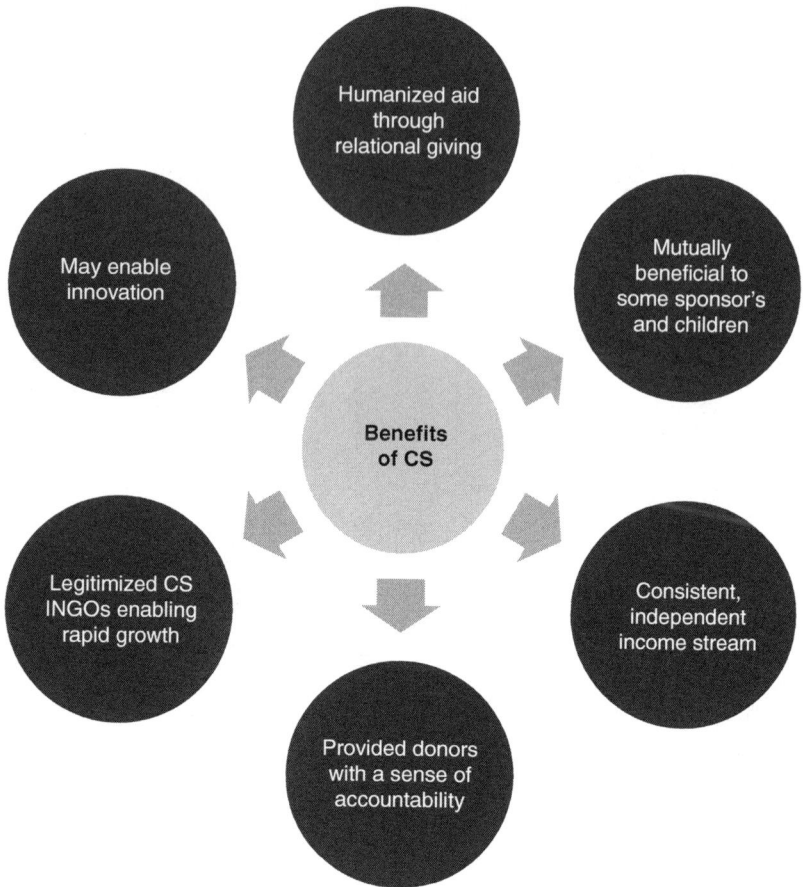

Figure 15.1 Commonly identified benefits of CS used to fund IICS and IFCS programmes

described a 'terrific personalness' leading to bonds so powerful that '...many Foster Parents offered to underwrite a Foster Child's continuing college education or special medical care' (Plan International, 1998, pp.23–24). Clearly, proponents of CS have and continue to view the relational side of traditional CS as a remarkable historic innovation in terms of its ability to attract support using specific children. Though the emphasis on personal, meaningful connection has waned in some organizations over time, this is not to undervalue the perceived benefits.

Mutually beneficial to sponsors and children

Referring to the psychological impact of images used by CS INGOs, *The New York Times* (1998, p.4) observed that 'A picture of a sad-eyed child can cut through politics, religion, even racial prejudice to touch whatever is maternal or paternal in the human heart'. Historically, donors to CS INGOs have been encouraged to bond with an individual, receiving cards, letters and updates over time. For some sponsors this can lead to a meaningful attempt to form a relationship if not a genuine friendship. After examining many carefully edited, cropped, depersonalized, depoliticized and de-identified letters to sponsored children in Zimbabwe, Bornstein (2001, p.604) concluded 'I was amazed at the intimacy, the pieces of lives shared, and the worlds translated in these packages, in the care that had gone into assembling them. I was touched by the letters; many seemed reasonable attempts to bridge the intimacy and strangeness of sponsoring a child in a country the sponsors had never visited.'

For some sponsors, the results are profound. Rabbitts (2012, p.930) accords significance of the act of sponsorship beyond a 'a tear-jerking campaign, or as a mundane regular commitment, but also as a deeply personal engagement that draws into play multiple different aspects of people's lives and intersects with existing identity- and community-building projects'. It is not clear what proportion of sponsors feel this way, or what sort of sponsorship programmes foster this deep engagement, and few researchers have stopped to consider that sponsorship may enrich the lives of those who give.

Benefits for sponsored children of a direct relationship with sponsors have also been frequently cited in the absence of scholarly research. Writing as an insider about Christian Children's Fund in the mid-1970s, Herrell observed that sponsored children could benefit from the 'emotional prop' provided by sponsors who cared, were likely to perform better at school when correspondence was regular, and benefited from the personal interest of sponsors who humanized the system and kept it 'sensitive to the ultimate implications of broad decisions upon the little guy at the end of the line, whose rice bowl may bear the agency's logo' (Herrell, 1974, pp.688–689). This remains true for many CS INGOs that retain an emphasis on child welfare and direct benefits rather than community development or rights-based development.

Consistent, independent income stream

It is an understatement to say that traditional CS has been 'very effective at raising funds' (Waters, 2001, p.5) or remains so. The promise of a personal relationship with a sponsored child has and continues to be attractive to individual donors, resulting in sustained funding flows for CS INGOs and flexible income. For Plan International (2008, p.2) the regular, sustained nature of CS allows longer-term commitments to communities than possible with official aid and '...allows Plan International to remain considerably more flexible and politically independent than if reliant on government grants for a large portion of funding'. CS is also valued for the fact that it provides a relatively consistent income stream, over long periods of time. At a pragmatic level, this provides a stable funding platform for interventions insofar as 'long term relationships translate into long-term financial commitments' (Oprandi in Plan International, 1998, p.64).

Provided donors with a sense of accountability

For many individual donors a personal relationship with a beneficiary has been synonymous with oversight, accountability and a degree of development education. Don Paterson, a vice-president for donor and field relations at World Vision in the mid-1990s observed (in Moore, 1998, p.2). 'The sponsor has the opportunity to correspond with that child, and if they are able, to visit their family and community and hold us accountable to the work that we're doing.' Further, in organizations with a strong development emphasis there has been some consensus that, 'The personal and emotional appeal of child sponsorship also appears to strengthen supporter commitment and loyalty to the cause of development and has the potential to develop the sponsor's understanding of the development process' (Plan International, 2008, p.2). A 1998 history of Plan International noted that exchanges between sponsors and Plan families '...achieves three things: development education, personal linkage and accountability' (Plan International, 1998, p.64). According to staff from two very large CS INGOs consulted with during the writing of this chapter, sponsors may provide an unprecedented level of accountability by writing to children, asking the organization questions, answering surveys, visiting their children and even discontinuing.

Legitimized CS INGOs enabling rapid growth and expansion

Within many CS INGOs the historic commitment to child well-being has functioned as a motivator for staff, key feature of organizational identity, signifier of their legitimacy and principal reason for being. Manzo (2008, p.652) argues that the iconography of childhood continues to reinforce '...an impression of both institutional efficacy and the power to act in *loco parentis* by tapping into cultural associations of childhood with dependence, innocence, and the need for protection and care'. In providing a direct link to individual children and their communities, CS functions as a bridge across cultures and communities, with CS INGOs as mediators and facilitators of two-way relationships. There can be no doubt that the influx of CS income allowed for remarkable growth of some INGOs. When Foster Parents Plan Netherlands initiated a nation-wide appeal for new sponsors in the early 1980s 'Phone lines in Amsterdam were knocked out as more than 50,000 new sponsors called in response'. Such booms 'Fuelled PLANs rapid expansion into some of the most challenging environments it had ever worked in, most notably Africa and South Asia' (Plan International, 1998, pp.50–51).

Enabled innovation over time

Arguably, long-term funding catalyses innovation. In the case of World Vision (2006, p.3) CS has been described as 'a dynamic mix of two ideas: brilliant fundraising (the child focus) and brilliant development (the community)'. In the Case of Save the Children (see Chapter 5 of this book) funds from CS are cited as a key to programmatic innovation, resulting in 'CS having a disproportionate influence on the way Save the Children makes large-scale, sustainable change for children.' Despite claims to the contrary, CS funding has been identified as a platform for innovation and engagement for long periods of time as evidenced in World Vision's Area Development Programs which remain active in particular locations for up to ten years. For CCF's early orphan care work, the purpose-built Hong Kong Children's Garden (constructed in the mid-1950s) housed 1,000 children in 98 cottages, each with house-parents, providing both formal and vocational education. CCF's experimentation with master-planned orphanages incorporating innovative family substitution and vocational education programmes verged on radical at the time though perhaps not pioneering. Though critics may counter that fundraising success and sponsor expectations hinder radical change, several large CS INGOs would argue that this is a simplistic analysis.

CS INGO response to critique

Public, media-led critique of CS INGOs, their fundraising and programmes peaked in the 1990s. However, critique has long been a part of CS INGO history, a matter explored in Chapter 3 of this volume devoted to evolution over time. Criticisms are discussed at length in Chapter 4. However, it is worth noting Ove's point that 1990s media critique, in

324 Child Sponsorship: A Path to its Future

the USA in particular, emphasized the message that 'in order to "fix" CS, these organizations needed to improve their "development" practices in the "South" and their accountability in the "North"' (Ove, 2013, p.3). Collectively, CS INGOs were depicted as negligent in regards to their responsibilities towards sponsors and to sponsored children.

The untold part of the CS story thus far (in this volume at least) is the way leading INGOs responded to vociferous, sweeping, and often generalized critique based on anecdotes and isolated examples taken to represent systemic failure. Pointing out that many of the articles were published in a short period of time and were not well supported by facts, a senior staff member in one large CS INGO asked for acknowledgement that '...a group of agencies decided to take a disciplined approach to dealing with criticisms whether they were based on fact or perception. This led to accredited external agencies certifying sponsorship agencies on standards that address these issues' (Personal correspondence). Thus, an important piece of the story is the InterAction Accreditation and Certification work carried out to address the issues raised.

At time of writing InterAction is the largest alliance of USA-based international NGOs with over 180 members. In 1992, InterAction members agreed to self-monitor their activities and benchmark against a common set of standards – known as the PVO standards. Responding to critique, World Vision, Plan International-USA/Childreach, Christian Children's Fund, Children International and Save the Children formed a sub-group to formulate and adopt additional standards which were integrated with InterAction's broader PVO standards in 1999.

At considerable cost to the CS INGOs involved, the CS certification audits were launched in October 2004 and completed in July 2005 (InterAction, 2005, p.1). Completed audits were submitted to a multi-stakeholder Certification Review Panel (CRP), consisting of 'a child sponsor (an individual US citizen, who sponsors children), an institutional donor, a representative of the auditing firm awarding certification, and a subject matter expert, who was familiar with CS programs in the field.' In reality, the auditing process was expensive, problematic to facilitate, and dependent on a very small team visiting a very small proportion of project activity. However, in theory, the principle was excellent. For CS INGOs accustomed to operating with little external oversight, the auditing process provided a unique opportunity for peer review, especially when the subject matter expert came from another leading INGO.

Although there is much merit in the InterAction Child Sponsorship standards, and they have undoubtedly impacted perceptions of best practice in the CS sector in the USA, it is worth noting that CS INGOs in various Northern countries abide by alternative codes of conduct. What is lacking though is a set of specific principles for CS applicable internationally. The principles set out below are presented in order to generate a dialogue amongst CS organizations, the children and local communities with whom they partner, and the supporters and donors that financially and emotionally commit themselves to this type of programming.

Principles for a child sponsorship code of conduct

Given the amount of funds raised by NGOs utilizing CS as model of development, it is imperative that these organizations are as efficient and effective as possible in both their programming and their fundraising. Based on the lessons learned from various contributions to this volume, the following principles for a Global Child Sponsorship Code of Conduct are suggested to aid and abet this efficiency and effectiveness. It is important therefore to note two things with regards to these proposed principles. Firstly, they are very likely to be already current practice for a number of INGOs. Secondly, these suggested principles are just that – principles that provide a framework for practices, not definitive prescriptions to homogenize CS INGOs so they are indistinguishable from one another. It is important that INGOs are distinct and serve various communities (both in developed and developing countries) as the uniqueness of responses to poverty aligned to the uniqueness experiences of poverty is central to effective outcomes. While often linked, these principles for a Child Sponsorship Code of Conduct will be presented – apart from the first and last – along the programming and fundraising divide. Such division though should be thought of as an inferred weighting of importance between the two. They are symbiotic. Indeed, the very first principle is the recognition of this interdependence.

Overarching

Principle 1: Recognizing child sponsorship as both a programming and fundraising model

The success of the CS interventions, especially as a development model, is the symbiotic relationships between fundraising and development work. The child as the focal point allows a relationship to be presented that directly links the sponsor and the recipient. This linkage of those with excess resources and those with limited resources results in a resilient model upon which funds can be raised and expended. Organizations utilizing this model should explicitly recognize the intertwined components of this model. It is important that there be public recognition that this powerful tool has value because it is both a programming approach and fundraising activity.

Fundraising

Principle 2: Education of donors/sponsors

Development education as a concept reached its zenith in developed countries during the mid to late1980s. Since that time, aid agencies have invested less resources and efforts into informing and educating their donors and supporters around development issues, structural justice and distortions in the global economic system of trade. While there are clearly instances and examples of these education programmes in place, it is important to recognize that across the sector they are less prominent than more than two decades ago. Rather, the 'marketing' of development has seemly overtaken development education so that information concerning complex humanitarian emergencies, economic vulnerability, malnutrition, and so forth are parceled with appeals and the fundraising campaigns. As such, the information shared has shifted to support the imperative of fundraising. The consequence is that donors and supporters receive significant information that ties development 'success' to specific programming initiatives, rather than information that considers larger issues of inequity, power imbalances, national security, et cetera. Donors and supporters are therefore limited in their knowledge of the causes of international poverty and to their potential non-financial responses to such poverty. Given the close relationships organizations which utilize the CS model have with donors and supporters, there is a need to strengthen development education and decouple – to a large extent – knowledge transfer of development from further fundraising appeals and campaigns.

Principle 3: Clarity of primary beneficiaries

As has been clearly identified and illustrated with various case studies within this volume, there are a number of distinct approaches to programming premised upon the CS model of fundraising. This continuum of models is best illustrated by the primacy of the child as beneficiaries within programming. Indeed, across this range, children are variously the sole beneficiary of any implementation to being a member of a much wider community to whom the implementation is targeted. Yet, despite where along this continuum the model sits, the fundraising material largely highlights the child as the focal point of concern. While a value judgment is not being made as to the effectiveness or efficiency of the programming model, it is important that organizations utilizing CS be more explicit and transparent as to the primacy of beneficiaries. If the child is the sole beneficiary of programming then that should be made clear. If though, the child is not the primary beneficiary and is just a member of a wider targeted community, then this also should be made clear in the fundraising materials. The latter does not preclude a child being a 'representative' member of the community or a 'window' into a community, but it should be made quite clear that this is indeed the case.

Principle 4: Images of children with family

The historical basis of the present CS model does have its roots in supporting children whom either did not have families or had been separated from families. In this sense they were orphaned and financial support was sought from sponsors to provide for their care. Within these circumstances, presenting the child in isolation was understandable. Since that time though, the absolute numbers of sponsored children who are orphaned as a proportion of total children sponsored is quite small. Yet, it remains a common practice to present the child in isolation from their family and their community. This gives rise to the sponsor incorrectly imagining that the child is reliant on the sponsor (and CS organization) for continuing well-being. It is important for the sponsor to better understand that the child whom they support is (most likely) a member of a family and (in most cases) a member of a community that plays central roles in their welfare. Organizations utilizing the CS model ought to recognize this familial and community connection through including families and communities in their images and place children in these social settings to limit sponsors inclinations of sole responsibility.

Principle 5: Offering funding choices to donors

The long history of CS speaks directly to its success. The simplicity of linking a child to a sponsor replicates the parent-child relationship and the attendant feelings of obligation, care and responsibility. Thus, it is not uncommon for sponsors to feel unable to cease their sponsorship before the child's circumstances naturally bring about a point of closure (normally when the child reaches a certain age). As such, the length of financial support towards a CS organization is quite significant and thus becomes a regular and dependable source of funding. However, CS requires heavy administration, adding to its cost of delivery. These costs of administration fall on both aspects of the model – fundraising and programming. The fundraising costs may involve the receiving and translating of letters and communication between sponsor and child (which are encouraged) and the maintenance of records regarding the child's progress in school, et cetera. There is often additional personalized communication at times of significant events, especially Christmas celebrations, for instance. In addition to the programming costs, there are additional costs again associated with the communication between sponsor and child, photo updates, and monitoring of children's whereabouts. Alternative fundraising schemes do not carry such administrative costs and so alternatives to CS that are less expensive to maintain should be offered to sponsors to increase the organization's efficiency. Providing sponsors with informed choices can be key to developing in them awareness of alternatives.

Principle 6: Promoting equality of participants

That a child is dependent upon its parents or primary care givers is uncontested. Indeed, this dependency is the hallmark trait of the historic use of CS. CS works because the sponsor is moved to believe that their support is necessary for the child's well-being and as such the sponsor assumes a sort of parental responsibility. Such dependency also results in an unequal relationship between the sponsor and the child in which the sponsor holds a dominant position – that is, if the sponsor withholds their financial support the child is powerless to object. Such a dependency can then feed into other aspects which may lend to the sponsor viewing the child (and their community) as helpless and hopeless. Such views do not accord with a sense of partnership that is appropriate. To counter such critique, organizations utilizing CS need to promote the equality of the child and sponsor, emphasizing the capacity of the child, their family and community. Orphan care providers should take special care to empower families and communities rather than isolate children in institutions.

Programming

Principle 7: Non-discrimination of beneficiaries

Selection of children to be sponsored is a core activity of organizations utilizing CS. As evidenced from a number of personal stories contained within this volume, receiving support through CS can bestow significantly improved life chances. Again, whilst there are numerous CS models that differ in regard to the primacy of the child in terms of programming beneficiary, those models that still make prominent the child have a great responsibility in the selection of children to be sponsored. It is essential therefore that these choices are not biased to favour one ethnicity, religious adherence, gender or ability. It is also essential that considerations of whom sponsors may 'prefer' are also excluded from these decisions. The primary determinant of inclusion should be that of need or ability to represent the needs and progress of the community.

Principle 8: Community involvement in selection of children for sponsorship

As discussed above, the inclusion of a child into a sponsorship programming can be life-changing. Thus, the non-selection of a child can similarly be life-denying through the lack of access to those benefits. Just as the selection of these children should be non-discriminatory, it is also important that the community in which those children belong be heavily involved in the selection of those children. Given the importance of being non-discriminatory in selection, it is not recommended that the community make the selection without consultation with the organization, but rather that these two work together to identify those children best included for a range of reasons based foremost on need. The needs of children and their families are best understood by communities themselves and the empowerment of communities necessitates, wherever possible, that children should be carefully selected by members of their own community, regardless of whether they are direct beneficiaries or representative beneficiaries.

Principle 9: Alignment with current development best practice

Remaining cognizant of the differing models of CS, it is important that organizations utilizing CS implement their programmes in alignment with current ideals of best practice. In this way, it is essential that these organization fund activities that have been identified, designed, and implemented through community-led participatory practices, that gender analysis is central to these determinations, and that activities are sustainable so that upon cessation of funding there remains a persistence of benefits from these activities. Constant monitoring and evaluation of CS activities are necessary to minimize unintended negative outcomes and to maximize both planned and unplanned benefits to the child and community. Where CS activities are essentially child-welfare oriented, such as in orphan care, conceptual understanding of best practice should ensure that orphans are cared for in their communities as a priority, in institutions as a last resort, and when institutional care is unavoidable, that it occur to the highest standard. In all cases, the true cost of quality interventions should not be hidden from sponsors.

Principle 10: Integration of programming activities

As with the importance of utilizing best practice, CS programming should be integrated with other activities if they are implementing non-sponsorship programming within the same community. This integration reduces duplication of effort, but also maximizes synergies that may exist between programming. Thus if an organization utilizing the CS model was supporting the school of sponsored children as well as implementing a water, sanitation and hygiene programme for the child's wider community, integrating the WASH education into the school curriculum would maximize the success of intended behavior change.

Principle 11: Greater public dissemination of programming evaluation

High quality monitoring and evaluation of CS programmes is not common place and wide dissemination of findings remains rather limited. This is even more so when less than optimal outcomes are reported. However, given the scope of use of CS funded interventions across a large number of small, medium and large aid agencies, it is important that the lessons learned around successes and failures be more widely shared to improve practice across all these organizations. Given the amount of information garnered by these organizations through their regular monitoring and evaluation activities, it would be beneficial that this be shared to enhance efficiency and effectiveness. This dissemination should not just be limited to other organizations utilizing the CS model but made available to sponsors and the general public in order to further educate people as to the reality of poverty and development.

Principle 12: Maintaining the dignity and agency of the child

Central to all these principles should be the guiding principle that the dignity of the child be maintained at all times. This does mean that images of the child used to encourage sponsorship do not represent the child as dependent, helpless or hopeless. Sponsors should not be encouraged through marketing or communication to pity the child they are sponsoring and feel that the child is utterly reliant upon their charity to survive. Further, the strengths and capacities of the child and their families and communities should be identified and celebrated in all communication with the sponsor to ensure that there is a clear understanding of equality between child and sponsor. It is important to highlight that children (and their families) do have agency within their lives and are not passive recipients of CS support and programming. As such their involvement and contribution to community development outcomes should not be minimized.

Principle 13: Ensuring good governance

Historic misuse of CS for both fundraising and programmes may be partially attributable to the governance structures of INGOs. As CS INGOs have prospered, it has become increasingly common to appoint senior managers without experience in the development or humanitarian aid sector. Ensuring that management boards have at least one expert positioned to counter the narrow imperatives of senior staff who are fixated on growth or donor relations, with concurrent peer review of programmes would be invaluable for both large and smaller organizations.

Consequences and challenges

These 13 principles, if implemented, will continue the positive trajectory of evolution displayed by some CS INGOs. As noted though, these principles are not a straightjacket of conformity, but do – if adhered to – contribute to a consistency of practice that ensures the primacy of the child in activities whether those activities are occurring within a developing country or a developed country. Further, while adhering to these principles, CS INGOs will continue to be able to operate in line with their own principles and histories and continue and build their relationships with their donor markets, but be assured that as a sector CS will be less a target for criticism.

How these principles can be codified into a Code of Conduct remains to be seen. Certainly there are instances of NGOs co-operating and working together to advocate on a range of development issues and in various countries there are already codes of conduct applying to them. For example, within the United Kingdom, 13 leading NGOs (including World Vision UK, CARE, and OXFAM amongst others) cooperate in a formal way to raise funds for complex humanitarian emergencies. Formed in 1963, the Disaster Emergency Committee (DEC) undertakes to provide an efficient appeal mechanism through the media for national fundraising and public responses. It was formed in 1963 as a response to the BBC not wishing to refuse requests of publicity by NGOs for fundraising activities for a cyclone in Sri Lanka (at that time known as Ceylon). It was thought that a more effective public response would be gained if a single entity sought to raise funds rather than a number of NGOs seemingly competing for public donations.

It is possible and indeed to be encouraged that those international NGOs utilizing CS advertising techniques and expending funds through various modes of intervention, form an association of some form to provide forums for the debate and codification of these principles. Such a grouping could also provide opportunities for the realization and support of common research needs within this mode across these agencies. As noted at the start of this chapter, there is scant academic research into CS, with this volume representing this first significant work in this area to be published commercially. Clearly further research is required and this is in the interests of all key stakeholders, including the beneficiaries of CS, donors or supporters, and the NGOs themselves.

Further research into child sponsorship

Given the focus of improving the lives of the world's poor, it is unsurprising that the development sector garners significant research and academic interest. It is certainly not overstating the issue to claim that lives are at stake in this field of endeavor. For practitioners working in this area, more effective and efficient programming does save lives but also provides increased opportunity and hope to beneficiaries whose lives would without intervention be characterized by hunger, illiteracy, gendered violence, lack of access to clean and safe water or sanitation, ill-health and premature death. Better understanding the effectiveness of development interventions will enhance development outcomes and increase the impact of these interventions.

Knowing the value of better development programming and implementation has resulted in much research and academic analysis of activities across the development sector. There is significant (and often daunting) literature addressing foreign aid effectiveness, governance, water and sanitation, health, education, rural agricultural, urban development, participation, gender and the environment – all of which is focused on learning from past experience to improve future practice in these sectors. As previously noted however, one of the founding models of development practice has been largely left untested and critically analysed. While there is no doubt that CS NGOs do invest considerable resources and time evaluating their own programming and that these reviews do shape and enhance approaches to CS, these reviews remain predominately available only to those within the NGO itself and are not publicly disseminated (see Wydick et al, 2013 and Glewwe and Wydick, 2013 as rare exceptions).

This lack of public dissemination has various consequences that constrain further potential improvements in CS. By not making these studies widely available, other CS INGOs are not only unable to take advantage of the lessons learned by INGOs with similar models, but must also expend further resources and time replicating evaluations (and mistakes) until they themselves generate these lessons for their own consumption. The lack of public dissemination also does not allow public scrutiny of actions by donors and supporters who must rely upon purposely prepared marketing documents to gain more knowledge of CS outcomes. Given the expressed purpose of these documents is to increase fundraising, it is rare (though not impossible – see Newmarch, 2011) to find information highlighting failures. Thus there is an unrealistic expectation of the good (and only the good) that can be expected from CS. When critical stories then do appear in the public press, donors and sponsors can feel particularly aggrieved or deceived.

To minimize these outcomes, it is important not only to make more public the existing internal research around CS but to actually increase the academic analysis of these specific models of intervention. There are a number of areas that it would be valuable to have greater understanding:

- Mapping of CS: a greater understanding of the scope and size of CS activities is fundamental before significant research can be undertaken of its efficacy and efficiency. It is not well understood as to where CS is taking place or the actual size of these programmes. A basic stock take across all organizations involved in this work would be of benefit as a starting point. Of particular interest is CS, child rights and potential to integrate CS with effective advocacy.
- Typologies of CS: Initial work has been presented in this volume regarding the typology of CS-funded intervention. Further testing

and development of this typology is now needed to help improve the overall model.

- Longitudinal studies of beneficiaries: Despite limited work, there is very little known as to the efficacy of CS over the longer term. Given its long history and the amount of resources expended, it is important to better understand the impact of CS over the longer term and the persistence of benefits associated with CS. Such studies are needed across all models of CS programming to assist in determining positive as well as negative lessons around practice.
- CS effectiveness in comparison to other development models: The administration of CS adds an impost to development programming both at the sponsorship end as well as the programming end. It is not known whether this impost results in more effective and efficient outcomes or is a cost that results in less beneficial outcomes. Comparison with other modes of programming would provide new knowledge to assist organizations utilizing CS to determine how they should prioritize CS programming within a range of non-sponsorship programming options to affect the greatest positive impact.
- Sponsor engagement and education: The number of citizens in developed nations sponsoring children is sizable. Better understanding the impact of the marketing and communications information received by these sponsors throughout their involvement with CS would provide great insights into the sophistication (or otherwise) of knowledge concerning development issues. These insights would allow great testing of sponsors' engagement with development issues both associated with their sponsorship but also independently of it.
- CS INGO institutional histories: For such resilient and publicly known organizations, little is widely known as to the institutional history of the major organizations utilizing CS. It is important to have stronger links to historical practices and policies to better understand contemporary practices and policies.

Research in each of these areas would likely provide valuable lessons and insights into not only just how CS is operationalized in developed and developing countries, but the impact of these activities both in the short and longer term. Given the billions of dollars provided each year to fund these interventions it is incumbent upon CS INGOs to undertake this research but to also work in partnership with academia to facilitate such research and ensure it is publicly and freely disseminated. Such transparency is in the best interest of the

INGOs, their supporters, but most importantly their intended beneficiaries.

Conclusion

Throughout this volume, the CS model has been discussed in ways that have rarely been seen before in public publication. Despite the size and history of CS, very little of its history and operations have been rigorously researched and analysis subjected to peer review. The importance of this volume therefore will be measured by the growth in such analysis and discussion in the future. Far more work is required to ensure that the great potential of child sponsorship is fulfilled to the point that it is universally accepted as a pathway for a brighter future for the world's children.

The absolute number of children, families, sponsors and financial resources involved in CS demand a greater level of scrutiny and understanding. Child sponsorship is so ubiquitous in so many countries yet this familiarity with it does not invite more than a cursory or veneer consideration. It is hoped that this volume has succeeded in doing more than this and while much more is required, that this will provide an appropriate starting point.

Bibliography

Bornstein, E. (2001) 'Child sponsorship, evangelism, and belonging in the work of World Vision Zimbabwe', *American Ethnologist*, 28, 3, 595–622.

Burman, E. (1994) 'Poor children: Charity appeals and ideologies of childhood', *International Journal of Psychology and Psychotherapy*, 12, 1, 29–36.

Clarke, M. (2008) 'Raising the funds – Spending the funds: A case study of the effectiveness of BOTH roles of NGOs', in A. Renzao (ed.) *Measuring Development Effectiveness* (New York: Nova).

Feeny, S. and Clarke, M. (2007) 'What determines Australia's responses to emergencies and natural disasters', *Australian Economic Review*, 40, 1, 24–36.

Feeny, S. and McGillivray, M. (2008) 'What determines bilateral aid allocations?: New evidence from time-series data', *Review of Development Economics*, 12, 3, 515–529.

Glewwe, P. and Wydick, B. (2013) *Child Sponsorship and Child Psychology: Evidence from Children's Drawings in Indonesia*, Working paper, University of San Francisco.

Herrell, D.J. (1974) 'The effects of Sponsorship on child welfare', *Child Welfare*, LIV, 10, 684–691.

InterAction (2005) *Interaction Child Sponsorship Certification: Executive Summary*, as of 18 July 2005, http://ec.europa.eu/dgs/home-affairs/what-is-new/public-consultation/2005/pdf/contributions/interaction3_en.pdf, date accessed 15 October 2013.

InterAction (2008) *Guidance Document For the Interaction Child Sponsorship Certification Standards and Certification Manual*, http://www.saasaccreditation. org/docs/InterAction%20Guidance%20Document,%20revision%203,%20 August.2008.pdf, date accessed 15 October 2013.

Kharas, H. (2008) *The New Reality of Aid* (Washington, DC: Wolfensohn Centre for Development, Brookings Institute).

Maizels, A. and Nissanke, M. (1984) 'Motivations for aid to developing countries', *World Development*, 2, 9, 879–900.

Manzo, K. (2008) 'Imaging humanitarianism: NGO identity and the iconography of childhood', *Antipode*, 40, 4, 633–659.

Moore, A. (1998) 'The myth of the needy child?' *Christianity Today*, 42, 6, 18 May, p.16.

New York Times (1998) 'Donations from the heart, greetings from the grave', *New York Times*, 5 April, p.4.

Newmarch, A. (ed.) (2011) *World Vision Australia Annual Program Review*, World Vision Australia, Melbourne, https://www.worldvision.com.au/Libraries/ Annual_Program_Review_2011_Full_Report/Annual_Program_Review_2010.sfl b.ashx, date accessed 16 August 2013.

Ove, P. (2013) *'Change a Life. Change Your Own': Child Sponsorship, the Discourse of Development, and the Production of Ethical Subjects*, Doctoral thesis, Faculty of Graduate Studies, University of British Columbia.

Plan International (1998) *A Journey of Hope – The History of Plan International 1937–1998* (London: Plan International).

Plan International (2008) *The Development Impact of Child Sponsorship: Exploring Plan International's Sponsorship-Related Processes and Materials, Their Effects, and Their Potential Evolution* (Woking, UK: Plan International).

Rabbitts, F. (2012) 'Child sponsorship, ordinary ethics and the geographies of charity', *Geoforum*, 43, 926–936.

S.C.F. (1925) *The World's Children: Journal of Child Care and Protection Considered from an International Viewpoint*, 5, 2, November, pp.21–38, SCF Box A670.

Waters, K. (2001) 'The art and ethics of fundraising', *Christianity Today*, 46, 15, 3 December, 50–52.

World Vision (2006) *Contemporary Approaches to Child Sponsorship: A Discussion Reflecting Contemporary Approaches to Child Sponsorship within the World Vision Partnership* (Melbourne: World Vision Australia).

Wydick, B., Glewwe, P. and Rutledge, L. (2013) 'Does international child sponsorship work? A six-country study of impacts on adult life outcomes', *Journal of Political Economy*, 121, 2, 393–436.

Index